Ius Gentium: Comparative Perspectives on Law and Justice

Volume 130

Ius Gentium is a book series which discusses the central questions of law and justice from a comparative perspective. The books in this series collect the contrasting and overlapping perspectives of lawyers, judges, philosophers and scholars of law from the world's many different jurisdictions for the purposes of comparison, harmonisation, and the progressive development of law and legal institutions. Each volume makes a new comparative study of an important area of law. This book series continues the work of the well-known journal of the same name and provides the basis for a better understanding of all areas of legal science.

The *Ius Gentium* series provides a valuable resource for lawyers, judges, legislators, scholars, and both graduate students and researchers in globalisation, comparative law, legal theory and legal practice. The series has a special focus on the development of international legal standards and transnational legal cooperation.

Valéria Emília de Aquino
Claudia Loureiro • Vinicius Villani Abrantes
Editors

Climate Litigation in a Changing World

A Comparative Analysis of Similarities, Challenges and Pathways

Springer

Editors
Valéria Emília de Aquino
Federal University of Goiás
Goiânia, Goiás, Brazil

Claudia Loureiro
Federal University of Uberlândia
Uberlândia, Minas Gerais, Brazil

Vinicius Villani Abrantes
Direito Internacional sem Fronteiras
Juiz de Fora, Minas Gerais, Brazil

ISSN 1534-6781 ISSN 2214-9902 (electronic)
Ius Gentium: Comparative Perspectives on Law and Justice
ISBN 978-3-032-05529-3 ISBN 978-3-032-05530-9 (eBook)
https://doi.org/10.1007/978-3-032-05530-9

This Springer imprint is published by the registered company Springer Nature Switzerland AG
The registered company address is: Gewerbestrasse 11, 6330 Cham, Switzerland

We dedicate this work to all activists, researchers and professionals who advocate for the protection of the environment, and also to climate migrants, whose vulnerability is so enormous that it becomes imperative to advocate for the environment and give voice to these individuals and communities. Finally, we also dedicate this book to our sacred and beloved Pachamama.

Acknowledgments

We are very grateful to everyone who supported this book and made it possible. Special thanks to the Springer team, especially to Laura Hofmann and Pradeep Kuttysankaran, who kindly assisted and supported us to publish this work, and to all the authors for their valuable contributions and for taking on the challenge of writing about the topic, since addressing climate change in the current global context means persisting, resisting, and persevering. Also we would like to thank all the authors who entrusted us with their manuscripts so that we could produce a work as rich and fruitful in discussion as this one.

Valéria Aquino extends her special thanks to her family, who supported her during the most difficult moments of her life, and who always encouraged her to pursue an academic career and to work in whatever made her happy, in this case, as a lawyer and researcher in the area of human rights. She also expresses her gratitude to her partner, to the Federal University of Goiás, and to all professors and researchers who believed in her over the years, especially Professor Cláudia and Professor Vinicius. And finally, she is also grateful to her emotional support dogs, who despite not knowing how to read were always by her side during the writing and revision process.

Claudia Loureiro would like to thank the Jean Monnet Chair at the Federal University of Uberlândia, Global Crossings Project, for the opportunity to conduct a research project with relevant results for the academic community, such as this book, which contains texts that make a scientific contribution to the evolution of the debate on climate change. Claudia would also like to thank her family for their support, without which no project could be structured on solid and lasting foundations.

Vinicius Villani Abrantes would like to extend his thanks to the entire International Law without Borders (Direito Internacional sem Fronteiras, in Portuguese) team. He is also grateful for his mother's generous love and *listening*. Vinicius also expresses his thanks to his colleagues Professors Cláudia and Valéria—*whom I take with me as great inspirations in my personal and professional life*.

Contents

Editors and Contributors

About the Editors

Valéria Emília de Aquino Lawyer and Human Rights Consultant, Human Rights PhD (Federal University of Goiás). Master's in Fundamental Rights and Sustainability (Federal University of Uberlândia). Member of the Editorial Board and Senior Research Member of "Direito Internacional sem Fronteiras" (Brazil). Researcher at "Global Crossings" (Jean Monnet Chair at Federal University of Uberlândia). Former scholar at CAPES and FAPEG. International Law and Environmental Law Professor. Researcher in International Law, Environmental Law, International Security, and Human Rights. Former Visiting fellow at the Mercosur Institute of Public Policies on Human Rights (Argentina).

Claudia Loureiro Coordinator of the Jean Monnet Chair at the Federal University of Uberlândia with the GLOBAL CROSSINGS Project. Post-doctorate in Law at Nova School of Law—Lisbon (2021), in Human Rights from the Faculty of Law of the University of Coimbra (2016), and International and Comparative Law from the Faculty of Law of the University of São Paulo (2019). PhD in Law from Universidade Nova de Lisboa (2020). PhD (2015) and Master's (2006) in Comparative Civil Law from the Pontifical Catholic University of São Paulo. Professor of Environmental Law and Biolaw at the Faculty of Law of the Federal University of Uberlândia. Permanent Professor of the Postgraduate Program in Law at the Federal University of Uberlândia. Associate member of the International Law Association—ILA BRASIL and the Ibero-American Institute of Legal Studies—IBEROJUR. She is a researcher at the Nova Refugee Legal Clinic at Universidade Nova de Lisboa-Portugal. She is an associate member of the Brazilian Society of Bioethics—SBB. She is leader of the Biolaw and Human Rights Research Group—UFU and the Inter-American and European Observatory of Sustainable Development Goals—UFU, both certified by CNPq.

Vinicius Villani Abrantes PhD Candidate and Master's in Linguistic Studies at Federal University of Minas Gerais, with an emphasis on language and migration law. He is a specialist in "Public Law" and "International Law" at Centro Universitário União das Américas (UniAmérica). He has "Applied Practical Training in Human Rights in the Brazilian Context" from Centro de Direito Internacional (CEDIN) and is Founder and General Director of the "Direito Internacional sem Fronteiras—Brazil" Research Center.

Contributors

Vinicius Villani Abrantes Direito Internacional sem Fronteiras, Juiz de Fora, Minas Gerais, Brazil

María Cristina Alé UCSF - UM, Mendoza, Argentina

Ibrahim Badawi Seattle University, Seattle, WA, USA

Sumanta Bhattacharya Makaut, Kolkata, India

Ana María Bonet IHUCSO–CONICET–UCSF, Santa Fe, Argentina

Dora Cristina Ribeiro Cabete CEDIS, Nova School of Law, Universidade NOVA de Lisboa - School of Law, Lisbon, Portugal

Ana Elizabeth Lapa Wanderley Cavalcanti Mackenzie Presbyterian University, São Paulo, Brazil

Cássius Guimarães Chai Federal University of Maranhão (PPGDIR and PPGAERO/UFMA) and Vitória School of Law – (PPGD/FDV), Vitória, Brazil

Mariana Cofferri Ferreira da Silva Centro de Ensino Unificado de Brasília (CEUB), Brasília, Brazil

Valéria Emília de Aquino Federal University of Goiás, Goiânia, Goiás, Brazil

Adriana Isabelle Barbosa Sá Leitão Di Pasquale University of Pisa, Tuscany, Italy

Elisa Maffassiolli Hartwig University of Vale do Rio dos Sinos, São Leopoldo, Brazil

Javier Palummo Lantes Inter-American Commission on Human Rights, Washington, DC, USA

Natalia Lorena Losccoco Buenos Aires University (UBA) and University of Belgrano (UB), Buenos Aires, Argentina

Claudia Loureiro Federal University of Uberlândia, Uberlândia, Minas Gerais, Brazil

Janny Carrasco Medina Universidade de Brasília, Brasília, Brazil

Tarin Cristino Frota Mont'Alverne Faculty of Law, Federal University of Ceará (UFC), Fortaleza, Brazil

Alex Silva Oliveira Centre de Recherche sur la Régulation et le Droit de la Gouvernance - CrRDG, Sherbrook, Canada

José Noronha Rodrigues School of Business and Economics, the University of Azores, Azores, Portugal

Thiago Giovani Romero IBMEC/SP and Universidade Federal de Uberlândia (UFU), São Paulo, Brazil

Marlon Antônio Rosa Araxá Municipal Pension Institute, Federal University of Uberlândia, Uberlândia, Brazil

Muriuki Sharon Human Rights Measurement Initiative, Wellington, New Zealand

Gianpaolo Poggio Smanio Mackenzie Presbyterian University, São Paulo, Brazil

Cósimo Gonzalo Sozzo FCJS/UNL – Institute for Advanced Studies of the Litoral, Santa Fe, Argentina

Shuma Talukdar Mahindra University, Hyderabad, India

Julia Schutz Veiga Nippon Foundation Ocean Voices Programme, University of Edinburgh, Edinburgh, UK

NOVA School of Law, Universidade Nova de Lisboa, Lisbon, Portugal

Gabriel Wedy University of Vale do Rio dos Sinos, São Leopoldo, Brazil

Alexandra Wenzel Paris, France

Introduction

Valéria Emília de Aquino, Claudia Loureiro, and Vinicius Villani Abrantes

Fighting climate change and advocating for a healthy, clean and sustainable environment is a task that requires the combined efforts for the common good: Mother Earth or *Pachamama*. It also requires persistence and perseverance to continue in a seemingly endless struggle that clashes with the interests of several global actors, including States, large corporations, and even international and regional organizations.

In a way, it resembles a utopia, since netting zero carbon emissions—among other forms of pollution—in a capitalist and extremely consumerist society is a difficult and complex task. However, although far from our reality, it is not impossible. On the contrary, it is a task that will require international cooperation for the sake of a common benefit: protecting the environment for present and future generations.

The externalities of climate change cannot be understood and faced with resilience without observing the principle of solidarity from an intergenerational perspective. Anthropogenic actions in the past, present and future are timelessly connected, so that past choices influence the present and determine the future of the planet. In this sense, it is necessary to revisit the past, correct the present and rethink the future, so that anthropogenic actions connect with the principle of sustainable development.

V. E. de Aquino (✉)
Federal University of Goiás, Goiânia, Goiás, Brazil

C. Loureiro
Federal University of Uberlândia, Uberlândia, Minas Gerais, Brazil
e-mail: claudia.loureiro@ufu.br

V. V. Abrantes
Direito Internacional sem Fronteiras, Juiz de Fora, Minas Gerais, Brazil
e-mail: viniciusabrantes@ufmg.br

V. E. de Aquino et al. (eds.), *Climate Litigation in a Changing World*, Ius Gentium: Comparative Perspectives on Law and Justice 130,
https://doi.org/10.1007/978-3-032-05530-9_1

It is the responsibility of current generations, based on the lessons learned from the past, to leave a legacy of respect for the environment to future generations, preserving the rights of future generations to make use of the natural resources that exist on Planet Earth today. Based on this understanding, it is understood that it is the duty of the entire international community to adopt cooperative measures to deal with global warming and other externalities, since the effects of the degradation of the right to an ecologically balanced environment are felt and experienced throughout the world and are not restricted to the borders of one state.

Any action taken by any human being in any corner of the Earth can have global consequences, transcending the borders of a state and re-signifying the concepts of citizenship, nationality and sovereignty. Thus, starting from the consideration of the right to an ecologically balanced environment as a human right, it is clear that the universal conscience of humanity must be led to the realization that protecting the environment for current and future generations is an imperative norm for the entire international community, which transcends the borders and interests of states and connects with the interests of humanity as a whole.

It's worth considering that climate migration is a direct consequence of environmental change. Millions of people are already facing forced displacement due to natural disasters, desertification and rising sea levels, making up the phenomenon of climate migration. These populations, often coming from countries that have contributed the least to the environmental crisis, face enormous challenges when seeking refuge in other territories. The lack of an international legal framework that recognizes climate migrants as a specific category of displaced persons exacerbates the situation, leaving these people without adequate protection and exposed to human rights violations.

Even if "smog is democratic",[1] that is, even if climate change affects everyone on the globe, it is essential to recognize that the impacts of climate change are unevenly distributed, deepening existing social and economic inequalities. Historically marginalized communities, especially in developing countries, suffer the most severe consequences of environmental degradation, which is also a cause of tension between the Global North and the Global South.[2] This highlights the need to link the fight against climate change to the defense of human rights.

A healthy environment is a fundamental right, and its guarantee is essential for the dignity and security of populations around the world. Governments, international organizations and civil society must work together to protect these rights. In addition, it is necessary to invest in public policies that strengthen the resilience of the communities most affected by climate change.

Environmental governance must adopt an inclusive approach, ensuring that the voice of local communities is heard and that their needs are prioritized in decision-making processes. Only with this inclusion will it be possible to build a fairer and more sustainable future.

---

[1] Beck (2011).

[2] Brown (2019).

The transition to a sustainable development model also requires a transformation of the collective mentality. Environmental awareness must be promoted from an early age, encouraging behaviors that value the preservation of natural resources and the reduction of waste.

The articulation between the human rights and sustainability agendas is essential to face contemporary challenges. Respect for human rights must be the basis of any climate change adaptation strategy, ensuring that no one is left behind.[3] At the same time, it is fundamental to promote climate justice, recognizing that the countries and communities most affected by the environmental crisis are entitled to technical and financial support to address its impacts. This support must be guided by the ethics of global co-responsibility.

Once these introductory remarks have been made, we present the chapters that make up this book, which deepen the reflections and debates on the themes introduced here. Each chapter has been structured to address different aspects of climate, environmental, social and human rights issues, exploring theoretical perspectives, practical experiences and critical analyses.

1 Part I: General Aspects of Climate Litigation

The first part of this work focuses on the general study of climate litigation, presenting concepts and actors that are essential to the climate fight, such as climate justice, climate-washing, procedural rights. Therefore, the aim of Part I is to begin this book by introducing general concepts that will also be addressed and link directly or indirectly to other chapters.

In Chapter "The Role of International and National Courts in Climate Disputes", the authors Rodrigues, Bhattacharya, Medina and Cabete present an important critique of the inequalities between the Global North and South in relation to climate change, adopting an intersectional perspective and addressing cases that discuss topics such as climate justice, environmental constitutionalism, accountability, and the role of international courts and human rights non-governmental organizations (NGOs).[4]

In Chapter "Litigation for Climate Justice: The Case of Procedural Rights Under the Aarhus Convention", Wenzel also discusses the role of NGOs in climate litigation, but the core of the research lies in the approach to procedural rights, provided for in the Aarhus Convention, which are essential to the realization of the right to a healthy environment. The author addresses how access to information, decision-making on climate matters and access to justice are rights frequently violated by States, which has led to a global increase in climate cases around the world.[5]

[3] Boyle (2015).

[4] Rodrigues et al. (2025).

[5] Wenzel (2025).

In Chapter "Climate Disinformation and Climate-Washing: Litigation in Defense of Human Rights and Transparency", Hartwig and Wedy discuss how climate disinformation is one of the greatest evils in the fight against climate change. By supporting the right to information, in climate matters, as a human right intrinsically related to the right to a healthy environment, the authors reinforce the State's duty to combat disinformation and fake news on the subject.[6]

2 Part II: Jurisdictional Analysis of Climate Litigation Around the World

Considering that a legal analysis should not be restricted to the presentation of concepts, Part II intends to present the jurisprudence on climate litigation around the world, not only addressing cases and advisory opinions from international courts, but also pointing out legal aspects of the laws already existing in certain jurisdictions, and how they can be used to strengthen the international climate regime in some cases, while in other cases the laws may be incipient for climate protection.

In the second part of the book, readers will find international, regional and national climate cases that span the five continents and the most varied jurisdictions. In Chapter "Recent Trends in Climate Justice Before the European and Inter-American Human Rights Systems", Loureiro and Oliveira promote a debate essential to the dialogue of international courts. The authors present cases in the European Court and the Inter-American Court, and question the difficulties and advances in achieving climate justice through climate litigation.[7]

In Chapter "Climate Litigation in Oceania: The Case of Insular Countries", Aquino and Rosa bring an important reflection on the different cases on the continent, also discussing two other cases in the UN system, reinforcing the obligation of States in climate matters and the applicability of the principles of International Environmental Law.[8]

In Chapter "Diving Into the Synergies Between the Climate and Ocean Emergencies: An Analysis of the International Tribunal for the Law of the Sea Advisory Opinion on Climate Change", di Pasquale, Mont'Alverne and Veiga address the dynamics between climate change and ocean protection, by discussing Case 31 of the International Tribunal for the Law of the Sea, and working with other international documents that intersect the disciplines.[9]

In Chapter "The Legal Treatment of Ecocide in Brazil", Cavalcanti and Smanio provide a perspective on the historical evolution and legal implications of the crime of ecocide, bringing together the main global trends and movements on the subject,

---

[6] Hartwig and Wedy (2025).

[7] Loureiro and Oliveira (2025).

[8] Aquino and Rosa (2025).

[9] Di Pasquale et al. (2025).

until reaching the proposed thematic focus: the study of ecocide in Brazil. The authors address the legal treatment of ecocide in the country, by analyzing the existing Bills aimed at conceptualizing and typifying the crime of ecocide in the Brazilian legal system, an arduous task that involves the natural unfolding of the Brazilian legislative process.[10]

In Chapter "The Ecological Footprint: A Tool for Decision Making in the Legal Field", Bonet, Sozzo and Alé work with concepts essential to climate litigation and environmental protection, such as ecological footprint, socio-environmental crises, and the legal approach to the environment. The authors seek to align these concepts to understand ecological responsibility and the technical and legal implications for society.[11]

In Chapter "Transboundary Environmental and Climate Responsibility: Guarani Aquifer", Loscocco and Chai discuss the Guarani aquifer, contextualizing it historically and presenting its main geographic and hydrographic characteristics, in addition to its social and ecological relevance, especially with regard to the macro and micro climate of the region. Furthermore, the authors present the legal framework of the aquifer, addressing the transboundary and climate responsibility of the countries in which the aquifer is located.[12]

In Chapter "Climate Change and Air Pollution in Africa: Legal Precedents and Their Impact on Environmental Justice", Badawi discusses how climate change impacts the African continent, especially in terms of climate displacement, whether through erosion, droughts, floods, among other phenomena. The author also discusses the social and economic impact in the field of agriculture and food security, and exposes some climate and environmental disputes in the African countries.[13]

In Chapter "The Role of Courts and the Legal Profession in Climate Litigation: A Tripartite Analysis of Access to the Kenyan, East African, and African Court Systems", Muriuki introduces concepts such as climate justice and access to justice, and then presents an analysis of how the legal systems of these countries address the issue. The author highlights the crucial role of judges, courts, registries, lawyers, and Law schools in climate litigation, presenting the main laws and cases in the region.[14]

In Chapter "Challenges in Climate Litigation in India: Analyzing the Legal Framework and Its Effects on Climate Action", Talukdar addresses a critical analysis on the existing legal frameworks on climate change in India, and presents the main climate cases before Indian courts, the Law invoked and their current status. The author also explores the challenges and obstacles that must be overcome by the country.[15]

---

[10] Cavalcanti and Smanio (2025).

[11] Bonet et al. (2025).

[12] Loscocco and Chai (2025).

[13] Badawi (2025).

[14] Muriuki (2025).

[15] Talukdar (2025).

3 Part III: Climate Litigation Through the Lenses of Individuals

Having presented the main climate cases around the world, the third, and last part of this book seeks to highlight the essential role of scientists, activists, experts and international organizations in climate litigation, both in its legal and social aspects. Without the exhaustive work of these professionals, the Paris Agreement and many other international documents would not have been created, nor would there be any talk of reducing GHG emissions.

The purpose of Part III is, therefore, to conclude the work with the contribution of professionals working on the front lines of climate activism. To this end, it presents a historical evolution of climate governance, which includes the teachings of El-Hinnawi and his construction of "environmental refugees" in the 1980s, and the experiences lived in recent years by the Special Rapporteur for the Economic, Social, Cultural and Environmental Rights at the Inter-American Commission on Human Rights.

In Chapter "El-Hinnawi's Legacy and his Contribution to Climate Litigation", Romero and Silva present the valuable contribution made by El-Hinnawi, who was the first UNEP scientist to formally defend the idea of the existence of environmental refugees before the UN. His pioneering work left an indispensable legacy for climate litigation, by linking environmental degradation to climate change and, consequently, to environmental migration.[16]

In Chapter "Climate Emergency and Human Rights: Perspectives of the Consultative Process of the Inter-American Court", the Special Rapporteur for the Economic, Social, Cultural and Environmental Rights at the Inter-American Commission on Human Rights, Dr. Javier Palummo Lantes, brings his expertise to address the link between the right to a healthy environment and climate change. For this purpose, the author discusses the impact of climate change over human rights, and explains how the process of issuing an advisory opinion works, along the work of Special Rapporteurship on Economic, Social, Cultural and Environmental Rights—REDESCA (in Spanish, Relatoría Especial sobre Derechos Económicos, Sociales, Culturales y Ambientales), has been essential to enhance the protection of the environment in the region.[17]

Finally, we hope that the book can serve as an important instrument and source of International Law, by bringing together the doctrinal contributions of several experts on climate change and human rights.

---

[16] Romero and Silva (2025).

[17] Palummo Lantes (2025).

References

Aquino VE, Rosa MA (2025) Climate litigation in Oceania: the case of insular countries. In: Aquino VE, Loureiro C, Abrantes VV (eds) Climate litigation in a changing world – a comparative analysis of similarities, challenges and pathways, this volume. Springer Nature, Berlin

Badawi I (2025) Climate change and air pollution in Africa: legal precedents and their impact on environmental justice. In: Aquino VE, Loureiro C, Abrantes VV (eds) Climate litigation in a changing world – a comparative analysis of similarities, challenges and pathways, this volume. Springer Nature, Berlin

Beck U (2011) Sociedade de risco. Editora 34, São Paulo.

Bonet AM, Sozzo G, Alé MC (2025) The ecological footprint: a tool for decision making in the legal field. In: Aquino VE, Loureiro C, Abrantes VV (eds) Climate litigation in a changing world – a comparative analysis of similarities, challenges and pathways, this volume. Springer Nature, Berlin

Boyle A (2015) In: BOER B (ed) Human rights and the environment: where next? Oxford University Press, Oxford

Brown W (2019) Nas ruínas do neoliberalismo: a ascensão da política antidemocrática no ocidente. Editora Filosófica Politeia, São Paulo

Cavalcanti AELW, Smanio GP (2025) The legal treatment of ecocide in Brazil. In: Aquino VE, Loureiro C, Abrantes VV (eds) Climate litigation in a changing world – a comparative analysis of similarities, challenges and pathways, this volume. Springer Nature, Berlin

Di Pasquale AIBSL, Veiga JS, Mont'alVerne TCF (2025) Diving into the synergies between the climate and ocean emergencies: an analysis of the international tribunal for the law of the sea advisory opinion on climate change. In: Aquino VE, Loureiro C, Abrantes VV (eds) Climate litigation in a changing world – a comparative analysis of similarities, challenges and pathways, this volume. Springer Nature, Berlin

Hartwig EM, Wedy G (2025) Climate disinformation and climate-washing: litigation in defense of human rights and transparency. In: Aquino VE, Loureiro C, Abrantes VV (eds) Climate litigation in a changing world – a comparative analysis of similarities, challenges and pathways, this volume. Springer Nature, Berlin

Loscocco NL, Chai CG (2025) Transboundary environmental and climate responsibility: the Guarani aquifer. In: Aquino VE, Loureiro C, Abrantes VV (eds) Climate litigation in a changing world – a comparative analysis of similarities, challenges and pathways, this volume. Springer Nature, Berlin

Loureiro C, Oliveira AS (2025) Recent trends in climate justice before the European and Inter-American Human Rights Systems. In: Aquino VE, Loureiro C, Abrantes VV (eds) Climate litigation in a changing world – a comparative analysis of similarities, challenges and pathways, this volume. Springer Nature, Berlin

Muriuki S (2025) The role of courts and the legal profession in climate litigation: a tripartite analysis of access to the Kenyan, East African, and African Court Systems. In: Aquino VE, Loureiro C, Abrantes VV (eds) Climate litigation in a changing world – a comparative analysis of similarities, challenges and pathways, this volume. Springer Nature, Berlin

Palummo Lantes J (2025) Climate emergency and human rights: perspectives of the consultative process of the Inter-American Court. In: Aquino VE, Loureiro C, Abrantes VV (eds) Climate litigation in a changing world – a comparative analysis of similarities, challenges and pathways, this volume. Springer Nature, Berlin

Rodrigues JN, Bhattacharya S, Medina JC, Cabete DCR (2025) The role of international and national courts in climate disputes. In: Aquino VE, Loureiro C, Abrantes VV (eds) Climate litigation in a changing world – a comparative analysis of similarities, challenges and pathways, this volume. Springer Nature, Berlin

Romero TG, Silva MCF (2025) El-Hinnawi's legacy and his contribution to climate litigation. In: Aquino VE, Loureiro C, Abrantes VV (eds) Climate litigation in a changing world – a comparative analysis of similarities, challenges and pathways, this volume. Springer Nature, Berlin

Talukdar S (2025) Challenges in climate litigation in India: analyzing the legal framework and its effects on climate action. In: Aquino VE, Loureiro C, Abrantes VV (eds) Climate litigation in a changing world – a comparative analysis of similarities, challenges and pathways, this volume. Springer Nature, Berlin

Wenzel A (2025) Litigation for climate justice: the case of procedural rights under the Aarhus convention. In: Aquino VE, Loureiro C, Abrantes VV (eds) Climate litigation in a changing world – a comparative analysis of similarities, challenges and pathways, this volume. Springer Nature, Berlin

Valéria Emília de Aquino Lawyer and Human Rights Consultant, Human Rights PhD (Federal University of Goiás). Master in Fundamental Rights and Sustainability (Federal University of Uberlândia). Member of the Editorial Board and Senior Research Member of 'Direito Internacional sem Fronteiras' (Brazil). Researcher at 'Global Crossings' (Jean Monnet Chair at Federal University of Uberlândia), former scholar at CAPES and FAPEG. International Law and Environmental Law Professor. Researcher in International Law, Environmental Law, International Security, and Human Rights. Former Visiting fellow at the Mercosur Institute of Public Policies on Human Rights (Argentina). valeriaemiliaa@gmail.com

Claudia Loureiro Coordinator of the Jean Monnet Chair at the Federal University of Uberlândia with the GLOBAL CROSSINGS Project. Post-Doctorate in Law at Nova School of Law - Lisbon (2021), in Human Rights from the Faculty of Law of the University of Coimbra (2016) and International and Comparative Law completed by the Faculty of Law of the University of São Paulo (2019). PhD in Law from Universidade Nova de Lisboa (2020). PhD (2015) and Master (2006) in Comparative Civil Law from the Pontifical Catholic University of São Paulo. Professor of Environmental Law and Biolaw at the Faculty of Law of the Federal University of Uberlândia. Permanent Professor of the Postgraduate Program in Law at the Federal University of Uberlândia. Associate member of the International Law Association - ILA BRASIL, and the Ibero-American Institute of Legal Studies - IBEROJUR. She is a researcher at the Nova Refugee Legal Clinic at Universidade Nova de Lisboa-Portugal. She is an associate member of the Brazilian Society of Bioethics-SBB. She is leader of the Biolaw and Human Rights Research Group-UFU and the Inter-American and European Observatory of Sustainable Development Goals-UFU, both certified by CNPq. claudia.loureiro@ufu.br

Vinicius Villani Abrantes PhD Candidate and Master in Linguistic Studies at Federal University of Minas Gerais, with an emphasis on language and migration law. Specialist in "Public Law" and "International Law" at Centro Universitário União das Américas (UniAmérica). He has "Applied Practical Training in Human Rights in the Brazilian Context" from Centro de Direito Internacional (CEDIN); Founder and General Director of the "Direito Internacional sem Fronteiras - Brazil" Research Center. viniciusabrantes@ufmg.br

General Aspects of Climate Litigation

The Role of International and National Courts in Climate Disputes

José Noronha Rodrigues, Sumanta Bhattacharya, Janny Carrasco Medina, and Dora Cristina Ribeiro Cabete

1 Introduction

Climate change has enormous societal, economic, and environmental ramifications, making it one of the greatest threats mankind faces in the modern era. The necessity for legal action to address the causes and mitigate the repercussions of climate change is being more acknowledged as the impacts of the phenomenon become more apparent. In light of this critical need, climate litigation has grown in importance, with national and international courts taking the lead in influencing climate policy, bringing governments and companies to account, and promoting environmental justice (Abbass et al. 2022. pp. 42439–42559).

Individuals, communities, and NGOs bring claims against governments and companies for their involvement in contributing to climate change, and national courts play a crucial role in deciding these cases. These courts can determine the meaning and application of domestic rules and laws pertaining to public health, human rights, and environmental preservation, and they can hold those in power to account for their acts or lack thereof. The authority to issue injunctions, sanctions,

J. N. Rodrigues (✉)
School of Business and Economics, the University of Azores, Azores, Portugal
e-mail: jose.n.rodrigues@uac.pt

S. Bhattacharya
Makaut, Kolkata, India

J. C. Medina
Universidade de Brasília, Brasília, Brazil

D. C. R. Cabete
CEDIS, Nova School of Law, Universidade NOVA de Lisboa - School of Law, Lisbon, Portugal
e-mail: dora.cr.rodrigues@uac.pt

V. E. de Aquino et al. (eds.), *Climate Litigation in a Changing World*, Ius Gentium: Comparative Perspectives on Law and Justice 130,
https://doi.org/10.1007/978-3-032-05530-9_2

and orders for remedial actions to mitigate environmental harm and avoid additional deterioration also lies with national courts. In addition to national courts, international tribunals and courts can mediate conflicts between governments and bring them to account for climate change-related breaches of international law (UNEP 2021).

Cases involving transboundary environmental degradation, treaty violations, and human rights abuses caused by climate change can be heard by international arbitration panels and the International Court of Justice (ICJ), among other entities. When it comes to resolving climate change on a worldwide basis, the role of international courts in interpreting and creating environmental law is vital. Many climate litigation cases incorporate both local and international legal frameworks and concepts, making the junction of these two sets of laws an important component of the field. When making decisions, national courts can look to international treaties, conventions, and customary international law; when dealing with conflicts involving private entities or governments, international courts can look to domestic laws and regulations. Coordinated action at both the national and international levels is crucial to produce effective and fair solutions to climate change, since this connection between the two systems highlights how interrelated the challenges are (Singh 2022) like as jurisdictional concerns, evidence requirements, and the necessity for judicial competence in intricate scientific and technological issues persist despite the increasing visibility of climate litigation.

Nevertheless, there are also chances for creativity and teamwork, as the relevance of public involvement, multidisciplinary methods, and the incorporation of indigenous and local knowledge in climate-related issues is becoming more acknowledged by the courts. (Kodiveri 2020, June). For the benefit of all generations, national and international courts have the authority to use the rule of law to advance sustainable development, protect human rights, and ensure climate justice.

2 Climate Litigation Before the European, Inter-American and African Human Rights Systems

As a result of climate change litigation, which are regarded as posing significant threats to both human rights and the environment, an increasing number of cases are being filed before regional human rights institutions. In this comparative analysis, all of the cases that have been brought before the European Court of Human Rights. The promotion of climate justice, environmental protection, and human rights are the goals of all three systems; yet, they accomplish these goals in contexts that are distinct from one another geographically. Through the process of comparing and contrasting various approaches to climate litigation, we may be able to gain insight into new opportunities, challenges, and trends in the legal responses of regional governments to climate change. The European Union's Framework for the Protection of Human Rights (Mayer and Van Asselt 2023).

The European Court of Human Rights was an early adoption of the concept that climate change is related with human rights violations. This concept was particularly applicable to situations involving environmental degradation, relocation, and insufficient action on the part of the government. Environmental pollution, for example, violates the right to private and family life, which is outlined in Article 8 of the European Convention on Human Rights. This right was established in the key case of López Ostra v. Spain, which was handed down by the European Court of Human Rights. As a result of following rulings such as Hatton v. UK and Budayeva v. Russia, the obligation of governments to protect their citizens from environmental damage and to give sufficient reparation for victims of climate-related offences has been further cemented (ECHR 2013, June).

In the course of its work on issues pertaining to the rights of indigenous peoples, the destruction of the environment, and the industrialization of natural resources, the International Court of Human Rights has also taken into consideration climate change in the context of human rights. In the case of Saramaka People v. Suriname, the International Court of Human Rights supported the collective land rights of indigenous peoples as well as their right to participate in development projects that have an impact on their territory. Back in 2007, the Inter-American Court of Human Rights handed down a decision that many folks now see as a turning point for indigenous rights.

The case, known as Saramaka People v. Suriname, came about when the Saramaka—a Maroon community in Suriname—argued that their ancestral lands were being exploited. They claimed that logging and mining concessions were handed out without any proper consult, win, or compensation. This meant that the government didn't really give them a chance to express their concerns, a move that many believe trampled on the rights outlined in the American Convention on Human Rights. In its ruling, the Court sided with the Saramaka. It pointed out that Suriname had, in most cases, failed to respect the community's rights. Specifically, there were clear breaches related to property (Article 21), judicial protection (Article 25) and equal protection (Article 24). Generally speaking, the judgment brought forward the idea of "free, prior, and informed consent" (FPIC) as crucial when any major development projects intersect with indigenous lands.

The notion here is simple: big projects shouldn't endanger communities, and any plan for resource use should involve a fair share of benefits as well as thorough checks for both environmental and social impacts. Some scholars, like Shelton (2011) and Anaya (2009), often refer to the Saramaka case as a pivotal mix of environmental safeguards and human rights law. They see it as setting the stage for later debates on climate issues and environmental litigation, not only in international circles but within regional systems too.

Kichwa Indigenous People of Sarayaku v. Ecuador was the case in which the Supreme Court of the United States affirmed the right of indigenous peoples to be consulted and given the opportunity to provide their consent prior to the extraction of oil from their ancestral lands. The ACHPR has been more active in addressing climate-related concerns, despite the fact that its climate jurisprudence is still in the process of development for the time being. (ESCR 2007, November). In 2012, the

Kichwa Indigenous People of Sarayaku v. Ecuador was brought before the Inter-American Court of Human Rights (IACtHR) rather than being decided by the U.S. Supreme Court. This proceeding, generally speaking, stands as a pivotal moment for both Indigenous rights and environmental justice within the framework of international human rights law.

The Kichwa community, long-established in the Ecuadorian Amazon, initiated legal action against the Ecuadorian government. They contended that the state had authorized oil exploration on their ancestral lands without obtaining the community's free, prior, and informed consent (FPIC)—a process that, notably, is essential for respecting Indigenous sovereignty. Moreover, deploying explosives for seismic testing not only compromised the local ecology but also threatened the community's spiritual and cultural fabric. In its judgment, the Inter-American Court ruled in favor of the Sarayaku. The decision, which in many cases underscores evolving legal norms, determined that Ecuador had violated the rights to property (Article 21), as well as to life and physical integrity (Article 4), alongside the community's cultural identity. The court's reasoning, lightly punctuated by clarifications and measured qualifiers, emphasized the necessity of securing FPIC and safeguarding Indigenous territories prior to embarking on development projects. Rodrigo Uprimny (2013) has, in most instances, portrayed this case as a benchmark—one that not only integrates Indigenous cosmologies into formal legal reasoning but also reinforces international standards regarding FPIC.

A number of issues, including environmental degradation, natural resource management, and the rights of pastoralists and indigenous peoples, are brought before the African Commission on Human and People's Rights (ACHPR) for consideration. Cases such as Endorois Welfare Council v. Kenya, Centre for Minority Rights Development (Kenya), and Minority Rights Group International v. Kenya have dealt with related issues, such as the right to a healthy environment and the rights of indigenous peoples. However, the ACHPR has not yet issued specific rulings on climate change (Ashamu 2011, pp. 300–313).

Climate litigation in the human rights systems of Europe, the Americas, and Africa have comparable themes and techniques, although differences in regional settings and legal frameworks. The obligation of states to avoid and mitigate climate-related harm is one of these. Another is the right of vulnerable groups to participate in decision-making processes that affect them. A few more include the awareness of the connection between human rights and environmental protection. Victims of climate-related offences should have access to appropriate remedies, such as compensation, restitution, and assurances of non-repetition, according to all three systems.

African, Inter-American, and European human rights systems have all taken important steps towards resolving climate-related disputes, but they are still struggling to put their findings into action. Among these obstacles is the complexity of climate change on a global scale, in addition to scarce resources, weak institutions, and a lack of political will (Aristova and Lim 2024, March).

On the other hand, regional human rights systems and other national and international actors may work together, share information, and strengthen their capacities to make a greater collective influence on climate justice. There is an increasing tendency to call states and other entities responsible for their part in causing climate change and its effects on human rights to account through climate litigation in the human rights systems of Europe, the Inter-American system, and Africa. Environmental protection, social justice, and sustainable development are shared concepts and aims across all systems, despite the fact that each system functions within its own distinct geographical context. In order to combat the effects of climate change and ensure that all people are able to exercise their human rights, these regional human rights systems should encourage communication, collaboration, and the sharing of knowledge.

3 Climate Litigation and Advisory Opinion as a Pathway to Address Loss and Damage

Damage and loss caused by climate change endangers ecosystems, livelihoods, and human lives, making it a major problem for people throughout the world. Climate lawsuits and advisory opinions are new but equally important strategies to deal with loss and harm as conventional methods of adaptation and mitigation fail. In this article, we will look at these paths and how they help with repairing harm and loss, what they can't do, and how they can help with climate justice. Litigation involving climate change occurs when private parties (such as people, communities, or organisations) sue public bodies (such as governments or companies) for their role in causing or failing to address climate change. Responsible parties must be held accountable for their acts or inactions as part of climate litigation in order to remedy loss and harm. Damages produced by climate-related consequences, such as rising sea levels, harsh weather, and biodiversity loss, can be recovered, for instance, by suing fossil fuel firms for their part in contributing to greenhouse gas emissions (Toussaint 2021, pp. 16–33).

Communities hit hard by climate change may be able to find legal recourse through climate lawsuit. Damage to property, loss of income, or compelled relocation as a result of environmental deterioration may be compensable. For example, climate change-related financial aid, mitigation measures, or ecosystem restoration may be mandated as a consequence of judgements or settlements rendered by national courts or international tribunals. The power of climate lawsuits to encourage policy shifts and hold governments and businesses to account is an asset. Changes in government policy, business practices, and public views on climate change can result from high-profile instances that raise public awareness and put political pressure on relevant parties. Legal precedents established via successful litigation can also serve to fortify environmental rules, hold corporations more accountable, and bolster safeguards for marginalised populations (Verheyen and Franke 2023).

Nevertheless, there are a number of obstacles to climate litigation, such as a lack of resources, difficulty in establishing culpability and causation, and other similar issues. Many impacted populations, especially those in low-income nations or marginalised regions, lack access to legal processes due to their lengthy, costly, and resource-intensive nature. Additionally, it may be difficult to fulfil the legal requirements for demonstrating causality and assigning blame in climate-related disputes, especially when dealing with complicated scientific data and situations involving several parties.

The Inter-American Court of Human Rights (IACHR or IACtHR), the International Court of Justice (ICJ), and other regional and international agencies offer legal advice on complicated matters pertaining to environmental protection, human rights, and international law in advisory opinions. When it comes to climate change, advisory opinions are really useful for guiding the legal and policy reactions to harm and loss. To address a worldwide danger to human security, the ICJ issued an advisory opinion on the legitimacy of nuclear weapons, which outlined how international law should be interpreted and applied.

Damage and loss-related legal duties, principles, and standards, such as the duty to avoid harm, the principle of common but differentiated responsibilities, and the rights of impacted communities to involvement, justice, and reparations, can be better understood through advisory opinions on climate-related matters. Governments, legislators, and stakeholders can benefit from advisory views in resolving loss and damage and advancing climate justice because they offer authoritative interpretations of international law and legal frameworks. Advisory opinions can clarify and harmonise the process of creating and implementing legal frameworks to deal with loss and damage because they offer expert interpretations of international law and legal concepts (Simlinger and Mayer 2019).

In addition to helping with international coordination and collaboration in the aftermath of climate disasters, advisory views can help nations and stakeholders reach an agreement on critical climate change concerns. Not only are advisory opinions not legally enforceable, but states and other actors may politicise them or selectively interpret legal principles according to their own interests. Advisory opinions, however helpful, do not have the same weight in law as decisions or judgements handed down by tribunals or courts. Advisory views are only useful if governments and other interested parties are prepared to put their suggestions into action and incorporate them into policy and practice. (Kosolapova 2024, March).

Important avenues for resolving climate change-related loss and harm include climate lawsuits and advisory opinions, which provide chances for responsibility, restitution, and policy direction. Advisory opinions give authoritative interpretations of international law and legal concepts related to loss and damage, whereas climate litigation focuses on holding responsible parties accountable for their affects on impacted populations and their contributions to climate change. Advocates for sustainable development, climate justice, and increased resilience may benefit current and future generations by making good use of these channels. Climate lawsuits and advisory opinions have their merits, but they must be supplemented with larger initiatives to tackle the causes of climate change and create more fair and resilient communities (Nobre 2022, November).

4 Overcoming Climate Neocolonialism: Achieving Climate Justice in Vulnerable Communities in the Global South

The most marginalised and oppressed regions of the world are suffering the brunt of the climate crisis, which is already producing severe difficulties with inequality and injustice. These regions are also the primary victims of the climate disaster. Some of the ways in which disadvantaged groups are experiencing the consequences of climate change include the destruction of the ecosystem, an increase in the frequency and severity of weather events, and a decrease in income. The concept of climate neocolonialism is explored in depth in this article, along with its impact on vulnerable communities in the southern regions of the world and the strategies that may be used to achieve climate justice in spite of these challenges. The examination of climate neocolonialism in the realm of climate litigation has assumed an urgency that goes well beyond the straightforward task of holding states and corporations accountable for their roles in climate change. In many cases, while litigation focuses on externalizing responsibility for environmental degradation on major emitters, closer scrutiny reveals underlying issues of historical accountability, justice, and equity—concerns that too often resonate with longstanding critiques of neocolonial practices. These debates challenge us to rethink how legal responses operate within the broader framework of global climate governance. At its core, climate neocolonialism describes a process where legal and policy frameworks, along with financial mechanisms, tend to impose disproportionate burdens on developing nations while allowing historically industrialized countries to maintain economic and geopolitical advantage. Frequently, international courts are perceived not merely as neutral arbiters but as institutions that echo the values and legal traditions of the Global North. For instance, nations from the Global South may be pressured into adhering to rigorous international environmental standards without receiving equivalent financial, technological, or capacity-building support—a dynamic that reinforces pre-existing asymmetries of power. Litigation brought forward by vulnerable communities—including Indigenous peoples and Small Island Developing States (SIDS)—serves to further illuminate these disparities. Such legal actions underscore how the communities most affected by climate harms are often not the ones predominantly responsible for historical emissions. As international tribunals are increasingly called upon to assess claims invoking principles like common but differentiated responsibilities (CBDR) and intergenerational equity, the outcomes of these cases bear significant influence on whether the judicial system will serve as a catalyst for change or inadvertently sustain neocolonial patterns.

This multifaceted discussion also prompts critical reflection on whose voices are prioritized in legal discourses, which normative frameworks are elevated, and whether current legal structures can adequately address postcolonial realities. For example, Indigenous knowledge systems and community-based environmental management—though rich in practical wisdom—are frequently marginalized in formal proceedings. Such omissions raise important questions about whether the prevailing model of climate litigation genuinely promotes global justice or simply reaffirms traditional power hierarchies under an environmentally progressive veneer (Yip 2022, November).

In the context of efforts to adapt to and mitigate the consequences of climate change, the term "climate neocolonialism" refers to the manner in which governments, companies, and international organisations exploit and marginalise people in the developing countries of the Global South. This particular form of neocolonialism maintains power relations that are unequal, economic reliance that is strong, and environmental injustice that is kept at bay. It does this by reinforcing patterns of exploitation and inequality that have been carried down from colonial centuries.

Neocolonialism in the context of climate change refers to the uneven distribution of climate-related finances and resources. The advantages of climate-related investments and initiatives are reaped by developed nations and corporations, but at the expense of communities in the South that are more economically disadvantaged. Top-down, technocratic solutions to climate change, such as large-scale infrastructure development and carbon offset initiatives, typically disrespect local knowledge, priorities, and rights. This is a common occurrence. This further marginalises afflicted groups and diminishes their agency and autonomy, further reducing their effectiveness. Indigenous peoples, smallholder farmers, and coastal inhabitants in the Global South are susceptible to the effects of climate neocolonialism because of their historical marginalisation, poor socioeconomic status, and geographical isolation.

This makes them particularly sensitive to the effects of climate change. The fact that these communities do not have access to essential resources such as clean water, food security, and healthcare, amongst other essential resources, renders them even more susceptible to the stresses and fluctuations that are brought on by climate change. In addition, the support that neocolonial agendas provide for extractive industries and land-use practices like as deforestation, large-scale farming, and mining results in the destruction of ecosystems, the displacement of people from their homes, and the weakening of local economies, all of which contribute to the cycle of poverty and inequality. Communities who are already at a disadvantage are frequently excluded from decision-making processes on adaptation and mitigation to climate change. This only serves to further isolate and disenfranchise these communities (Baue and Vieira 2023).

The resolution of the underlying causes of climate neocolonialism and the encouragement of disadvantaged communities to participate in decision-making, obtain access to resources, and advocate for their rights are crucial steps towards achieving climate justice. Decolonizing climate finance requires taking a number of crucial steps, one of which is to redirect climate finances and resources to fulfil the needs of indigenous peoples, women, and youth in the Global South. This is a population that is particularly vulnerable. Increasing funding for adaptation and resilience-building activities that are driven by communities is a component of this, as is providing support for sustainable livelihoods and traditional knowledge systems (Datta and Kairy 2024).

When it comes to combating the consequences of climate change and neocolonial exploitation, it is of the utmost importance to empower disadvantaged populations to take control of their land, resources, and self-determination. In order to do this, it is necessary to ensure that individuals have a genuine voice in decision-making, to respect and acknowledge the land tenure systems of indigenous peoples, and to encourage community-based management of natural resources. It is the purpose of fostering South-South collaboration to assist countries in the Global South in working together to find solutions to the climatic challenges that they all face. This may be accomplished by the exchange of knowledge, the enhancement of their capacities, and the demonstration of solidarity. This includes pushing for collaborative research initiatives that give emphasis to local opinions and context-specific techniques for adapting to and reducing the effects of climate change, as well as for the transfer of technology and learning from one another (Etchart 2017).

When the Establishment of Neocolonial Power is called into question: In order to resist climate neocolonialism, we must first address its core causes, which include economic exploitation, environmental degradation, and power imbalances. This may be accomplished by asking for fundamental reforms in international law and development policy. It is imperative that human rights, social justice, and environmental sustainability be given top priority in every facet of global government, including investment programmes, trade agreements, and international institutions (Baue and Vieira 2023).

Putting an emphasis on indigenous knowledge and wisdom means recognising and honouring indigenous ways of knowing, doing, and being as essential resources for coping with, adapting to, and surviving the effects of climate change. Providing indigenous people with a role in the planning and policymaking process about climate change, providing support for conservation activities that are leading by indigenous people, and respecting indigenous peoples' rights to cultural autonomy and self-determination are all instances of this. In order to overcome climate neocolonialism and achieve climate justice for marginalised communities in the South, it is vital to implement a plan that is both all-encompassing and all-inclusive, and that addresses the basic reasons for oppression, exploitation, and marginalisation. By decolonizing climate finance, encouraging community ownership and control, strengthening South-South cooperation, challenging neocolonial power structures, and putting indigenous knowledge and wisdom at the centre, we can create societies that are more just and sustainable, and that put people and the earth at the forefront of their priorities (Datta and Kairy 2024).

Ultimately, in order to achieve climate justice, it is not enough to only address the impacts of climate change; you must also remove the power structures, privileges, and repressive institutions that are responsible for maintaining environmental injustice and inequality. We need to come together, collaborate, and take collective action on a global, national, and even micro level in order to construct a society that is better and more equal for the generations who are currently living and those that will come after us.

4.1 Cases in Pacific Islands

The nations of the Pacific, which are particularly vulnerable to the effects of climate change, rely heavily on national and international courts to hear climate lawsuit claims. The role of these courts is to handle the legal elements of climate change, such as ensuring that governments and companies are held responsible for their roles in causing and coping with global warming. To seek compensation for damages caused by climate change, some Pacific Island nations have employed national and international legal systems.

Notable examples include the Republic of the Marshall Islands' (RMI) use of the International Court of Justice (ICJ) to sue nuclear-armed states for violating the Non-Proliferation Treaty (NPT's) requirement that they engage in good faith negotiations to disarm their nuclear arsenal. Although not directly related to climate change, this case shows how Pacific Island states have used international tribunals to tackle serious dangers to their safety and security, even those made worse by the phenomenon (International Court of Justice n.d.)

The Teitiota v. Chief Executive of the Ministry of Business, Innovation and Employment case in New Zealand garnered interest from across the world when it was decided on a national basis. Ioane Teitiota, a citizen of Kiribati, said that his country was becoming unsuitable as a result of climate change and sought refuge in New Zealand. His case may have failed in the end, but it brought attention to the increasing overlap between refugee law and climate change and opened up conversations about nations' responsibility to those displaced by the latter. (United Nations Environment Programme 2015, July 20).

Tavua District (and others) v. The Attorney-General, a case heard in Fiji, demonstrated how national courts may hold governments to account when they fail to adequately address climate change. The plaintiffs, who lived in coastal settlements in Fiji, sued the government for not doing more to prevent the destruction of their homes and the flooding that comes with climate change. Precedent for future climate litigation in Fiji was established by the case, which led to the acknowledgment of the government's legal obligation to defend citizens' rights in confronting climate change (Yuen and Madraiwiwi 2015).

In addition, a world-renowned precedent in climate litigation was established in the case of Urgenda Foundation v. The State of the Netherlands. Even if it has nothing to do with the countries of the Pacific, the effects will be felt all around the globe. An environmental group from the Netherlands called Urgenda prevailed in court, and the judge ordered the government to drastically raise its goals for reducing emissions of greenhouse gases. This case demonstrated that governments had a responsibility to aggressively combat climate change, and it served as a precedent for other nations, particularly those in the Pacific, to pursue similar measures through the legal system (Environmental Law Alliance Worldwide 2015, June 24).

Climate litigation cases in Pacific Island states are greatly aided by both national and international courts. These courts provide opportunities to seek justice, hold governments responsible, and advance legal ideas that tackle the intricate problems caused by climate change. By taking part in these lawsuits, Pacific Island nations are doing double duty: standing up for their rights and helping shape climate legislation on a global and national scale.

4.2 Cases in Europe

When it comes to climate litigation, European courts—both national and international—are essential, touching on issues like government duties, business responsibility, and environmental protection. Activists, governments, and environmental groups are battling it out in these courtrooms to ensure that those responsible for climate change are held responsible and to enforce stronger climate legislation.

There has been a recent in cases involving climate change and other environmental concerns brought before the European Court of Human Rights (ECtHR). Urgenda Foundation v. The Netherlands is a case that stands out. The Dutch Supreme Court's 2019 judgement confirms a lower court's finding that the government has an obligation to drastically cut emissions of greenhouse gases in order to safeguard the human rights of its inhabitants. As a result of this lawsuit, human rights law now requires nations to take action to reduce the effects of climate change (Environmental Law Alliance Worldwide 2015, June 24).

Urgenda Foundation v. The Netherlands stands out as a turning point in the fight against climate change. In 2015, a case by the Urgenda Foundation—joined by 886 Dutch citizens—challenged how little the government had cut greenhouse gas emissions, arguing that such slack action clashed with what Dutch tort law and the rights to life and privacy (as outlined in Articles 2 and 8 of the European Convention on Human Rights) would demand. The matter, which later gained affirmation from the Dutch Supreme Court in 2019, has often been invoked in academic debates as evidence that states must shoulder responsibility for mitigating climate change. In one remarkable decision, Dutch judges ordered the government to lower GHG emissions by 25% by 2020 relative to 1990 levels—a directive that, in most cases, underscores the belief that human safety outweighs bureaucratic hesitations. The Supreme Court, citing human rights concerns, backed the move and essentially reminded everyone that climate change risks force governments, in a very real sense, to act actively under the ECHR's umbrella. It's a ruling that, frankly speaking, reshaped the conversation around state obligations and environmental protection. Peel and Osofsky (2018) and Voigt (2020), for instance have remarked that this case set an international benchmark by linking human rights directly to climate measures. Its influence has spilled over into other legal battles, notably in European Court of Human Rights climate cases, and even sparked similar challenges elsewhere.

Overall, a growing number of judges seem increasingly willing to view environmental harm as not just a policy issue but really as a violation of fundamental rights.

Climate litigation has also made significant progress at the national level in a number of European countries' courts. As an example, in 2021, Germany's top court said that the government's climate protection policies were inadequate and infringed against the basic rights of generations to come. In order to guarantee more aggressive reduction objectives for emissions, the government was compelled by the Constitutional Court to amend its climate legislation (Weise 2024, April 9).

In a similar vein, Irish people challenged their government's climate policies in court. The claimants were upheld by the Irish Supreme Court in 2019, who found that the government's national mitigation plan did not meet its responsibilities as outlined in the Irish Constitution and international agreements. The government was forced to update its climate policy in order to comply with the court's ruling. The French government was sued by environmental organisations for its failure to fulfil its climate pledges. In a historic ruling in 2021, the French Administrative Court ruled the government liable for ecological damage and deemed them guilty of climate change inaction. The government was compelled by the court to implement more stringent policies aimed at reducing emissions and safeguarding the environment (McIntyre 2020, August 27).

The increasing involvement of national and international courts in influencing climate policy and enforcing corporate and government responsibility for environmental degradation is highlighted by these cases. Their actions demonstrate the efficacy of legal action in pressuring governments to take climate action and meet their responsibility to preserve the earth and the rights of present and future generations.

4.3 Cases in Africa

Africa is bearing a disproportionate share of the world's climate change consequences, making it all the more important for national and international courts to handle climate lawsuit claims. The purpose of these courts is to provide a platform for communities impacted by climate change to seek justice, hold governments and companies responsible for their actions, and advance their rights. When it comes to dealing with climate-related problems on the continent, a number of high-profile cases show how important national and international legal procedures are.

Urgenda Foundation v. The State of the Netherlands is a well-known lawsuit that started in the Netherlands but has worldwide consequences. A non-profit group called Urgenda won a 2015 case in which the Dutch Supreme Court upheld a legal requirement that the Dutch government cut emissions of greenhouse gases by 25% from 1990 levels by 2020. As a precedent for future cases of its kind, this historic ruling demonstrated that governments must act swiftly to curb climate change while safeguarding their citizens' rights. One African case that exemplifies how national courts may call businesses responsible for their part in climate change and environmental degradation to account is Friends of the Earth Africa v. Shell Nigeria. Oil spill victims in Nigeria sued oil behemoth Shell, claiming the company failed to do enough to stop the damage to the environment and pay them fairly. The fact that a Nigerian court decided to punish Shell shows that national legal systems may help fix climate-related injustices and safeguard the rights of marginalised groups (Princewill and Shveda 2022, May 26).

When it comes to human rights breaches caused by climate change, international courts like the African Court on Human and Peoples Rights (AfCHPR) are crucial. Cases involving environmental degradation, displacement, and infringement of indigenous peoples' rights sometimes connect with climate concerns, although these courts do not explicitly handle climate change litigation. Deforestation and land degradation caused by climate change have contributed to the displacement of the Ogiek people from their ancestral lands in Kenya. This was the central issue in the case of Ogiek People v. Republic of Kenya, which was heard by the AfCHPR. Human rights breaches caused by climate change have also been addressed in the jurisprudence of the African Commission on Human and Peoples' Rights (ACHPR). The African Court of Human Rights upheld the right to a healthy environment as a basic human right in the case of Centre for Human Rights and Others v. Nigeria. The court found the Nigerian government liable for the Niger Delta region's environmental degradation, including oil pollution and its negative impacts on local communities' livelihoods (ESCR-Net 2017, October 29).

To ensure that governments and companies are held responsible, that impacted people' rights are protected, and that environmental justice is advanced, climate litigation claims in Africa must be heard in both national and international courts. The promotion of sustainable development and the mitigation of its negative affects on vulnerable people are greatly aided by these courts, which also operate as vital venues for resolving the complicated legal concerns caused by climate change.

4.4 *Cases in Latin America and Caribbean*

There has been a noticeable uptick in climate change lawsuits throughout Latin America and the Caribbean, with national and international courts being engaged more and more. These lawsuits are critical in bringing companies and governments to justice for their involvement in causing climate change and in promoting measures to lessen the impact of this global warming. Among the most prominent cases heard by the Inter-American Commission on Human Rights (IACHR) is that of the Indigenous Kichwa People of Sarayaku v. Ecuador. This case involves the Kichwa people of Sarayaku, Ecuador, who took legal action against the government for permitting oil drilling on their ancestral grounds without their permission. A ruling in favour of the Kichwa people by the court highlights indigenous peoples' rights and the need for governments to have free, prior, and informed permission before developing projects that can harm indigenous peoples' homes and ecosystems. In a similar vein, the Colombian government was sued by a group of twenty-five young

Colombians in what is formally called the Climate Change Lawsuit. Their constitutional rights to a healthy environment, life, food, water, and health were allegedly breached since the government did not sufficiently address climate change. In a unanimous decision, Colombia's highest court has ruled that the government must act immediately to stop the destruction of the Amazon rainforest and cut emissions of greenhouse gases (International Centre on Human Rights and Drug Policy 2012, June 27).

Significant climate litigation has also occurred at the national level in Brazil. The Brazilian government was mandated to create a comprehensive strategy to decrease emissions of greenhouse gases and fight against deforestation in the Amazon by the Federal Court of Rio Grande do Sul in a historic decision. The court upheld Brazil's international obligations under the Paris Agreement and the government's constitutional duty to safeguard the environment (Kossoy 2018, October 8).

Small island republics in the Caribbean are particularly susceptible to the effects of climate change, as was demonstrated in the case Maurice et al. v. the Attorney General of Trinidad and Tobago. The claimants, who were resident of Trinidad and Tobago, said that their fundamental rights to life, liberty, and property were violated by the government's insufficient response to climate change, namely its reliance on fossil fuels. This lawsuit is far from over, but it does show how critical it is to include climate change in national policy and legislation.

The importance of national and international courts in promoting climate justice in the Americas is highlighted by these instances. These legal processes help safeguard human rights, the environment, and the future of our planet by making governments and businesses answer for their deeds.

5 Environmental Constitutionalism

The idea that environmental protection should be included in a country's constitution, typically next to other basic rights like the right to life, health, and a healthy environment, is known as environmental constitutionalism. This idea highlights the significance of regulatory frameworks in dealing with environmental issues, such as global warming. Through climate litigation, which seeks judicial remedies for environmental harm and promotes greater climate action, national and international courts play an essential role in maintaining environmental constitutionalism.

The role of international courts like the ICJ and regional human rights courts in climate litigation has grown in recent years. In order to ensure that governments fulfil their responsibilities under international environmental and human rights treaties and accords, these tribunals provide interpretations of these documents. When it comes to climate litigation, national courts are crucial because they interpret environmental protection statutes and constitutional issues at the national level. More and more claims involving climate change have been brought before courts in nations like Ecuador and Colombia, where environmental rights are clearly stated in the constitution. As an example, the Ecuadorian government was found to have infringed upon the rights of indigenous people when it permitted oil drilling on ancestral grounds without their agreement, according to the Inter-American Court of Human Rights' ruling in the Indigenous Kichwa People of Sarayaku v. Ecuador case (Mayer and Van Asselt 2023, pp. 175–184).

Environmental laws can be enforced and governments can be held responsible for non-compliance with environmental duties through national courts. As an example of the judiciary's involvement in ensuring environmental promises are met, consider the Brazilian case where the Federal Court of Rio Grande do Sul ordered the government to create a national strategy to fight deforestation in the Amazon and decrease emissions of greenhouse gases. When it comes to climate litigation, both national and international courts play a crucial role in pushing environmental constitutionalism forward. Jurisprudence that acknowledges the inherent connection between environmental rights and human rights is advanced by these courts via their interpretation and application of constitutional and legislative provisions pertaining to environmental preservation. The courts have the power to ensure that governments address climate change, safeguard vulnerable groups, and respect the right of current and future generations to an environmentally safe and sustainable environment through their rulings (UN Environment Programme 2019, January 29).

6 Environmental and Climate Responsibility

More and more, legal and governmental frameworks throughout the world are beginning to acknowledge environmental and climate responsibilities as critical components. As the threat of climate change has grown in recent years, litigation in both domestic and international courts has played an increasingly important role in resolving environmental and climate-related disputes. The goal of this legal movement is to make governmental and corporate institutions answerable for their roles in causing environmental degradation and global warming. In this article, we delve into the ways in which national and international courts have been involved in climate litigation and how they have helped to forward the cause of environmental and climate accountability.

Environmental and climate responsibility law has been significantly shaped by regional human rights tribunals and the International Court of Justice (ICJ) on a global scale. These tribunals apply human rights and environmental law concepts to the interpretation of treaties and international accords in order to bring nations to account for their behaviour. The interdependence of environmental and security concerns was demonstrated, for instance, in the Marshall Islands' case against nuclear-armed states for their failure to disarm. The ICJ underlined states' obligations to prevent environmental harm, including the risks associated with nuclear weapons testing (Kipane and Vilks 2022).

The European Court of Human Rights has also heard cases involving claims of human rights breaches by communities or people as a result of environmental degradation or authorities' lack of effective action on climate change. According to the court's ruling in López Ostra v. Spain, the Spanish government's inaction on pollution violated the right to privacy guaranteed by the European Convention on Human Rights. International courts have played a crucial role in establishing a connection between human rights, environmental preservation, and state accountability, as these rulings demonstrate (Letzing and Sung 2024, April 9).

The role of the courts in combating climate change and fostering environmental responsibility has grown in recent years on a national scale. The courts play a crucial role in implementing environmental laws and bringing governments and companies to account in nations that have robust environmental protection legal frameworks. An example of this is the United States, where the Supreme Court's decision in the seminal case of Massachusetts v. EPA mandated EPA regulation of automobile emissions due to the classification of greenhouse gases as pollutants under the Clean Air Act.

Significant climate lawsuit cases have occurred in Latin American nations such as Colombia and Brazil, where national courts have addressed environmental and climate responsibilities. Recognising the state's constitutional duty to safeguard the environment, the Brazilian Federal Court of Rio Grande do Sul mandated that the government establish a comprehensive strategy to lessen emissions of greenhouse gases and fight against the destruction of the Amazon rainforest. In a similar vein, a group of juvenile plaintiffs in Colombia's Climate Change Lawsuit were upheld by the country's highest court, which then mandated that the government immediately implement policies to decrease emissions of greenhouse gases and halt the cutting down of trees. When it comes to taking action to protect the environment and mitigate climate change, the role of national and international courts is critical. To ensure that governments and other entities are held responsible for their acts, courts play an important role in deciding issues involving environmental damage, pollution, and climate change. Furthermore, judicial rulings have the power to bind lawmakers into concrete measures to combat climate change, safeguard marginalised populations, and preserve human and environmental rights. Thus, climate litigation is crucial in promoting global and national environmental and climatic responsibilities (Colby et al. 2020, pp. 168–185).

7 Role of Non-Governmental Organizations (NGOs) and National Human Rights Institutions (NHRIs)

Around the globe, climate litigation is a major arena for non-governmental organisations (NGOs) and national human rights institutions (NHRIs), which help push for environmental justice, safeguard human rights, and advance sustainable development. These groups frequently take on the role of advocates, helping those in need who are pursuing legal action to hold governments and businesses responsible for climate-related damages and who may not have access to the legal representation they need.

Non-governmental organisations (NGOs) play an important role in climate litigation by representing impacted populations and initiating legal cases based on their knowledge of environmental legislation, advocacy, and community mobilisation. Frequently, these groups speak for underrepresented populations, indigenous peoples, and communities on the front lines of the fight against climate change. In order to combat development projects, government policies, and corporate practices that lead to deforestation, greenhouse gas emissions, and other forms of environmental degradation, non-governmental organisations (NGOs) resort to strategic litigation (Jans and Marseille 2010, pp. 373–390).

In a similar vein, NHRIs are vital in climate litigation by keeping an eye out for human rights abuses caused by environmental degradation and fighting for changes in legislation and legal solutions. The right to a healthy environment is one of the human rights guaranteed by international human rights treaties, and NHRIs are obligated to uphold and defend this right. In order to promote environmental justice and address human rights abuses connected to climate change, these institutions undertake investigations, publish findings, and collaborate with governments, civil society, and international organisations (Luporini and Kodiveri 2021).

For example, SUHAKAM, Malaysia's Human Rights Commission, has brought attention to the fact that climate change threatens several human rights, such as the right to exist, to eat, to drink, and to be healthy. In order to combat climate change and shield at-risk populations from its consequences, SUHAKAM has demanded stricter legislative and policy measures. In their work to ensure that national laws and constitutions adequately protect environmental rights and to ensure that countries adhere to international human rights norms, non-governmental organisations (NGOs) such as SUHAKAM play an important role in climate litigation. Climate litigation is one area where NHRIs and NGOs frequently work together, combining forces to increase the impact of lawsuits and provide impacted communities a stronger voice. Collaborations like this make it easier for underrepresented communities to get the justice they need and boost the impact of advocacy efforts for climate and environmental justice. As a team, NHRIs and NGOs can make the most of each other's expertise to achieve shared objectives and ensure that those responsible for protecting human rights and the environment live up to their promises (Suhakam 2024, January, 18).

Communities are empowered to participate in climate litigation and advocate for their rights successfully through capacity-building efforts conducted by NGOs and NHRIs. These groups help communities get the knowledge and tools they need to participate in legal procedures, train future lawyers, and encourage grassroots organising. In their work towards environmental justice, NGOs and NHRIs help impacted communities become more self-advocate, which in turn democratises climate governance and gives voice to underrepresented groups.

Non-governmental organisations (NGOs) and non-governmental research institutes (NHRIs) are vital in global climate litigation, achieving environmental justice, safeguarding human rights, and fostering sustainable development. These groups work to hold governments and businesses responsible for their part in causing climate change and environmental degradation, as well as to help communities who have been impacted by these issues and to seek legal remedies. A more equitable and sustainable future may be achieved when NHRIs and NGOs collaborate and strengthen local communities.

8 Gendered and Intersectional Analysis on Climate Litigation

Litigation over climate change, like many other parts of the issue, does not respect gender. A gendered and intersectional approach to climate litigation acknowledges that people and communities are impacted differently by climate change depending on factors such as gender, socioeconomic background, race, ethnicity, and other intersecting identities. If climate litigation is serious about promoting gender equality and social justice and addressing the varied needs of all impacted individuals, it must first have a firm grasp of these dynamics.

Climate change has a disproportionate effect on women and other marginalised genders, and gendered analysis in climate litigation takes this into account. Because of preexisting gender inequality, socioeconomic inequities, and cultural norms, women typically take the hit when natural catastrophes and environmental degradation strike. Droughts, floods, and deforestation disproportionately affect women since they often bear the primary responsibility for providing their family with water, food, and fuel. Climate change already puts women at a disadvantage, and their lack of agency, land, and resources further makes the situation worse.

When we use intersectional analysis, we may learn even more about the ways in which racism, colonialism, and classism interact with climate change. For example, women from low-income communities, indigenous groups, and women of colour may experience different forms of discrimination and marginalisation, which might make them more susceptible to the effects of climate change. Various identities influence how people are able to engage in climate litigation and decision-making, the resources they have access to, and the risks they face from the environment (Djoudi et al. 2016, pp. 248–262).

Climate litigation has the potential to disrupt or reinforce preexisting power relations and disparities; gendered and intersectional analyses illuminate this process. Limitations in legal representation, language obstacles, and general ignorance of rights are just a few examples of the ways that women and other marginalised genders may encounter obstacles on the path to justice. Litigation over climate change that disregards these obstacles runs the risk of further marginalising marginalised communities and reiterating existing gender and socioeconomic disparities.

Contrarily, climate litigation that is gender-responsive and intersectional aims to reduce these inequalities by fostering inclusive and participative practices, including varied viewpoints, and giving a stronger voice to oppressed groups. A good example of this is the work of groups like What we do (WEDO), which seeks to ensure that women and other marginalised genders have their unique climate policy, financial, and legal demands and objectives met.

By including gender and intersectional analysis into climate litigation, new avenues for legal action may be explored, leading to remedies and strategies that combat structural inequality and bring about revolutionary change. For instance, by establishing precedents that acknowledge the significance of Indigenous knowledge, traditional practices, and women's leadership in climate adaptation and mitigation initiatives, lawsuits aiming to hold governments and corporations responsible for infringing upon the rights of indigenous women or communities can be a powerful tool. In order to comprehend the uneven effects of climate change, to challenge current power systems, and to advance gender parity and social justice, gendered and intersectional analysis is crucial in climate litigation. Through the integration of varied viewpoints and experiences into advocacy and legal tactics, climate litigation has the potential to be a potent instrument for combating structural injustices, promoting human rights, and constructing a future that is both sustainable and egalitarian for everyone (Rainard et al. 2023).

9 Future Perspective

When it comes to protecting environmental constitutionalism, encouraging environmental stewardship, and achieving climate justice on a global scale, climate litigation—in which both domestic and international courts play critical roles—is essential. The climate change cases that these courts decide help shape legal frameworks that value sustainable development, human rights, and environmental preservation as interdependent issues. Climate litigation that includes non-governmental organisations (NGOs) also helps impacted communities get their voices heard and supports advocacy efforts to make governments and companies pay for their dirty deeds.

The foundation of legal initiatives aiming to address climate change through the courts in several nations is environmental constitutionalism. In a similar vein, litigants requesting government action on climate change have been successful in national courts in Pakistan and Colombia, which have acknowledged the constitutional right to a healthy environment. Recognising the state's responsibility to preserve the environment for present and future generations, Colombia's Supreme Court of Justice mandated that the government establish a strategy to combat Amazon deforestation. Judicial activism on environmental concerns is on the rise in Pakistan after the Lahore High Court delivered a historic ruling establishing the right to a clean environment as a basic constitutional right.

Non-governmental organisations (NGOs) are vital in climate litigation because they aid impacted communities in their pursuit of justice by offering legal knowledge, resources, and emotional support. To combat ecologically detrimental activities and promote stricter environmental legislation, groups such as Earthjustice in the US and Client Earth in Europe have taken legal action by suing governments and businesses. Frequently, these non-governmental organisations (NGOs) speak on behalf of underrepresented groups who are being unduly affected by climate change, bolstering their claims in legal proceedings and fighting for their entitlements.

The transboundary character of climate change and its effects on human rights have also led to an increase in the number of climate-related cases heard by regional human rights courts and the International Court of Justice (ICJ). The Inter-American Commission on Human Rights, for instance, recognised that indigenous peoples' rights are being affected by climate change and encouraged nations to take immediate measures to lessen the impact of this phenomenon in the case of the Inuit Circumpolar Conference v. United nations and others. Environmental constitutionalism, environmental responsibility, and accountability for climate change can only be advanced via the involvement of national and international courts in climate litigation. These courts help establish norms and standards in law that put an emphasis on sustainable development and environmental preservation by defending the rights of people and communities hit hard by climate change. Involvement of non-governmental organisations (NGOs) augments these endeavours by offering disadvantaged populations advocacy, assistance, and legal representation; this, in turn, advances global climate justice and environmental sustainability.

10 Conclusion

When it comes to tackling the pressing issues caused by climate change and promoting global environmental justice, the involvement of both domestic and international courts in climate litigation is crucial. In order to ensure that governments and businesses are held responsible for their roles in climate change and that communities and individuals impacted by it are able to assert their rights, these courts play an essential role. International and national courts have laid the basis for revolutionary change by establishing legal precedents and historic verdicts that acknowledge the interdependence of sustainable development, human rights, and environmental preservation. Furthermore, grassroots movements and non-governmental organisations (NGOs) fighting for climate justice and environmental sustainability are amplifying the voices of underrepresented communities through climate litigation, which in turn strengthens advocacy efforts and encourages more openness, accountability, and participation.

References

Abbass K, Qasim MZ, Song H et al (2022) A review of the global climate change impacts, adaptation, and sustainable mitigation measures. Environ Sci Pollut Res 29:42539–42559. https://doi.org/10.1007/s11356-022-19718-6

Anaya SJ (2009) International Human Rights and Indigenous Peoples. Aspen Publishers. https://www.wklegaledu.com/Anaya-InternationalHumanRights

Aristova E, Lim J (2024, March). Climate Litigation in Europe Unleashed: Catalysing Action against States and Corporations. https://www.law.ox.ac.uk/sites/default/files/2024-03/Climate%20Litigation%20in%20Europe_Catalysing%20Action%20against%20States%20and%20Corporations.pdf

Ashamu E (2011) Centre for Minority Rights Development (Kenya) and Minority Rights Group International on Behalf of Endorois Welfare Council v Kenya: A Landmark Decision from the African Commission. J Afr Law 55(2):300–313. http://www.jstor.org/stable/41709865

Baue L, Vieira RS (2023) Climate Neocolonialism – The Carbon Metric under the Intergenerational Justice; SSRN; https://doi.org/10.2139/ssrn.4452354

Colby H, Ebbersmeyer AS, Heim LM, Røssaak MK (2020) Judging climate change: the role of the judiciary in the fight against climate change. Oslo Law Rev 7(3):168–185. https://doi.org/10.18261/ISSN.2387-3299-2020-03-03

Datta R, Kairy B (2024) Decolonizing climate change adaptations from indigenous perspectives: learning reflections from munda indigenous communities, coastal areas in bangladesh; MDPI. Sustainability 16(2):769. https://doi.org/10.3390/su16020769

Djoudi H, Locatelli B, Vaast C, Asher K, Brockhaus M, Sijapati BB (2016) Beyond dichotomies: gender and intersecting inequalities in climate change studies. Springer Link, Ambio, 45:248–262

ECHR (2013) Environment and the European Convention on Human Rights. https://www.echr.coe.int/documents/d/echr/fs_environment_eng

ESCR (2007) Case of the Saramaka People v. Suriname. https://www.escr-net.org/caselaw/2014/case-saramaka-people-v-suriname

ESCR-Net (2017) African Commission on Human and Peoples' Rights v. Republic of Kenya, ACtHPR, Application No. 006/2012; https://www.escr-net.org/caselaw/2017/african-commission-human-and-peoples-rights-v-republic-kenya-acthpr-application-no

Etchart L. (2017). The role of indigenous peoples in combating climate change; Palgrave Communications, humanities and social sciences communications 3, Article number: 17085. https://doi.org/10.1057/palcomms.2017.85

International Centre on Human Rights and Drug Policy (2012) Kichwa Indigenous People of Sarayaku v. Ecuador (Merits, Reparations, Costs) IACtHR Series C No 245; https://www.hr-dp.org/contents/700

International Court of Justice (n.d.) Obligations concerning Negotiations relating to Cessation of the Nuclear Arms Race and to Nuclear Disarmament (Marshall Islands v. India); https://www.icj-cij.org/case/158

Jans JH, Marseille AT (2010) The role of NGOs in environmental litigation against public authorities: some observations on judicial review and access to Court in the Netherlands. J Environ Law 22(3):373–390. https://doi.org/10.1093/jel/eqq021

Kipane A, Vilks A (2022) Legal framework for environmental protection in the context of sustainable development. Eur J Sustain Dev 11(4). https://doi.org/10.14207/ejsd.2022.v11n4p169

Kodiveri A (2020) The promises and challenges of climate change litigation in India, Open Global Rights, https://www.openglobalrights.org/promises-and-challenges-of-climate-change-litigation-in-india/

Kosolapova E (2024) ICJ to Rule on States' Climate-related Obligations: How Did We Get Here?, IISD, https://sdg.iisd.org/commentary/policy-briefs/icj-to-rule-on-states-climate-related-obligations-how-did-we-get-here/

Kossoy A (2018) No mystery: What is Brazil doing to address climate change?; Woeld Bank Blogs; https://blogs.worldbank.org/en/latinamerica/no-mystery-what-brazil-doing-address-climate-change

Letzing J, Sung M (2024) Is climate inaction a human rights violation?; World Econ Forum. https://www.weforum.org/agenda/2024/04/climate-progress-human-rights-violation/

Luporini R, Kodiveri AU (2021). The role of human rights bodies in climate litigation. European University Institute. https://hdl.handle.net/1814/72765

Mayer B, van Asselt H (2023) The rise of international climate litigation. Rev Int Corp Int Environ Law, Special Issue: International Climate Litigation, 32(2):175-184. https://doi.org/10.1111/reel.12515

McIntyre O (2020.) The Irish Supreme Court Judgment in Climate Case Ireland: 'One Step Forward and Two Steps Back'; IUCN; https://www.iucn.org/news/world-commission-environmental-law/202008/irish-supreme-court-judgment-climate-case-ireland-one-step-forward-and-two-steps-back

Nobre JA (2022, November). Legal Avenues to Fight Climate Change , IPI Global Observatory. https://theglobalobservatory.org/2022/11/legal-avenues-to-fight-climate-change/

Peel J, Osofsky HM (2018) Climate change litigation: regulatory pathways to cleaner energy. Cambridge University Press

Princewill N, Shveda K (2022, May 26) Shell escaped liability for oil spills in Nigeria for years. Then four farmers took them to court – and won. CNN. https://edition.cnn.com/2022/05/25/africa/shell-oil-spills-nigeria-intl-cmd/index.html

Rainard M, Smith, CJ, Pachauri S (2023) Gender equality and climate change mitigation: are women a secret weapon? Front Clim 5. https://doi.org/10.3389/fclim.2023.946712

Shelton D (2011) Advanced introduction to international human rights law. Edward Elgar Publishing. https://doi.org/10.4337/9781781005212

Simlinger F, Mayer B (2019) Legal responses to climate change induced loss and damage. In: Mechler R, Bouwer L, Schinko T, Surminski S, Linnerooth-Bayer J (eds) Loss and damage from climate change. Climate risk management, policy and governance. Springer, Cham. https://doi.org/10.1007/978-3-319-72026-5_7

Singh MW (2022) Climate Change in an Unequal World: Do International Courts and Tribunals Matter?, NUS. https://cil.nus.edu.sg/blogs/climate-change-in-an-unequal-world-do-international-courts-and-tribunals-matter/

Suhakam (2024, January 18) A Year of Paradoxes: Human Rights Triumphs and Challenges in 2023. https://suhakam.org.my/category/press-statement/write-up/

Toussaint P (2021) Loss and damage and climate litigation: the case for greater interlinkage. RECIEL 30:16–33. https://doi.org/10.1111/reel.12335

UNEP (2015) Teitiota vs. Chief Executive Ministry of Business, Innovation and Employment; Supreme Court of New Zealand; https://leap.unep.org/en/countries/nz/national-case-law/teitiota-vs-chief-executive-ministry-business-innovation-and

UNEP (2019) Dramatic growth in laws to protect environment, but widespread failure to enforce, finds report; https://www.unep.org/news-and-stories/press-release/dramatic-growth-laws-protect-environment-widespread-failure-enforce

UNEP (2021) May In battle against climate change, courts become a new frontier https://www.unep.org/news-and-stories/story/battle-against-climate-change-courts-become-new-frontier

Uprimny R (2013) The Sarayaku Judgment: a new step in the development of indigenous rights in the Inter-American system. Sur Int J Human Rights 10(18):117–125. https://sur.conectas.org/wp-content/uploads/2017/11/sur18-eng-rodrigo.pdf

Verheyen R, Franke J (2023) Climate change litigation: a reference area for liability. In: Gailhofer P, Krebs D, Proelss A, Schmalenbach K, Verheyen R (eds) Corporate liability for transboundary environmental harm. Springer, Cham. https://doi.org/10.1007/978-3-031-13264-3_8

Voigt C (2020) Climate litigation as climate regulation. J Environ Law 32(3):417–441. https://doi.org/10.1093/jel/eqaa020

Weise Z (2024). Climate protection is now a human right — and lawsuits will follow. Politico; https://www.politico.eu/article/monumental-climate-ruling-europe-top-human-rights-court-heralds-new-era-climate-litigations/#:~:text=That%20same%20year%2C%20Germany's%20Constitutional,cutting%20burden%20on%20future%20generations.

Yip L (2022) How marginalised groups are disproportionately affected by climate change, Earth.org. https://earth.org/marginalised-groups-are-disproportionately-affected-by-climate-change/

Yuen C, Madraiwiwi J (2015) Pacific human rights law digest - Volume 5. Pacific Islands Legal Information Institute; http://www.paclii.org/other/PHRLD/pacific-human-rights-law-digest-5.html#2015_UPDATES_VOL_1

J.N. Rodrigues Professor at University of the Azores, School of Business and Economics, Rua da Mãe de Deus, 9500-321 Ponta Delgada, Researcher at CEDIS, Nova School of Law, FD, Universidade NOVA de Lisboa - School of Law, Campus de Campolide, 1099-032 Lisboa, Portugal. Chairman of the Board of the Gaspar Frutuoso Foundation. Scientific Coordinator of the Master's Degree in Company and Employment Law, as well as of the Degree in Law at the University of Santiago - Cape Verde, Visiting Professor in the Master's Degree in Civil Law and in the Master's Degree in Tax Law at the Catholic University of Mozambique. Doctor in Law (PhD) "CUM LAUDE", by the University of Santiago de Compostela (Spain), recognized the equivalence of the degree of Doctor in Law by the Lisbon University Faculty of Law, DEA in European Union Law (2008), Master's in International Relations (2004), Post-Graduate in Regional Law (1998), Post-Graduate in Labor Law (2003) and Graduated in Law (1996). He is also the Delegate for the Azores of the Instituto de Derecho Iberoamericano and holds the Chair of the Policy Center for the United Nations Convention on the Rights of the Child.

S. Bhattacharya Research scholar at Makaut, Public - Foreign-Defence Policy Analyst, C.E, Ch. E, M. Tech., Ma in Development Studies, LLB, MA in Security and Defence Law, DIA&D, DG&GS, PGFEDS, MPI (Oxford University).

J.C. Medina Postdoctor in Social Justice and Inequality in Latin America from the Universidade de Brasília, UnB. Post-Graduate Professor at the Pontifícia Universidade Católica de Minas, PUC-MG. PhD in International Law from the Universidade de Brasília, UnB. Assistant Professor at Marta Abreu las Villas Universidad, Cuba. Master in Higher Education from the Universidad Marta Abreu Las Villas, Cuba. Law Degree from Marta Abreu las Villas Universidad, Cuba.

D.C.R. Cabete Guest lecturer at University of Azores, School of Business and Economics, Rua da Mãe de Deus, 9500-321 Ponta Delgada, Portugal. Researcher at CEDIS, Nova School of Law, FD, Universidade NOVA de Lisboa - School of Law, Campus de Campolide, 1099-032 Lisboa, Portugal Doctor (PhD) in Business Economic Sciences – specialization in Economics - at the School of Business and Economics approved with distinction and praise by the University of the Azores (UAc), PhD candidate in Law at the Universidade Nova de Lisboa - School of Law, Lisboa, Master's and postgraduate degree in Social Sciences at the University of the Azores (UAc) and in Law by the Universidade Autónoma de Lisboa (UAL). She is also a guest lecturer at the University of Santiago - Cape Verde and a lawyer.

Litigation for Climate Justice: The Case of Procedural Rights Under the Aarhus Convention

Alexandra Wenzel

1 Introduction

Climate change litigation has seen a substantial rise in recent years. As of 2017, 884 climate change cases were brought forward. As of 2022, only 6 years later, this number more than doubled to 2180 cases.[1] This increase is indicative of the growing trend of climate change litigation. Climate change litigation is enacted as a last resort; it can only be used when policymakers or corporations violate rights, including substantive and procedural rights.[2] As the effects of climate change worsen, causing impacts including but not limited to a lack of potable water, loss of livelihood, and loss of life, there is a greater possibility for human-rights based claims for climate justice.[3] As a result, civil society has increasingly gone to the courts to demand climate justice.[4] Litigation, in this context, is used as a tool by civil society

[1] United Nations Environment Programme (2023), p. 12. This number represents a floor, as there may be other climate change cases not captured in the data collection.

[2] Peel and Osofksy (2018), p. 43.

[3] Peel and Osofksy (2018), p. 40.

[4] Find here the UNEP definition of climate justice, "Climate justice is a term used for framing global warming as an ethical and political issue, rather than one that is purely environmental or physical in nature. This is done by relating the effects of climate change to concepts of justice, particularly environmental justice and social justice and by examining issues such as equality, human rights; collective rights, and the historical responsibilities for climate." https://leap.unep.org/en/knowledge/glossary/climate-justice.

A. Wenzel (✉)
Paris, France
e-mail: alexandra.wenzel@graduateinstitute.ch

V. E. de Aquino et al. (eds.), *Climate Litigation in a Changing World*, Ius Gentium: Comparative Perspectives on Law and Justice 130,
https://doi.org/10.1007/978-3-032-05530-9_3

to hold policymakers and corporate actors accountable and rectify a lack of ambition to act on climate change.[5]

This chapter will analyze the increased use of procedural rights as a pathway for climate justice. It will do this by analyzing climate change litigation cases which are brought forward by civil society, including individuals and non-governmental organisations (NGOs). This chapter finds that cases brought forward on the grounds of a violation of procedural rights are being used as a tool for climate justice. NGOs and individuals use environmental democracy rights such as those guaranteed under the Aarhus Convention to pursue climate change litigation thereby holding actors accountable for their climate commitments. However, it is critical to note that the rise in Strategic Litigation Against Public Participation (SLAPP) suits, threats to environmental defenders, and the shrinking of civil space in many countries poses a threat to achieving climate justice. Protecting civic space is therefore crucial.

This chapter first will investigate the role of climate change litigation as a tactic by civil society to attain climate justice. Next, it will address the procedural rights granted to civil society and go on to analyze the documents which codify these rights. Specifically, it will assess the importance of the Aarhus Convention and its implications for climate change litigation. This chapter will then analyze climate change case studies which use procedural rights with reference to the Aarhus Convention. It will conclude by looking at the findings to discuss the future of procedural rights in climate change litigation.

2 A Rise in Climate Change Litigation

Climate change litigation has seen a significant rise in the past decade. Speech makers, particularly policymakers, have clearly articulated the adverse connection between climate change and human rights.[6] These cases against states and corporations present another avenue for civil society to ensure climate change commitments are enforced and to ensure climate justice in the face of human rights violations. Climate change litigation allows civil society to present a counterbalance to the climate change-causing activities of states and corporations.[7] Climate change litigation is important not only for its legal implications; it also can illuminate failures of states and corporations, resulting in an increase in media and public discourse on climate injustices.[8] These cases also lead to broader discussions about the

[5] Alogna et al. (2021), p. 3.

[6] Hall (2014), p. 17.

[7] Alogna et al. (2021), p. 141.

[8] Peel and Osofksy (2018), p. 67.

role of science in climate change attribution and historical responsibility.[9] Such discussions have connected to environmental justice principles including common but differentiated responsibilities (CBDR) and the Polluter Pays Principle.[10]

As will be analyzed in the case studies section, climate change cases can come in two forms: strategic cases which feature climate change as the main goal and central feature of the case, and routine cases which focus on specific issues and may not state an explicit link to climate change.[11] Climate change cases are increasingly based in rights claims, using a human rights framing.[12] This human rights-based approach to climate action has provided an avenue to demand accountability and, as seen in the significant uptick in cases, has been increasingly used by civil society.

Climate change cases which use a rights claim can lead to important shifts in the understanding of the legal obligations of states. These rights claims can be divided into the two types of obligations under international environmental law; procedural and substantive obligations.[13] Substantive obligations address conduct and includes rights such as the right to life. Procedural obligations deal with observing set procedures such as the right of access to information, as will be explored in the following section. The enforcement of such procedural obligations can lead to a better enforcement of substantive obligations. Climate change cases can be both substantive and procedural and many of the cases which have gained significant media traction are primarily based on a violation of substantive rights. However, these cases are only possible if procedural rights are upheld.

One of the most historic climate change cases is the case *Urgenda Foundation v. State of the Netherlands* (2020).[14] The court in the Hague found that the Netherlands must improve their actions to prevent global climate change and ordered the Dutch state to reduce GHG emissions to 25% below 1990 levels by 2020. The ruling was based on a combination of agreements and commitments, including; the UNFCCC, binding EU climate targets, and the European Convention on Human Rights Articles 2 and 8 corresponding, respectively, to the right to life and the right to private and family life.[15] This landmark case crystallized the link between human rights and climate change litigation.[16] Climate litigation in this case established jurisprudence

---

[9] United Nations Environment Programme (2023), p. 74.

[10] Cullet (2016), p. 498.

[11] Alogna et al. (2021), p. 18.

[12] Peel and Osofsky (2018), p. 40.

[13] Peters (2018), p. 2.

[14] *Urgenda Foundation v. State of the Netherlands.* (2015). HAZA C/09/00456689. http://climatecasechart.com/climate-change-litigation/non-us-case/urgenda-foundation-v-kingdom-of-the-netherlands/.

[15] Alogna et al. (2021), pp. 202–203.

[16] Alogna et al. (2021), p. 222.

through enshrining rights related to climate change, such as the rights of future generations and the duty of care. This case has been noteworthy for garnering media attention on the legal obligation of states to act on climate change as well as provided a key reference for lawyers to learn from. Procedural rights must be protected and upheld for such substantive cases to take place and the final judgement itself references the right of civil society to have access to justice in environmental matters.[17]

3 The Case of Procedural Rights

Procedural rights play an important role in environmental democracy and holding governments accountable as they protect civic space, allowing for public participation. Procedural rights are a category of normative principles under human rights. Upholding these rights can lead to processes which improve the agency of the public.[18] The right of access to information allows citizens to read governmental decisions on climate change which in turn creates a space of criticism necessary for a healthy democracy.[19] Procedural rights have been associated with both better respect of environmental laws and a democratic legitimacy of processes.[20] Procedural rights include the right of access to information, public participation in decision making, and the right to access justice on environmental issues to citizens and NGOs. These rights can also be expanded or be used to enforce procedural principles of prevention: cooperation, notification and consultation, prior informed consent, and environmental impact assessment.[21] It is important to note that procedural rights are not only used by groups seeking to advance climate action and have been also used to pushback against climate policy.[22] In some cases, the difference between climate action and climate justice is made clear: cases have been brought against unjust, inequitable climate policies and have thus ensured greater justice and democratic legitimacy in policy.[23]

The current legal opportunity structure has led to an increased use of procedural rights-based cases to advance climate litigation.[24] In the case of climate change, it can be more straightforward to demonstrate a breach of legal duty and prove a viola-

[17] Find the reference on page 30, https://climatecasechart.com/wp-content/uploads/non-us-case-documents/2020/20200113_2015-HAZA-C0900456689_judgment.pdf.

[18] Hall (2014), p. 15.

[19] Kravchenko (2010), p. 618.

[20] Peters (2018), p. 6.

[21] Dupuy and Vinuales (2018), p. 62.

[22] Peeters and Nóbrega (2014), p. 364.

[23] United Nations Environment Programme. (2023). *Global Climate Litigation Report: 2023 Status Review.* https://wedocs.unep.org/bitstream/handle/20.500.11822/43008/global_climate_litigation_report_2023.pdf?sequence=3.

[24] Vanhala (2018), p. 112.

tion of procedural rights than in substantive rights, which often involves important discussions around attribution science and historical responsibility.[25] The use of procedural rights has been found to make policies more transparent and responsive, and result in better protection for substantive rights, such as the right to life.[26] Increased transparency as a result of enforced procedural rights can be used to hold institutions accountable to their climate commitments through greater scrutiny.[27] Procedural rights have enabled NGOs to in turn expand the legal opportunity structure to enforce substantive environmental law.[28] However, this legal opportunity structure may change given recent political shifts including a rise in far-right populism and a reduced civic space which includes a crack-down on environmental defenders.[29]

3.1 The Codification of Procedural Rights

Procedural rights have been codified in multiple international agreements on climate change. Principle 10 of the Rio Declaration states that "environmental issues are best handled with the participation of all concerned citizens."[30] The Declaration goes on to include the right to access of information, participation in decision-making processes, as well as access to judicial and administrative proceedings including redress and remedy. This is also included in the United Nations Framework Convention on Climate Change.[31] Article 6 of the UNFCCC on education, training, and public awareness declares that states must allow for "public access to information on climate change and its effects" as well as "public participation in addressing climate change and its effects and developing adequate responses."[32] These procedural rights have continued to be enshrined in international treaties and agreements; the preamble to the 2015 Paris Agreement also affirms these rights of public participation. Procedural rights have also been codified in regional agreements. Regionally, procedural environmental rights have been codified in texts including the Regional Agreement on Access to Information, Public Participation and Justice in Environmental Matters in Latin America and the Caribbean, also referred to as the Escazú Agreement.[33] This article will focus on the Convention on Access to

[25] Cullet (2016), p. 502.

[26] Bodansky et al. (2017), p. 309.

[27] Ibid.

[28] Hofmann (2019), p. 357.

[29] Barritt (2024), pp. 77–79.

[30] United Nations (1992a).

[31] United Nations (1992b).

[32] Ibid.

[33] United Nations (2018).

Information, Public Participation in Decision-Making and Access to Justice in Environmental Matters, or the Aarhus Convention.[34]

3.2 *The Aarhus Convention*

The Aarhus Convention, is a historic document enshrining procedural rights to the public under the UN Economic Commission for Europe (UNECE). The Convention was signed in Aarhus, Denmark on June 25th, 1998.[35] There are 39 signatories and 47 parties to the Aarhus Convention. Members States are primarily from Europe and Central Asia but any state is permitted to join. The Aarhus Convention, under Article 1, sought to extend procedural environmental rights, namely: the right of access to information, public participation in decision making, and the right to access justice on environmental issues to citizens and NGOs. It is a noteworthy document as the focus of the Convention is upon the relation of governments to civil society. It includes both passive duties which include responding to requests for information and active duties such as making information public.[36] Article 9 notably guarantees access to justice for persons who were wrongfully denied access to information under Article 4.[37] The Aarhus Convention covers a broad array of environmental activities, listed in Annex I, from activities in the chemical industry to the energy sector. The Convention is presented as a "floor but not a ceiling," in that governments are encouraged to go beyond the provisions.[38] It is also important as the European Court of Human Rights (ECtHR) has relied upon the Aarhus Convention in its interpretation of the European Convention on Human Rights.[39] According to former UN Secretary-General Kofi Annan, the Aarhus Convention is "one of the most far-reaching international treaties in the field of environmental democracy. Its core principles . . . empower citizens to hold governments accountable."[40] The noteworthiness of the Aarhus Convention also applies to the participation of civil society.

[34] United Nations (1998).

[35] Ibid.

[36] Wates (2005), p. 3.

[37] United Nations (1998).

[38] Wates (2005), p. 2.

[39] Peter (2018), p. 10.

[40] Annan (2005).

3.3 *The Role of Civil Society in the Aarhus Convention*

The unusually high involvement by NGOs in the Aarhus Convention, from its conception to present day, has contributed to the current legal opportunity structure. It was NGOs which proposed the development of the Aarhus Convention.[41] Additionally, domestic NGOs envisioned the Aarhus Convention to have a boomerang effect; domestic NGOs can use the Aarhus Convention to bring international pressure back to their domestic context.[42] This effect thereby expands access to courts at the domestic level.

In the present day, NGOs are still actively involved in the Aarhus Convention, as seen in the Aarhus Convention Compliance Committee which includes both Member States and NGOs.[43] One outcome of this NGO involvement is a trend of the EU Commission of increasingly allowing NGOs to enforce EU environmental law, rather than enforce it directly themselves.[44] The role of NGOs is permitted through the liberalizing of national procedural rules under the Aarhus Convention. One such case of environmental NGOs leveraging the Aarhus Convention, which was brought to the Court of Justice of the European Union, is the amendment of the 'loser pays rule' which led to a more equitable distribution of UK court fees.[45] This use of procedural rights has led to more equitable access to justice. One example of the public understanding the value of the Aarhus Convention is the Lights on Aarhus project by Youth and Environment Europe (YEE), a network of environmental youth organizations. The organization hosted a series of events related to the project to create an "opportunity for an increased engagement of young activists in legal processes."[46] As a part of this project, YEE members also published a handbook, *Understanding Aarhus*.[47] This handbook describes avenues to attain climate justice in EU courts. The Aarhus Convention is powerful as it is binding for EU Member States as well as the EU institutions themselves.[48] Thus, the YEE discusses the use of the Aarhus Convention as a compelling leverage point. YEE's handbook outlines the opportunities, and issues, of the Aarhus Regulation, the EU's document on the implementation of the Convention. One issue they point to is that when challenging an act only NGOs, and not individuals, are covered by the Aarhus Regulation.[49] YEE calls for a stronger, more inclusive Aarhus Regulation which allows for increased participation of the public and particularly youth. This example shows the awareness of the

[41] Wates (2005), p. 9.

[42] Vanhala (2018), p. 124.

[43] Peeters and Nóbrega (2014), p. 362.

[44] Hofmann (2019), p. 343.

[45] Vanhala (2018), p. 125.

[46] Youth and Environment Europe (2021a).

[47] Youth and Environment Europe (2021b).

[48] Peeters and Nóbrega (2014), p. 356.

[49] Youth and Environment Europe (2021b), p. 19.

Aarhus Convention, and procedural rights as whole, as a relevant avenue to pursue climate change litigation.

4 Climate Change Litigation Case Studies

The chapter will now turn to analyzing three sets of climate change case studies which illustrate the use of procedural rights and make reference to the Aarhus Convention: access to information, public participation in decision-making, and access to justice.[50] These case studies rely upon procedural rights to different extents, with some cases using procedural rights outlined under the Aarhus Convention to base their case or some solely for their appeal. These cases include both strategic cases and routine cases.

4.1 Access to Information

Access to information is a key feature of procedural rights. In *ClientEarth v. European Investment Bank* (2019), ClientEarth, an environmental NGO working on environmental law, filed suit against the European Investment Bank (EIB) over rejecting their petition for an internal review on EIB's decision to finance a biomass power plant.[51] ClientEarth argued that the EIB's actions constituted an administrative act and therefore must abide by the Aarhus Convention. The EU General Court's findings agreed with ClientEarth's claim.

In *Environment-People-Law v. Cabinet of Ministers of Ukraine and National Agency of Environmental Investments (2009),* the Ukrainian NGO Environment-People-Law filed suit to gain access to information on international GHG emissions trading, based on rights given in both the Aarhus Convention and the Constitution of Ukraine.[52] The case was won in part as the court ruled that the information on international GHG emissions trading must legally be provided but it dismissed the request for information on the price of GHG emission quotas. Both of these cases led to increased transparency surrounding climate policies as a result of attaining access to information.

[50] Further case law related to the Aarhus Convention can be found here: https://aarhusclearinghouse.unece.org/jurisprudence.

[51] *ClientEarth v. European Investment Bank.* (2019). C-212/21 P http://climatecasechart.com/non-us-case/clientearth-v-european-investment-bank/.

[52] *Environment-People-Law v. Cabinet of Ministers of Ukraine and National Agency of Environmental Investments.* (2009). K/9991/29050/11 https://climatecasechart.com/non-us-case/environment-people-law-v-cabinet-of-ministers-of-ukraine-and-national-agency-of-environmental-investments/.

4.2 Public Participation in Decision-Making

In *Greenpeace v. Secretary of State for Trade and Industry* (2007), Greenpeace argued that the consultation process, which the NGO took part in, of building a nuclear power plant in the United Kingdom was flawed.[53] The High Court agreed with the claim and invoked the ratification of the Aarhus Convention as a legally binding document which required a fair consultation process. This case is an example of how leveraging procedural rights can lead to improved quality and effectiveness of substantive decision-making, as Greenpeace proved in court that consultations processes must be fair.[54]

Cases which are lost nonetheless can lead to important developments and increase existing climate change case law. The *Friends of the Irish Environment CLG v. Fingal County Council* (2007) was a case by the NGO Friends of the Irish Environment CLG filed against the construction of a new runway at the Dublin Airport Authority.[55]

They claimed that there must be further public participation in granting an extension of a planning permission, in part based upon the Aarhus Convention. While the claim was denied, the judgement by the Irish High Court found that there was a constitutional right to an environment. Thus, while the case based on procedural rights did not succeed, it did make remarkable progress in guaranteeing substantive rights.

4.3 Access to Justice

A group of senior Swiss women filed a petition against the Swiss government for failure to mitigate climate change in the case *Verein Klimaseniorinnen Schweiz v. Bundesrat* (2016).[56] The Swiss Supreme Court had denied their case on the basis that their rights had not been affected with sufficient intensity. The women then filed an application to the ECtHR with one of their complaints being that the Swiss authorities and courts violated Article 13 on the right to an effective remedy as they

---

[53] *Greenpeace v. Secretary of State for Trade and Industry.* 2007. EWHC 311. https://climate-laws.org/geographies/united-kingdom/litigation_cases/greenpeace-v-secretary-of-state-for-trade-and-industry-queen-s-bench-division-administrative-court-2007.

[54] Hall (2014), p. 16.

[55] *Friends of the Irish Environment CLG v. Fingal County Council.* (2017). No.344 JR. https://climatecasechart.com/non-us-case/friends-irish-environment-clg-v-fingal-county-council/.

[56] *Verein KlimaSeniorinnen Schweiz v. Bundesrat.* (2016). No. A-2992/2017. https://climatecasechart.com/non-us-case/union-of-swiss-senior-women-for-climate-protection-v-swiss-federal-council-and-others/.

did not deal with the content of their complaints.[57] The ECtHR gave the case priority status and ordered Switzerland to submit a response by July 16, 2021.

This case exemplifies the use of procedural rights to advance climate change litigation at a significantly high level of authority, the ECtHR. The giving of priority to the case is also noteworthy as it demonstrates the ECtHR's willingness to discuss climate change cases. On *Verein KlimaSeniorinnen Schweiz and Others v. Switzerland* ECtHR gave a judgement on April 9, 2024 finding a violation of access to court.[58] Regarding substantial rights, the court also found that there was a violation of the right to respect for private and family life. The Aarhus Convention was also specifically mentioned in the ECtHR's judgement as relevant international material. This case is noteworthy as it was successful in both the substantive and procedural elements of the claim.

Another case is the *People's Climate Case* or *Armando Ferrão Carvalho and Others v. The European Parliament and the Council* (2021).[59] The case was brought forward by multiple families alleging that the greenhouse gas emission reduction targets set by the EU are insufficient and threaten multiple rights of the applicants including the right to life and the right to health. The European General Court dismissed the case on the basis of procedure for not having adequate standing, as also confirmed in the appeal to the European Court of Justice. In the appeal, the applicants referenced the Aarhus Convention in the need to provide sufficient access to justice.

In a more successful example, *VZW Klimaatzaak v Kingdom of Belgium & Others* (2023)[60] reference the Aarhus Convention in defending their standing to access justice. This case is similar to *Urgenda* as it is a strategic case against the applicant's national government for failing to implement and credit adequate climate action plans. The case thus focuses on substantive rights but relies upon procedural rights to have standing. The applicants make reference to Article 9.3 of the Aarhus Convention, on the right of access to justice. This case upholds the ability of civil society to access justice related to environmental matters.

[57] Find the judgement here: https://climatecasechart.com/wp-content/uploads/non-us-case-documents/2024/20240409_Application-no.-5360020_judgment-1.pdf. Accessed September 29, 2024.

[58] *Verein KlimaSeniorinnen Schweiz and Others v. Switzerland.* (2024). 53600/20 https://hudoc.echr.coe.int/eng/#{%22itemid%22:[%22002-14304%22]}.

[59] *Armando Ferrão Carvalho and Others v. The European Parliament and the Council* (2021). Case C-565/19 P. https://eur-lex.europa.eu/legal-content/EN/TXT/?uri=CELEX:62019CJ0565.

[60] *VZW Klimaatzaak v Kingdom of Belgium & Others.* (2023). 2023/8411. https://climatecasechart.com/non-us-case/vzw-klimaatzaak-v-kingdom-of-belgium-et-al/.

5 Analysis

5.1 *The Use of Procedural Rights*

From this selection of case studies, procedural rights are used, often successfully, in both routine and strategic cases on climate change. Procedural rights are also used to support cases based on substantive claims. This use of climate change litigation can be seen as a demand for states to be accountable to act on climate change and provide adequate climate targets. Procedural rights are thus one avenue for climate justice because they force states to adhere to their legal obligations of responsive and inclusive climate change decision-making.[61]

The routine cases discussed above differ greatly from the tactics and potential impact of the strategic cases analyzed under access to justice, *Verein KlimaSeniorinnen Schweiz, the People's Climate Case,* and *VZW Klimaatzaak.* Strategic cases have the potential to set new precedents with courts outlining the obligations of actors to climate action and these three cases used procedural rights to ensure access to justice. Nonetheless, it also is evident from the result of *Friends of the Irish Environment CLG v. Fingal County Council* that procedural, routine cases can have an important impact on furthering substantive rights. These cases show an important interplay between the use of substantive and procedural rights in both strategic and routine cases. It shows a promising pathway for the public to leverage procedural rights as a tool to ensure climate justice. As seen in these cases, by successfully taking these issues to the courts, civil society has made clear the connection between human rights and climate change.

5.2 *Difficulties in Climate Change Litigation*

Climate change is a super wicked problem, and its legal remedies are no less complicated than its political ones.[62] Climate change poses new legal challenges on all three fronts of mitigation, adaptation, and loss and damage. As the impacts of climate change are incredibly diverse, it can be a difficult role for courts to place responsibility and determine victimhood. In the case discussed in the section above, *Verein KlimaSeniorinnen Schweiz v. Bundesrat,* the Swiss courts dismissed the case on the grounds that senior Swiss women are not the only group affected by climate change and that their rights were not affected with sufficient intensity and in the *People's Climate Case* the European Court of Justice dismissed the case for a lack of proper standing.

Using the law as an avenue for climate justice is also difficult when the case discusses impacts related to slow-onset events. The impacts of slow-onset events are

[61] Hall (2014), p. 17.

[62] Levin et al. (2012), p. 123.

complex and from a legal perspective proving causation is still in the early stages.[63] The transboundary nature of climate change leads to questions on the attribution of responsibilities and holding countries and multinational corporations to account for their historical role in causing global climate change. While these strategic cases are still in the early stages, the law must adapt to the challenges of the present day and the courts have demonstrated a readiness to address these questions.

5.3 Threats to Procedural Rights

Shrinking civic space and threats to environmental defenders in many countries threatens the possibility of civil society to engage in climate change litigation. Environmental defenders, defined by the Aarhus Convention as being anyone seeking to protect rights in line with the Aarhus Convention, face increased threats.[64] However, the Aarhus Convention can respond to such issues, and has, in the appointment of a UN Special Rapporteur on Environmental Defenders under the Aarhus Convention, Michel Forst. In his role, Forst cites concern of a "chilling effect" where a climate of fear restricts the civic space for environmental defenders to act. The Aarhus Convention Compliance Committee is another mechanism which can be used to ensure accountability with environmental procedural rights. It can be triggered by any member of the public, including citizens and NGOs, as well as Parties to the Convention, the secretariat, and the Meeting of the Parties.[65] Another threat to civic space is SLAPP lawsuits.[66] SLAPP suits are used to intimidate environment defenders and reduce civic space. The reduction of civic space is particularly concerning as these cases have been brought forward by civil society to increase awareness on the violation of human rights resulting from climate change and pathways for remedy.

5.4 The Evolving Role of Procedural Rights

Given the rapidly unfolding impacts of climate change, and their potential to infringe on human rights, asserting the right to legal remedy is a form of taking a stand to demand accountability from the states and corporations which have knowingly contributed disproportionately, both historically and presently, to creating climate change. Access to information, public participation in decision-making, and

---

[63] Bodansky et al. (2017), p. 314.

[64] Forst (2024), p. 2.

[65] For more details on the Compliance Committee look here: https://unece.org/DAM/env/pp/Publications/Guide_to_the_Compliance_Committee__second_edition__2019_/English/Guide_to_the_Aarhus_Convention_Compliance_Committee__2019.pdf.

[66] Mugga et al. (2023), pp. 47–49.

access to justice are cornerstones in any well-functioning democratic society and the use of such procedural rights by NGOs and individuals is a key piece of ensuring both justice in relation to the impacts of climate change and that climate policy is just.

6 Conclusion

This chapter has analyzed the importance of procedural rights, specifically the three rights of access to information, public participation in decision-making and access to justice, as outlined in the Aarhus Convention, in pursuing climate change litigation. By doing so, this chapter has argued there is considerable potential in the legal opportunity structure for using procedural rights in climate litigation cases. It has looked at both routine and strategic examples of climate change cases which have leveraged procedural rights on which to either base their case or appeal their case.

Additionally, this chapter has found that the cases which rely upon procedural rights are often routine cases. Routine cases have important victories in transparency which can bring about improved compliance and accountability. Strategic cases use procedural rights in combination with substantive rights. Procedural cases can also lead substantive gains as seen in *Friends of the Irish Environment CLG v. Fingal County Council.*

Climate change litigation cases which rely on procedural rights, whether strategic or routine, have the capability to make important gains for climate justice. And, as outlined by UNEP, the protection of civic space and environmental human rights defenders is crucial. Annan said that "the success of the [Aarhus] Convention will depend not only on the political will of governments but also on the readiness of the public to exercise the rights that the Convention seeks to guarantee."[67] From these cases, the public has been more than willing to exercise these rights.

References

Alogna I, Bakker C, Gauci J (2021) Climate change litigation: global perspectives. Koninklijke Brill NV

Annan K (2005). Secretary-General Welcomes Active Involvement of Civil Society in Aarhus Convention on Access to Information. [Press Release]. May 27, 2005. https://www.un.org/press/en/2005/sgsm9896.doc.htm

Barritt E (2024) The Aarhus convention and the latent right to a healthy environment. J Environ Law 36(1):67–84. https://doi.org/10.1093/jel/eqae003

Bodansky D, Brunnée J, Rajamani L (2017) International climate change law. Oxford University Press

[67] Annan (2005).

Cullet P (2016) Human rights and climate change: broadening the right to environment. In: Gray KR, Tarasofsky R, Carlarne CP (eds) The Oxford handbook of international climate change law. Oxford University Press, pp 496–509
Dupuy P-M, Vinuales JE (2018) International environmental law. Cambridge University Press
Forst M (2024) State repression of environmental protest and civil disobedience: a major threat to human rights and democracy [Position Paper]. https://unece.org/sites/default/files/2024-02/UNSR_EnvDefenders_Aarhus_Position_Paper_Civil_Disobedience_EN.pdf
Hall MJ (2014) Advancing climate justice and the right to health through procedural rights. Health Hum Rights 16(1):8–18
Hofmann A (2019) Left to interest groups? On the prospects for enforcing environmental law in the European Union. Environ Polit 28(2):342–364. https://doi.org/10.1080/09644016.2019.1549778
Kravchenko S (2010) Procedural rights as a crucial tool to combat climate change. Georgia J Int Comp Law 38(3):613–648
Levin K, Cashore B, Bernstein S, Auld G (2012) Overcoming the tragedy of super wicked problems: constraining our future selves to ameliorate global climate change. Policy Sci 45(2):123–152. https://doi.org/10.1007/s11077-012-9151-0
Mugga JI, Gupta J, Lefeber R (2023) Shaping Africa's climate action through climate litigation: an impact assessment. Recht in Afrika 26(1):26–54. https://doi.org/10.5771/2363-6270-2023-1-26
Peel J, Osofsky HM (2018) A rights turn in climate change litigation? Transnatl Environ Law 7(1):37–67. https://doi.org/10.1017/S2047102517000292
Peeters M, Nóbrega S (2014) Climate change-related Aarhus conflicts: how successful are procedural rights in EU climate law? Rev Eur Comp Int Environ Law 23(3):354–366. https://doi.org/10.1111/reel.12076
Peters B (2018) Unpacking the diversity of procedural environmental rights: the European convention on human rights and the Aarhus convention. J Environ Law 30(1):1–27. https://doi.org/10.1093/jel/eqx023
United Nations (1992a) Rio Declaration. UN Doc A/CONF.151/26 (vol. I), 31 ILM 874
United Nations (1992b) United Nations framework convention on climate change. https://unfccc.int/files/essential_background/background_publications_htmlpdf/application/pdf/conveng.pdf
United Nations (1998) Convention on access to information, Public Participation in Decision-Making and Access to Justice in Environmental Matters. Aarhus, Denmark
United Nations (2018) Regional agreement on access to information, public participation and justice in environmental matters in Latin America and the Caribbean. Escazú, Costa Rica. https://treaties.un.org/doc/Treaties/2018/03/20180312%2003-04%20PM/CTC-XXVII-18.pdf
United Nations Environment Programme (2023) Global Climate Litigation Report: 2023 Status Review. https://wedocs.unep.org/bitstream/handle/20.500.11822/43008/global_climate_litigation_report_2023.pdf?sequence=3
Vanhala L (2018) Shaping the structure of legal opportunities: environmental NGOs bringing international environmental procedural rights back home. Law Policy 40(1):110–127. https://doi.org/10.1111/lapo.12093
Wates J (2005) The Aarhus convention: a driving force for environmental democracy. J Eur Environ Plan Law 2(1):2–11. https://doi.org/10.1163/187601005X00561
Youth and Environment Europe (2021a, July 14) Lights on Aarhus. https://yeenet.eu/project_item/lights-on-aarhus/
Youth and Environment Europe (2021b) Understanding Aarhus: a simple handbook on access to justice at EU level. https://yeenet.eu/wp-content/uploads/2021/12/YEE_Understanding-Aarhus_Handbook-

Alexandra Wenzel Bachelor of Arts with Major in International Relations at the University of British Columbia. Master of Arts in International Affairs, Specialization in Environment and Sustainability at Geneva Graduate Institute.

Climate Disinformation and Climate-Washing: Litigation in Defense of Human Rights and Transparency

Elisa Maffassiolli Hartwig and Gabriel Wedy

1 Introduction

Climate disinformation is identified as the greatest global risk of our time and consists in a political process of dissemination of false or distorted information in a systematic and organized way, with the aim of discrediting climate science and the existence of anthropogenic climate change. It consists in a great threat precisely because of the importance of the current generation in reversing the trajectory of global warming, which depends on cutting greenhouse gas emissions immediately.

Climate disinformation is not a new phenomenon and has already generated a delay of decades in taking effective actions to combat the climate crisis. Faced with a consensus of almost 100% of climate scientists about the existence of anthropogenic climate change,[1] climate disinformation has increasingly lost its theoretical respectability. From this, the climate disinformers and "merchants of doubt" began to use grey areas of misinformation, such as greenwashing and climate-washing. These terms designate misleading and inaccurate communications from corporations and governments, which advertise products, actions and measures as sustainable, when in fact they contribute to climate change or do not properly address environmental and social issues.

[1] Danowski (2022), p. 109.

E. M. Hartwig (✉) · G. Wedy
University of Vale do Rio dos Sinos, São Leopoldo, Brazil
e-mail: gabrielWEDY@unisinos.br

V. E. de Aquino et al. (eds.), *Climate Litigation in a Changing World*, Ius Gentium: Comparative Perspectives on Law and Justice 130,
https://doi.org/10.1007/978-3-032-05530-9_4

In recent years, there has been a great growth in cases of climate litigation involving greenwashing and climate-washing claims, mainly against large corporations. Initially concentrated on fossil fuel giants, this movement is now addressing other sectors of the economy in a significant way,[2] such as aviation[3] and meat processing, which are also major emitters of greenhouse gases.

Thus, climate litigation integrates the complex global governance system of climate change and has been shown as an important instrument to combat the climate crisis, in view of the failure of governments and companies to reduce emissions. This resistance demonstrates a concern with the preservation at all costs of the old business model, prioritizing the generation of profit over all other values and over the preservation of the environment for current and future generations.

For all these reasons, the objective of this study is to verify how the climate-washing litigation trend can find common ground with another trend in the transnational climate litigation movement that has been documented for many years: cases involving climate rights. The hypothesis of the research is that cases involving climate-washing and climate disinformation can and should use argumentation based on human rights, especially procedural rights of access to information, access to justice and public participation in environmental issues, which form the basis of the concept of environmental democracy.

2 Climate Disinformation and Climate-Washing

On 10 January 2024, the World Economic Forum published the 19th edition of its Report on the main Global Risks. About 1500 experts were interviewed with the aim of identifying the major threats to global society, in different time frames.

Disinformation has been pointed out as the risk of greater severity in the short term (2-year period) by global leaders and researchers, while extreme weather events occupy second place. In the long-term analysis (10 years), extreme weather events are identified as the greatest global threat, followed by critical change to Earth systems, biodiversity loss and ecosystem collapse, natural resources shortages, and disinformation in fifth place.[4]

Regarding the risk of disinformation, the main interconnections observed were with societal polarization, censorship and surveillance measures and the erosion of human rights.[5] However, the report does not speak of a significant risk that emerges from the interrelation between the two main global threats identified by experts: climate disinformation.

[2] Tigre and Spijkers (2023).

[3] Balounová (2023).

[4] World Economic Forum (2024), p. 8.

[5] World Economic Forum (2024), p. 21.

With the launch of the twentieth edition of the Global Risks Report in January 2025, disinformation remains, for the second consecutive year, the main threat identified over a short to medium-term period. The Report also recognizes that the accelerated spread of false information and disinformation amplifies other risks faced by the global community, such as armed conflicts and extreme weather events.[6]

There are different possible conceptualizations for disinformation, with no consensus among scholars about its definition. However, the subject has been much researched internationally in several areas of knowledge such as psychology, communication and law, especially with the advent of the internet and social networks, that enable the formation of communication bubbles and alternative information systems, beyond traditional media. For the European Commission's Expert Group, disinformation can be understood as "false, inaccurate, or misleading information designed, presented and promoted for profit or to intentionally cause public harm".[7]

According to the UN, there is a clear difference between the concepts of "disinformation" and "false information". While the latter refers to unintentional dissemination of inaccurate information, shared in good faith by those who do not know that they are transmitting falsehoods, the first designates a content that is not only inaccurate, but intended to deceive people and causa harm. It can be disseminated by state or non-state actors and can affect all areas of development, such as peace, security, public health, humanitarian aid and climate action.[8]

Fallis (2015) understands that the existing analyses of the concept of disinformation usually fail to be very broad, very narrow, or both. The author examines several proposals of conceptualization of disinformation, from authors such as Luciano Floridi, Brian Skyrms and some of his own works, through conceptual analysis. First, he understands that the concept of disinformation is composed of three essential characteristics: (1) it is a type of information, while something that represents some part of the world in a certain way; (2) it is a type of misleading information that because of the potential to create false beliefs in its recipient, puts people at risk of suffering some damage, whether or not epistemic; and, (3) it is not accidental, distinguishing itself, for example, from honest errors.

After pointing out flaws in the analyzed conceptualizations, Fallis (2015) formulates his own concept of disinformation, which would be: misleading information that has the function of deceiving people. This function, according to him, can manifest itself in two ways: either through the intention of its source (most forms of disinformation such as lies and propaganda); or because the source systematically benefits from misleading information (as in the case of conspiracy theories).

Disinformation can target various topics on the public agenda, such as economy, education, health, security, tourism, culture, environment and climate, with harmful consequences for human rights.

---

[6] World Economic Forum (2025), p. 13.

[7] European Commission (2018).

[8] United Nations (2023), p. 5.

Some organizations have been focusing on the task of formulating a definition of "climate disinformation". In November 2022, the Climate Action Against Disinformation (CAAD), a coalition of more than 50 leading organizations on climate and disinformation formulated the following definition:

> Recognising the shift in messaging, tactics, and the overall ecosystem, the CAAD coalition defines climate disinformation as content that:
>
> - Undermines the existence or impacts of climate change, the unequivocal human influence on climate change, and the need for corresponding urgent action according to the IPCC scientific consensus and in line with the goals of the Paris Climate Agreement;
> - Misrepresents scientific data, including by omission or cherry-picking, in order to erode trust in climate science, climate-focused institutions, experts, and solutions; or
> - Falsely publicizes efforts as supportive of climate goals that in fact contribute to climate warming or contravene the scientific consensus on mitigation or adaptation.[9]

It should be stressed that climate disinformation is not something new. Oreskes and Conway demonstrated how climate disinformation has existed since at least the 1980s, from which a small group of denier scientists, linked to fossil fuel companies and associations, as well as governments committed to these sectors of the economy, have begun organizing real campaigns against scientific evidence about the relationship between burning fossil fuels and global warming. The authors showed that the climate "disinformers" were inspired by the strategy of disinformation used by the tobacco industry a few years before.[10]

Oreskes and Conway emphasize that this pattern of disinformation and "commercialization of doubt" in relation to various environmental issues aims not only to delay public awareness and the institution of effective climate policies, but also to shield industries (e.g. tobacco, fossil fuels, fashion, aviation and meat processing) from litigation and regulation.[11]

In Brazil, the scientific denialism of the climate crisis has particularities consistent in the protagonism of institutions and scientists linked to agribusiness, as well as its relationship with organizations dedicated to the defense of neoliberal ideals and linked to economic liberalism. Denialism acts as a strategic device of the permanent effort of environmental deregulation, with the aim of benefiting selective economic interests of agribusiness and other economic sectors.[12]

The Intergovernmental Panel on Climate Change recognized in its 2022 report on Climate Change, "Impacts, Adaptation and Vulnerability", that hidden interests have been generating, in the public environment, disinformation that harms climate science and ignores the risks and urgency of the situation.[13]

It is important to note that in recent years, some "disinformants" have gone from an absolute denial of the existence of climate change to a strategy of actions aimed at preventing effective and necessary changes in climate policies, mainly because of

---

[9] Climate Action Against Disinformation (2022), p. 7.

[10] Oreskes and Conway (2011), p. 213.

[11] Oreskes and Conway (2011), pp. 1–14.

[12] Miguel (2022), p. 304.

[13] Intergovernmental Panel on Climate Change (2022), p. 1931.

the lower theoretical respectability that denialism has in relation to revisionism. Thus, current revisionist tactics include narratives that promote inertia (through the idea that it is too late to prevent the climate crisis), ineffective solutions to this crisis or the imposition of the burden to prevent it on individuals and individual actions, instead of governments and industries.[14]

There are also grey areas of disinformation such as greenwashing, a term created in the late 1980s to refer to various sustainable practices and discourses adopted by companies and governments that contradict their actions of exploitation of fossil fuels and greenhouse gas emissions. Among the forms that the broad concept can take, it is worth highlighting the selectivity in publicizing certain sustainable actions, without presenting its efficiency against harmful activities, or even to assume a visual identity associated with sustainability, without proving or maintaining any action of the genre in practice.[15]

Recently the term climate-washing has appeared in discussions on transparency and the right to information of consumers and citizens. Climate-washing can be considered a type of greenwashing that refers to the gap between the speeches and actions of state and non-state actors regarding climate change. But climate-washing can cover concerns that go beyond and are more specific than environmental issues, such as claims related to human health, the economy, or other aspects of climate change.[16]

Researchers performed an analysis of speech, promises, actions and investments of four major oil and gas companies (Chevron, ExxonMobil, Shell and BP), using data collected from 2009 to 2020, and concluded that the transition to clean energy business models is not occurring, since the magnitude of investments and actions does not match the discourse of companies.[17]

These large companies (BP, Shell, Chevron, ExxonMobil, and TotalEnergies) continue to promote campaigns of climate disinformation, albeit in different forms. This was confirmed by a study from InfluenceMap, which identified investments of over one billion dollars in greenwashing and lobbying against climate regulations in the 3 years following the celebration of the Paris Agreement.[18]

In a second report, the discrepancy between the sustainability discourse and the real clean energy policies of the same corporations was verified. Analysis suggested that they are spending around $750 million a year on greenwashing-related communication activities, while in contrast, only 12% of their 2022 capital expenditures were directed to low-carbon activities.[19]

This also explains the importance of using the term "disinformation" instead of "denialism", since the former covers practices that cannot be precisely referred to as

---

[14] Schiffman (2021).

[15] de Freitas Netto et al. (2020).

[16] Benjamin et al. (2022), p. 4.

[17] Li et al. (2022).

[18] InfluenceMap (2019).

[19] InfluenceMap (2022).

negationists. In this perspective, both greenwashing and climate-washing can be understood as forms of disinformation. It is understood that a clear and unequivocal distinction must be drawn between an individual and personal denial of the climate crisis (which may include skepticism[20]) and the process of active and coordinated production of false information distributed systematically to the general public, including by members of the public administration.[21] The term misinformation is also not appropriate, since it refers to inaccurate, false or misleading information in general, but which may include honest errors.[22]

Having conducted this introductory analysis of the concepts of climate disinformation, greenwashing, and climate-washing, we now will turn to the examination of the relationship between these practices and potential human rights violations, such as the right to information, drawing on innovative positions taken by international and constitutional bodies.

3 Can Climate Disinformation and Climate-Washing Lead to Human Rights Violations?

It is found that on many occasions disinformation, greenwashing and climate-washing can generate or hide violations of human and fundamental rights of consumers, citizens and vulnerable populations. According to the United Nations, the spread of disinformation on a large scale and the denial of scientifically established facts is an existential risk for humanity.[23] In addition, the UN recognizes that disinformation is a threat to democratic institutions and fundamental human rights.[24]

The existence of a political strategy of climate disinformation, often manifested through greenwashing and climate-washing is now fully recognized, but many people differ about its consequences. In this sense, there is a discourse that aims to reduce the role of this disinformation, claiming to be something harmless and underestimating its impacts on the formation of environmental awareness by the

[20] We must be especially careful with the use of the term skepticism, given the absence of scientific controversy about global warming and its anthropic character. According to Danowski (2012) "there is no more reason, scientifically speaking, for us to ask ourselves whether climate change is real or not, if it is anthropogenic or not, nor whether its consequences are or will be serious or not". Danowski prefers to use the term denialism to refer to various types of people and practices, including those that accept and recognize climate change, but do not see possible solutions beyond a supposed improvement of the capitalist society. This would be the theories of green capitalism, ecocapitalism or sustainable capitalism, which ignore that this system is precisely responsible for ecological collapse.

[21] Hartwig (2023), p. 73.

[22] Fallis (2015).

[23] United Nations (2021), p. 17.

[24] United Nations (2023), p. 3.

public. Often, this speech is accompanied by claims that climate disinformation would be protected by the right to freedom of expression.

The dangers of this discourse were observed all over the world during the covid-19 pandemic, which began at the end of 2019. This pandemic has generated nearly 15 million direct or indirect deaths in a period of less than two years.[25]

The number of deaths could have been much lower if the pandemic had not been accompanied by scientific disinformation by several global leaders, a phenomenon that replicated the populist strategy of climate disinformation and the systematic undermining of scientific authority driven by economic interests. In Brazil, which became known as the epicenter of the pandemic in Latin America, the consequence of the political process of scientific disinformation was an aggravation of the covid-19 pandemic, which contributed to the hundreds of thousands of deaths of Brazilians.[26]

Examples of this disinformation in Brazil were campaigns made through social networks by the government leaders, especially the Presidency of the Republic at that time, with content clearly contrary to technical and scientific evidence, as incentives for people not to be vaccinated, not to use protective equipment such as facial masks and to use medications that are not effective in treating the disease.[27]

This process of scientific disinformation occurred during the covid-19 pandemic was recognized by the World Health Organization through the concept of "Infodemic", which according to such agency, corresponds to a situation of overload of information systems, including false and misleading information, in digital and physical environments, during a disease outbreak.[28]

There is no doubt that the scientific disinformation practiced during the covid-19 pandemic, including by state agents, has led to serious violations of human rights, especially the right to integrity, to life, health and access to information of several populations, especially in a historical moment so delicate that these same populations were facing an outbreak of an unknown disease, requiring the positive action of states.

Another situation recently experienced by the Brazilian people clearly illustrates the implications of disinformation for the effective realization of human rights. In Brazil, the Supreme Court has established few precedents specifically addressing disinformation, but this subject is more developed in the field of electoral law. In this context, the Constitutional Court broadly affirms that there is no right to disseminate false information on social networks and the internet during the electoral process, since such dissemination would restrict the free exercise of the right to information, resulting in violations of popular sovereignty and democracy.[29]

---

[25] UN News (2022).

[26] Fonseca et al. (2021).

[27] Federal Senate of Brazil (2021), p. 1273.

[28] World Health Organization (2025).

[29] Fachin and Silva (2024), p. 64.

In the case of Climate Law, human rights violations caused by disinformation become even more evident when related to environmental and climatic disasters. In recent disasters, patterns of indiscriminate use of digital media have been observed with recurrence, from photos and videos taken by local citizens near their homes, exaggerated or falsely altered articles, to false information, disinformation, conspiracy theories and rumors (hoaxes),[30] including those disseminated and promoted by public agents.

In this sense, there is already research that argues that digital disinformation, especially in disaster contexts, can lead to violations of the right to life and the right to access information. This happens, for example, when social media and the internet prioritize engagement over accuracy, basing their business models on the "economy of attention" and actively manipulating the content that their users receive. False statements about and during disasters are much more damaging than false publicity or damage to an individual's reputation, since false information during disasters can result in the loss of human lives.[31]

The right to information is encompassed by the right to freedom of expression and thought,[32] a fundamental human right widely recognized in international treaties and conventions[33] and in the constitutions of modern states. In this sense, international law recognizes freedom of expression as a basic human right, along with the extension of that right that allows freedom of access to information to be as grounded as the rights of those who speak or express.[34]

Traditionally, the main threat to freedom of expression was direct punishment by the government, which translated into contemporary constitutional provisions such as the First Amendment to the United States Constitution and the 1988 Brazilian Citizen's Constitution. However, conditions have changed radically in recent years, constituting the "age of disinformation", in which the lens to face disinformation must be people's right to receive quality information, and no longer necessarily freedom of expression.[35]

Thus, many authors argue that disinformation would not be covered by the free exercise of freedom of expression, on the contrary, it would be an attack on this same freedom.[36] This is because freedom of expression must be exercised in harmony with other constitutional rights and values, such as the right to information, knowledge and democratic dialogue, since it is impossible to exercise free individual thought and action amid mistrust and uncertainty, which ends up making

---

[30] Kubo et al. (2024), p. 555.

[31] Mai (2021).

[32] Inter-American Court of Human Rights (2017), p. 85.

[33] The right to freedom of expression, which includes the freedom to seek and receive information, is provided for, for example, in Article 19 of the International Covenant on Civil and Political Rights of 1966; in Article 13 of the American Convention on Human Rights, of 1969; and, in Article 19 of the Universal Declaration of Human Rights, adopted in 1948.

[34] Mai (2021).

[35] Mai (2021).

[36] Morales (2018), p. 110.

democracy unfeasible.[37] In the words of the Brazilian Supreme Court Minister, Luiz Edson Fachin:

> in hard and difficult times, the freedom that vilifies the own freedom reconceive challenges of known conceptual parameters as new continents devoid of borders. (…) Disinformation is an erasure; information is a belonging.[38]

The fact is that legal parameters about disinformation and freedom of expression are still being built in philosophy, constitutional theory and dogmatic law and international law, being still a topic in expansion and development.[39] There is not yet a fully recognized right of individuals to be free from disinformation, nor is there a clear duty of states to combat disinformation, even when it affects human rights.

However, there are indications that the formation of such a right is underway. This can be observed through resolutions of the World Health Organization, urging member states to "take measures to strengthen health literacy and to counter misinformation, disinformation and stigmatization, including by providing access to other sources of fact- and science-based information". International actors, partners, civil society and the private sector were also called on to address "the proliferation of disinformation and misinformation particularly in the digital sphere, as well as the proliferation of malicious cyber-activities that undermine the public health response; and to support the timely provision of clear, objective and science-based data and information to the public".[40]

Meanwhile, the Joint Declaration on the climate crisis and freedom of expression of the OAS Special Rapporteur for Freedom of Expression and other bodies, published in 2024, determined that disinformation and false information about the climate crisis can have a serious detrimental effect on the actors involved, undermine public confidence and hinder effective participation in decision-making. The declaration sustains that "States and other relevant actors, including companies, online platforms and media, shall refrain from creating or disseminating false or misleading information, and take appropriate and proportionate measures to mitigate the risks arising from disinformation".[41]

There is no doubt that climate misinformation and practices such as greenwashing and climate-washing damage democratic dialogue and deteriorate environmental democracy, since they prevent the formation of a true environmental and climate conscience by the public.[42] The foundations of environmental democracy are precisely the procedural rights of access to information, public participation in decision-

[37] Toffoli (2021).

[38] Fachin and Silva (2024), p. 70.

[39] Fachin and Silva (2024), p. 59.

[40] World Health Organization (2021).

[41] Comisión Interamericana de Derechos Humanos (2024). In the original: "Los Estados y otros actores relevantes, incluidas las empresas, las plataformas en línea y los medios de comunicación, deben abstenerse de crear o difundir información falsa o engañosa, y tomar medidas adecuadas y proporcionadas para mitigar los riesgos derivados de la desinformación".

[42] Hartwig (2023), p. 102.

making and access to justice in environmental matters, guaranteed by the Aarhus Convention at a European level and by the Escazú Agreement in Latin America and the Caribbean.[43]

As recognized by the Bali Guidelines, access to environmental information is a prerequisite for effective public participation in environmental decisions.[44] These rights are intrinsically related and allow the realization of human rights and environmental democracy, which is prevented by climate disinformation and climate-washing. By distorting and denying the gravity of environmental problems, disinformation distorts public understanding, hampers the implementation of measures to combat climate change and other global environmental challenges, and foster polarization and mistrust between different social and political groups.[45] It is possible to say that disinformation, in its different forms, constitutes a threat to the future of the environment and undermines the realization of the principle of intergenerational equity. In addition, greenwashing and climate-washing may violate the rules of Consumer Law, characterizing, for example, misleading advertising and unfair commercial practice. Because of this, companies are increasingly required to comply with due diligence duties, as is the case with the European Union's Directive on Corporate Sustainability Due Diligence. This directive sets out obligations for companies with respect to the risks of their activities to human rights and the environment, including their global chain of activities. In addition, the regulations require compliance with transparency and reporting obligations, for example, the publication of annual statements, and the fight against climate change, through a transition plan compatible with a sustainable economy and with the limiting of global warming to 1.5 °C, in line with the Paris Agreement and with the objective of achieving climate neutrality.[46]

The Inter-American Court of Human Rights holds that the duty of due diligence is applicable to actions by both public and private entities carrying out activities that constitute a possible risk to the environment. Thus, based on the principle of prevention, which is part of customary international law, States have an obligation to regulate, control and mitigate any activities potentially harmful to the environment and human rights under their jurisdiction.[47] Therefore, in the next item of this article we will address some cases in which these practices violate human rights, relating the issue with climate litigation. It must be borne in mind that this is still a topic under

[43] Both Conventions consist of legally binding instruments in environmental matters and also human rights treaties, whose main beneficiaries should be the most vulnerable populations. According to the Preface of the Escazú Agreement, one of its objectives is to guarantee the right of all people to participate in a meaningful way in decisions that affect their lives and their environment, in very relevant areas such as land degradation, environmental disasters and climate change. It also aims to guarantee access to information and access to justice when these rights are violated, forming the triad of public participation in a broad sense.

[44] United Nations Environment Programme (2010).

[45] Rehbein and Alves (2024), p. 219.

[46] European Union (2024).

[47] Inter-American Court of Human Rights (2023), p. 64.

construction and that access to courts can often represent the recognition of new rights, such as the right to a stable climate, which can assist in an even greater justification of the duty of climate transparency and the construction of a right of citizens to be free from any form of climate disinformation.

4 Climate-Washing Litigation Meets the Rights Turn in Climate Change Litigation

Climate litigation is a transnational movement that integrates the multidimensional system of climate change governance, demanding that governments and private actors adopt the necessary measures for mitigation, adaptation, and climate regulation.[48] It is, in fact, a supplementary measure in light of the failures to implement the principles of precaution and prevention, as well as the lack of awareness regarding the principle of environmental and climate education. Given the current generations' inability to curb anthropogenic climate change, climate litigation emerges as an instrument of intergenerational significance for the protection of the environment for future generations.[49]

The United Nations Environment Programme (UNEP) reports an exponential increase in climate litigation in recent years, spanning at least 65 jurisdictions, non-judicial bodies, and international or regional courts. According to UNEP, all existing climate cases can be classified into six main categories: (i) the use of "climate rights" in climate litigation; (ii) domestic enforcement; (iii) keeping fossil fuels and carbon sinks in the ground; (iv) corporate liability and responsibility; (v) climate disclosures and greenwashing; and (vi) failure to adapt and the impacts of adaptation.[50]

The cases of "climate rights" (i) are those in which the plaintiffs allege that insufficient action to mitigate climate change violates their human and fundamental rights to life, health, adequate food, water, freedom, family life, a healthy environment, a safe climate, among others. In these cases, petitioners typically assert climate rights derived from constitutional and fundamental provisions in domestic legislation, often linking them to international obligations under the Paris Agreement.[51] The number of cases involving "climate rights" has been increasing, with discussions today focusing on a true human rights turn in climate litigation.[52]

This turn is primarily influenced by various resolutions from the UN General Assembly and its Human Rights Council, which have recognized the intrinsic link between the climate crisis and human rights violations, especially affecting

---

[48] Peel and Osofsky (2015), p. 35.

[49] Wedy and Kokke (2021), p. 40.

[50] United Nations Environment Programme (2023), p. 26.

[51] United Nations Environment Programme (2023), p. 27.

[52] Peel and Osofsky (2018).

vulnerable populations such as women, the elderly, indigenous and traditional communities, and persons with disabilities Human Rights Council (2015). These positions culminated in the UN General Assembly's recognition of the right to a clean, healthy, and sustainable environment as a human right in a landmark and historic resolution,[53] which has been influencing the filing of climate cases in all regions of the globe.

The hypothesis of this study is that climate rights cases may be related to another category of climate litigation identified by UNEP: v) climate disclosures and greenwashing. These cases are primarily concerned with holding corporations accountable for incorrect statements about climate change. UNEP categorizes these cases into three main areas: (a) protection of investors: climate disclosures; (b) protection of consumers: greenwashing complaints; (c) protection of consumers: misrepresentation of products.[54]

Beyond greenwashing, a significant trend in climate litigation today is the cases aimed at corporate accountability for climate-washing. The number of cases involving climate-washing has been increasing in recent years, with 47 petitions filed in 2023 alone, bringing the total number of litigations recorded to over 140. These cases have seen notable success, with more than 70% of completed cases decided in favor of the plaintiffs.[55]

Climate-washing litigation is part of the broader climate litigation movement and aims to hold governmental and non-governmental actors legally accountable for their actions and products that falsely claim to address climate change. This type of litigation relies primarily on consumer protection laws and civil and commercial regulations, using accessible and understandable arguments for the general public, which helps raise consumer awareness. Climate-washing litigation is not used in isolation but often in conjunction with other tools, such as government regulation and campaigns by non-governmental organizations.[56]

Thus, it is evident how governments and companies are being held accountable for the dissemination of climate disinformation, as well as misleading information about products and investments that actually contribute to anthropogenic climate change. An example of this is the claims by governments and companies of achieving "net zero" by mid- or late-century, which often serve as an excuse for a "burn now, pay later" approach.[57]

All these movements that emerge within "green capitalism" create the appearance of genuine concerns for sustainability but ultimately serve to legitimize economic growth at any cost. They disguise environmental damage and risks yet are embedded within the very logic of capitalist consumption, cloaked in green and eco-friendly rhetoric. They also act as a form of greenwashing, perpetuating a false

[53] United Nations (2022).

[54] United Nations Environment Programme (2023), p. 55.

[55] Setzer and Higham (2024).

[56] Benjamin et al. (2022), p. 5.

[57] Dyke et al. (2021).

belief in a supposed "technological salvation", which diminishes the sense of urgency to cut emissions now.[58]

Not only that, but recent analyses have highlighted the dangers of blind faith or exacerbated "techno-optimism" regarding technologies that supposedly could solve the problem of climate mitigation. An example is the hype surrounding CCS—carbon capture and storage—while the current state of knowledge suggests we are still far from the accessible and scalable implementation of this technology. It is clear that technologies have much to contribute to climate mitigation and adaptation; however, claiming that they alone can solve the problem delays the adoption of honest, effective, and imperative measures, such as cutting greenhouse gas (GHG) emissions.[59]

Traditionally, climate litigation against large corporations has focused on fossil fuel giants, given their significant contribution to GHG emissions. However, many climate litigations are now being filed against corporations from various sectors of the economy, such as large meat processing companies and the aviation industry, for misleading claims about their products and practices.

An example of this is the recent lawsuit filed by the State of New York against the meat processing giant JBS USA Food Company and JBS USA Food Company Holdings (JBS USA). The climate case, presented on February 28, 2024, is primarily based on the company's commitment to "Net zero by 2040", which was deemed misleading and inconsistent with the company's actions. The complaint also argued that JBS's calculations of greenhouse gas emissions have not accounted for emissions resulting from deforestation in the Amazon and other land-use changes in its supply chain, and that the company has violated consumer protection standards and should return profits traceable to these violations.[60] The case is currently pending a decision.

As for the aviation sector, it is possible to identify at least five types of climate litigation in relation to this industry, but cases involving climate-washing were the only ones so far with favorable results for companies to be held accountable for their practices that favor the climate crisis. These cases usually question misleading advertisements from companies, such as those that claim they are "carbon neutral" or that they are the airline with the "lowest carbon emissions".[61]

An example is the case *FossielVrij NL v. KLM*, filed in the District Court of Amsterdam, which questions KLM's CO2ZERO program, through which consumers donate to reforestation or biofuels schemes. The plaintiffs considered that such practices violate the EU's Directive on unfair commercial practices, since it leads consumers to believe that their flights would not worsen the climate emergency,

[58] Dyke et al. (2021).

[59] Wiseman and Alexander (2017), p. 95.

[60] Sabin Center for Climate Change Law (2024).

[61] Balounová (2023), p. 296.

which also draws attention to offset marketing as a form of greenwashing or climate-washing.[62]

Another interesting case, directed against government bodies, is the case *ClientEarth v. European Investment Bank*, filed before the EU General Court in August 2019. This litigation falls under the category of climate transparency in investments, as it concerns a dispute over the European Investment Bank's (EIB) decision to grant a €60 million loan for the construction of a biomass plant in Spain. The NGO ClientEarth challenged this decision, arguing that the project overstated the environmental benefits of biomass and underestimated the risks associated with emissions from logging and forest fires.[63]

It is important to note that the petition filed by ClientEarth is based on the Aarhus Convention, primarily concerning the human right to access justice in environmental matters. This aims to ensure rights related to access to information and public participation in environmental decision-making, which are also guaranteed by the convention. Indeed, the primary objective of the Aarhus Convention, as stated in its Article 1, is to protect the right of present and future generations to live in an environment adequate for health and well-being, for which these instrumental rights are essential.[64]

From this perspective, it is possible to see a connection between climate-washing litigation and human and climate rights cases. This happens because climate disinformation, greenwashing, and climate-washing not only mislead the public about governmental and corporate practices regarding the environment and climate change but can also conceal and contribute to serious human rights violations.[65]

This is the case of two judicial disputes that focus on situations experienced in the Brazilian Amazon, highlighting both climate-washing practices by companies and human rights violations against traditional communities.[66]

The first case was a Public Civil Action filed in December 2021 by two Associations of Residents of Extractive Reserves in the Federal Court of the State of Pará against more than 18 companies, including Sustainable Carbon - Projetos Ambientais Ltda. The petitioners claim that these companies are unlawfully trading carbon credits generated in the Extractive Reserves in Pará, which are environmentally preserved by the traditional extractive communities. However, the communities have reportedly received no remuneration or compensation, allowing the companies to gain an economic advantage through the illegal appropriation of credits.[67]

The carbon credit sale project, titled Ecomapuá Project, allegedly used the name, image, and cultural heritage of the communities, claiming to hold "social carbon"

[62] Balounová (2023), p. 297.

[63] General Court of the European Union (2021), § 57.

[64] General Court of the European Union (2021), § 2.

[65] Setzer and Higham (2024), p. 39.

[66] Setzer and Higham (2024), p. 38.

[67] Pará Federal Court (2021), p. 4.

certification due to supposed benefits for the communities, which never materialized. It is noteworthy that a large part of the farms covered by the Ecomapuá Project were in overlap with extractive reserves, using environmental preservation carried out by traditional communities to sell carbon credits without their consent. Considering this, the petitioners alleged a violation of the human right to prior, free and informed consent of the traditional population, as provided in Articles 6 and 7 of the International Labour Organization Convention No. 169 and sought compensation for material and collective moral damages.[68]

Although the legal action does not expressly mention the practice of greenwashing or climate-washing, it refers to the illegal practices of companies, including foreign ones, to trade or acquire carbon credits in the voluntary market, with the aim of presenting themselves as environmentally conscious to the public, while violating the human rights of traditional communities in Brazil.

The second case was presented by the Pastoral Land Commission of Brazil and the French jurists' association Notre Affaire à Tous against BNP Paribas in February 2023. The petitioners allege that BNP Paribas provides financial services without due diligence to companies like Marfrig, one of the world's largest beef producers. The case is based on the Law on the duty of vigilance of the French Commercial Code, which requires the development of plans to prevent human rights violations and environmental harm that may occur in the course of their business. According to the organizations, BNP Paribas's vigilance plans are inadequate, as they do not address the practices of Marfrig's suppliers that involve Amazon deforestation, appropriation of protected indigenous territories, and forced labor on cattle farms. In this regard, the bank's environmental commitments and public communication are said to be ambiguous, contributing to greenwashing practices and human rights violations.[69]

It is interesting to note that states can also violate human rights when they do not comply with due diligence obligations in relation to private business activities carried out on their territory. The case *Community La Oroya v. Peru*, sentenced by the Inter-American Court of Human Rights, dealt with a situation of industrial and chemical pollution that created a "sacrifice zone" in the city of La Oroya, with systemic and massive violations of the human rights of residents. In this case, the Court recognized the violation by the State of Peru of the right to information, provided for in Article 13 of the American Convention on Human Rights, since the State did not comply with its duty of active transparency, that is, it did not take sufficient measures to inform the population about the situation of environmental contamination and its health risks.[70]

It is possible to observe, in this context, that climate-washing litigation is increasingly intersecting with litigation grounded in human and climate rights, particularly concerning vulnerable populations and based on procedural or instrumental

---

[68] Pará Federal Court (2021), pp. 52–53.

[69] Sabin Center for Climate Change Law (2023).

[70] Inter-American Court of Human Rights (2023), p. 98.

environmental rights, which are fundamental to environmental democracy and the Environmental Rule of Law. In this sense, the rights to access information, public participation, and access to justice in environmental matters are essential for ensuring other substantive rights that are commonly violated due to the climate crisis. Climate disinformation, greenwashing, and climate-washing often violate the right to information, making it necessary and crucial to foster connections between arguments based on human rights and the lack of transparency for the future of climate litigation.

5 Final Considerations

Considering all that has been discussed, it is evident that the transnational climate litigation movement has proven to be of great importance in holding corporations and governments accountable for disseminating misleading and inaccurate information about their actions and products in addressing the climate crisis. Specifically in the case of climate-washing litigation, the results have been quite promising, with a high success rate in the cases that have already been resolved.

These cases offer various advantages, such as raising greater awareness among consumers about the products and companies they consume from, which contributes to the principles of environmental and climate education.

Based on the analysis conducted, it was possible to confirm the hypothesis that, in many instances, the presented climate cases can be classified under both the category of litigation based on human and climate rights and climate-washing litigation, which seeks greater transparency and accountability from both state and non-state actors.

Although each case presents various nuances, it is safe to say that in many climate disinformation and climate-washing cases, there is an attempt to conceal abuses of human rights, particularly against vulnerable populations that contribute to environmental preservation. These harmful practices developed by corporations and governments ultimately result in violations of the fundamental rights of consumers and communities, such as the right to environmental information and the right to self-determination, outlined in several international treaties.

In light of the recognition by international bodies of the interconnections between the climate crisis and human rights, it is crucial for more litigants to base climate-washing and greenwashing cases on internationally and domestically recognized human rights. This is because the dissemination of climate disinformation and climate-washing, aimed at deceiving the public and causing confusion and delays in essential measures to curb the climate crisis, should be understood not only as an abusive practice by companies and governments but as a violation of human rights.

References

Balounová E (2023) Climate litigation: targeting the aviation sector. Chinese J Environ Law 7(2):288–300

Benjamin L et al (2022, January 13) CSSN Research Report 2022:1: Climate-Washing Litigation: Legal Liability for Misleading Climate Communications. Retrieved September 21, 2024, from https://cssn.org/cssn-research-report-20221-climate-washing-litigation-legal-liability-for-misleading-climate-communications/

Climate Action Against Disinformation (2022, November 15) The Impacts of Climate Disinformation on Public Perception. Retrieved September 21, 2024, from https://caad.info/analysis/reports/the-impacts-of-climate-disinformation-on-public-perception-2/

Comisión Interamericana de Derechos Humanos (2024, May 3) Relatoría Especial para la Libertad de Expresión. Declaración conjunta sobre crisis climática y libertad de expresión. Retrieved April 10, 2025, from https://www.oas.org/es/CIDH/jsForm/?File=/es/cidh/expresion/documentos_basicos/declaraciones/20241.asp

Danowski D (2012) O hiperrealismo das mudanças climáticas e as várias faces do negacionismo. Sopro (Panfleto Político-Cultural), 70. http://www.culturaebarbarie.org/sopro/outros/hiperrealismo.html

Danowski D (2022) A zona cinzenta de negação ontem e hoje. In: Lessa R, Bines RK (Orgs.). Mundos de Primo Levi. Editora PUC-Rio; Editora Numa

de Freitas Netto SV et al (2020) Concepts and forms of greenwashing: a systematic review. Environ Sci Europe 32:19. https://doi.org/10.1186/s12302-020-0300-3

Dyke J et al (2021) Climate scientists: concept of net zero is a dangerous trap. The Conversation. https://theconversation.com/climate-scientists-concept-of-net-zero-is-a-dangerous-trap-15736

European Commission (2018, March 12) Tackling disinformation online: Expert Group advocates for more transparency among online platforms. European Commission. https://ec.europa.eu/commission/presscorner/detail/en/IP_18_1746

European Union (2024, June 13) Directive (EU) 2024/1760 of the European Parliament and of the Council of 13 June 2024 on corporate sustainability due diligence and amending Directive (EU) 2019/1937 and Regulation (EU) 2023/2859. Retrieved April 10, 2025, from https://eur--lex.europa.eu/eli/dir/2024/1760/oj

Fachin LE, Silva COP (2024) Livres e (des) informados? A liberdade de expressão e informação pelas lentes da jurisprudência do Supremo Tribunal Federal. In: Osorio ARP et al (Orgs.). Desinformação o mal do século: o futuro da democracia: inteligência artificial e direitos fundamentais. Brazilian Supreme Court (Supremo Tribunal Federal - STF)

Fallis D (2015) What is disinformation? Libr Trends 63(3):401–426. https://sci-hub.se/10.1353/lib.2015.0014

Federal Senate of Brazil (2021, October 26) Parliamentary Committee of Inquiry about the pandemic. Final Report. Retrieved April 9, 2025, from https://download.uol.com.br/files/2021/10/3063533630_relatorio_final_cpi_covid.pdf

Fonseca EM et al (2021) Political discourse, denialism and leadership failure in Brazil's response to COVID-19. Global Public Health 16(8–9):1251–1266. https://doi.org/10.1080/17441692.2021.1945123

General Court of the European Union (2021, January 27) ClientEarth v. European Investment Bank. Retrieved September 21, 2024, from https://climatecasechart.com/non-us-case/clientearth-v-european-investment-bank/

Hartwig EM (2023) Quando a mentira ameaça o futuro: desinformação climática e seus impactos na democracia. Blimunda

Human Rights Council (2015, June 30) Human rights and climate change. Retrieved September 21, 2024, from https://ap.ohchr.org/documents/dpage_e.aspx?si=A/HRC/29/L.21

InfluenceMap (2019, March) How the oil majors have spent $1Bn since Paris on narrative capture and lobbying on climate. Retrieved September 21, 2024, from https://perma.cc/UW6A-KSBE

InfluenceMap (2022, September) Big Oil's Real Agenda on Climate Change 2022. Retrieved September 21, 2024, from https://influencemap.org/report/Big-Oil-s-Agenda-on-Climate-Change-2022-19585
Inter-American Court of Human Rights (2017, November 15) Advisory Opinion OC-23/17. The Enviornment and Human Rights. Retrieved April 12, 2025, from https://corteidh.or.cr/docs/opiniones/seriea_23_ing.pdf
Inter-American Court of Human Rights (2023, November 27). Caso Habitantes de la Oroya Vs. Perú. Sentencia de 27 de Noviembre de 2023 (Excepciones Preliminares, Fondo, Reparaciones y Costas). Retrieved April 10, 2025, from https://cdn.www.gob.pe/uploads/document/file/6927310/5979293-sentencia-la-oroya.pdf?v=1726087384
Intergovernmental Panel on Climate Change (2022) Climate Change 2022: impacts, adaptation and vulnerability. Retrieved September 21, 2024, from https://www.ipcc.ch/report/ar6/wg2/
Kubo M et al. (2024) Preventing the diffusion of disinformation on disaster SNS by collective debunking with penalties. J Robot Mechatr 36(3):555–567. https://www.fujipress.jp/jrm/rb/robot003600030555/
Li M et al (2022) The clean energy claims of BP, Chevron, ExxonMobil and Shell: A mismatch between discourse, actions and investments. PLoS ONE 17(2):e0263596. https://doi.org/10.1371/journal.pone.0263596
Mai B (2021, June 8) Digital Disinformation During Declared Disasters: a First Amendment Storm Warning. https://doi.org/10.2139/ssrn.3862803
Miguel JCH (2022) The "mesh" of climate denialism and the obstruction of environmental governmentalization in Brazil. Revista Sociedade e Estado 37(1):293–315. https://periodicos.unb.br/index.php/sociedade/article/view/39014
Morales UR (2018) Richter. El ciudadano digital: fake news y posverdad em la era de internet. Editorial Océano de México
Oreskes N, Conway EM (2011) Merchants of doubt: how a handful of scientists obscured the truth on issues from tobacco smoke to global warming. Bloomsbury Press
Pará Federal Court (2021, December 20) AMOREMA e AMORETGRAP vs. Sustainable Carbon and others (Carbon credits and Extractive Reserves). Retrieved September 21, 2024 from https://climatecasechart.com/non-us-case/amorema-e-amoretgrap-vs-sustainable-carbon-and-others-carbon-credits-and-extractive-reserves/
Peel J, Osofsky HM (2015) Climate change litigation: regulatory pathways to cleaner energy. Cambridge University Press
Peel J, Osofsky HM (2018) A rights turn in climate change litigation? Transnatl Environ Law 7(1):37–67. https://doi.org/10.1017/S2047102517000292
Rehbein KDS, Alves FD (2024) A desinformação como fenômeno de risco para o futuro do meio ambiente. In: Osorio ARP et al. (Orgs.). Desinformação o mal do século: o futuro da democracia: inteligência artificial e direitos fundamentais. Brazilian Supreme Court (Supremo Tribunal Federal - STF)
Sabin Center for Climate Change Law (2023) Comissão Pastoral da Terra and Notre Affaire à Tous v. BNP Paribas. Climate Case Chart. https://climatecasechart.com/non-us-case/comissao-pastoral-da-terra-and-notre-affaire-a-tous-v-bnp-paribas/
Sabin Center for Climate Change Law (2024) People v. JBS USA Food Co. Climate Case Chart. https://climatecasechart.com/case/people-v-jbs-usa-food-co/
Schiffman R (2021, January 12). Climate deniers shift tactics to 'Inactivism'. Scientific American. https://www.scientificamerican.com/article/climate-deniers-shift-tactics-to-inactivism/
Setzer J, Higham C (2024, June 24) Global Trends in Climate Change Litigation: 2024 Snapshot. Grantham Research Institute on Climate Change and the Environment, London School of Economics and Political Science, London. Retrieved September 21, 2024, from https://www.lse.ac.uk/granthaminstitute/publication/global-trends-in-climate-change-litigation-2024-snapshot/
Tigre MA, Spijkers O (2023) Introduction to the special issue on climate litigation. Chinese J Environ Law 7(2):163–171

Toffoli JAD (2021) Fake News, desinformação e liberdade de expressão. In: Abboud G, Nery Jr N, Campos R (Org.). Fake news e regulação. Thomson Reuters Brasil

UN News (2022, May 5) Nearly 15 million deaths directly or indirectly linked to COVID-19. Retrieved April 9, 2025, from https://news.un.org/en/story/2022/05/1117582

United Nations (2021, August 5) Our Common Agenda. Report of the Secretary-General. Retrieved September 21, 2024, from https://documents.un.org/doc/undoc/gen/n21/217/01/pdf/n2121701.pdf

United Nations (2022, August 1) Resolution adopted by the General Assembly on 28 July 2022. The human right to a clean, healthy and sustainable environment. Retrieved September 21, 2024, from https://documents.un.org/doc/undoc/gen/n22/442/77/pdf/n2244277.pdf?OpenElement

United Nations (2023, June) Our Common Agenda Policy Brief 8: Information Integrity on Digital Platforms. Retrieved September 21, 2024, from https://www.un.org/en/civil-society/information-integrity-digital-platforms

United Nations Environment Programme (2010, February 26) Guidelines for the development of national legislation on access to information, public participation and access to justice in environmental matters. Retrieved April 12, 2025, from https://www.unep.org/resources/publication/guidelines-development-national-legislation-access-information-public

United Nations Environment Programme (2023, July 27) Global Climate Litigation Report: 2023 Status Review. Retrieved September 21, 2024, from https://www.unep.org/resources/report/global-climate-litigation-report-2023-status-review

Wedy G, Kokke M (2021) Climate litigation in international plan: comparative analyses. Revista dos Tribunais 110(1023):39–58

Wiseman J, Alexander S (2017) The degrowth imperative: reducing energy and resource consumption as an essential component in achieving carbon budget targets. In: Garcia E et al (eds) Transitioning to a post-carbon society: degrowth, austerity and wellbeing. Palgrave Macmillan

World Economic Forum (2024, January).Z The Global Risks Report 2024. Retrieved September 21, 2024, from https://www3.weforum.org/docs/WEF_The_Global_Risks_Report_2024.pdf

World Economic Forum (2025, January). The Global Risks Report 2025. Retrieved April 11, 2025, from https://www.weforum.org/publications/global-risks-report-2025/

World Health Organization (2021, May 25) Seventy-fourth world health assembly. Strengthening WHO preparedness for and response to health emergencies. Retrieved April 9, 2025, from https://www.who.int/health-topics/infodemic#tab=tab_1

World Health Organization (2025) Infodemic. Retrieved April 9, 2025, from https://www.who.int/health-topics/infodemic#tab=tab_1

Elisa Maffassiolli Hartwig is a PhD Candidate and Master in Public Law by the University of Vale do Rio dos Sinos. Scholarship holder of the Academic Excellence Program of the Coordination for the Improvement of Higher Education Personnel of the Ministry of Education in Brazil. Bachelor of Laws and Erasmus Exchange student at the University of Lisbon.

Gabriel Wedy holds a Post-doctoral degree in Law from PUCRS, with research period at Columbia Law School - Sabin Center for Climate Change Law (United States) and at the Universitat Heidelberg Instituts für deutsches und europäisches Verwaltungsrecht (Germany). Professor of the Graduate Program in Law of the University of Vale do Rio dos Sinos, Brazil.

Climate Jurisprudence Across the Globe

Emerging Trends in Climate Change Litigation in the European and the Inter-American Human Rights Systems

Alex Silva Oliveira and Claudia Loureiro

1 Challenges in Defining Climate Change Litigation: A Possible Solution in Public Interest Litigation?

The topic of climate change litigation crosses multiple social layers: economy, diverse areas of law and governance. On this basis, this phenomenon would be apprehended as "virtually all litigation" given that "climate change is the consequence of billions of everyday human actions, personal, commercial, and industrial".[1]

As a tentative to summarize the complexity related to climate change litigation, some authors have categorized the cases according to the relational extent of the centrality of climate change itself in the issues raised in the litigation, or 'where addressing climate change is a clear motivation for, or consequence of, bringing a case but it is not part of the legal arguments put to the court'.[2]

[1] Hilson (2010), p. 421.

[2] Peel and Osofsky (2020), pp. 23–24.

A. S. Oliveira
Centre de Recherche sur la Régulation et le Droit de la Gouvernance - CrRDG, Sherbrook, Canada
e-mail: alexsilva_22@hotmail.com

C. Loureiro (✉)
Federal University of Uberlândia, Uberlândia, Minas Gerais, Brazil
e-mail: claudia.loureiro@ufu.br

V. E. de Aquino et al. (eds.), *Climate Litigation in a Changing World*, Ius Gentium: Comparative Perspectives on Law and Justice 130,
https://doi.org/10.1007/978-3-032-05530-9_5

As pointed out by scholars' assessments of the impact of public interest[3] litigation programs, 'litigation is an imperfect but indispensable strategy of social change'.[4] However, litigation is just one tool among other tools, such as the policy advocacy work and social campaigns, that convey needed climate policy and behavioral responses.[5]

Intuitively, scholars and common sense highlight the public interest feature in climate change litigation so it could be categorized under the umbrella of public interest litigation. Yet, international legal grammar could not provide a clear definition of what international 'public interest'—nor its litigation—is.[6]

In fact, the notion of 'public interest'[7] in international litigation must consider other three important features to be useful and appropriate: "the systematic link to a specific set of values and an identified group of beneficiaries on the one hand, and, on the other, a designated authority entrusted with its interpretation and defence".[8]

The approach regarding the aim of public interest at protecting a specific cause beforehand[9] can be debated because the beneficiaries[10] and the substantive international law potentially covered by the notion are still undefined.[11] Moreover, the ineptitude of the development of an autonomous "notion of 'public interest stand-

[3] The term 'interest' can be defined as "the relation of being objectively concerned in something, by having a right to, a claim upon, or a share in"(interest - Advanced search results in Meanings | Oxford English Dictionary. https://www.oed.com/search/advanced/Meanings?partOfSpeech=noun&languageOfOrigin=english&subject=law%2Clanguage&textTermText0=interest&textTermOpt0=Definition&dateOfUseFirstUse=false&page=1&sortOption=AZ. Accessed 15 August 2024). Interests become public "if and when a broader group of (potential) individuals draws benefit from it" (Belohlavek (2012), p. 126).

[4] Cummings and Rhode (2009), p. 604.

[5] Cummings and Rhode (2009). Some authors suggest the environment can be seen as a global public good, as it "requires global common action, that gives rise to a legitimate interest of the whole international community and to a common responsibility to assist in their protection" (Morgera 2012, p. 749).

[6] Delbruck (1998), pp. 33–34. Another common concept generally used in this context is 'climate justice' which may be interpreted in different ways. According to Mary Robinson, it involves placing people at the center of solutions to ensure human rights and justice for the most vulnerable individuals and nations—those who typically contribute the least to environmental degradation. Additionally, Robinson emphasizes that the ideal of climate justice includes the possibility of living in harmony with nature, guided by compassion and international cooperation (Robinson 2021, p. 31 e 36). Procedurally speaking, it is also possible to argue that climate justice is a way to guarantee access to justice in a strict sense through multiple international courts (Cançado Trindade 2013, pp. 39–43; 45 e 46)).

[7] Public interests are value-driven and aspirational in their nature—interests which "promote […] collective welfare" (McHarg 1999, p. 677).

[8] Esnault (2023), p. 11.

[9] Mingde and Fengyuan (2011), p. 219.

[10] Those beneficiaries can be: (a) a community of individuals within a nation; (b) a group of states parties to a multilateral treaty; (c) international community of states, at large; or (d) based on the letter (c), the "international community" extending beyond states to their citizens (Suedi and Bendel 2024, pp. 42–44).

[11] Esnault (2023), p. 11.

ing' in areas which appear to involve multilateral rights and obligations"[12] may be challenging for the consolidation of the term in international litigation. Whether enough jurisdictional basis is present, the court may give states standing for "the protection of a collective interest of the group".[13] In this regard, public interest litigation is a tool used to "promote structural change".

However, a difference between beneficiaries and parties[14] to international litigation seems to be pertinent. Delineating, by the hands of the judges during the procedures, the public interest, it may affect third parties. An international judge may contribute to the "further specification, coordination and, eventually, enforcement" of common interests.[15]

Before the European Court of Human Rights (ECtHR), its Practice Directions specify: the "Contracting Party [i]s responsible for the public interest".[16] The Court underscored that, "because of their direct knowledge of their society and its needs, the national authorities are in principle better placed than the international judge to appreciate what is 'in the public interest'".[17]

In a similar venue, although in a larger scale, the InterAmerican Court on Human Rights (IACtHR) asserted in its Rules of Procedure that the InterAmerican Commission is to be the "guarantor of the public interest under the American Convention" (ACHR).[18]

Indeed, the term 'public interest' can assume different meanings in different contexts.[19] The context of the use of the term 'public interest' is the international litigation before the ECtHR and the IACtHR and how climate change litigation is comprehended by those judicial bodies. Litigation takes the form of dispute, "a disagreement on a point of law or fact, a conflict of legal views or of interests between two persons".[20] In other words, litigation focuses on the contentious jurisdiction of international courts.

However, in this paper, advisory opinions are also analyzed and understood in the light of providing consistency to international legal system, of preventing future litigation and of solving implicit legal conflicts. Advisory opinions, especially in public interest cases, are observed as a mean of regulating political interests and legal expectations of stakeholders: "regardless of their non-binding nature, advisory

[12] Crawford (2006), p. 422.

[13] International Law Commission, *Draft Articles on Responsibility of states for Internationally Wrongful Acts*, Supplement n. 10 (A/56/10), November 2001, Article 48(1)(a). See also: Jeßberger and Steinl (2022), p. 379.

[14] The standing in public interest litigation should include who suffered, on behalf of a wider public, or not suffering any harm, but altruistically defend others (Suedi and Bendel 2024, pp. 56–58).

[15] Benzing (2006), p. 372.

[16] European Court of Human Rights, *Practice Directions*, 3 June 2022, I(2).

[17] European Court of Human rights, *Béláné Nagy v. Hungary*, 53,080/13, Judgment of 13 December 2016, [113].

[18] InterAmerican Court on Human Rights, *Rules of Procedure*, 16–25 November 2000, Article 34(3).

[19] Gruner (2003), p. 929.

[20] PCIJ, *Mavrommatis Palestine Concessions (Greece v. UK)*, Ser. B n. 3, Judgment of 1924.

opinions enshrine authoritative statements of law which may inform further legal and political actions”.[21]

In addition, this paper will analyze the evolution of climate litigation at the European Court of Human Rights, based on three recent cases judged by the European Court. The article will also present a reflection on the European Green Deal as one of the main representations of the greening of human rights.

Finally, the paper will address the synergies between the Inter-American and European systems of human rights protection about climate litigation.

2 International Environmental Law Intertwined with International Human Rights Entities: An Issue or a Vein for Climate Change Litigation?

The contributions made by international human bodies are often ignored in international environmental law.[22] Nonetheless, environmental concerns have increasingly been an object through human rights law and institutions. Using legal grammar, both procedural and substantive, litigants have been able to bring important environmental claims before human rights complaints procedures.[23]

Some legitimate concerns about the appropriateness of changing issues of environmental preservation and protection into the anthropocentric terminology of human rights must be cautiously observed by the practitioners.[24] In fact, safeguarding human rights and preserving ecosystems are in most cases complementary objectives.

The rise of international human rights case law concerning environmental issues offers a potentially rich venue of jurisprudence for the development of international environmental law, although the particularities of human rights discourse can create obstacles to the extrapolation of rules generally applicable in the environmental context.[25]

Despite the absence of express environmental rights from human rights texts, global, and regional human rights entities including the Human Rights Committee, the ECtHR, and the InterAmerican Commission on Human Rights (IAComHR) are confronting a growing number of environmental cases and interpreting human rights instruments to accommodate environmental issues.[26] This is mainly because

[21] Carrillo (2023).

[22] Stephens (2009), p. 53.

[23] Taillant and Picolotti (2003), p. 1.

[24] Redgwell (1998), p. 72.

[25] Stephens (2009), p. 54.

[26] Acevedo (2000), p. 439.

they hold out international procedures for individuals to challenge governmental action or inaction in relation to environmental matters.[27]

Procedural rights have been developed whereas environmental protection, through substantive human rights (such as a right to an 'adequate', 'decent', or 'healthy' environment), has met strong resistance. This is because procedural rights are concerned with enhancing the level of public participation in environmental decision-making, and both environmental and human rights texts recognize this as an important objective.[28]

The Aarhus Convention was the first treaty to guarantee procedural rights in a legally binding instrument. It imposes states' obligations to implement these rights not only at a national level, but also that they promote their application in international environmental decision-making processes.[29]

The IAComHR has recognized that participatory rights contained in the 1969 American Convention on Human Rights (ACHR) extend to include involvement in decision-making on environmental matters. In its report on the human rights situation of indigenous peoples in Ecuador affected by rapid development, the IAComHR asserted that article 23 of the ACHR, which provides that all persons enjoy a right 'to take part in the conduct of public affairs', implied a right 'to participate, individually and jointly, in the formulation of decisions which directly concern their environment'.[30]

The Commission resolved that 'the quest to guard against environmental conditions which threaten human health requires that individuals have access to information, participation in relevant decision-making processes, and judicial recourse'.[31] In this regard, Ecuador was stimulated to take affirmative actions to advance the exercise of those rights. Although adopting a restrictive approach only to participatory rights concerning to a human rights treaty, the Commission's decision would appear coherent with the reasoning adopted in environmental texts, including the Aarhus Convention.

The ECtHR has repeatedly referred to international instruments that support these procedural rights, including principle 10 of the Rio Declaration[32] and the Aarhus Convention.[33] Regarding substantive human rights law, the ECtHR considered the violation of the right to life because of environmental negligence in

[27] Taillant and Picolotti (2003), p. 2.

[28] Stephens (2009), p. 312.

[29] United Nations (1998) Convention on Access to Information, Public Participation in Decision-Making and Access to Justice in Environmental Matters,Treaty Series, vol. 2161. Art. 3(1) and art. 3(7). ECtHR [GC], *Guerra and Others v. Italy*, 58,135/09, Judgment of 19 February 1998, [357].

[30] InterAmerican Commission on Human Rights, *Report on the Situation of Human Rights in Ecuador*, OEA/Ser.L/V/II.96 Doc. 10 Rev. 1, 1997, p. 93.

[31] Ibid., p. 92.

[32] ECtHR, *Okyay and Others v. Turkey*, 36220/97, Judgment of 12 July 2005, [51–52].

[33] ECtHR, *Taşkin and Others v. Turkey*, 46117/99, Judgment of 10 November 2004, [99].

Öneryildiz v. Turkey.[34] In this case, the court concluded that a violation of the right to life 'can be envisaged in relation to environmental issues'.[35]

While the Human Rights Committee has emphasized that there is no *action popularis* in international human rights law that would allow individuals to commence proceedings to protect human health and the environment in abstract,[36] the international judicial practice shows the contrary.

The *Yanomami v. Brazil,*[37] the IAComHR decided that Brazil violated the rights to life and health of a group of indigenous people. These violations resulted from a variety of factors, including the construction of a highway through indigenous lands, the failure to establish a promised Yanomami Park, the authorization of resource exploitation, and allowing outsiders carrying contagious diseases to penetrate Yanomami territory.

In the European human rights system, article 8(1) of the European Convention on Human Rights (ECHR) has offered the most prominent venue to address environmental-focused human rights litigation, which provides that 'everyone has the right to respect for his private and family life, his home and his correspondence'.[38] ECtHR has confirmed on numerous occasions that 'no right to nature preservation is as such included' in the ECHR.

Most of the cases involving article 8 of the ECHR have concerned noise pollution. In *Powell and Rayner v. United Kingdom,*[39] the ECtHR decided that although the applicants' properties were adversely affected by noise emanating from aircraft arriving or departing from London's Heathrow airport, there was no violation of article 8. The Court stated that 'regard must be had to the fair balance that has to be struck between the competing interests of the individual and of the community as a whole'.[40]

In the case *López-Ostra v. Spain*, the ECtHR decided on the case of the applicant's health issues as an effect of the fumes emitted from a tannery waste-treatment plant located only 12 meters from her home. The start-up of the plant had emitted noxious fumes causing health problems for a number of residents, and as a result the town council evacuated those affected, including the applicant, and rehoused them

---

[34] ECtHR [GC], *Öneryildiz v. Turkey*, 32009/16, 38889/16, 42872/16, 44485/16, 45155/16, 45189/16, 45915/16, 46283/16, 46341/16, 67614/16, 68678/16, 68872/16, 44243/17, 47834/17, 65248/17, 69602/17, 69924/17, Judgment of 30 November 2004, [491].

[35] Ibid., [64].

[36] Human Rights Committee, *André Brun v. France*, CCPR/C/88/D/1453/2006, Judgment of 2006, [6.3].

[37] InterAmerican Commission on Human Rights, *Yanomami v. Brazil*, 7615 (Brazil) OAE/Ser. I./VII.66 Doc. 10 Rev. 1, Judgment of 1985.

[38] European Court of Human Rights, *Fadeyeva v. Russia*, 55723/00, Judgment of June 2005, [68] citing *Kyrtatos v. Greece* [2003], ECHR 242 ('the Court cannot accept that the interference with the conditions of animal life in the swamp constitutes an attack on the private of family life of the applicants').

[39] European Court of Human Rights, *Powell and Rayner v. United Kingdom*, 9310/81, Judgment of 1990, [355].

[40] Ibid., p. 41.

free of charge in the town centre. The authorities also ordered a partial closure of the plant.[41]

Limited efforts by the authorities to mitigate the pollution issue, and despite their margin of appreciation, Spain had been successful in striking a fair balance between the interest of the town's economic well-being and the applicant's effective enjoyment of her right to respect for her home and family life.[42]

The great synergy between procedural rights in human rights and environmental contexts, in issues such as access to information, participation in decision-making, and right to legal redress for injury, creates an important body of precedent for the implementation of similar rights recognized in environmental law. Those cases will enhance the understanding and application of Aarhus Convention's provisions.

However, this relationship between human rights guarantees and international environmental law can assume challenging contours. It can be envisaged conflicting scenarios in which the recognition of economic, cultural, or social rights may involve collision with norms requiring the protection of environments, ecosystems, or species.

A State policy imposing limits upon restricted protected areas to preserve its biodiversity, or other environmental aspects may attract opposition by a local community on the grounds that such limitations constituted an infringement of 'cultural rights', or perhaps even the 'right to development'.[43] The balance and the application in concrete cases of the right to development and the right to environment is by no means clear.[44]

---

[41] European Court of Human Rights, *López-Ostra v. Spain*, 16,798/90, Judgment of 1995, [51].

[42] European Court of Human Rights, *Guerra and others v. Italy*, 116/1996/735/932, Judgment of 1998, [58].

[43] United Nations (1992) Rio Declaration on Environment and Development, A/CONF.151/26 (Vol. I). Principle 3: "The right to development must be fulfilled so as to equitably meet developmental and environmental needs of present and future generations". See also: United Nations (1987) Declaration on the Right to Development, General Assembly resolution 41/128, adopted on 04 December 1986; United Nations (1966) International Covenant on Economic, Social and Cultural Rights, General Assembly resolution 2200A (XXI), adopted on 16 December 1966, art. 1(2).

[44] Stephens (2009), p. 321.

3 InterAmerican Court of Human Rights' Advisory Opinions and its Contributions to Climate Change Litigation

3.1 Advisory Opinion 23/2017

The first Advisory Opinion to be analyzed responded to a request submitted by the Republic of Colombia on 14 March 2016 (Request) to the IACtHR.[45] Three questions on the interpretation of the ACHR were requested, namely:

(i) Can a state party ('State X') to the ACHR be made the respondent to a claim by an individual living in another state ('State Y') for violations of justiciable human rights recognized in the ACHR where those violations are caused by environmental harms emanating from the first state and, in particular, where the two states are parties to a treaty-based system of environmental protection, such as the Convention for the Protection and Development of the Marine Environment of the Wider Caribbean Region (Cartagena Convention)?[46]
(ii) If so, would it be a breach of the ACHR for State X, by act or omission, to cause serious transboundary environmental damage that undermined the rights to life and personal integrity protected by Articles 4 and 5 of the ACHR?
(iii) Does the ACHR require (with the purpose of protecting the individuals in State Y whose rights are in danger of being violated) State X to comply with the norms of international environmental law and does that include, as one necessary mode of compliance, a requirement to carry out an environmental impact assessment of proposed projects, and, if so, what does that obligation generally entail?

Colombia's request was brought within the context of effects of major infrastructure projects on the marine environment. Climate change, whereas it was not the focus of this Advisory Opinion, would be another example of those effects.

Colombia's request was made 5 years after 2011 Maastricht Principles[47] and in reference to civil rights (life and personal integrity) rather than economic, social and cultural rights. It remarked 'an important data point of state practice as well as an occasion for considered international jurisprudence on the topic'.[48]

Concomitantly, an inherent political context was adhered to Colombia's request. It was made in context where: proposal for Nicaragua to build, with Chinese

---

[45] IACtHR, *Request for an Advisory Opinion, Presented by the Republic of Colombia, Concerning the Interpretation of Article 1(1), 4(1) and 5(1) of the American Convention on Human Rights*, 14 March 2016.

[46] UNTS (1983) Convention for the Protection and Development of the Marine Environment of the Wider Caribbean Region, 1506 UNTS 157.

[47] ETO Consortium (2012) Maastricht Principles on the Extraterritorial Obligations of States in the Area of Economic, Social and Cultural Rights.

[48] Feria-Tinta and Milnes (2016), p. 67.

founding, a canal to rival the Panama Canal which would affect the shipping and coastal communities in the Caribbean region; and the ICJ had concluded a dispute on maritime boundaries between Colombia and Nicaragua adversely to Colombia.[49]

In *Territorial and Maritime Dispute* case, Colombia had withdrawn its optional clause declaration under Article 36(2) of the ICJ Statute,[50] with the consequence that Colombia would no longer have a right to recourse to ICJ against Nicaragua, i.e. in cases of environmental harm. In this sense, the request could be interpreted as Colombia opening up a new front in that political dispute. The IACtHR avoided this aspect and concentrated on the issues of principle and prevented itself from expressing any concrete views on particular instances of pollution sources or their victims.

Under the view of a wider interpretative power, the IACtHR stated broadly affirmative to Colombia's three questions, except that on question (i). The IACtHR declined Colombia's invitation to base either substantive state human rights obligations, or the scope of 'jurisdiction' under Article 1(1) of the ACHR, upon the existence or otherwise of any other treaty regime, such as the Cartagena Convention.[51]

Some important legal considerations[52] can be highlighted from IACtHR decision:

(i) the court recognizes the right to a healthy environment as an autonomous right 'which protects the components of the environment such as woodlands, rivers, sea and others, as legal interests in their own right' (para. 62) and as a fundamental right for the existence of humanity (para. 59);
(ii) it acknowledges the right to a healthy environment as a right with individual and collective connotations (para. 47);
(iii) it recognizes the relationship between the protection of the environment and the realization of other human rights, stating that 'environmental degradation and the adverse effects of climate change affect the effective enjoyment of human rights' (para. 47);
(iv) it acknowledges an interdependence and indivisibility between human rights and the protection of the environment, giving rise to state obligations (para. 55);
(v) it acknowledges that the majority of the environmental obligations rest on a duty of due diligence on the part of the state (para. 124);
(vi) environmental obligations become stricter if, in addition to a human rights treaty, there is also an environmental treaty (such as the Cartagena Convention) (para. 126); and
(vii) it identifies a connection between (1) a number of substantive human rights (including the right to life and right to integrity and to dignity), and, indeed, the right to a healthy environment, and their correlative obligations on the part of the state, such as the obligation to prevent (including the duty to regulate,

---

[49] International Court of Justice, *Territorial and Maritime Dispute (Nicaragua v. Colombia)*, Judgment of 19 November 2012, ICJ Repots 624.

[50] United Nations (1945) Statute of the International Court of Justice, 1 UNTS 993.

[51] UNTS (1983) Convention for the Protection and Development of the Marine Environment of the Wider Caribbean Region, 1506 UNTS 157.

[52] Feria-Tinta and Milnes (2016), pp. 68–69.

supervise, and inspect, to require and approve environmental impact assessments, to establish contingency plans), precaution, and cooperation (including the duty to consult and negotiate with a potentially affected state) and (2) procedural rights such as access to information, public participation, and access to justice. The court held, in particular, that in order to respect and guarantee rights to life and integrity states are under a duty to:

(a) prevent significant environmental damage, both inside and outside their territory;
(b) regulate, oversee, and control the activities under their jurisdiction that may give rise to significant damage to the environment, carry out studies on environmental impact when there exists the risk of significant damage to the environment, draw up a contingency plan so as to have in place safety measures and procedures for minimizing the possibility of major environmental accidents, and mitigate any significant environmental damage that would have ensued, even when this may have occurred in spite of the preventive actions on the part of the state;
(c) act in accordance with the precautionary principle when faced with possible severe or irreversible damage to the environment, even in the absence of scientific certainty;
(d) cooperate in good faith for the protection against damage to the damage to the environment;
(e) pursuant to that duty of cooperation, notify other states that may be potentially affected when they become aware that a planned activity under their jurisdiction could give rise to a risk of significant cross-border damage and in cases of environmental emergencies as well as consulting and negotiating, in good faith, with the states potentially affected by significant cross-border damage;
(f) guarantee the right to access to information relating to possible negative impact upon the environment, enshrined in Article 13 of the ACHR;
(g) guarantee the right to public participation of people under their jurisdiction, which is enshrined in Article 23(1) of the ACHR, in the making of decisions and policies that may affect the environment; and
(h) guarantee access to justice, with regard to state obligations for the protection of the environment (para. 242).

The interdependence and indivisibility across human rights, notably, on the one hand, between civil and political rights, and, on the other hand, economic, social and cultural rights, are evident throughout the Advisory Opinion. It helped to synchronize both the environment and the right to development in human rights' grammar. Moreover, the role of soft law as source is carefully considered by the IACtHR.

Interesting to note as well that the Court recognized nature and the environment as subjects of rights with an entitlement to protection, which is becoming a legal venue to ensure the preservation of rivers, forests and areas where extractive industries and energy-related mega projects are located.

What is new in the Advisory Opinion was its analysis of individual rights in relation to the environment in a central and systematic manner.[53] The IACtHR concluded that Article 11 of the Protocol of San Salvador incorporates the "Right to a Healthy Environment".[54] The preamble to the Protocol of San Salvador recognizes the close relationship between those indivisible human rights which are 'based on the recognition of the dignity of the human person'.[55]

The IAComHR already pronounced, and quoted by the Advisory Opinion, about the necessity of 'a minimum of environmental quality' as a precondition to exercise several fundamental rights that 'are profoundly affected by the degradation of natural resources'.[56] The Advisory Opinion also quoted the special rapporteur on the issue of human rights obligations relating to the enjoyment of a safe, clean, healthy, and sustainable environment, who stated: 'Human Rights and the protection of the environment are inherently interdependent'.[57]

The Advisory Opinion clarifies that, in principle, the InterAmerican system permits cross-border human rights claims with respect to other types of conduct, such as transboundary pollution and ecological damage. It also holds that jurisdiction extends to activities over which a state exercises 'effective control'.[58] The IACtHR held that,

> [a]s regards transboundary harms, a person is under the jurisdiction of the State of origin if there is a causal relationship between the event that occurred in its territory and the affectation of the human rights of persons outside its territory. The exercise of jurisdiction arises when the State of origin exercises effective control over the activities carried out that caused the harm and consequent violation of human rights.[59]

---

[53] InterAmerican Court of Human Rights, *Environment and Human Rights (State Obligations in Relation to the Environment in the Context of the Protection and Guarantee of the Rights to Life and to Personal Integrity—Interpretation and Scope of Articles 4(1) and 5(1) in Relation to Articles 1(1) and 2 of the American Convention on Human Rights)*, Advisory opinion OC-23/18, Ser A (No 23), Judgment of 15 November 2017, para 46.

[54] OEA (1988) Additional Protocol to the American Convention on Human Rights in the Area of Economic, Social and Cultural Rights, 28 ILM 156 (1989).

[55] Ibid. Preamble, recital 3.

[56] InterAmerican Commission on Human Rights, *Indigenous and Tribal People's Rights over Their Ancestral Lands and Natural Resources, Norms and Jurisprudence of the Inter-American Human Rights System*, OEA/Ser.I/L/V/ II. Doc 56/09, Judgment of 30 December 2009, para 190.

[57] Knox JH (2012) Preliminary Report of the Independent Expert on the Issue of Human Rights Obligations Relating to the Enjoyment of a Safe, Clean, Healthy and Sustainable Environment, UN Doc A/HRC/22/43, para 10.

[58] The European Court of Human Rights (ECtHR) recognized 'effective control' of territory as a basis for jurisdiction under Article 1 in *Loizidou v Turkey*, Application no 15318/89 (ECtHR), Judgment, 23 March 1995, para 52 (*Loizidou*).

[59] InterAmerican Court of Human Rights, *Environment and Human Rights (State Obligations in Relation to the Environment in the Context of the Protection and Guarantee of the Rights to Life and to Personal Integrity—Interpretation and Scope of Articles 4(1) and 5(1) in Relation to Articles 1(1) and 2 of the American Convention on Human Rights)*, Advisory opinion OC-23/18, Ser A (No 23), Judgment of 15 November 2017, para 104(h).

In the Advisory Opinion, regarding transboundary environmental harms, 'effective control' is no longer something that must be exercised over the territory where the victim was, nor over the victim herself. It is highlighted that what matters is whether the source state has effective control over the activities that caused the transboundary harm. However, the IACtHR was careful to emphasize in the Advisory Opinion that extraterritorial obligations are exceptional and should be restrictively built.[60]

As remarked, the Advisory Opinion did not address climate change *per se*, but some of the IACtHR's observations on states' duties are applicable to this ultimate example of transboundary pollution. Using the court's reasoning, an argument that a state's contribution to the accumulation of greenhouse gases in the atmosphere should result in state responsibility and accountability under the ACHR to victims living in other states seems plausible. For example, the Advisory Opinion was later cited by the UN Committee on the Rights of the Child in a case affirming countries' 'extraterritorial responsibilities for carbon pollution'.[61]

3.2 The 2023 Advisory Opinion Request by Chile and Colombia on "Climate Emergencies and Human Rights," and the Resulting 2025 Advisory Opinion No. 32 on the Climate Emergency and Human Rights

The climate emergency is not new to the Inter-American System. It was the first regional and international forum to address climate change as a human rights issue, starting with the Inuit case (*Sheila Watt-Cloutier* et al. *v. United States*).[62] This 2005 claim, brought on behalf of Arctic Inuit communities, argued that global warming had the most severe impact on the Arctic, leading to human rights violations under the American Declaration of the Rights and Duties of Man.[63] Though dismissed by the Inter-American Commission, the issue has returned, now before the Court as an Advisory Request.

As a progressive litigation development of the Advisory Opinion 23/2017, the request for an advisory opinion made by Chile and Colombia in 2023 aimed at clarifying the scope of state obligations, in both their individual and collective dimensions, to address the climate emergency within the framework of International Human Rights Law, taking into account, in particular, the differentiated effects of

[60] Ibid, paras 81, 104(d).

[61] Committee on the Rights of the Child, *Decision adopted by the Committee under the Optional Protocol to the Convention on the Rights of the Child on a communications procedure, concerning communication*, CRC/C/88/D/105/2019, Judgment of 22 September 2021, pp. 7–8, 11–13.

[62] InterAmerican Commission on Human Rights, *Petition Seeking Relief from Violations resulting from Global Warming caused by Acts and Omissions of the United States*, Judgment of 7 December 2005.

[63] Adopted by the Ninth International Conference of American States, Bogotá, Colombia, 1948.

this emergency on people and population groups from various regions, nature, and human survival on our planet.[64]

The proliferation of droughts, floods, landslides, and wildfires due to climate change highlighted, according to Colombia and Chile, the need to respond urgently and based on the principles of equity, justice, cooperation, and sustainability, with a human rights perspective. Colombia and Chile emphasized the need for regional standards to accelerate action to confront climate change.

Colombia and Chile's petition covers several key topics[65]:

(i) State Obligations and Climate Emergencies: The petitioners sought clarity on state responsibilities to prevent and address human rights impacts of climate emergencies, focusing on actions required under the Paris Agreement to prevent exceeding the 1.5-degree global temperature threshold. They requested the Court to outline the necessary measures to address climate impacts, particularly for vulnerable communities, including regulation, monitoring, environmental impact assessments, contingency plans, and mitigation efforts. They also requested guidance on the principles that should guide these actions, specifically in adaptation, mitigation, and loss and damage.

(ii) Right to Life and Climate Change: The petitioners asked for an opinion on how states must uphold the right to life amid climate emergencies, in line with human rights and scientific standards. They emphasized the importance of access to information to protect other rights, such as life, property, health, and participation.

(iii) Protection of Children and Future Generations: Colombia and Chile sought clarification on states' differentiated obligations to safeguard the rights of children and future generations from climate change, citing specific articles of the American Convention. They also inquired about the right of children to access justice to prevent potential climate-related harms.

(iv) Judicial Actions and Procedural Obligations: The petitioners asked the Court to define the nature of states' obligations to provide judicial actions for adequate protection and reparation of rights affected by the climate emergency, including the need for consultations on the climate impacts of certain activities.

(v) Protection of Environmental Defenders: Referring to the American Convention and the Escazú Agreement, the petitioners focused on state obligations to protect environmental defenders, especially indigenous people and women, who are critical in protecting ecosystems amid the climate crisis.

(vi) Regional Cooperation and Climate Justice: Finally, the petition emphasized the need for regional cooperation to address climate change, particularly

[64] InterAmerican Court of Human Rights, *Request for an Advisory Opinion I/A Court H.R., Request for an Advisory Opinion submitted by Chile and Colombia before the Inter-American Court of Human Rights*, 1st September 2023.

[65] Request for an advisory opinion on the scope of the state obligations for responding to the climate emergency. In: Climate Change Litigation. https://climatecasechart.com/non-us-case/request-for-an-advisory-opinion-on-the-scope-of-the-state-obligations-for-responding-to-the-climate-emergency/. Accessed 18 August 2024.

clarifying shared and differentiated obligations among nations. They also sought guidelines on how states should address migration triggered or exacerbated by climate effects, considering equity and climate justice principles.

To provide answers to those questions, Advisory Opinion 32 of May 29, 2025 (OC-32/25) was divided into two main parts. The first provides an overview of the factual background of climate change, its impacts on people and the environment, international responses, regulatory developments in the Americas, and the current climate emergency. The second part interprets relevant inter-American legal provisions, focusing on general obligations related to substantive and procedural rights, including the rights of individuals and vulnerable groups.

To address this Advisory Opinion, the Court primarily relied on IPCC reports due to their credibility and broad international recognition. It interpreted the relevant legal provisions using both specific rules from the American Convention (notably Article 29 and the pro persona principle) and general principles from the Vienna Convention on the Law of Treaties. These included interpreting treaties considering their object and purpose—particularly the protection of human rights—and as evolving instruments responsive to changing conditions. The Court also considered the broader *corpus iuris* of the Inter-American system, international human rights law, and relevant international environmental and climate change norms. Additionally, it may refer to case law and treaties such as the UNFCCC, the Paris Agreement, the Convention on the Rights of the Child, and the Escazú Agreement to ensure a harmonized interpretation of international obligations.

The Court highlighted that its interpretation of the American Convention and the Protocol of San Salvador in this Advisory Opinion applies not only to States Parties to these instruments but to all OAS member states. This is because all OAS members are bound by the obligations of the American Declaration, the OAS Charter, and the Inter-American Democratic Charter.

Overall, three major states' obligations concerning human rights towards climate crisis were recognized by the Court. The first one is the obligation to respect human rights. The second is the obligation to protect human rights and the last one the obligation to cooperate.

The obligation to respect embodies a negative and positive aspect. The former states that the States must refrain from any kind of action that may set back, slow down, or undermine the results of measures necessary to protect human rights from the impacts of climate change—this negative aspect of the obligation derives from the principles of progressivity and non-regression. The latter asserts that policies must be justified scientifically and must observe the principles of proportionality and necessity to promote a decrease in risk.

The obligation to protect human rights and to prevent its violations is deeply connected with the idea of due diligence. The Court affirms that due diligence must be proportionate to the level of environmental risk. It agrees with the International Tribunal for the Law of the Sea that due diligence is a flexible standard, shaped by specific circumstances, available scientific and technological knowledge, international norms, the likelihood of harm, and the urgency of the situation.[66]

To achieve this standard, the Court indicated that States, when they elaborate their policies and legislate their law, must identify and evaluate in a comprehensive way all the risks, based on the principle *pro persona*; take proactive and ambitious actions to prevent disastrous scenarios caused by climate crisis; use the best science available to design and implement climate action; consider the implementation of a human right perspective in the monitoring, design and execution of these policies. States must ensure that their policies will not lead to new vulnerabilities or enhance the existent ones. They must also implement a monitoring system to improve transparency and accountability in the States' actions. Moreover, the Court innovated by addressing directly the regulation and supervision of due diligence specifically in business and companies.

The obligation to cooperate is essentially embodied in the support of technology transfer funding and in the support of capacity building. Both actions should be performed according to the principles of good faith, equity and common but differentiated responsibilities (CBDR). Important to mention that the Court emphasized the relevance of States to cooperate and be able to receive cooperation as well.

In fact, the Court stated that the obligation to cooperate on environmental issues extends beyond transboundary harm and applies broadly when addressing global challenges like climate change. In such contexts—especially in cases of climate disasters and climate-induced migration—cooperation is essential and must reflect the principle of equity. This involves considering differences among States, including their capacities and responsibilities, to ensure fair and effective international action.

The Court reiterated that the obligation to cooperate includes financial and economic support for less developed countries, technical and scientific collaboration, implementing measures that benefit other states, and creating international forums and joint policies. This obligation also involves sharing resources, expertise, policy advice, information, and technologies to promote collective action and a just transition.

Some other obligations arising from substantive rights were specified by the Court. This was organized in two distinct categories of environment-related rights: (i) substantive rights, such as the rights to life, health, integrity, and property, which are directly threatened by environmental harm; and (ii) procedural rights, like access to information, participation in decision-making, freedom of expression and association, and the right to an effective remedy, which help ensure sound environmental governance.[67]

---

[66] ITLOS. Request for an Advisory Opinion Submitted by the Commission of Small Island States on Climate Change and International Law, Case No. 31, Advisory Opinion, ITLOS Reports 2024, par. 239.

[67] IACtHR, *Request for an Advisory Opinion, Presented by the Republic of Colombia, Concerning the Interpretation of Article 1(1), 4(1) and 5(1) of the American Convention on Human Rights*, 14 March 2016, par. 64.

With regard to the first category, the Court has (1) reiterated its jurisprudence on the right to a healthy environment; (2) clarified its position on the protection of nature as a subject of rights; (3) ruled on the *jus cogens* nature of the obligation not to cause irreversible damage to the climate and the environment; (4) referred to the obligation to protect the climate system as well as the (5) right to a healthy climate; and, finally, developed (6) the obligations derived from the right to a healthy environment in the context of the climate emergency.

The right to a healthy environment is a fundamental human right with both collective and individual dimensions. Collectively, it represents a universal interest owed to present and future generations. Individually, its violation can directly or indirectly affect other rights, such as health, personal integrity, and life.

This Court has pointed out that the principle of prevention forms part of customary international law. The Court has found that, although the principle of prevention in environmental matters was established in the context of inter-state relations, the obligations it imposes are similar to those arising from the general duty to prevent human rights violations. The exercise of jurisdiction by the State of origin in relation to transboundary harm is based on the understanding that it is the State in whose territory or under whose jurisdiction these activities are carried out that has effective control over them and can prevent transboundary harm that affects the enjoyment of human rights outside its territory. Potential victims of the negative consequences of these activities fall under the jurisdiction of the State of origin for the purposes of the State's possible responsibility for failing to fulfill its obligation to prevent transboundary harm.

Another innovation from this advisory opinion is the recognition of Nature as a subject of Law. This shift from object to subject of Law means highlighting Nature's structural role in the vital balance of conditions that make the planet habitable. This approach strengthens a paradigm focused on the protection of ecological conditions essential for life and empowers local communities and indigenous peoples, who have historically been guardians of ecosystems and possess deep traditional knowledge about how they function.[68] It represents a contemporary manifestation of the principle of interdependence between human rights and the environment. This interpretation is also in line with advances in international environmental law, which has affirmed structural principles such as intergenerational equity, the precautionary principle, and the duty of prevention, all of which are aimed at preserving the integrity of ecosystems in the face of current and future threats.

Additionally, the OC-32 has expressly affirmed that the obligation to preserve the common ecosystem is so essential to the enjoyment of fundamental rights that it constitutes a *jus cogens* norm, meaning it cannot be overridden by any contrary *posteriori* or *priori* agreement. In other words, the Court affirmed the legal nature of *jus cogens* to the prohibition of creating massive and irreversible damage to nature.[69]

[68] IACtHR. OC-32/25, 29 May 2025, par. 280.

[69] IACtHR. OC-32/25, 29 May 2025, paras. 291–292.

Although it is undeniable the avant-garde character of the IACtHR jurisprudential position in this OC-32 regarding the legal nature of *jus cogens*, the Court did not categorize what acts that cause 'massive' and 'irreversible' damage would be. These concepts fell short in terms of achieving objective parameters to be assessed thus making the task of identifying accountability and responsibility of actors, in this context, very impractical. Moreover, the Court has established a high standard of burden of proof. In other words, it has coordinated a double adjectivization and standard to the damage derived from the act: it must be 'massive' **and** 'irreversible'.

This discussion is very similar to the characterization of ecocide in international criminal law. According to the International Commission of Jurists, ecocide would refer to any unlawful or arbitrary act committed with the knowledge that there is a significant probability of causing serious, extensive, or lasting damage to the environment.[70] With the help of the InterAmerican Court of Human Rights, these elements could be better explained and later be used by international organs and jurists to finally build a consensus about how to frame and criminalize internationally these damages considered as 'massive' and 'irreversible'. It was a great recognition towards the peremptory legal nature of the prohibition to cause irreversible and massive damage, but a clearly missed opportunity to set interpretative limits on these two abstract concepts.

Relevant to address that this prohibition is not only for States' actions. Other actors, such as individuals, private and public companies, must refrain from damaging Nature. Ultimately, States must promote restauration of ecosystems with help to the best sciences available which includes traditional and indigenous knowledge. This obligation to preserve the balance and the equilibrium of Nature constitutes, according to the Court, an international and an imperative duty for States.

Derived from the notion of the right to a healthy environment, the Court stated the right to a healthy climate. The Court defined it as a climate system that has no anthropogenic interferences that may be dangerous to human beings and Nature as a whole. The right to a healthy climate would have an individual and a collective dimension. The first dimension protects the possibility of every person developing themselves in a climate system that is free from dangerous anthropogenic interferences. The second dimension protects the collective interests of present and future generations of human beings and other species to maintain a climate system that is adequate to ensure their well-being and balance among the species considering the serious existential threats derived from the effects of climate emergency.

In this latter dimension, the Court ensured the application of the principle of intergenerational and intragenerational equality in which States must vigorously take actions through environmental policies in accordance with other environmental principles, such as the principle of prevention, principle of precaution and principle of progressiveness. As derived from human rights, the right to a healthy climate is

---

[70] This concept can be found in https://www.stopecocide.earth/polly-higgins. Consulted on 6 July 2025.

also both indivisible and non-exclusive, belonging collectively to all those who share this common interest. Failure to comply with international obligations to protect the global climate system necessarily affects that interest and generates State responsibility. Therefore, measures aimed at ending the violation, preventing its recurrence, and repairing its consequences must simultaneously benefit present and future humanity, as well as Nature as a whole.

The right to a healthy climate has a huge impact on Nature, considered as the physical and the biological foundation of life. To promote balance between climate stability and ecological equilibrium, it is imperative to articulate an integrative legal approach between human rights and rights of Nature with the harmonious interpretation of principles of *pro persona* and *pro natura.*[71] This recognition of Nature as a subject to autonomous legal protection reinforces and strengthens the response of States considered in the context of climate emergency.

From the right to a healthy climate, the Court recalled some obligations regarding the causes of climate change and the mitigation of Greenhouse gas (GHG) emissions. Likewise, from the right to a healthy environment derive specific obligations related to (i) the protection of nature and its components and (ii) the progressive advancement towards sustainable development.[72]

Besides regulation, supervision and monitoring, States must also demand and approve Environment Impact Assessments (EIAs), based on the principles of progressiveness, CBDR, equality, prevention and precaution, by defining a mitigation goal or target. In this definition, States must consider the best available science; their current contribution to GHG emissions; their past and historical contribution accumulated to climate change; the capacity to contribute to mitigation targets; and the circumstances in which they are inserted. The design of a domestic strategy to meet those targets must be built on human rights approach and must be as ambitious as possible including a binding standard and regulation for the State with specific deadlines for its compliance and progressively increase it.

The Court highlighted that it is fundamental States regulate the behavior of companies and enterprises. Thus, States should (i) urge all companies domiciled or operating in their territory and jurisdiction to adopt effective measures to combat climate change and related human rights impacts; (ii) enact legislation requiring companies to conduct human rights and climate change due diligence along the entire value chain; (iii) require companies, public and private, to disclose in an accessible manner the greenhouse gas emissions of their value chain; (iv) require companies to take measures to reduce such emissions, and to address their contribution to climate mitigation goals, throughout their operations; and (v) adopt a set of standards to discourage greenwashing and undue influence by companies in the political and regulatory sphere in this area, and support the actions of human rights advocates.[73] The Court considered that the development of compliance monitoring

[71] IACtHR. OC-32/25, 29 May 2025, par. 315.
[72] IACtHR. OC-32/25, 29 May 2025, par. 320.
[73] IACtHR. OC-32/25, 29 May 2025, par. 347.

mechanisms within companies is a good practice to ensure the effective implementation of environmental and human rights regulations.[74]

The Court affirmed, therefore, that States should establish differentiated climate action obligations based on the current and historical contribution of companies to climate change and imposed stricter obligations on companies that carry out activities that generate higher GHG emissions. Such obligations may refer, for example, to business operating conditions, tax burdens, contributions to fair transition plans and strategies, investment in education, adaptation measures, and loss and damage, among others. The distinctions thus established should be aimed at putting into practice the polluter pays principle and ensuring the effectiveness of national mitigation measures. The Court also stressed the importance of considering the role played by the different components of economic conglomerates and transnational corporations, so that States can attribute legal responsibilities to parent companies, or those that exercise control over others, in terms of the GHG emissions generated by their subsidiaries or by the companies they control.[75]

Within the microsystem constituted by the UNFCCC and the Paris Agreement, states must adopt measures to adapt to climate impacts, which triggers common obligations for all states to protect human rights affected by climate change. Both documents determine the establishment of adaptation plans to increase the capacity to absorb the effects of climate change and to promote resilience.[76]

The Conference of the Parties, as the planning body, establishes the need to assess the risks caused by climate change, outline strategies, implement adaptation measures, monitor and evaluate the results and adjust and improve, in accordance with the principle of progressiveness and with the precautionary principle,[77] the adoption of the measures taken. In this context, it is necessary to observe the impacts on gender equality, participation and transparency.[78]

In addition, the IACHR has established a fruitful debate with the European Court of Human Rights and, especially with regard to the Case of the Elderly Swiss Ladies, has pointed out the need to adopt plans to guarantee the adaptation and the mitigation of adverse impacts on people's health and human rights, since the lack of response by states poses a risk of persistent violation of human rights.

The Inter-American Court has also emphasized the need for states to keep their national adaptative plans up to date. Therefore, the measures followed by states must be capable of preventing and mitigating the degradation of human rights caused by climate impacts to the greatest extent possible and with enhanced due diligence.

Such adaptative plans must be designed according to the particularities of each state, considering the risks of affecting human rights and their technical capacities

[74] IACtHR. OC-32/25, 29 May 2025, par. 349.

[75] IACtHR. OC-32/25, 29 May 2025, par. 350.

[76] IACtHR. OC-32/25, 29 May 2025, par. 379–381.

[77] IACtHR. OC-32/25, 29 May 2025, par. 390.

[78] IACtHR. OC-32/25, 29 May 2025, par. 383–389.

in line with the principle of CBDR. Moreover, these plans must be based on the best science, including the local traditional and indigenous knowledge with no discrimination as all people have the right to the benefits of scientific and technological progress.

More precisely, the IACHR pointed out that climate change can affect the right to life, personal integrity, health, present and future generations and health.[79] In one hand, global warming may impact on the right to life and physical integrity, in such a way it can increase the number of deaths and new illnesses because of weakened access to public facilities and health infrastructures, which obliges states to increase the resilience of national healthcare systems.

On the other hand, global warming can directly impact rights such as the right to private and family life, the right to property, and the right to adequate housing. Rising sea levels, for instance, can undermine access to employment, housing, and land suitable for agriculture, thereby threatening the conditions necessary for a dignified life.

The Court also emphasized the link between environmental degradation and forced displacement, affirming that States must adopt public policies to address this reality in accordance with the principles of international cooperation and solidarity. In this context, the right to mobility must be safeguarded—both within national borders and across them—especially in response to climate-induced migration. States must also ensure continuous access to essential rights such as water, adequate food, employment, and social security, all of which are increasingly threatened by the impacts of climate change.

Furthermore, access to culture and education must be treated as a priority in mitigating the adverse effects of climate change on the enjoyment of human rights. Cultural heritage is at risk from rising sea levels and environmental disasters, while the right to education may be undermined by the deterioration of infrastructure, disruptions caused by natural disasters, and health crises linked to environmental degradation. Children and adolescents, in particular, face heightened vulnerability, as climate impacts can significantly hinder their access to and enjoyment of educational opportunities.

The protection of human rights in the context of climate change is inseparable from the preservation of scientific knowledge and local, traditional expertise—especially the role of Indigenous peoples in safeguarding ecosystems, as already recognized by the Inter-American Court in Advisory Opinion 23/2015.

In the face of the disruptive and often dystopian consequences of climate change, a broad range of rights must be safeguarded, including the right to access, produce, and disseminate information; the right to political participation; and the fight against disinformation.

The principles of equality and non-discrimination must be applied in a way that acknowledges and addresses the specific vulnerabilities of groups disproportionately affected by climate change, ensuring differentiated and inclusive protection.

[79] IACtHR. OC-32/25, 29 May 2025, par. 392–588.

In summary, the Court affirmed that under the general obligation to respect human rights, States are required to act with due diligence to protect both human rights and the right to a healthy environment, not only for current but also for future generations. This includes the duty to pursue sustainable and progressive development and to incorporate these obligations into domestic legal systems.

The OC 32/25 also reaffirmed States' obligations to guarantee a broad range of rights threatened by climate change, including the rights to property and housing, freedom of movement and residence, access to water and food, work, social security, culture, education, scientific progress, and the recognition of traditional and Indigenous knowledge systems.

In conclusion, the OC 32/25 consolidates the foundations for autonomous climate litigation within the Inter-American System, strengthens the principle of sustainable development, affirms intergenerational justice, elevates the value of local knowledge, and reinforces the integration between the United Nations climate framework (UNFCCC and the Paris Agreement) and the human rights standards of the Inter-American system.

4 European Union and Climate Litigation: A Shift in Paradigm

The greening of human rights[80] is a movement that is intensifying in various parts of the world and in various human rights protection systems. As we have seen so far, the inter-American system has been making progress on this issue, trying to establish standards for environmental protection by outlining the obligations of states, a reality that is also seen in the European Union and the in the European human rights system, as we will see in this section.

With the development of green practices in normative, institutional and organizational aspects, states, international organizations, non-governmental organizations, companies and civil society have been working to meet the demands of the Sustainable Development Goals, coined by the United Nations' Agenda 2030,[81] whose guiding principle is to ensure that no one is excluded or left behind.

This whole movement is corroborated by the United Nations which, in two Resolutions from two of its bodies, emphasized that the right to an ecologically balanced environment is a human right.

Despite the non-coercive nature of the UN Resolutions, the resolutions reflect the involvement of international organizations with the issue of climate change and the important role they play in consolidating greening movements worldwide. Moreover, they trigger a movement for states to recognize the right to the environment as a

[80] Loureiro (2022), pp. 216–236.

[81] United Nations (2015) Agenda 2030.

human right in their national constitutions and for international organizations to do the same in regional international treaties.

Thus, at the global level, on October 8, 2021, the United Nations Human Rights Council adopted Resolution A/HRC/48/13[82] recognizing the right to an ecologically balanced environment as a human right and the duty of due diligence of States to adopt the necessary measures to protect the environment.

One of the most important aspects of this Resolution is the possibility of autonomous protection of the right to the environment, which could strengthen litigation on this right at a national and an international level. In turn, on July 28, 2022, the United Nations General Assembly issued Resolution A/RES/76/300,[83] also on the human right to a clean, healthy and sustainable environment, in the same vein as the aforementioned Human Rights Council Resolution.

The recognition of the human right to an ecologically balanced environment is a consequence of the transnational social movements unleashed by the international community to protect the environment and comes at a crucial time for environmental protection, since there has been a considerable loss of biodiversity on Planet Earth, a scenario that has been reproduced by the Conferences of the Parties every year, with emphasis on the need for immediate action to contain global warming.

The Resolutions under analysis also reflect the emergency of adopting measures to contain the escalation of the catastrophic society that has taken hold in the international community because of the Anthropocene era, with overdevelopment and the accumulation of wealth in the rich part of the world.[84]

The documents also reflect the need to adopt measures to contain the negative effects of the risk society, sharing the global risks generated by climate change with the entire international community.[85]

The United Nations' stance is also a response to the social movements that have been unleashed with the aim of building an international document with binding

[82] United Nations. (2021). Resolution A/HRC/48/13. The human right to a clean, healthy and sustainable environment.

[83] United Nations (2022). Resolution A/RES/76/300. The human right to a clean, healthy and sustainable environment.

[84] According to Delanty, The Anthropocene is, first and foremost, a temporal concept in geological time: the Human Age. It is the time when human beings caused a major transformation in the physical structure of the Earth. Until now—since August 2016—this has been accepted by the Anthropocene Working Group of the International Commission on Stratigraphy. It refers to a time when the human world and the physical Earth are entering a new phase. Of course, it is also a political concept in that it implies a critical position on the consequences of "what I call the "world-Earth relationship" and, as I will argue later, it is also a cultural concept in that it implies an interpretation of current times. These three dimensions - the temporal, the political and the cultural - make it potentially relevant to social science and directly related to the central concerns of classical sociological theory, as it faces new challenges arising from new insights emerging from the natural sciences. Developments in the fields of geology and biology are forcing the social sciences beyond the scientific legacy of the nineteenth century". Delanty (2018), p. 377.

[85] Beck (2010).

force for all states to protect the environment on a global scale, such as the Global Pact for the Environment.[86]

These actions also reflect the emergence of measures that must be adopted to contain the transnational effects of climate change, through the union of states in international cooperation, as a consequence of the principle of solidarity, reflecting borders between the Global North and South and highlighting the responsibility of rich countries to reverse the risks they have created for humanity with their inadequate actions in relation to the environment.[87]

The emergence of actions to tackle climate change is recorded annually by the Intergovernmental Panel on Climate Change—IPCC, which in 2023 recorded the need to adopt immediate measures.[88]

The United Nations Framework Convention on Climate Change (UNFCCC)[89] establishes an open and collaborative dialogue with institutions and organizations for the benefit of improving the International Agenda on Climate Change. It defines climate change as a change in the climate attributable directly or indirectly to human activity that alters the composition of the global atmosphere (art. 1, § 2, UNFCCC).

In this sense, the main objective of the United Nations Framework Convention on Climate Change is to achieve stabilization of the concentration of greenhouse gases in the atmosphere at a level that could prevent anthropogenic damage to the climate system (art. 2, UNFCCC).

In this sense, art. 3 of the UNFCCC establishes the common but differentiated responsibility among States, considering the capacities, specific needs and special circumstances of developing Member States for the adoption of preventive measures in the pursuit of sustainable development through cooperation.

In the context of common responsibility, a discussion has arisen about the classification of the crime of ecocide by states, i.e. a crime that causes serious damage to the environment and interferes with the achievement of human and fundamental rights of people around the world.[90] States would have the responsibility to classify the crime of ecocide in their legal systems as an international crime, to exercise universal jurisdiction in primacy.

Improving the issue in the regulatory sphere is an action/measure that can contribute to achieving the objectives of the Kyoto Protocol and the Paris Agreement to prevent, reduce and control the practice of heinous crimes against the environment. Therefore, it is proposed that a debate on ecocide as an international crime and as the fifth crime against peace.

[86] Regarding the Global Environment Pact, see https://globalpactenvironment.org/en/.

[87] The principle of solidarity concerns the preservation, conservation and protection of an asset shared by all, which exists for the benefit of the community. (Forst 2021, pp. 3–4).

[88] Ipcc. (2023). Report on Climate Change. https://www.ipcc.ch/report/ar6/syr/.

[89] United Nations (1992). United Nations Framework Convention on Climate Change. https://unfccc.int/resource/docs/convkp/conveng.pdf.

[90] Loureiro (2023), pp. 344–374.

Aware of its position in this scenario, the European Union has worked intensively to draw up the European Green Deal,[91] with various measures to deal with the externalities of climate change, but above all with measures and policies to restructure all sectors of the economy, social and cultural sectors of the European Union with the aim of promoting a just energy transition, which also includes investments for third countries.

The European Green Deal has also led to changes in the European Union's regulatory framework. For the purposes of this study, we would like to highlight the acts considered to be equivalent to ecocide and the work that has been carried out to achieve this consideration of ecocide as an international crime, an aspect that will be detailed in due course.[92]

The European Union's primary objective, as articulated in the European Green Deal (EGD), is to protect the natural environment, safeguard the planet, and support the economy by achieving climate neutrality by 2050. This initiative represents a comprehensive strategy aimed at reducing greenhouse gas emissions and fostering job creation. The EGD has translated the EU's political commitment to the 2030 Agenda into a binding legal framework, requiring the active cooperation of all EU member states.

Key measures within the EGD include the decarbonization of the energy sector, renovation of buildings, development of a leading green economy, and the promotion of cleaner transport solutions. Fig. 1 outlines the structural components of the European Green Deal.

The greening movement is evolving with the goal of preventing, reducing, and mitigating human-induced environmental damage, ultimately promoting climate justice as shown in section 1 of this study.

Climate justice can be interpreted in various ways. According to Mary Robinson, it involves placing people at the center of solutions to ensure human rights and justice for the most vulnerable individuals and nations—those who typically contribute the least to environmental degradation. Additionally, Robinson emphasizes that the ideal of climate justice includes the possibility of living in harmony with nature, guided by compassion and international cooperation.[93]

On the other hand, it is possible to say that climate justice also relates to access to justice in a strict sense, such as the multiple international courts that reflect the expansion of subjectivities and coexistence.[94]

It is also important to add the normative perspective of climate justice, with the development of the European Green Deal, as well as the consideration of ecocide as an international crime in the European Union.

---

[91] European Union (2019). European Green Deal.

[92] Regarding this issue, it should be highlighted that the European Union Directive that approved the extension of environmental crimes assimilated to ecocide can be found at https://www.europarl.europa.eu/doceo/document/TC1-COD-2021-0422_PT.pdf and at https://data.consilium.europa.eu/doc/document/ST-16069-2023-INIT/en/pdf.

[93] Robinson (2021), p. 31 e 36.

[94] Cançado Trindade (2013), pp. 39–43; 45 e 46.

From the perspective of access to justice, it is important to analyze how international courts have assimilated climate change into their judgments and advisory opinions.

The first part of this article presented the perspective of the Inter-American Court. This is followed by Section 5 which focuses on the contributions of the European Court of Human Rights to the consolidation of the greening of human rights.

5 Climate Litigation at the European Court of Human Rights: A Path to Climate Justice?

International courts play an important role in the interpretation and application of laws. The European Court of Human Rights has demonstrated its commitment to considering the environment as a human right by analyzing claims involving the negative effects of climate change.

To date, three prominent cases concerning climate justice have been brought before the European Court. Although not all have resulted in favorable rulings, they mark a significant development in the Court's role in environmental protection.

5.1 Case of Verein KlimaSeniorinnen Schweicz and Others V. Switzerland

The first case to be analyzed was brought by the Association of Elderly Ladies of Switzerland with the aim of expressing concern about the consequences of global warming on the lives and health of the elderly, given the inertia of the Swiss authorities in adopting mitigation measures, despite the country's international obligations.[95]

In this case, it is important to note that the plaintiffs claimed that Switzerland's inadequate climate policies violated their right to life and health, in accordance with Articles 2 and 8 of the European Convention on Human Rights. In addition, the plaintiffs claimed that the Swiss Federal Supreme Court's rejection of their case was arbitrary, thus violating Article 6 of the ECHR, which establishes the right to a fair trial. Finally, the plaintiffs claimed that the Swiss authorities and courts, by failing to rule on the merits of the case, violated Article 13 of the ECHR, which provides for the right to an effective remedy.

For its part, the Swiss state argued that the plaintiffs did not enjoy the status of victims and therefore could not benefit from the *locus standi* before the Court. The

[95] European Court of Human Rights (2024b). Verein KlimaSeniorinnen Schweiz and Others v. Switzerland [GC].

state also argued that the applicants had failed to prove the existence of an intrinsic link between the government's alleged omissions and the rights violated. The Swiss state also argued that the plaintiffs were claiming civil rights and not the protection of human rights.

Based on the parties' allegations and the evidence presented in the case file, the Court ruled that the plaintiffs had standing. On the merits, the Court held that the State should have adopted measures to achieve carbon neutrality and to promote the reduction of greenhouse gases, in order to give effect to Article 8 of the ECHR.

The Court also found that Switzerland had failed to comply with its obligations to reduce greenhouse gas emissions and had not acted in a timely, adequate and consistent manner so as not to violate Article 8 of the ECHR.

The case dealt with Article 8 of the European Convention on Human Rights, which governs the right to respect for private and family life. The Court held that the same legal provision applies to the right to effective protection by state authorities from the adverse effects of climate change on people's lives, health, well-being and quality of life.

The Court held that Switzerland failed in its duty of due diligence to observe the positive obligations arising from the Convention on Climate Change by not acting in a timely manner to adopt, develop and implement legislation and measures relevant to addressing the externalities of climate change.

In this case, the Court held that:

> The Swiss Confederation had therefore exceeded its discretion ("margin of appreciation") and had failed to comply with its duties in this respect. There had therefore been a violation of Article 8 of the Convention. [96]

The case has had a significant impact on the field of environmental protection, particularly by advancing climate litigation. In this regard, it illustrates a key contribution to the realization of the "greening" movement, notably through the recognition of climate change as a human rights issue. Furthermore, as previously noted, the case marks a crucial step forward in affirming states' due diligence in exercising precaution whenever the environment and the right to health are at risk.

In this context, it is important to emphasize the understanding of the European Committee of Social Rights, which asserts that individuals have a right to the highest attainable standard of health, a right that necessarily entails access to an ecologically balanced environment.[97]

Finally, the case demonstrates the intersectionality between the right to health and the right to a healthy environment as preconditions for the exercise and realization of human rights.

---

[96] European Court of Human Rights (2024b) Verein KlimaSeniorinnen Schweiz and Others v. Switzerland [GC]. The right to a private and familiar life, p. 5.

[97] European Committee of Social Rights, 2006, para. 196.

5.2 *The Carême V. France Case*

Another case that deserves to be highlighted in the context of climate litigation in the European Union is Carême v. France[98] which, despite being unanimously ruled inadmissible, demonstrates that climate litigation has become more intense as a result of the so-called greening movement, as mentioned above.

The lawsuit was filed by the former mayor of the town of Grande Synthe, who claimed that France had failed to adopt necessary and sufficient measures to prevent the harmful effects of climate change and had thus failed in its duty of due diligence to guarantee the right to family and private life, as set out in the aforementioned Article 8 of the European Convention on Human Rights.

However, the case was ruled inadmissible, since the plaintiff no longer resided in France, in the city where he had been mayor, and there was no longer any relationship with the municipality of Grande Synthe. The court therefore held that he no longer had the right to claim the violation of the aforementioned right, since he had lost his status as a victim.

Despite this, Carême said that France had failed to adopt the necessary measures to reduce greenhouse gas emissions, and had not adopted the legislative measures needed to make the climate issue a priority.

5.3 *Case of Agostinho Duarte and Others V. Portugal and Others*

The case of Agostinho Duarte and others v. Portugal and others [99] This completes the triad of leading climate justice cases before the European Court of Human Rights, in particular through the actions of young Europeans, precisely six young Portuguese men, who decided to file a lawsuit to claim rights arising from the future impacts of climate change, including changes in temperature and heat.

The plaintiffs claimed that they were exposed to a risk of harm as a result of climate change and that this harm would only increase over time, which demonstrates the intergenerational aspect of the risks that are being transferred to future generations, who will not have access to the same natural resources that exist today, due to the degradation of the environment.

The Court held that the petitioners did not have standing to bring the action against other states. In addition, the Court also held that the case against Portugal was also inadmissible because there had been no demonstration of the exhaustion of domestic remedies in that country.

---

[98] European Court of Human Rights (2024a). Case Carême v. France.

[99] European Court of Human Rights (2022). Case Duarte Agostinho and Others v. Portugal and Others.

5.4 Intersectional Analysis of the Three Cases

Firstly, it is worth highlighting the fact that citizens of a given EU member state are not allowed to bring actions against other member states, considering European citizenship and the cross-border effects of climate change.

From the Agostinho case, the Court held that young Portuguese citizens did not have the right to sue states other than their own, which at first seems incoherent considering the rights deriving from European citizenship. In this respect, Loureiro states that

> It can be said that European citizenship designates a relationship between the citizen and the Union characterized by rights, duties and participation in political life, with the aim of supplanting the democratic participation that would normally take place at national level. Article 15(3) of the TFEU gives all natural and legal persons the right of access to the documents of the institutions, bodies, offices and agencies that make up the EU. In turn, Article 2 of the TEU states that human dignity is the founding value of the European Union, together with equality, democracy, freedom, the rule of law, including minority rights (European Parliament, 2023). The legal framework for European citizenship is formed by the case law of the Court of Justice of the European Union, the Treaty of Lisbon and the Charter of Fundamental Rights of the European Union and, thus, according to Article 9 of the TEU and Article 2 of the TFEU, any person who has the nationality of a Member State is considered to be a citizen of the Union. European citizenship complements national citizenship, without claiming to replace it, and includes a set of rights and duties that derive from national citizenship (European Parliament, 2023). In this sense, it is worth noting that citizenship of the Union presupposes the legal-political link that a person has with their state, which must be a Member State of the Union, in other words, nationality is presupposed. At the same time as national and European citizenship are intrinsically linked, they are autonomous concepts, in that national citizenship confers Community rights on the citizen and makes them a citizen of the Union, with rights before it, as well as establishing a political link with European citizens to build a new form of civic and political solidarity (European Parliament, 2023). Thus, European citizenship does not depend on the existence of a people, but on the European political space, from which rights and duties emerge from the decomposition of nationality. On the other hand, European citizenship is not determined by nationality, since the denationalization of European citizenship strengthens the ties that bind citizens to their states and, at the same time, emancipates them to exercise citizenship beyond the borders of their states, with rights and duties that are set by Community law. [100]

In the *Carême* case, the Court adopted a formal position, deeming the plaintiff an illegitimate party because he no longer resided in the municipality of Grande-Synthe, where he served as Mayor at the time the lawsuit was initiated.

The Court acknowledged the transboundary and intergenerational nature of climate change's harmful effects, which persist over time. Climate change is seen as a continuous act that inflicts damage across generations, affecting the lives and health of both present and future populations.

In this instance, the plaintiff, while residing in the French city, recognized in his capacity as a public official that the French government had failed to take adequate

[100] Loureiro (2024), pp. 405–406.

measures to reduce greenhouse gas emissions. This failure, constituting a breach of due diligence, perpetuates harm to future generations.

The Court, as established in the *Augustine* case, generally adheres to territorial jurisdiction but makes exceptions for extraterritorial application when it is demonstrated that a state exercises control and authority beyond its borders. In this case, the Court held that the exception allowing extraterritoriality applied. Moreover, the UNFCCC's preamble obliges states to act with due diligence to prevent harm not only within their borders but also to other states.[101]

Thus, committing acts that cause damage to other states can characterize the jurisdiction of the European Court over that state, even when the plaintiff belongs to another state and as long as he or she is a European citizen. Furthermore, when it comes to protecting the environment, we can see the perspective of the interests of humanity, which would give rise to the use of universal jurisdiction, a topic that would require another article to delve deeper into the discussions, and therefore does not fit within the scope of this work.

Therefore, it becomes evident that the European Court of Human Rights itself uses the institute of jurisdiction in a restrictive way.

In sum, the European case-law in this paper need to be further detailed and compared, both in terms of their scientific and legal basis, as well as their contribution to climate litigation.

The case of the Elderly Swiss Ladies made an important contribution to the maturing of climate justice in the European Union, based on scientific studies proving the link between climate change and the health impacts of recent heatwaves. In addition to the IPCC reports, the European Commission's report shows that older people are being disproportionately affected by heatwaves. [102]

With regard to the legal basis of the case, the connection with the Swiss Constitution, Swiss environmental legislation and the European Convention on Human Rights stands out. In this context, it is clear from the case that there is a need to reduce greenhouse gas emissions by 50% by 2030.

In addition, the case's intrinsic link to the protection of human rights was an important argument to corroborate the intersectionality between climate change and the health of the elderly. In this case, this was the scientific evidence that made it possible to accept the Elderly Ladies as a vulnerable group, since they are particularly and disproportionally affected by climate change. For this reason, they were considered capable of bringing an action before the European Court.[103]

---

[101] European Court of Human Rights (2022). Case Duarte Agostinho and Others v. Portugal and Others.

[102] European Commission. **Temperature-related mortality burden to worsen in Europe. 2024.** Available in: https://joint-research-centre.ec.europa.eu/jrc-news-and-updates/temperature-related-mortality-burden-worsen-europe-2024-08-22_en. Last accessed in: 31st March 2025.

[103] BAHR, Cordelia C. KlimaSeniorinnen: lessons from the Swiss senior women's case for the future climate litigation. Journal of Human Rights and the Environment, vol. 9, n. 2, p. 194–221, 2018. Available in: https://www.elgaronline.com/view/journals/jhre/9/2/article-p194.xml. Last accessed in: 31st March 2025.

As for the offense against the European Convention on Human Rights, it was argued that there had been a violation of Articles 2 (right to life), 6 (1) (judicial protection) and 8 (private and family life). Furthermore, the discussion about a possible breach of the principle of separation of powers was refuted, since the core of the issue was the violation of human rights and not the powers of the Executive and Legislative Branches.

The case of the elderly women drew attention to the application of the precautionary principle, sustainable development, as well as the consideration of the Paris Agreement as mandatory and imposing legislation on states. It demonstrated that the deep relationship between the environment and human rights stands out as extremely important for the future of climate litigation, and this case is considered a paradigm for others to come.

The Carême v. France case is connected to the Elderly Ladies case, as it also rests on the claim that the authorities have failed to adopt the necessary measures to contain global warming. However, in terms of capacity to act, the Court held that the former mayor did not have legal standing, as our study has already been pointed out. It was asserted that Articles 2 and 8 of the European Convention on Human Rights had been violated.

Common aspects between the Carême case and that of the Elderly Ladies stand out, especially with regard to vulnerability, real immediate risk, the concept of victim directly affected by greenhouse gas emissions, as well as non-compliance with the Paris Agreement. In addition, in both cases, it seems that the Court has had difficulty in punctuating the rights of current and future generations. Despite not being admitted, the Carême case reinforces the need for justiciability of the right to an ecologically balanced environment.

The Augustine case seems the most controversial case, since the central aspect of the problem focused on the territorial scope of application of the European Convention on Human Rights.

As far as the legal basis is concerned, the case also revolved around Articles 2 and 8 of the ECHR, with the IPCC reports as its scientific basis, as well as the authorities' failure to adopt adequate and effective measures to reduce greenhouse gas emissions into the atmosphere.

As for the territoriality/extraterritoriality aspect, despite the fact that the case involved member states of the European Union and the transboundary aspect of the damage to the environment, the Court held that these two circumstances were not relevant to the case.

Therefore, the Court ruled that there was no responsibility of states beyond Portugal, considering the argument that damage to the environment causes damage beyond borders to be insufficient. Furthermore, the Court held that there was a need to exhaust domestic remedies.

Another relevant aspect of the Court's understanding concerns the refusal to use precedents from the Global South, from the Inter-American Court of Human Rights

(Case of Sacchi et al. v. Argentina et al.),[104] in which it was affirmed that extraterritorial jurisdiction applies to states that have caused damage through carbon emissions. Such a perspective would be extremely beneficial for broadening the debate and the scope of the European Court's decisions, especially considering the main contributions of Advisory Opinion 23/2017 of the Inter-American Court of Human Rights, which are connected to the standards advocated by the United Nations on the human right nature of the right to an ecologically balanced environment.

Despite the inadmissibility of the case, this had an impact on climate litigation, since the Court will no longer be able to neglect the issue of extraterritoriality when it comes to environmental damage caused by climate change.

This synergy would be extremely beneficial for the realization of human rights, since the reality of the Global South, often guided by its natural wealth, as well as the ideals of the Original Peoples, would provide a rich contribution for the perspective of the greening of human rights in Europe.

6 Conclusion: Synergies Between the European and Inter-American Systems

At first glance, it can be asserted that the term 'public interest' can indeed take on different meanings depending on the context. In the context of international litigation before the European Court of Human Rights (ECtHR) and the Inter-American Court of Human Rights (IACtHR), and in the light of their Advisory Opinions, the focus was to understand how these judicial bodies interpret and address climate change litigation.

It is possible to see that climate litigation in regional human rights protection systems has been evolving and, based on its peculiar characteristics, there are points of contact between the legal institutes of different systems.

The strong connection between procedural rights in human rights and environmental law, particularly regarding access to information, participation in decision-making, and the right to legal redress, has helped establish a valuable body of precedent. This synergy enhances the understanding and implementation of rights recognized in environmental law, including the provisions of the Aarhus Convention.

However, challenges can arise from this relationship. Conflicts may occur when economic, cultural, or social rights clash with norms aimed at protecting the environment, ecosystems, or species, creating complex legal scenarios.

From the analysis of the European Union, it is possible to emphasize its legal nature as a supranational organization, as well as its implications for the consolidation of the European Green Deal.

---

[104] Available in: https://harvardlawreview.org/print/vol-135/isacchi-v-argentina/#footnote-5. Last accessed in: 31st March 2025.

The European Union is an international organization of a supranational nature, meaning that there are structures that operate above the member states and are binding upon them. In this context, the sovereignty of member states is considered in a broader sense, taking into account that there is a shared communal ideal among all European citizens, thus certain common goals pertain to the collective as a whole.[105]

In this scenario, there are bodies and decisions issued within the EU that are binding on member states, due to the primacy of European Union law. European citizenship also gains prominence, since it is one of the most relevant legal institutes that contribute to the achievement of the European community ideal. [106]

In the same way, the development of actions aimed at implementing the European Green Deal is highlighted, since it comes from the perspective of complying with the United Nations 2030 Agenda, with its 17 Sustainable Development Goals, with the aim of promoting the Agenda in the regional context.

Another right that deserves to be highlighted in the European regional context is the direct access of individuals to European justice, something that does not occur in the inter-American system.[107]

Within the inter-American system, there is no Community ideal, and it does not have the legal institutes that are pertinent to the European system, such as European citizenship and direct access to the inter-American Court, so that it is necessary to use the Inter-American Commission and strategic litigation to gain access to the Inter-American Court of Human Rights.

It is in this context that the *amicus curiae* presented as a preparatory phase for the issuance of Advisory Opinions gains strength to legitimize the system and to make it more democratic and accessible to the reality of Inter-American citizens.

This was seen in the case of OC 23/2017, the hearings that took place for the issuance of the future OC that is about to be issued. Another important feature of this Advisory Opinion on transboundary environmental harm was the concept of "effective control" that no longer requires control over the territory where the victim is located or over the victim themselves. Instead, what matters is whether the state has effective control over the activities that caused the transboundary harm. However, the Inter-American Court of Human Rights (IACtHR) emphasized that extraterritorial obligations are exceptional and should be applied restrictively.

While OC 23/2017 did not specifically address climate change, some of the IACtHR's observations on state duties were applied to climate-related transboundary pollution in the OC 32/2025. Based on the Court's reasoning, it is plausible to argue that a state's contribution to the accumulation of greenhouse gases could lead to state responsibility under the American Convention on Human Rights (ACHR) for harm caused to victims in other countries. For instance, the UN Committee on the Rights of the Child later cited the Advisory Opinion in a case affirming states' extraterritorial responsibilities for carbon pollution. This highlights how Advisory

[105] Borchardt (n.d).

[106] Loureiro (2024), pp. 405–406.

[107] Council of Europe (2020). European Convention on Human Rights.

Opinion OC-23/17 was pivotal in deepening regional understanding of the interdependence between human rights and the environment and its influence on policymaking.

More specifically on the grounds of the Advisory Opinion OC-32/25 of the Inter-American Court of Human Rights, it marks an important development in the intersection between international human rights and environmental law. In response to the climate emergency, the Court articulates a holistic and legally binding interpretation of States' obligations under the Inter-American human rights system, drawing on international environmental law, customary principles, and cutting-edge scientific evidence, particularly from the Intergovernmental Panel on Climate Change (IPCC).

By recognizing three core obligations—to respect, to protect, and to cooperate—the Court frames climate change not merely as an environmental issue but as a matter of fundamental human rights. The incorporation of procedural and substantive environmental rights—including the right to a healthy environment and the newly emphasized right to a healthy climate—signals a deepening of the legal architecture supporting climate justice in the Americas.

Critically, the Court breaks new ground by affirming the *jus cogens* nature of the prohibition against massive and irreversible environmental harm and by recognizing Nature as a subject of law.[108] These steps push the legal frontier toward a more ecocentric paradigm, supporting the integration of indigenous knowledge and reinforcing intergenerational equity, revisiting the anthropocentric paradigm, as stated by Kotzé (2004). Yet, the lack of clear definitions for key terms such as 'massive' and 'irreversible' damage represents a missed opportunity to enhance the practical enforceability of this norm.

The Opinion further strengthens the accountability of non-state actors, especially corporations, by establishing detailed duties related to due diligence, emissions disclosure, and regulation aligned with the polluter pays principle. The emphasis on regulating business conduct and enabling robust monitoring mechanisms reflects an urgent call for systemic transformation toward sustainability.

Ultimately, OC-32/25 consolidates the Court's leadership in the global jurisprudence of climate and environmental justice. While challenges remain in operationalizing some of its broad concepts, the Opinion lays a comprehensive normative foundation for future litigation, legislation, and cooperative international action. It is both a doctrinal milestone and a moral imperative for states and societies confronting the climate crisis.

This whole structure reveals that the Inter-American system is still influenced, in the long run, by the interstate structure, which still leaves room for the state centric narrative. Despite the supranational structure of the European Union, the European Court's stance was not very different when it ruled the *Agostinho* case inadmissible, in view of the argument that the young Portuguese could not litigate against other

[108] The IACHR also stressed the need for states to observe the Sendai Framework to prevent environmental disasters.

states, despite the supranational nature of the organization and the dialogue between the Charter of Fundamental Rights of the European Union and the Convention on Human Rights.

Synergies can thus be seen between international courts belonging to different systems in terms of advancing environmental protection through climate litigation. Setting interpretations and directives on States' obligations before the European law, the Inter-American law or the international law, and adequate standards to a health environment are visible efforts of Inter-American and European systems. Although limited in their jurisdiction and followed by some criticism, both regional human rights systems provided substantive advancements in reaffirming the interconnection and the interdependence between human rights and environmental law in shaping domestic policies.

References

Acevedo M (2000) The intersection of human rights and environmental protection in the European court of human rights. New York Univ Environ Law J 8:437–496

Beck U (2010) Sociedade de risco. Rumo a uma outra modernidade. Trad. Sebastião Nascimento. Editora, São Paulo, p 34

Belohlavek AJ (2012) Public Policy and Public Interest in International Law and EU Law. CZECH YEARBOOK OF INTERNATIONAL LAW: Public Policy and Ordre Public III:117–147

Benzing M (2006) Community interests in the procedure of international courts and tribunals. Law Prac Int Cts Trib 5:369–408

Borchardt K-D (n.d.) O ABC da União Europeia. Publicações da União Europeia. Available at: https://edisciplinas.usp.br/pluginfile.php/5505853/mod_resource/content/1/o%20abc%20do%20direito%20na%20união%20europeia.pdf

Cançado Trindade AA (2013) Os tribunais internacionais contemporâneos. Brasília, FUNAG

Carrillo CAC (2023) The role of advisory opinions in addressing public interest issues. In: Public interest litigation in international law. Routledge

Council of Europe (2020) A Convenção Europeia dos Direitos do Homem. Um instrumento vivo. 2020. Available at: https://edoc.coe.int/en/european-convention-on-human-rights/9419-a-convencao-europeia-dos-direitos-do-homem-um-instrumento-vivo.html

Crawford J (2006) Multilateral rights and obligations in international law. Brill, The Hague

Cummings S, Rhode D (2009) Public interest litigation: insights from theory and practice. Fordham Urban Law J 36:603

Delanty G (2018) Os desafios da globalização e a imaginação cosmopolita: as implicações do Antropoceno. Revista Sociedade e Estado 3:373–388. Available at: https://www.scielo.br/pdf/se/v33n2/0102-6992-se-33-02-00373.pdf. Acesso em: 22 de fev. 2021

Delbruck J (1998) 'Laws in the public interest' - some observations on the foundations and identification of Erga Omnes norms in international law. In: Jaenicke G, Götz V, Selmer P, Wolfrum R (eds) Liber amicorum Günther Jaenicke--zum 85. Geburtstag. Springer, Berlin, New York

Esnault M (2023) On the pertinence of "public interest" for international litigation. In: Public interest litigation in international law. Routledge

European Committee of Social Rights, Marangapoulos Foundation for Human Rights (MFHR) v. Greece, decision on the merits, Complaint n. 30/2005, 6 december 2006, para. 196

European Court of Human Rights (2022) Case Duarte Agostinho e outros v. Portugal and others. Disponível em https://hudoc.echr.coe.int/eng#_Toc162284518. Acesso em: 11 set. 2024

European Court of Human Rights (2024a) Case Carême v. France. Available at:: https://hudoc.echr.coe.int/eng#{%22itemid%22:[%22001-233174%22]}
European Court of Human Rights (2024b) Verein KlimaSeniorinnen Schweiz and Others v. Switzerland [GC]. Available at: https://hudoc.echr.coe.int/eng/#{%22itemid%22:[%22002-14304%22]}
European Union (2019) European Green Deal. Available at: https://www.consilium.europa.eu/pt/policies/green-deal/; https://commission.europa.eu/strategy-and-policy/priorities-2019-2024/european-green-deal_pt; https://eur-lex.europa.eu/legal-content/PT/TXT/HTML/?uri=CELEX:52019DC0640&from=FR
European Union (2023). Diretiva da União Europeia sobre o alargamento dos crimes ambientais equiparados ao ecocídio. Available at: https://www.europarl.europa.eu/doceo/document/TC1-COD-2021-0422_PT.pdf; https://data.consilium.europa.eu/doc/document/ST-16069-2023-INIT/en/pdf
Feria-Tinta M, Milnes SC (2016) The rise of environmental law in international dispute resolution: the inter-American court of human rights issues a landmark advisory opinion on the environment and human rights. Yearb Int Environ Law 27:64–81. https://doi.org/10.1093/yiel/yvy004
Forst R Solidarity: concept, conceptions, and contexts. Normative orders working paper. 02/2021. Researche Centre of Goethe University Frankfurt am Main
Gruner DM (2003) Accounting for the public interest in international arbitration: the need for procedural and structural reform. Columbia J Transnatl Law 41:923–964
Hilson C (2010) Climate change litigation in the UK: an explanatory approach (or bringing grievance Back in). In: Fracchia F, Occhiena M (eds) Climate change: LA Riposta del Diritto. Editoriale Scientifica, Naples
Intergovernmental Pannel on Climate Change (2023) Report on Climate Change. Available at: https://www.ipcc.ch/report/ar6/syr/
Jeßberger F, Steinl L (2022) Strategic litigation in international criminal justice: facilitating a view from within. J Int Crim Just 20:379–401. https://doi.org/10.1093/jicj/mqac008
Kotzé LJ (2014) Human rights and the environment in the Anthropocene. Anthrop Rev 1(3):252–275. https://doi.org/10.1177/2053019614547741
Loureiro C (2022) Greening: o esverdeamento dos direitos humanos e o protagonismo da Corte Interamericana de Direitos Humanos. Relações Internacionais no mundo atual 5:216–236. Available at: http://revista.unicuritiba.edu.br/index.php/RIMA/article/view/6209
Loureiro C (2023) Ecocídio perante o Estatuto de Roma. Revista de Direito Internacional 20:344–374. Available at: https://www.publicacoes.uniceub.br/rdi/article/view/9184
Loureiro C (2024) Cidadania global: uma perspectiva a partir da cidadania europeia. Revista Jurídica da Presidência 26:396–422. https://doi.org/10.20499/2236-3645.RJP2024v26e139-3048
McHarg A (1999) Reconciling human rights and the public interest: conceptual problems and doctrinal uncertainty in the jurisprudence of the European court of human rights. Mod Law Rev 62:671–696
Mingde C, Fengyuan W (2011) Environmental public interest litigation in China. Asia Pac Law Rev 19:217–235. https://doi.org/10.1080/10192557.2011.11788249
Morgera E (2012) Bilateralism at the Service of Community Interests? Non-judicial enforcement of global public goods in the context of global environmental law. Euro J Int Law 23:743–767. https://doi.org/10.1093/ejil/chs037
Peel J, Osofsky HM (2020) Climate change litigation. Ann Rev Law Soc Sci 16:21–38. https://doi.org/10.1146/annurev-lawsocsci-022420-122936
Redgwell C (1998) Life, the universe and everything: a critique of anthropocentric rights. In: Boyle AE, Anderson MR (eds) Human rights approaches to environmental protection. Oxford University Press
Robinson M (2021) Justiça climática. Esperança, resiliência e a luta por um futuro sustentável. Trad. Leo Gonçalves e Clóvis Marques. 1ª ed. Rio de Janeiro: Civilização Brasileira
Stephens T (2009) International courts and environmental protection. Cambridge University Press, Cambridge

Suedi Y, Bendel J (2024) Public interest litigation - a pipe dream or the future of international litigation? In: Suedi Y, Bendel J (eds) Public interest litigation in international law. Routledge, New York, pp 34–62

Taillant JD, Picolotti R (2003) 1 the environmental jurisprudence of international human rights tribunals. In: Linking human rights and the environment. University of Arizona Press, pp 1–30

United Nations (1987) Report of the World Commission on Environment and Development (Our Common Future)

United Nations (1992) United Nations Framework Convention on Climate Change. Available at: https://unfccc.int/files/essential_background/background_publications_htmlpdf/application/pdf/conveng.pdf

United Nations (2015) Agenda 2030. Available at: https://brasil.un.org/pt-br/sdgs

United Nations (2021) Resolution A/HRC/48/13. The human right to a clean, healthy and sustainable environment. Available at: https://documents.un.org/doc/undoc/gen/g21/289/50/pdf/g2128950.pdf

United Nations (2022) Resolution A/RES/76/300. The human right to a clean, healthy and sustainable environment. Available at: https://documents.un.org/doc/undoc/gen/n22/442/77/pdf/n2244277.pdf

Alex Silva Oliveira Researcher at the Centre de Recherche sur la Régulation et le Droit de la Gouvernance - CrRDG, University of Sherbrooke, Canada. PhD in public International law at the University of Montreal. MSc and bachelors in law at the University of São Paulo".

Claudia Loureiro Coordinator of the Jean Monnet Chair at the Federal University of Uberlândia with the GLOBAL CROSSINGS Project. Post-Doctorate in Law at Nova School of Law - Lisbon (2021), in Human Rights from the Faculty of Law of the University of Coimbra (2016) and International and Comparative Law completed by the Faculty of Law of the University of São Paulo (2019). PhD (2015) and Master (2006) in Comparative Civil Law from the Pontifical Catholic University of São Paulo. Professor of Environmental Law and Biolaw at the Faculty of Law of the Federal University of Uberlândia. Permanent Professor of the Postgraduate Program in Law at the Federal University of Uberlândia. Permanent Professor of the Postgraduate Program in International Relations at the Federal University of ABC. She is leader of the Biolaw and Human Rights Research Group-UFU and the Inter-American and European Observatory of Sustainable Development Goals-UFU, both certified by CNPq.

Climate Litigation in Oceania: Understanding Differences and Similarities Across the Continent

Valéria Emília de Aquino and Marlon Antônio Rosa

1 Introduction

We are currently experiencing one of the most serious environmental and climate crises in the history of humanity. Although planet Earth goes through cycles of cooling and warming, human action has never affected this process as much as it does now. According to the IPCC report,[1] a 1.5 °C increase in global temperature will lead to ecosystems reaching their peak, putting human life and other species at risk. Furthermore, according to the Panel, climate change has led to humanitarian crises, in which the impacts of these changes, combined with the vulnerability of certain populations, have caused displacement in all regions of the world, especially in small island countries.

Consequently, due to climatic inclement weather and slow processes of climate change, humanity is also experiencing a complex crisis in human mobility across the globe, especially with regard to climate migration or climate displacement, which has imposed unprecedented challenges on States and International Organizations, especially given the regulatory gap regarding the international protection of these individuals.

The exhaustion of the current protection model requires a paradigm shift towards more humane, fair and dignified decisions that not only place human beings at the

[1] IPCC. Summary for policymakers (2022). Available at: https://www.ipcc.ch/report/ar6/wg2/downloads/report/IPCC_AR6_WGII_SummaryForPolicymakers.pdf. Accessed on: 30 Aug. 2024.

V. E. de Aquino (✉)
Federal University of Goiás, Goiânia, Goiás, Brazil

M. A. Rosa
Araxá Municipal Pension Institute, Federal University of Uberlândia, Uberlândia, Brazil

V. E. de Aquino et al. (eds.), *Climate Litigation in a Changing World*, Ius Gentium: Comparative Perspectives on Law and Justice 130,
https://doi.org/10.1007/978-3-032-05530-9_6

center of protection, but also include the environment, due to its intrinsic value to humanity. In other words, it is urgent that humanity return to ensuring an ecocentric paradigm, since there is no dignified human life without the existence of a healthy, safe and sustainable environment.

Given the interdependence of human rights, the right to an ecologically balanced environment is a premise for the full guarantee and enjoyment of other human rights. When States are unable to guarantee the minimum existence for their individuals, the right to sue them in court arises. Cases of violations of the right to a healthy environment are even more emblematic, because they result in a cascade effect of human rights violations. Furthermore, since environmental damage can be transboundary and future, these cases are mostly complex and are still commonly rejected in the name of legal uncertainty and insecurity.

The current triple planetary crisis also reflects a global crisis of inequality, and although it affects all countries, it is important to highlight that those that have contributed least to this result are, for the most part, those that suffer most from the effects of these changes. There is a clear asymmetry between the global North and South in terms of resilience, coping, mitigation and adaptation to the effects of climate change. At the international level, the requirement for environmental commitments and accountability by States has gained greater relevance after the 2015 Paris Agreement, which aims to reduce greenhouse gas emissions and reduce global temperature rise to 1.5 degrees. In fact, the Paris Agreement is one of the main documents used to force States to fulfill their environmental commitments.[2]

Thus, this article will address the case of the Pacific countries, firstly: (I) addressing data on these States and their human rights protection systems; (II) discussing cases related to climate change before the UN system of international protection of human rights, considering the lack of a regional system of protection of human rights; and, finally, (III) exploring emblematic cases from Australia and New Zealand, involving climate litigation in the countries of the region.

The method used in this research is descriptive and analytical, which is based on a bibliographic review combined with a documentary analysis and, above all, case law, when addressing climate disputes in the Pacific. In addition, it also includes a survey of data on the Pacific countries that are signatories to human rights treaties within the scope of the United Nations, specifically the International Covenant on Civil and Political Rights (ICCPR) and the International Covenant on Economic Social and Cultural Rights (ICESCR), which are the two main treaties that can be interpreted to enhance the protection of the right to a healthy, safe and sustainable environment.

Finally, the work aims to serve as an instrument for strengthening climate research, as well as a political instrument, with the goal of giving greater visibility to the cause and to the individuals and States most affected by climate change. If refuge places human beings in a situation of vulnerability, climate refuge, which has

[2] MMA – MINISTÉRIO DO MEIO AMBIENTE. Acordo de Paris. 2019. Disponível em: https://www.mma.gov.br/clima/convencaodas-nacoes-unidas/acordo-de-paris. Acesso em: 24 set. 2024.

no legal provision, places individuals in a situation of hyper vulnerability, since they find themselves in a true normative limbo. Unfortunately, this is a reality that many people in the region live in, and recognizing the existence of these people and the precarious conditions in which they live is a first step towards expanding their legal protection.

2 How Has Climate Change Been Affecting Pacific Countries?

The Oceania is one of the most critical regions in terms of the effects of climate change, since most of the countries that comprise it are island countries, and are particularly prone to hurricanes, storms, floods and rising sea levels. The region is made up of the following countries: Australia, Cook Islands, Fiji, Kiribati, Marshall Islands, Micronesia, Nauru, New Zealand, Niue, Palau, Papua New Guinea, Samoa, Solomon Islands, Tonga, Tuvalu and Vanuatu.

Over the years, the sea temperatures in the continent have been rising, and in 2018, it increased 1.2 °C above average, which can result in rising sea levels and potentially risk the existence of many low-lying islands, such as Tuvalu, Kiribati, Marshall Islands, Solomon Islands, Cook Islands, Tonga and Vanuatu. These countries are in the imminence of sinking due to sea level rise, and they are currently facing many climate-environmental problems, such as: erosions, loss of infrastructure and coastal land, disappearance of freshwater sources, coral bleaching and ocean acidification, land scarcity, among others.[3]

In addition to the aforementioned environmental problems, the countries in the region have also suffered from socioeconomic and health problems, since the lack of arable land and the reduction in fishing have led to a decrease in income, especially for the islanders who rely on the ocean as a source of income. Furthermore, health is also directly affected by salinity, the lack of fresh food (since many depend on food exports), water contamination,[4] as well as the stress and anxiety that rising sea levels and the lack of resources have caused in the lives of these people,[5] faced with potentially unsurvivable habitats. In Fiji, for instance, sugar cane crops are declining due to the rising salinity in the country:

> The Pacific region is already suffering from the effects of climate change. With its low-elevation island nations, it has long been considered particularly vulnerable. All states of the region are expected to be affected to some extent, but the small atoll islands of Kiribati, the Marshall Islands, Tokelau and Tuvalu are considered at the frontline, with their population threatened by impacts ranging from resource degradation and weather extremes to irreversible sea level rise. Commonly underrepresented in research, but central for local and

[3] IYOPS. *Climate change effects in Oceania – World Series Part 4*. Available at: https://www.iyops.org/post/climate-change-effects-in-oceania. Accessed on: 25 Sep. 2024.

[4] *Ibid.*

[5] Dodds (2021), pp. 222–226.

> regional efforts to address climate change impacts is the social meaning of land for processes of identity and place-making as well as notions of belonging in the region. The identity of Pacific Islanders is built around the land of their ancestors and related ideas of home, so that the loss of land potentially causes deep alienation.[6]

All of these factors have led many people to migrate from their countries to other, closer countries, such as Australia and New Zealand, which are typically the countries that receive the most climate migrants in the region. Although internal migration is more common in the case of climate migration, international migration is more common in Oceania, since the countries mentioned are small, so there is nowhere to flee to escape climate change.

In 2023, IDMC recorded 46.9 million internally displaced persons (IDP) people worldwide, of which 26.4 million were displaced by disasters. In Oceania and East Asia alone, approximately 9,309,000 internally displaced people were recorded by disasters and 1,462,000 by conflicts, which corresponds to 22.4% of the total displaced people in the world.[7] However, these figures do not account for international climate migrants, also called climate refugees, which are a category of environmental refugees.[8]

According to Mahlke, the ever-increasing need to welcome an ever-increasing number of refugees globally encounters a real obstacle in the current global political architecture of refuge, which has not been able to offer concrete solutions to the current complex demands, whether due to the difficulty of agencies acting, mobilizing resources and cooperation between countries, or even due to the obstacles imposed by States themselves, which prevent the recognition of new flows as a transnational issue or even the expansion of the concept of refuge.[9] Migration surely is not a new phenomena in Oceania, but climate change is reshaping the current migration flows in the region:

> One exception might be the case of Kiribati. Its government bought over 2000 ha of land in Vanua Levu Island, Fiji, so that it could sustain agricultural as well as fisheries development for its people, and maybe also to use the land for resettlement (Campbell and Bedford 2012; Hermann and Kempf 2017). Examples for in-country resettlement can be found in Fiji, the Solomon Islands, Vanuatu and Papua New Guinea. In Fiji, for example, the village of Vunidogoloa has been relocated recently. Other communities have been actively trying to relocate, like the Carteret Islands inhabitants in the Autonomous Region of Bougainville in Papua New Guinea (McNamara and Des Combes 2015). Nothing is as evolved (at least in theory) as Kiribati's "migrate with dignity"-strategy though.[10]

---

[6] FRÖHLICH, Christiane; KLEPP, Silja. Climate Change and Migration Crises in Oceania. *Toda Peace Institute*, Policy Brief No. 29, November 2018. Available at: https://png-data.sprep.org/system/files/Climate_Change_and_Migration_Crises_in_Oceania.pdf. Accessed on: 30 Sep. 2024.

[7] IDMC. *Global Report on Internal Displacement (2024)*. Available at: https://api.internal-displacement.org/sites/default/files/publications/documents/IDMC-GRID-2024-Global-Report-on-Internal-Displacement.pdf. Accessed on: 27 Sep. 2024.

[8] El-Hinnawi (1985)..

[9] Mahlke (2017), p. 29.

[10] FRÖHLICH, Christiane; KLEPP, Silja. Climate Change and Migration Crises in Oceania. *Toda Peace Institute*, Policy Brief No. 29, November 2018. Available at: https://png-data.sprep.org/sys-

Although the term 'climate refugee' is controversial, these migrants exist and should not be made invisible by mere political choice. Even though there is no international treaty that grants protection to this group, and no treaty that recognizes the right to a healthy, safe and sustainable environment,[11] these individuals can avail themselves of the current system of protection provided by the United Nations. That is, it is possible to avail themselves of the protection provided by the nine core human rights treaties,[12] especially the International Covenant on Civil and Political Rights (ICCPR) and the International Covenant on Economic, Social and Cultural Rights (ICESCR).

The ICCPR, in its Article 6, proclaims the right to life, while Article 9 establishes the right to liberty and security of person. However, it is Article 12 that addresses one of the most important rights for migrants: the right to freedom of movement and freedom to choose his residence, which includes the right to leave any country, including its own. The ICESCR, in its Article 3, states that the States Parties must ensure equal right of women and men to the enjoyment of all economic, social and cultural rights. This article allows for a broader interpretation of the rights guaranteed in the treaty, since, as human rights are interdependent, it is not possible to fully access and enjoy these rights and, especially, to guarantee an adequate standard of living (Article 11) and the highest attainable standard of physical and mental health (Article 12), without the protection of the right to a healthy, safe and sustainable environment.

Table 1 provides a survey of the countries in Oceania that have ratified the nie core human rights treaties, so that it is possible to understand the developments in climate litigation cases in the region. Furthermore, knowing which countries have ratified the ICCPR and ICESCR makes it easier to understand the aforementioned migration flows:

The only treaty that has full adherence is the CRC, followed by the CRPD, which has a high adherence rate in the region. Although the ICCPR and the ICESCR are the two most important human rights treaties, we can observe that several countries

---

tem/files/Climate_Change_and_Migration_Crises_in_Oceania.pdf. Accessed on: 30 Sep. 2024.

[11] The Convention relating to the Status of Refugees (1951) and its Protocol (1967) do not mention 'climate change' or "environment" as motivations to justify the status of refugees. However, the Resolution 48/13 of the Human Rights Council, recognized the right to a clean, healthy and sustainable environment as a human right. United Nations. **A/HRC/RES/48/13**: The human right to a clean, healthy and sustainable environment. 2021. Human Rights Council - 48th Session. Available at: https://documents-dds-ny.un.org/doc/UNDOC/GEN/G21/289/50/PDF/G2128950.pdf?OpenElement. Accessed on: 17 Sep. 2024.

[12] The nine core human rights treaties are: (1) the Convention on the Elimination of All Forms of Racial Discrimination (ICERD); (2) the International Covenant on Economic, Social and Cultural Rights; (3) the International Covenant on Civil and Political Rights; (4) the Convention on the Elimination of All Forms of Discrimination against Women (CEDAW); (5) the Convention against Torture and Other Cruel, Inhuman or Degrading Treatment or Punishment (CAT); (6) the Convention on the Rights of the Child (CRC); (7) the International Convention on the Protection of the Rights of All Migrant Workers and Members of Their Families (ICMW); (8) the Convention on the Rights of Persons with Disabilities; and, (9) the Convention for the Protection of All Persons from Enforced Disappearance (CPED).

Table 1 UN Human Rights Treaties in Oceania

	ICCPR	ICESCR	ICERD	CEDAW	CAT	CRC	ICMW	CPED	CRPD
Australia	X	X	X	X	X	X	–	–	X
Cook Islands	–	–	–	X	–	X	–	–	X
Fiji	X	X	X	X	X	X	X	X	X
Kiribati	–	–	–	X	X	X	–	–	X
Marshall Islands	X	–	X	X	X	X	–	–	X
Micronesia	–	–	–	X	–	X	–	–	X
Nauru	Signed	–	Signed	X	X	X	–	–	X
New Zealand	X	X	X	X	X	X	–	–	X
Niue	–	–	–	–	–	X	–	–	–
Palau	Signed	Signed	Signed	Signed	Signed	X	Signed	Signed	X
Papua New Guinea	X	X	X	X	–	X	–	–	X
Samoa	X	–	–	X	X	X	–	X	X
Solomon Islands	–	X	X	X	–	X	–	–	Signed
Tonga	–	–	X	–	–	X	–	–	Signed
Tuvalu	–	–	–	X	–	X	–	–	X
Vanuatu	X	–	–	X	X	X	–	Signed	X

Source: OHCHR Interactive Dashboard (2024) Available at: https://indicators.ohchr.org/. Accessed 30 Sept 2024.

have not signed and/or ratified them. One possible hypothesis is that, as these small island states are familiar with their own realities and their peculiar geographies, the ratification of three instruments could bring real difficulties for these countries in guaranteeing the aforementioned rights, especially in the context of climate change.

It is important to highlight that the mobilization of international human rights treaties has been reshaping climate litigation in Oceania, albeit in contrasting ways between Australia and New Zealand - whose disputes are mainly developed in federal courts, under common law system - and small island states in the Pacific, which resort to international bodies to protect their own survival.

Climate litigation in the Pacific develops along two axes: Island countries such as Kiribati, Tuvalu and Palau seek existential claims centered on loss of territory and displacement, while Australia and, to a lesser extent, New Zealand face lawsuits that target gaps in domestic mitigation. Thus, the difference between these two points arises from two factors: I—unequal exposure to sea level rise and II—disparate institutional capacity.

As stated in the report 'Providing legal options to protect the human rights of persons displaced across international borders due to climate change' by the former Special Rapporteur on the promotion and protection of human rights in the context of climate change, Ian Fry, climate displaced persons "face the risk of being subjected to a number of human rights violations", which lead the Office of the United Nations High Commissioner for Refugees (UNHCR) understand, in special circumstances (e.g.: intersection between climate change, disasters and conflicts), that the Convention may be applicable.[13] That said, the next topic will analyze cases in the UN system, since both cases deal with human rights violations due to climate change, with the first specifically dealing with climate migration.

3 Cases Before the United Nations' Treaty Bodies

Firstly, it is important to emphasize that although the decisions of UN treaty bodies are not binding, since they are not judicial bodies, they are extremely important for giving visibility to human rights violations that occur around the world and because they also issue recommendations to countries that have violated such rights. In other words, it is a powerful mechanism of 'naming and shaming', since these decisions can exert political pressure on States, with the aim of preventing further actions.

The opinions of treaty bodies can also be used to give voice to and amplify the demands of the most marginalized individuals, and they also serve to form an international custom, which may later even be recognized by international courts and tribunals. It is worth noting that, although Article 38 of the Statute of the International Court of Justice points out as sources of International Law international treaties, customs, general principles of law, case law of international courts and doctrine, resolutions and opinions issued within the scope of the UN system can be considered as sources by analogy, since: (I) they take into account the opinion of acclaimed jurists and experts; (II) they help to solidify international custom.

In this sense, this topic intends to address two cases before the Human Rights Committee (HRC) concerning countries in the Pacific. Furthermore, although the International Court of Justice (ICJ) is a judicial body linked to the UN—and, therefore, not to the treaty bodies -, this topic will also analyze the request for an Advisory Opinion formulated by the Vanuatu Initiative. Thus, by understanding how the largest international organization has been dealing with climate disputes, it is possible to draw up an analysis of how the environment and the climate have been conceived in the international context.

3.1 Case Ioane Teitiota v. New Zealand Before the HRC

This case was the first case on climate displacement brought before the UN, and can be considered a milestone in the application of the principle of non-refoulement with regard to climate displacement. Although it was unsuccessful and the term

[13] FRY, Ian. *A/HRC/53/34: Providing legal options to protect the human rights of persons displaced across international borders due to climate change* (2023). Available at: https://documents.un.org/doc/undoc/gen/g23/073/25/pdf/g2307325.pdf. Accessed on: 30 Sep. 2024.

'climate refugee' was not used, the recognition of the interdependence of the right to the environment with other human rights is certainly a victory for the discipline.

The case concerns an asylum claim by Mr. Ioane Teitiota and his family, born in Kiribati, who migrated to New Zealand in search of better living conditions. He claimed to the immigration authorities that climate change has made Kiribati uninhabitable due to rising sea levels, which are affecting the water and food supply, as well as creating a shortage of arable and habitable land. Therefore, his and his family's right to life would have been affected, leaving him with no other option but to migrate to New Zealand.[14]

New Zealand rejected the asylum claim because it did not recognize climate change as a justification. As a result, Mr. Teitiota and his family were deported to Kiribati. However, he submitted a request, in 2015, to the UN Human Rights Committee for consideration of his case, arguing that the decision handed down by New Zealand and the referral represented a violation of his right to life. Although the UN Human Rights Committee ruled that Mr. Teitiota could not prove that his right to life was violated, the case represents a historic advance in terms of recognizing climate migration, as it emphasizes that States must respect the principle of non-refoulement, which is a *jus cogens* norm, which should have been applied in the case in question, since his family's life in Kiribati had become unbearable.[15]

It worth noting that the decision at the HRC was not unanimous: two members dissented, one defended that the HRC "placed an unreasonable burden of proof on Teitiota to establish a real risk of danger of arbitrary deprivation of life, while the other attacked the HRC's point on the lack of evidence that they were lacking potable water, stressing that potable does not mean safe drinking water, that they did not have.[16] Even though the principle of non-refoulement is related to refuge, the Committee understood that it would also be applicable to deportation cases, as such.

Therefore, by redefining the interpretation of the principle of non-refoulement, the HRC also ended up expanding the scope of the 1951 Convention, which, although it does not recognize climate change as a justification for asylum claims, allows this principle to be applied in cases of climate displacement.

[14] United Nations. Human Rights Committee Views adopted by the Committee under article 5 (4) of the Optional Protocol, concerning communication No. 2728/2016* , **, ***: CCPR/C/127/D/2728/2016. 2020. International Covenant on Civil and Political Rights. Available at: https://docstore.ohchr.org/SelfServices/FilesHandler.ashx?enc=6QkG1d%2fPPRiCAqhKb7yhsjvfIjqiI84ZFd1DNP1S9EKG9gxBGj9kie9DBbO0eH5N3hhnsj%2fmXyyUMRGqAMBUPEmGiVv1l5ueyf40YfsDu0dp9yZLW4jePTIgY0yjbRLVIKjUOSrHvJMn0qYD5THTtw%3d%3d. Accessed on: 17 Sep. 2024.

[15] Loureiro and Romero (2024).

[16] Climate Case Chart. *UN Human Rights Committee Views Adopted on Teitiota Communication* (2015). Available at: https://climatecasechart.com/non-us-case/un-human-rights-committee-views-adopted-on-teitiota-communication/. Accessed on: 27 Sep. 2024.

3.2 *Case Daniel Billy et al. v. Australia (Torres Strait Islanders' petitioning) Before the HRC*

The Torres Strait Islander case was filed in 2019 by eight Australian citizens and members of Aboriginal peoples, with the support of the environmental NGO Client Earth, and is based on the allegation of violation of the rights to life (Article 6), to private and family life (Article 17), the rights of future generations of the plaintiffs' community (Article 24) and to culture (Article 27) of the ICCPR, by Australia, of the inhabitants of the Torres Strait as a consequence of its clearly insufficient climate policies.[17]

Along with the petition, the authors included scientific reports that demonstrate that residents of the Torres Strait Islands are among the most vulnerable to the impacts of climate change, mainly due to rising sea levels, flooding, erosion and high temperatures. Another alleged point was the acidification of the ocean, the death of reefs and marine animals, impacts generated by high emissions of carbon dioxide into seawater.

Among the impacts generated by such effects, the petitioners report the impact on their physical, economic and mental well-being, including reduced rates of physical movement related to intense heat, forced migration as a consequence of rising sea levels, damage to infrastructure and loss of stocks and crops due to forest fires, inadequate housing and energy poverty. Another point raised is the concern about the disappearance of their culture in the long term and that the relocation of the population could make it difficult to transition their culture to future generations.[18]

The United Nations Human Rights Committee, in September 2022, issued a landmark ruling in the case, concluding that the Australian government is in breach of its obligations to protect the human rights of indigenous peoples of the Torres Strait Islands, given its failure to act in relation to climate change. With this understanding, the committee understood that, by its inaction, Australia violates the rights of these peoples to enjoy their culture and to be protected against arbitrary interference in their private, family and cultural lives. Another point addressed by the Committee is that Australia was among the largest producers of greenhouse gases in recent decades and that it has a high international economic and human development status.[19]

The Committee, referring to its decision in the Teitiota v. New Zealand case, recalled its case law based on Article 1 of the Optional Protocol, which states that a

---

[17] Face the Facts: Aboriginal and Torres Strait Islanders Peoples: Available at: https://humanrights.gov.au/our-work/education/face-facts-aboriginal-and-torres-strait-islander-peoples. Accessed on: 23 Sep. 2024.

[18] TSRA, 'Torres Strait Climate Change Strategy 2014–2018: Building Community Adaptive Capacity and Resilience' (June 2016) Available at: https://www.tsra.gov.au/__data/assets/pdf_file/0015/12372/TS-Regional-Adaptation-and-Resillience-Plan-Final.pdf Accessed on: 20 Sep. 2024.

[19] Sabin Center for Climate Changelaw. (2024). Available at: https://climatecasechart.com. Accessed on: 20 Sep. 2024.

person can only claim to be a victim if he or she can actually prove that he or she is affected by a serious individual risk. In this regard, the Committee acknowledged that the applicants had proven this requirement by showing that they already suffer from erosion, flooding and declines in marine species.[20] The Committee recalled that, according to General Comment No. 36, the positive obligation of States to respect and ensure the right to life "extends to reasonably foreseeable threats and life-threatening situations that may result in loss of life".[21]

This case is emblematic because it is the first time that a United Nations body has found that a State has violated international human rights law due to the absence of an adequate climate policy. It is also the first decision to recognize the impact of climate change on the right to culture of indigenous peoples. The decision also called on Australia to adopt significant climate adaptation measures. It is understood that the decision reaffirms the specific rights of indigenous peoples around the world to be protected from climate change and the obligation of States to pursue adequate climate policies.

3.3 Advisory Opinion Request by the Vanuatu Initiative Before the ICJ

According to the UN's 2021 World Risk Index (WRI), the Republic of Vanuatu, an island archipelago in the South Pacific, is considered the country with the highest risk of disasters in the world, and in the absence of swift action, will become uninhabitable by mid-century, threatening its culture, state and sovereignty. Vanuatu is a leading state in the movement for climate justice,[22] as states have duties under various international laws and treaties to reduce climate damage.

In coalition with 132 other nations, the country realized that the ICJ is the only main body of the UN system that has not yet been called upon in relation to climate crisis issues, which is why it requested an advisory opinion from the court. Thus, adopted by consensus climate resolution 77/276[23] on March 29, 2023 at the 77th session of the UN General Assembly and based on art. 96 of the United Nations

[20] Sabin Center for Climate Changelaw (2024). Available at: https://climatecasechart.com. Accessed on: 20 Sep. 2024.

[21] TSRA, 'Torres Strait Climate Change Strategy 2014–2018: Building Community Adaptive Capacity and Resilience' (June 2016) Available at: https://www.tsra.gov.au/__data/assets/pdf_file/0015/12372/TS-Regional-Adaptation-and-Resillience-Plan-Final.pdf Accessed on: 20 Sep. 2024.

[22] WRR (2021). Available at: https://www.preventionweb.net/publication/world-risk-report-2021-focus-social-protection#:~:text=The%20countries%20with%20the%20highest,exposure%20to%20extreme%20natural%20events. Accessed on: 25 Oct. 2024.

[23] RESOLUTION 77/276. ICJ Resolution, Available at: https://www-vanuatuicj-com.translate.goog/resolution?_x_tr_sl=en&_x_tr_tl=pt&_x_tr_hl=pt-BR&_x_tr_pto=sc. Accessed on: 25 Oct. 2024.

Charter, the ICJ was requested to provide an advisory opinion on the following issues:

> Having particular regard to the Charter of the United Nations, the International Covenant on Civil and Political Rights, the International Covenant on Economic, Social and Cultural Rights, the United Nations Framework Convention on Climate Change, the Paris Agreement, the United Nations Convention on the Law of the Sea, the duty of due diligence, the rights recognized in the Universal Declaration of Human Rights, the principle of prevention of significant harm to the environment and the duty to protect and preserve the marine environment,
>
> (a) What are the obligations of States under international law to ensure the protection of the climate system and other parts of the environment from anthropogenic emissions of greenhouse gases for States and for present and future generations?
> (b) What are the legal consequences under these obligations for States where they, by their acts and omissions, have caused significant harm to the climate system and other parts of the environment, with respect to: (i) States, including, in particular, small island developing States, which due to their geographical circumstances and level of development, are injured or specially affected by or are particularly vulnerable to the adverse effects of climate change? (ii) Peoples and individuals of the present and future generations affected by the adverse effects of climate change?[24]

The strategy is important since the advisory opinion issued by the ICJ has great legal weight and moral authority, and is an important instrument of preventive diplomacy, which helps in the elucidation and development of international law, in the search for peaceful solutions between States.[25] The Court has unanimously recognized that humanity is facing an "urgent and existential threat", and concluded that the harm due to human-caused climate change may entitle victims to reparations, since there is a causal link between the wrongful act attributable to the state and the harms suffered by the victims, which must be analyzed on "case-by-case" basis. Moreover, the ICJ stated that States have "binding obligations to ensure protection of the climate system", and in case of breaching this responsibility, then it arises the duty to repair for loss and damage.

Although this was the first time that the Court gave its opinion on climate change, it is important to highlight that it has already ruled in some cases on principles of International Environmental Law and on the obligations of States to protect the environment: Gabčíkovo-Nagymaros Case (Hungary v. Czechoslovakia, 1992), Nuclear Test Case I and II (Australia and New Zealand v. France, 1973, 1995), Uruguay River Paper Mills Case (Argentina v. Uruguay, 2006–2010), Whale Case (Australia v. Japan, 2010), San Juan River Case (Costa Rica v. Nicaragua, 2010).[26]

---

[24] ICJ. Obligations of States in respect of Climate Change. Available at: https://www.icj-cij.org/case/187 Accessed on: 25 Oct. 2024.

[25] The Republic of Vanuatu is leading the initiative at the UN International Court of Justice for an Advisory Opinion on the Obligations of States relevant to climate action. Available at: https://www-vanuatuicj-com.translate.goog/?_x_tr_sl=en&_x_tr_tl=pt&_x_tr_hl=pt-BR&_x_tr_pto=sc Accessed on: 25 Oct. 2024.

[26] Aquino (2020). Available at: https://repositorio.ufu.br/bitstream/123456789/29929/4/ResponsabilidadeCivilEstatal.pdf. Accessed 08 Oct 2024.

In these cases, the Court, whether in its judgment or in dissenting opinions, has expressed its views on the polluter-pays principle, on reparation in cases of transboundary environmental damage and the no harm principle, on the principle of sustainable development, on prevention and precautionary measures, on State responsibility, and also on the duty to carry out environmental impact studies and to consult States that share borders. It is important to emphasize that all these principles are directly related to the duty of States to adopt measures to mitigate the effects of climate change.

3.4 The ITLOS Advisory Opinion on Climate Change

On 12 December 2022, a group of States, known as 'Small Island Developing States'[27] requested an advisory opinion from the International Tribunal for the Law of the Sea in relation to two relevant issues:

> What are the specific obligations of State Parties to the United Nations Convention on the Law of the Sea (the "UNCLOS"), including under Part XJI:
>
> (a) to prevent, reduce and control pollution of the marine environment in relation to the deleterious effects that result or are likely to result from climate change, including through ocean warming and sea level rise, and ocean acidification, which are caused by anthropogenic greenhouse gas emissions into the atmosphere?
> (b) to protect and preserve the marine environment in relation to climate change impacts, including ocean warming and sea level rise, and ocean acidification?[28]

It is clear that the main concern is in relation to ocean warming, sea level rise and acidification of the marine environment, caused by greenhouse gases emitted by humans into the atmosphere. On May 21, 2024, the International Tribunal for the Law of the Sea issued a favorable and unanimous advisory opinion, recognizing its jurisdiction to hear the matter in question. This is the first time that an international tribunal has issued an advisory opinion on the obligations of States in relation to climate change mitigation.[29]

In the Advisory Opinion, the Court highlighted that anthropogenic emissions of greenhouse gases into the atmosphere constitute a form of pollution of the marine environment, and defined specific sources of pollution as emissions from land-based sources, vessels or from the atmosphere. The Court found that the definition of "marine pollution" has three elements: 1—there must be a substance or energy; 2—this substance or energy must be introduced by humans, directly or indirectly,

[27] The group is formed by the following States: Antigua and Barbuda; Tuvalu; Palau; Niue; Vanuatu; St. Lucia; St. Vincent and the Grenadines; St. Kitts and Nevis.

[28] ITLOS. Request for an Advisory Opinion submitted by the Commission of Small Island States on Climate Change and International Law (Request for Advisory Opinion submitted to the Tribunal). Available at: https://www.itlos.org/en/main/cases/list-of-cases/request-for-an-advisory-opinion-submitted-by-the-commission-of-small-island-states-on-climate-change-and-international-law-request-for-advisory-opinion-submitted-to-the-tribunal/ Accessed on: 25 Oct. 2024.

[29] Silverman-Roati and Bönnemann (2024).

into the marine environment; 3—such introduction must result or be likely to result in deleterious effects, which is seen, for example, in GHG emissions.[30]

Furthermore, it stated that countries have an obligation to take all necessary measures to protect and preserve the seas in the face of climate impacts and ocean acidification. The obligation to take all necessary measures is a "due diligence" obligation, which requires States to establish a national system to regulate polluting activities and to exercise surveillance to ensure the effectiveness of this system, which must be rigorous in the case of GHG emissions.

ITLOS concluded that States have a duty to take all "necessary measures" to control marine pollution associated with anthropogenic greenhouse gas (GHG) emissions.[31] The Tribunal clarified that the necessary measures must be "objectively determined," taking into account, among other factors, the "best available science." A key issue likely to come before many tribunals in climate litigation is the definition of what constitutes "best available science" as scientific evidence, as the Tribunal did not clarify this terminology. States also have an obligation to develop plans for the restoration of impacted habitats and ecosystems, including ensuring that non-State actors under their jurisdiction and control comply with these measures.[32]

The main external standards that ITLOS considered as complementary to the Convention include the United Nations Framework Convention on Climate Change (UNFCCC), the Kyoto Protocol, the Paris Agreement, the International Convention for the Prevention of Pollution from Ships (MARPOL), the Chicago Convention, the Montreal Protocol (including the Kigali Amendment) and the Convention on Biological Diversity (CBD).[33]

4 Regional Cases in National Jurisdictions in Australia and New Zealand

Although located in the Southern Hemisphere, Australia and New Zealand are part of the so-called "Global North", a designation based on political and economic criteria to qualify countries considered "developed".[34] Consequently, as mentioned, there is a clear distinction at the heart of climate litigation cases in these countries, when compared to other countries in the region.

While other countries litigate for existence (and subsistence), due to rising sea levels, which make life in these island countries unviable, climate litigation in Australia and New Zealand focuses on holding the public and private sectors

[30] Ibid.

[31] Ibid.

[32] ibid.

[33] Voigt (2024).

[34] Braff and Nelson (2022).

accountable for pollution and climate inaction. In addition, both countries have also received cases on the protection of the rights of traditional populations—including Aboriginal, Maori, and other ethnic minorities—populations who have seen their ways of life, culture, and spirituality threatened by climate change.

According to the University of Melbourne data center on climate change litigation, to date there are 625 climate change litigation cases, involving Australia, New Zealand, Kiribati, Fiji and Papua New Guinea. There are 69 cases concerning State accountability related to human rights claims, of which, 37 cases concerning human rights and refugee claims, 5 cases concerning the duty of care, and another 3 constitutional cases brought before the courts of these countries. There are another 58 cases related to access to justice, 100 cases related to corporate accountability, 212 cases related to project approval in the field of adaptation, and 186 cases related to project approval in the field of mitigation.[35]

At a regional level, this research proposed the thematic focus of three climate cases that can be considered relevant in this region and that raise fundamental questions about environmental responsibility and the actions of corporations and governments in the face of the climate crisis. These cases address large companies' responsibility for emitting greenhouse gases, as well as government decisions that directly affect local climate policy.

4.1 *Case Sharma et al. v. Minister of the Environment*

In September 2020, eight young people filed a class action lawsuit in the Federal Court of Australia seeking to prevent the Australian government from approving a proposed coal mining expansion at the Whitehaven Vickery mine. The petitioners represented all under-18s and argued that Minister Sussan Ley has a duty of care to young Australians, as mining and burning coal will worsen climate change and harm the future.[36]

In May 2021, the Court recognised a new duty of care owed by the government to avoid causing personal harm to children, but refused to grant an injunction to prevent the coal mine from expanding as it was not proven that the Minister would breach that duty of care. On 8 July 2021, the Court held that the Minister's duty of care applied to all Australian children under the age of 18, not just the claimants.[37]

Unfortunately, in March 2022, following an appeal by the Australian State, the full Federal Court of Australia reversed the initial decision, stating that policy issues such as this are not appropriate for the judiciary.[38] It is clear that the Court missed a

[35] University of Melbourne. *Australian and Pacific Climate Change Litigation*. Available at: https://law.app.unimelb.edu.au/climate-change/#litigation. Accessed on: 17 Oct. 2024.

[36] Sharma and others v. Minister for the Environment. Available at: https://climatecasechart.com/non-us-case/raj-seppings-v-ley/ Accessed on: 23 Sep. 2024.

[37] Ibid.

[38] Ibid.

great opportunity to link executive decisions to the duty of care towards Australian children.

4.2 Case Hauraki Coromandel Climate Action Incorporated v. Thames-Coromandel District Council

In 2019, Thames-Coromandel District Council decided not to endorse a Climate Change Declaration signed by Local Leaders, which committed the government to taking ambitious action to reduce greenhouse gas emissions and increase the resilience of local communities. Hauraki Coromandel Climate Action Incorporated (HCCA) challenged the decision in court, arguing that the Council's refusal was unreasonable given the urgency and global consensus on climate change.[39]

The High Court of New Zealand upheld the argument, holding that despite the political dimension of the decision, there was a strong public interest involved which made the decision not to approve reviewable. The Court accepted the evidence that anthropogenic climate change would significantly affect the District and concluded that the Council's decision was inconsistent with the Local Government Act 2002 and the Council's policy of engagement.[40]

Furthermore, the Court stated that decisions on climate change by public authorities deserve scrutiny comparable to that of human rights, requiring greater rigor in their analysis. As a result, the Court ordered the Council to reconsider its approval of the Declaration, in accordance with relevant law and policies.[41] The decision is yet another call for climate change to be scrutinized on the same level as human rights issues.

4.3 Case Smith v. Fonterra Co-Operative Group Limited

Michael John Smith, a Ngāpuhi and Ngāti Kahu elder and climate change spokesperson for the Iwi Chairs' Forum,[42] has filed a lawsuit against seven high-emitting New Zealand companies in the agriculture and energy sectors. In his submissions, Smith alleges that the defendants' actions constituted public nuisance, negligence and a breach of their duty to cease contributing to climate change. In March 2020, the High Court of New Zealand dismissed the first two claims but allowed the third

[39] Hauraki Coromandel Climate Action Incorporated v. Thames-Coromandel District Council. Available at: https://climatecasechart.com/non-us-case/hauraki-coromandel-climate-action-incorporated-v-thames-coromandel-district-council/. Accessed on: 23 Sep. 2024.

[40] Ibid.

[41] Ibid.

[42] Fórum nacional de líderes tribais.

to proceed, stating that Smith could not demonstrate public nuisance as the alleged harm was neither specific to him nor a direct consequence of the defendants' actions. The court also ruled that the negligence claim also failed to apply as there was no evidence that the defendants owed him a duty of care.[43]

On appeal, the Court dismissed Smith's appeal, stating that tort law was not the appropriate means of addressing climate change, since every person in New Zealand contributes to and is affected by the relevant harm. The Court warned that labelling the companies' conduct as unlawful would create an arbitrary system without democratic legitimacy. However, the Court of Appeal acknowledged that courts have a role in climate action, particularly in holding government accountable. In late 2021, Smith applied for leave to appeal to the High Court of New Zealand, which was granted on 31 March 2022, focusing on whether the Court of Appeal's dismissal of the appeal was correct.[44]

On 7 February 2024, the High Court of New Zealand handed down judgment and unanimously allowed the appeal to reaffirm Smith's statement of claim (comprising all three causes of action) against the seven companies alleged to have materially contributed to the climate crisis by being involved in an industry that emits greenhouse gases (GHGs) or by supplying products that facilitate the release of GHGs when burned.[45]

The case must now be determined by the High Court with full evidence and arguments, including tikanga evidence. Depending on the outcome of the trial, companies in certain industry sectors could be subject to huge legal risks in relation to their carbon emissions. Regardless of what happens at trial, the court's decision is likely to set an international precedent, encouraging further climate change litigation in countries beyond New Zealand.

5 Final Remarks

As outlined above, as the effects of the Anthropocene become increasingly noticeable, climate litigation has been increasing in global courts, in the quest for environmental protection and in the fight to avoid climate crises, since climate change has a multitude of factors that clash with national and international standards that require governments to act preventively to avoid environmental destruction and degradation.

When analyzing the cases above, it can be inferred that in the cases involving Australia and New Zealand, the judgments materialized the content of

[43] Smith v. Fonterra Co-Operative Group Limited. Disponível em: https://climatecasechart.com/non-us-case/smith-v-fonterra-co-operative-group-limited/ Acesso em: 24 set. 2024.

[44] Ibid.

[45] Courts of New Zealand. Michael John Smith v Fonterra Co-operative Group Limited - [2024] NZSC 5 Disponível em: https://www.courtsofnz.govt.nz/cases/michael-john-smith-v-fonterra-co-operative-group-limited Acesso em: 23 set. 2024.

environmental law protection standards and showed some tendencies of the courts to: 1—consider it the duty of States to protect their peoples against climate change, including the protection of their cultures and ancestry; 2—The perception, although defeated in the Sharma case, that there is a duty of care on the part of the State in the preparation of its acts; 3—The equivalence of climate rights to human rights; and 4—The possibility of analyzing the civil liability of companies for the environmental impacts generated.

It should also be noted that climate litigation cases have required not only positive actions from States to guarantee, promote, protect and fulfil the right to a healthy environment, but also requires the same from companies and other agents. Furthermore, it also requires States to take responsibility for these companies, since they also have a duty of due diligence and the duty to refrain from actions that could harm this right.[46] Accountability is, therefore, the central pillar of these cases.

In general, there has been a positive trend in the emergence of climate litigation, with environmental protection gaining strength, especially at the international level, and positioning the relevance of the environment in protecting against climate change as an *erga omnes* obligation. The use of litigation is an important tool in the search for environmental justice and in holding States and companies accountable, exposing regulatory failures and gaps in climate governance.

In this sense, it is also concluded that, due to the dialogue that exists between international Courts, advisory opinions play an indispensable role in protecting the environment and also in the fight against climate change, by guiding the international community on the role of States in this regard. In other words, advisory opinions or judgments issued by the international courts are commonly invoked by others to support the existence of an international obligation or custom. Moreover, they are an important tool to overcome these normative gaps.

In light of the cases analyzed in this paper, it is also clear that there is a regulatory gap regarding climate migration, which makes it essential to understand how climate change has affected the dynamics of current migration flows around the world. Finally, it is worth noting that the cases in Oceania are, unfortunately, a clear example of inequality and climate injustice, and that they illustrate the cascading effect of human rights violations.

Although the principle of common but differentiated responsibility is commonly mentioned in international forums and in the main documents that address climate change, the nations of the Pacific are among those most affected by this triple planetary crisis, whether due to their geomorphological characteristics or their low capacity for environmental resilience, in many cases resulting from years of exploitation of their resources by countries in the Global North.

---

[46] Boyle (2015).

References

Aquino VE (2020) Responsabilidade Civil Estatal E Direito Internacional Ambiental: danos ambientais transnacionais sob a perspectiva da Organização das Nações Unidas. Master thesis, Universidade Federal De Uberlandia. Available at: https://repositorio.ufu.br/bitstream/123456789/29929/4/ResponsabilidadeCivilEstatal.pdf. Accessed 8 Oct 2024

Boyle A (2015) Human rights and the environment: where next? In: BOER B (ed) Environmental law dimensions of human rights. Oxford University Press, Oxford

Braff L, Nelson K (2022) The global north: introducing the region. In: Fernandez NT, Nelson K (eds) Gendered lives: global issues. Sunny Press, New York

Courts of New Zealand. Michael John Smith v Fonterra Co-operative Group Limited - [2024] NZSC 5 Disponível em: https://www.courtsofnz.govt.nz/cases/michael-john-smith-v-fonterra-co-operative-group-limited. Acesso em: 23 set. 2024

Dodds J (2021) The psychology of climate anxiety. BJPsych Bull 45(4):222–226. https://doi.org/10.1192/bjb.2021.18

El-Hinnawi E (1985) Environmental refugees. UNEP, Nairobi

Face the Facts: Aboriginal and Torres Strait Islanders Peoples: Available at: https://humanrights.gov.au/our-work/education/face-facts-aboriginal-and-torres-strait-islander-peoples. Accessed in: 23 set. 2024

Hauraki Coromandel Climate Action Incorporated v. Thames-Coromandel District Council. Disponível em: https://climatecasechart.com/non-us-case/hauraki-coromandel-climate-action-incorporated-v-thames-coromandel-district-council/. Acesso em: 23 set. 2024

ICJ. Obligations of States in respect of Climate Change. Available at: https://www.icj-cij.org/case/187. Accessed: 25 Oct. 2024

International Court of Justice. Case 148 Whaling in the Antarctic (Australia v. Japan> New Zealand intervening). Disponível em: https://www.icj-cij.org/case/148. Acesso em 22 set. 2024

International Court of Justice. “Australia vs Japón: New Zealand intervening” (Separate Opinion of Judge Cançado Trindade), p. 17, ítem 42

ITLOS. Request for an Advisory Opinion submitted by the Commission of Small Island States on Climate Change and International Law (Request for Advisory Opinion submitted to the Tribunal). Available at: https://www.itlos.org/en/main/cases/list-of-cases/request-for-an-advisory-opinion-submitted-by-the-commission-of-small-island-states-on-climate-change-and-international-law-request-for-advisory-opinion-submitted-to-the-tribunal/. Accessed 25 Oct 2024

Loureiro CROMS, Romero TG (2024) Caso Ioane Teitiota e sua Família: O Marco Inicial na Judicialização dos Refugiados Ambientais em Face das Mudanças Climáticas para a garantia de Direitos Humanos. In: Nascimento ARd, Luz MF (orgs.) Pesquisa científica em Direito e Democracia: o papel dos Direitos Humanos como arma de construção ou de destruição. Liber Ars, São Paulo, SP

Mahlke H (2017) Direito Internacional dos Refugiados: novo paradigma jurídico. Arraes Editores, Belo Horizonte, p 29

MMA – MINISTÉRIO DO MEIO AMBIENTE. Acordo de Paris. 2019. Disponível em: https://www.mma.gov.br/clima/convencaodas-nacoes-unidas/acordo-de-paris. Acesso em: 24 set. 2024

RESOLUTION 77/276. ICJ Resolution, Disponível em: https://www-vanuatuicj-com.translate.goog/resolution?_x_tr_sl=en&_x_tr_tl=pt&_x_tr_hl=pt-BR&_x_tr_pto=sc. Accessed on: 25 Oct. 2024

Sabin Center For Climate Changelaw (2024). Climate Change Litigation Databases. Columbia Law School/ Columbia Climate Change. New York. Disponível em: https://climatecasechart.com. Acesso em: 20 set. 2024

Sharma and others v. Minister for the Environment. Disponível em: https://climatecasechart.com/non-us-case/raj-seppings-v-ley/. Acesso em: 23 set. 2024

Silverman-Roati K, Bönnemann M (2024) The ITLOS Advisory Opinion on Climate Change: An introduction into the joint blog symposium, VerfBlog, 2024/5/22, https://verfassungsblog.de/the-itlos-advisory-opinion-on-climate-change/, https://doi.org/10.59704/8034cca584b1594b

Smith v. Fonterra Co-Operative Group Limited. Disponível em: https://climatecasechart.com/non-us-case/smith-v-fonterra-co-operative-group-limited/ Acesso em: 24 set. 2024

The Republic of Vanuatu is leading the initiative at the UN International Court of Justice for an Advisory Opinion on the Obligations os States relevant to climate action. Disponível em: https://www-vanuatuicj-com.translate.goog/?_x_tr_sl=en&_x_tr_tl=pt&_x_tr_hl=pt-BR&_x_tr_pto=sc Accessed: 25 Oct 2024

TSRA (2016) 'Torres Strait Climate Change Strategy 2014–2018: Building Community Adaptive Capacity and Resilience' (June 2016) Disponível em: https://www.tsra.gov.au/__data/assets/pdf_file/0015/12372/TS-Regional-Adaptation-and-Resillience-Plan-Final.pdf. Acesso em: 20 set. 2024

Voigt C (2024) ITLOS e a importância de (obter) regras externas (corretas) na interpretação da UNCLOS, VerfBlog, 29/05/2024. https://verfassungsblog.de/itlos-and-the-importance-of-getting-external-rules-right-in-interpreting-unclos/. https://doi.org/10.59704/d9dfb01f480ab1b7.

WRR (2021) WorldRiskReport 2021. Alliance Development Works and United Nations University – Environment and Human Security (UNU-EHS). University Stuttgart. Available at: https://www.preventionweb.net/publication/world-risk-report-2021-focus-social-protection#:~:text=The%20countries%20with%20the%20highest,exposure%20to%20extreme%20natural%20events. Acessed em: 25 Oct. 2024

Valéria Emília de Aquino Lawyer and Human Rights Consultant, Human Rights PhD (Federal University of Goiás). Master in Fundamental Rights and Sustainability (Federal University of Uberlândia). Member of the Editorial Board and Senior Research Member of 'Direito Internacional sem Fronteiras' (Brazil). Researcher at 'Global Crossings' (Jean Monnet Chair at Federal University of Uberlândia), former scholar at CAPES and FAPEG. International Law and Environmental Law Professor. Researcher in International Law, Environmental Law, International Security, and Human Rights. Former Visiting fellow at the Mercosur Institute of Public Policies on Human Rights (Argentina). valeriaemiliaa@gmail.com

Marlon Antônio Rosa is a Municipal Attorney at the Araxá Municipal Pension Institute. Master's degree in Public Law at the Federal University of Uberlândia, researcher at Global Crossings and the Inter-American and European Observatory of Sustainable Development Goals, both at Federal University of Uberlândia. Member of the American Laboratory for Comparative Constitutional Studies. marlon1vsp@gmail.com

Diving Into the Synergies Between the Climate and the Ocean Emergencies: An Analysis of the International Tribunal for the Law of the Sea Advisory Opinion on Climate Change

Adriana Isabelle Barbosa Sá Leitão Di Pasquale, Julia Schutz Veiga, and Tarin Cristino Frota Mont'Alverne

1 Introduction

Even before the 2015 United Nations Summit on Sustainable Development, which culminated in the 2030 Agenda,[1] the international community was already noticing some of the adverse effects of its own actions. Since the 1979 World Climate Conference,[2] humanity has acknowledged that the combustion of fossil fuels and deforestation, along with shipping and other activities, are fundamentally associated with increased atmospheric concentrations of carbon dioxide (CO_2).[3]

This reconnaissance has prompted the formulation of theories that link human activities to natural phenomena, specifically climate change. For instance, Paul Crutzen introduced the term "Anthropocene" in 2000, designating it as a geological

[1] United Nations (UN) (2015).

[2] World Climate Conference, 1979. XX.

[3] Information Unit For Conventions (IUC) (2000). Climate Change Information Sheet 17. The international response to climate change: A history. Information Unit for Conventions – UN Environment Programme.

A. I. B. S. L. Di Pasquale (✉)
University of Pisa, Tuscany, Italy
e-mail: adrianasaleitaoadv@gmail.com

J. S. Veiga
Nippon Foundation Ocean Voices Programme, University of Edinburgh, Edinburgh, UK

NOVA School of Law, Universidade Nova de Lisboa, Lisbon, Portugal
e-mail: julia.schutz@novalaw.unl.pt

T. C. F. Mont'Alverne
Faculty of Law, Federal University of Ceará (UFC), Fortaleza, Brazil

V. E. de Aquino et al. (eds.), *Climate Litigation in a Changing World*, Ius Gentium: Comparative Perspectives on Law and Justice 130,
https://doi.org/10.1007/978-3-032-05530-9_7

period that signifies the profound influence of human activities on the Earth.[4] Its significance in the discussion is predicated on the understanding that only one planet exists, necessitating coordinated and collaborative efforts to devise solutions for these pressing contemporary challenges.

Theories of this kind have remarkably influenced the international agenda. For instance, the international environmental regime has expanded since the 1990s by establishing binding international legal instruments (e.g. the Kyoto Protocol[5] and the Paris Agreement).[6] Furthermore, non-binding international commitments have been instituted as a strategy to encourage states and other stakeholders to undertake actions aimed at minimising the adverse impacts of their activities, exemplified by the Sustainable Development Goals (SDGs).[7]

These commitments and obligations illustrate that the global community is poised to fundamentally alter the human paradigm to safeguard not only its own survival but also that of other species while simultaneously ensuring the continued functionality of ecosystems by prioritising nature as the central focus. In this context, one of the most pressing issues of the Anthropocene is the loss of marine biodiversity, which has undergone comprehensive analysis, establishing synergies between climate and ocean systems.[8]

The interdependencies between climate regulation and the ocean underpin the concept of the "ocean-climate nexus".[9] The ocean[10] plays a crucial role to humanity by providing oxygen, food, carbon storage, economic activities, and cultural inspiration,[11] besides regulating the climate by absorbing excess heat and CO_2[12]—which make this ecosystem essential for mitigating and adapting to the impacts of climate change.[13]

Climate change, however, threatens the resilience of the ocean and poses serious challenges to coastal communities that depend heavily on marine resources.[14]

---

[4] Barros-Platiau et al. (2015).

[5] The Kyoto Protocol is one of several international legal instruments established in the 90s. However, marine and ocean systems were not expressly recognised in that document. The turning point was the Paris Agreement in 2015, as it is analysed in subsection 2 of this chapter.

[6] Luomi (2020).

[7] UN (2015).

[8] Pörtner et al. (2021), p. 4.

[9] Pörtner et al. (2019), p. 1155; and Voigt (2023), p. 17.

[10] The IOC of UNESCO is the body of the United Nations which is responsible for supporting global ocean science and services. This organisation has been working to protect the health of "our shared ocean" by coordinating programmes in ocean observations, hazard mitigation, tsunami warnings and marine spatial planning, among others. For this reason, considering this choice of the IOC to refer to marine ecosystems as a single global ocean, this essay adopts the nomenclature "ocean" in the singular. For more, *see* IOC-UNESCO (2020). The Science we need for the ocean we want: the United Nations Decade of Ocean Science for Sustainable Development (2021–2030).

[11] Lubchenco and Haugan (2023), pp. 907–915.

[12] Hoegh-Guldberg et al. (2019), p. 1372.

[13] Morgera et al. (2023), p. 447.

[14] Popova et al. (2019), pp. 90–102.

Beyond the direct impact on human societies, climate change also endangers species, ecosystems, and biodiversity, either through direct harm or due to the loss of critical habitats, potentially leading to extinction in some cases.[15]

Since records began in 1955, the temperature of the ocean has increased steadily, setting new records in 2023. Marine heat waves are becoming more frequent and intense because of all this extra heat.[16]

Furthermore, ocean acidification is being intensified primarily due to the reaction between seawater and atmospheric CO_2 emissions originated from human activity. The ecological integrity of the ocean is already at risk, and acidification poses a serious compounding threat to it – not to mention the great menace that climate change poses to coral reefs and the various species that depend on them.[17]

Nevertheless, ocean acidification has also started to contribute to positive feedback loops related to the climate, which pose a risk to drive further climate change beyond the Paris Agreement's 1.5–2.0 °C temperature targets.[18]

Hence, ocean warming, acidification, deoxygenation, and changes in primary productivity are considered the four major climate change stressors of ocean ecosystems—and since they occur simultaneously, there is a high possibility that they will have synergistic effects.[19]

In addition, when it comes to the groups and coastal communities that compose the Small Island Developing States (SIDS), climate change is an existential menace to them. Its influences on the ocean is reflected in sea level rise, ocean warming, ocean acidification and greenhouse gases (GHG) concentrations, adversely affecting food production from fisheries and shellfish aquaculture in some oceanic regions and leading to the intensification of tropical cyclones and/or extratropical storms, flooding in coastal and other low-lying regions.[20]

The ocean is a key source of sustenance for these populations, therefore protecting its environmental health is essential[21]—especially because the ocean economy (or the blue economy) plays a crucial role in the future well-being and prosperity of humanity in general, providing essential resources like food, energy, minerals, health benefits, recreation, and transportation. It supports the livelihoods of hundreds of millions of people, making its sustainable management critical for global prosperity.[22]

Looking toward the future, there are nascent or still-developing sectors, such as carbon capture and storage and the management of large-scale ocean protected areas, which could become integral parts of the ocean economy. Managing these

---

[15] Nwabueze and Techera (2021), p. 217.

[16] National Aeronautics and Space Administration (2024). The Ocean and Climate Change.

[17] Telesetsky and Bratspies (2021).

[18] Taylor (2023).

[19] Gallo et al. (2017), p. 835.

[20] Intergovernmental Panel on Climate Change (IPCC) (2023), pp. 5–6.

[21] Cremean et al. (2021), p. 173.

[22] OECD (2016), p. 16. https://doi.org/10.1787/9789264251724-en.

economic activities, however, must consider the unique physical context of the ocean—a dynamic, buoyant, and three-dimensional environment that spans approximately two-thirds of the Earth's surface.[23]

The SIDS' vulnerabilities, thus, comprehend the impacts on fisheries—as they are an essential element of the livelihoods, economies and food security of their populations[24]–, but also forced migration from low-lying coastal zones[25] and even the real possibility of vanishing beneath the surface by the end of this century.[26]

In light of this context—in which interactions between ocean and climate have increasingly intensified and the most affected populations are those most dependent on sectors of the blue economy (and, consequently, the most vulnerable to the impacts of climate change on the ocean)–, the International Tribunal for the Law of the Sea (ITLOS)—going against a trend of narrowly focused governance frameworks[27]–, became the first International Court to issue an Advisory Opinion (AO) concerning the climate emergency.[28] This happened because the Commission of Small Island States on Climate Change and International Law (COSIS) requested ITLOS to provide an AO on the responsibilities of states to mitigate the effects of climate change on the ocean.[29]

In this scenario, this chapter concentrates on multidisciplinary legal research about ITLOS' AO on climate change through the perspective of the ocean-climate nexus. It integrates two significant legal domains, namely, the international law of the sea and international environmental law.

The methodology employed is desk research, featuring logical-systematic and critical analyses of selected sources, including international legislation, international organisations reports, and relevant literature.

The initial section presents an overview of the AO, followed by an examination of the evolution of international commitments established in accordance with scientific studies relevant to this nexus. Ultimately, this chapter investigates the complexities associated with the ocean and climate change regimes, highlighting the contributions of the AO in promoting synergies between these fields.

This essay is dedicated to supporting the exploration of collaborative approaches intended to enhance the interaction of these regimes, thereby strengthening the resilience and sustainability of vulnerable areas, such as SIDS, while also emphasising the role of the ocean in the climate emergency.

---

[23] Ibidem.

[24] Shelton et al. (2024).

[25] Vousdoukas et al. (2023), pp. 1552–1564.

[26] House of Commons International Development Committee (2024).

[27] Keohane and Victor (2011), pp. 7–23.

[28] Here referred as the emergency that is mainly related to the emission of GHG that contribute to rise temperatures, leading to increases in extreme heat events, substantial damages, increasingly irreversible losses, reduced food and water security, hindering efforts to meet Sustainable Development Goals (SDGs). In: Intergovernmental Panel on Climate Change (IPCC) (2023), pp. 5–6.

[29] ITLOS (2024).

The research aspires to contribute to developing effective policies grounded in scientific evidence and international cooperation.

2 Climate Change and Ocean Emergencies: Scientific Alerts and Implications

One of the biggest risks to the global economy, natural resources, and public health is the climate emergency—and the ocean is greatly threatened by it. Beyond the anthropocentric impacts, species, ecosystems and biodiversity are also negatively affected, either directly or as habitats are lost, and in some cases may result in extinction.[30]

The ocean ecosystem is not only in danger, but also serves as the world's largest carbon sink, which is essential for reducing the effects of climate change itself.[31]

Therefore, ocean and climate interactions have attracted greater attention, so much so that the presidency of the 23rd Conference of the Parties (COP) of the United Nations Framework Convention on Climate Change (UNFCCC) introduced the oceans pathway into the climate solutions arena. This acknowledges the significance of the ocean in the climate system and the availability of ocean commitments for adaptation and mitigation through Nationally Determined Contributions (NDCs) under the UNFCCC.[32]

Before that, although the 1992 UNFCCC formally acknowledged the value of marine ecosystems as sinks and reservoirs for GHG,[33] subsequent COP negotiations largely ignored ocean, marine, or coastal ecosystems. Given the rise in ocean-related side events, increased participation from ocean scientists and non-governmental organizations, and the signing of the "Because the Ocean" Declaration by 22

[30] Nwabueze and Techera (2021), p. 217.

[31] United Nations (UN) (2021).

[32] Abram et al. (2019), p. 92.

[33] Article 4 "COMMITMENTS" (…) (d) Promote sustainable management, and promote and cooperate in the conservation and enhancement, as appropriate, of sinks and reservoirs of all greenhouse gases not controlled by the Montreal Protocol, including biomass, forests and oceans as well as other terrestrial, coastal and marine ecosystems.

Parties,[34] the Paris Agreement marked a significant turning point for the recognition of the ocean[35] within the climate negotiations.[36]

Moreover, in contrast to the Kyoto Protocol of 1997, where marine and ocean systems are not expressly recognised, the Paris Agreement formally includes the ocean in the Preamble. Beyond that, recent COPs have also addressed the ocean-climate relations. For instance, the Global Environment Facility's report for the 26th COP recognised that life on Earth fundamentally depends on clean air and water, biodiversity, healthy oceans and lands, and a stable climate, and identified that the climate emergency influences rising sea levels, flooding, coastal erosion, increased extreme weather events, coral reef bleaching, and ocean acidification.[37]

The Sharm El Sheik decision from COP 27, instead, invited Parties to, when appropriate, take ocean-based actions into account for achieving their national climate goals and carrying them out, including (but not limited to) the NDCs, long-term plans, and communications on adaptation.[38] Whereas the COP 28's draft decision CMA.5 encouraged "*further strengthening of ocean-based action*".[39]

The growing recognition of the relationship between these climate and ocean emergencies has, ever since, raised increasing alerts about its implications for SIDS, mainly due to their geographic vulnerabilities. In the 1992 United Nations Conference on Environment and Development, in fact, the international community first acknowledged that SIDS are a "special case" for sustainable development, due to their unique social, economic and environmental vulnerabilities.[40]

Chapter 17 of the Agenda 21, which is entitled "*protection of the oceans, all kinds of seas, including enclosed and semi-enclosed seas, and coastal areas and the protection, rational use and development of their living resources*" also recognised that SIDS are vulnerable and ecologically fragile. The document emphasises that their small size, scarce resources, dispersed geographic location, and lack of market accessibility put them at a competitive economic disadvantage and hinder

---

[34] On the eve of COP21 in Paris, ministers and heads of state and government signed the first "Because the Ocean" Declaration.

[35] It should be noted that the term 'ocean' will be used in the singular to emphasise the interconnectedness of marine areas. There is only one global ocean: a vast body of water that covers 71 percent of the Earth and is geographically divided into distinctly named regions. The boundaries between these regions have evolved over time for a variety of historical, cultural, geographic, and scientific reasons. On this point, see, Laffoley et al. (2021), pp. 1512–1534; Intergovernmental Oceanographic Commission (IOC-UNESCO) (2017); National Oceanic and Atmospheric Administration (NOAA) (2024).

[36] Gallo et al. (2017). Op. cit., p. 835.

[37] UN (2020), p. 83.

[38] Conference of the Parties (COP) 27 (2022).

[39] United Nations Framework Convention on Climate Change (UNFCCC) (2023). First global stocktake Proposal by the President Draft decision -/CMA.5 Outcome of the first global stocktake. FCCC/PA/CMA/2023/L.17.

[40] Food and Agriculture Organization of the United Nations (FAO) (2014). Natural Resources Management and the Environment in Small Island Development States (SIDS).

economies of scale. Therefore, the ocean and coastal environment are strategically significant and a valuable resource for SIDS.[41]

Paragraph 130 of this chapter called, as well, for more international cooperation and summoned for the first Global Conference on the Sustainable Development of SIDS. Thus, the conference took place in in Bridgetown, Barbados, in April 1994, aiming to assist SIDS in resolving the development and environmental issues they were facing.[42]

The conference then adopted the Barbados Declaration and Programme of Action for the Sustainable Development of SIDS,[43] which emphasised the need for global cooperation, particularly in the areas of funding, technology transfer, information sharing, and capacity building. Follow-up conferences have since been held to assess the implementation of the Programme of Action, including two events held in Mauritius (2004) and in Samoa (2014).[44]

In 2014, in fact, Heads of State and Government and high-level representatives met at the third International Conference on SIDS, reaffirming their commitment to the sustainable development of SIDS and establishing the S.A.M.O.A. Pathway.[45] The aim of the pathway was to address the unique challenges faced by SIDS and to support their development through assisting in mobilizing international support and resources for the implementation of the Programme of Action; supporting a coordinated follow-up of the pathway; providing support to group consultations of SIDS, among others.[46]

It should also be noted that the 2030 Agenda recognises, as well, the challenges that SIDS face in order to achieve sustainable development. Among the 17 Sustainable Development Goals (SDGs), the SDGs 4, 7, 9, 10, 13, 14 and 17[47] explicitly address their struggle. More importantly, SDG 13 "climate action" mentions SIDS in target 13.b,[48] whereas SDG 14 "life bellow water" has two targets dedicated to SIDS (14.7[49] and 14.a[50]).

---

[41] UN (1992).

[42] UN (1994a).

[43] UN (1994b).

[44] Mead (2021), p. 4.

[45] S.A.M.O.A. stands for "SIDS ACCELERATED MODALITIES OF ACTION".

[46] UN (2023). Final report a toolkit for monitoring and reporting on the SAMOA Pathway.

[47] UN (2015). Transforming our world: the 2030 Agenda for Sustainable Development.

[48] Which brings the following goal: "promote mechanisms for raising capacity for effective climate change-related planning and management in least developed countries and small island developing States, including focusing on women, youth and local and marginalized communities;".

[49] Which brings the following goal: "by 2030, increase the economic benefits to Small Island developing States and least developed countries from the sustainable use of marine resources, including through sustainable management of fisheries, aquaculture and tourism".

[50] Which brings the following goal: "increase scientific knowledge, develop research capacity and transfer marine technology, taking into account the Intergovernmental Oceanographic Commission Criteria and Guidelines on the Transfer of Marine Technology, in order to improve ocean health and to enhance the contribution of marine biodiversity to the development of developing countries, in particular small island developing States and least developed countries".

Furthermore, the SDGs of the 2030 Agenda are an important example of the recognition that different phenomena and ecosystems establish synergies with each other. At this point, a brief digression is warranted to explore the content of the 2030 Agenda in more detail.

The SDGs' aim is to move beyond the fragmentation of technical and policy efforts by fostering integrated approaches to the interconnected economic, social, and environmental challenges that the planet is facing.[51]

The 17 SDGs provided by the 2030 Agenda are interconnected and cannot function in isolation, as each goal can influence others and be influenced in return. This creates a significant *cause-and-effect* relationship among the goals, which should not be overlooked.[52] Despite this horizontal nature of the SDGs—that is, they are not assigned any hierarchy or priority for implementation—it is essential to emphasise that SDG 14—"Life below water" presents itself as a central objective.

The ocean plays a pivotal role in achieving sustainable development for society. Many SDGs cannot be fully achieved without addressing SDG 14. For instance, SDG 14 aims to end overfishing and illegal practices, which are crucial for fulfilling other goals such as no poverty (SDG 1), zero hunger (SDG 2), good health and well-being (SDG 3), and reducing inequalities (SDG 10).

Marine ecosystems provide numerous ecosystem services,[53] which can be understood as benefits that people obtain from the environment. Some examples are regulatory and supporting ecosystem services, such as the distribution of heat around the planet, the functioning of the hydrological cycle and the absorption of CO_2 as part of the carbon cycle. Other ecosystem services are obtained as a result of human activity to acquire them, such as obtaining food provided by capture fisheries, providing significant quantities of the protein needed to feed the world's population. If such human activities are not carefully managed to maintain ecosystem structure and function, the acquisition of such ecosystem services may result in damage to the marine environment and the reduction or loss of these fundamental services.[54]

Hence the need to ensure that the implementation of the SDGs is carried out in a systemic and holistic manner, observing the interconnections between different environmental agendas, such as the ocean-climate nexus.

Well before the adoption of the 2030 Agenda, however, the SIDS had already effectively leveraged their shared vulnerabilities to the climate emergency to engage actively in global climate change negotiations.

---

[51] Servaes (2017), p. 9.

[52] Kumar et al. (2018), p. 2120.

[53] Ecosystem services, or environmental services, can be defined as flows originating from natural capital stocks that combine with human services capital to provide well-being to populations. These services can be classified into four categories: cultural services (aesthetic and recreational elements); regulatory services (which regulate the climate, the floods, the pests and water purification, for instance); support services (nutrient cycling and soil formation); and provision services (such as the supply of food, fresh water, fibre and fuels). In: Nusdeo (2016), pp. 619–643.

[54] United Nations Environment Programme (UNEP) (2016)

In 1990, they established a coalition, the Alliance of Small Island States (AOSIS), during the Second World Climate Conference in Geneva[55] and, later, an agreement for the Establishment of the Commission of Small Island States on Climate Change and International Law (COSIS) was signed prior to COP26, in 2021.[56]

It is interesting noting that the Agreement for the establishment of the COSIS expressly predicts in Article 2 (2) that "*having regard to the fundamental importance of oceans (…) the Commission shall be authorized to request advisory opinions*[57] *from the International Tribunal for the Law of the Sea (…)*"[58] and, in fact, on Decembre 2022, under Article 21 of the ITLOS Statute and Article 138 of the United Nations Convention on the Law of the Sea (UNCLOS),[59] the COSIS submitted a request for an AO, constituting Case 31/2022.[60]

3 Case 31 of ITLOS: Historical, Scientific and Legal Recognitions of the Procedure

The COSIS formally solicited an AO from ITLOS with the primary objective of attaining clarity from the international tribunal regarding the explicit responsibilities of States Parties to UNCLOS in relation to climate change and its subsequent impact on the marine environment.[61]

It should be clarified that the jurisdiction of ITLOS is underpinned by Article 21 of the ITLOS Statute and Article 138 of the UNCLOS.[62] ITLOS based its decision on the precedent established by ITLOS Case 21 in 2015,[63] which granted advisory jurisdiction to ITLOS, underscoring the majority support of UNCLOS States Parties for rendering an AO concerning fishing activities.[64]

---

[55] Alliance of Small Island States (AOSIS) (2023).

[56] Commission of Small Island States on Climate Change and International Law (COSIS) (2022).

[57] The COSIS Agreement was established against the backdrop of ITLOS Case 21, 2015. To pursue the ITLOS advisory opinion, West African states established the Sub-regional Fisheries Commission. Many states were in favour, while others were against it. Although there are these disagreements, ITLOS has set precedents by issuing the 2015 advisory opinion.

[58] Commonwealth Foundation (2021).

[59] Considering Article 2(2) of the COASIS Agreement, the Commission uttered, "[h]aving regard to the fundamental importance of oceans as sinks and reservoirs of greenhouse gases and the direct relevance of the marine environment to the adverse effects of climate change on Small Island States, *the Commission shall be authorized* to request advisory opinions from the International Tribunal for the Law of the Sea ("ITLOS") on any legal question within the scope of the 1982 United Nations Convention on the Law of the Sea, consistent with Article 21 of the ITLOS Statute and Article 138 of its Rules" (ITLOS, Case 31, para 4, 2024).

[60] Sabin Center For Climate Change Law (2024).

[61] ITLOS, Case 31, para 3(2), 138-144, 2024.

[62] ITLOS, Case 31, para 93, 2024.

[63] ITLOS Case 21, 2015. See footnote 25.

[64] ITLOS, Case 31, para 90, 2024.

The COSIS integrated the recommendations provided by a committee of legal experts[65] and considered the efforts undertaken by the Subcommittee on the Protection and Preservation of the Marine Environment in submitting its request for an AO. The COSIS request for ITLOS focused on

> what are the specific obligations of States Parties to UNCLOS, including Part XII: (a) to prevent, reduce and control pollution of the marine environment in relation to the deleterious effects that result or may result from climate change, including through ocean warming and sea level rise, and ocean acidification, which are caused by anthropogenic emissions of greenhouse gases into the atmosphere? and (b) protect and preserve the marine environment in relation to the impacts of climate change, including ocean warming and sea level rise, and ocean acidification?.[66]

In addition, the COSIS conveyed its endorsement of Vanuatu's initiative, which solicited an AO from the International Court of Justice (ICJ) regarding climate change.[67] Additionally, the Commission requested that the Subcommittees on Sea Level Rise, Human Rights, and Loss and Damage propose further actions that should be undertaken to aid in the definition, implementation, and progressive development of international legal rules and principles relating to climate change.[68]

Throughout 2023, 31 States, seven international organisations and many civil society representatives submitted written statements to ITLOS, expressing their perspectives on the request of the COSIS.[69] Furthermore, 33 States, four international organisations and one regional group intended to participate in the oral proceedings.[70] In addition, seven civil society representatives requested to act as *amicus curie*, which ITLOS denied.[71]

In September 2023, in addition to the requests made by the COSIS and the written submissions, along with requests for oral arguments from various stakeholders, Judge Kittichaisaree sought clarifications regarding the submissions that had been presented. The Judge emphasised the necessity for the COSIS and the International Union for Conservation of Nature (IUCN) to delineate, in accordance with Article 76 of the Rules of ITLOS, the obligations classified as obligations of conduct and those identified as obligations of result as well as the rationale underlying their distinctions.[72]

ITLOS based its decision on the precedent established by ITLOS Case 21 in 2015,[73] which granted advisory jurisdiction to ITLOS, underscoring the majority support of UNCLOS States Parties for rendering an AO concerning fishing

[65] Committee of Legal Experts. Recommendation CLE.1/2022/Rec, 2022.

[66] ITLOS, Case 31, para 3(1), 2024.

[67] ITLOS, Case 31, para 3(2), 2024.

[68] ITLOS, Case 31, para 3(3), 2024.

[69] ITLOS, Case 31, para 17-23 and 35, 2024.

[70] ITLOS, Case 31, para 28 and 36, 2024.

[71] ITLOS, Case 31, para 20, 2024.

[72] ITLOS, Case 31, para 40, 2024.

[73] ITLOS Case 21, 2015. See footnote 35.

activities.[74] ITLOS also recognised the interplay between the ocean and climate within the boundaries delineated by the COSIS, emphasising that anthropogenic activities induce substantial warming of the atmosphere, ocean, and land, thereby detrimentally impacting marine ecosystems.[75]

ITLOS asserts that climate change directly impacts the marine environment.[76] In this regard, ITLOS underscored that the UNCLOS general obligation of States Parties entails the protection and preservation of the marine environment, as stipulated in Article 192 of UNCLOS. Furthermore, ITLOS acknowledged that this obligation applies also to non-state Parties operating under the jurisdiction or authority of one or more State Parties.[77]

This general obligation signifies the inclusion of prevention, mitigation, and control of marine pollution as forms of preserving and conserving the marine environment. In this regard, ITLOS articulates the general rule of Article 192 of UNCLOS

> (…) applies to all maritime areas and can be invoked to combat any form of degradation of the marine environment, including climate change impacts, such as ocean warming and sea level rise, and ocean acidification. Where the marine environment has been degraded, this may require restoring marine habitats and ecosystems.[78]

Nonetheless, ITLOS underscored that pollution control represents merely one aspect of this context.[79] In conjunction with this observation, ITLOS articulated that the 'preservation of the marine environment' encompasses the 'restoration of marine habitats and ecosystems,' despite the absence of direct mention of 'restoration' in Article 192. In essence, the obligation to safeguard the marine environment extends to restoring compromised marine habitats and ecosystems, thereby ensuring the maintenance of ecological equilibrium.[80]

The noteworthy aspect of ITLOS lies in its recognition that a state must undertake all feasible measures, in alignment with its capacities and available resources, to prevent, diminish, and manage marine pollution caused by anthropogenic GHG emissions.[81]

This recognition does not conflict with applying the principle of common but differentiated responsibilities. For instance, the Paris Agreement establishes varying targets for gas emission reductions across different states.

The affirmation of the ocean-climate nexus by the court highlights the significance of climate change and its substantial consequences for small island states.[82] The international tribunal stressed the necessity for harmonisation between

[74] ITLOS, Case 31, para 90, 2024.

[75] ITLOS, Case 31, para 45–82.

[76] ITLOS, Case 31, para 107, 2024.

[77] ITLOS, Case 31, para 396, 2024.

[78] ITLOS, Case 31, para 400, 2024.

[79] ITLOS, Case 31, para 151–152, 2024.

[80] ITLOS, Case 31, para 386, 2024.

[81] ITLOS, Case 31, para 241, 2024.

[82] ITLOS, Case 31, para 121–122, 2024.

UNCLOS and external regulations (Article 237 of UNCLOS), particularly concerning compliance between Part XII of UNCLOS and other international legal instruments pertinent to the protection and preservation of the marine environment.[83]

ITLOS reinforces UNCLOS as a dynamic instrument by advocating for the coordination and harmonisation of UNCLOS with related legal frameworks, such as the Paris Agreement. This approach will also contribute to the progression of the law.[84] The evident disjunction within international environmental law underscores the intricate interplay of various regimes aimed at fortifying efforts to protect and preserve the marine environment, highlighting the limitations of the specific obligations imposed upon states and other stakeholders.

4 Diving Into a Regime Complexity: Between Fragmentation and Interactions

The considerations provided about the intrinsic relationship and interactions between ocean and climate—the ocean-climate nexus—highlight several key dimensions of the legal governance surrounding human activities in the ocean.

The increasing body of scientific evidence on climate change and its impacts—particularly in relation to the ocean, marine biodiversity, and non-living marine resources—further complicates the intricate web of interactions involved. It is not only the vast expanse of the ocean that connects the Law of the Sea with various aspects of environmental law. The ecosystem services the ocean provides along with its crucial role in regulating the global climate, underscore the distinctive position of the Law of the Sea as a regulatory framework. This framework, in turn, intersects with other global and regional governance structures.[85]

These "other" structures—or regimes—derive from the fragmentation of international law: the emergence of new branches that operate independently, cultivating their unique identities and governance structures, exemplifies one dimension of the broader issue concerning such fragmentation. The phenomenon of regime interaction, extensively explored in the literature, highlights the complexities inherent in overlapping different legal frameworks and the challenges posed by their coordination.[86]

For instance, the necessity of facilitating access to and the transfer of relevant marine technologies to combat detrimental impacts stimulates the convergence of

[83] ITLOS, Case 31, para 130–137, 2024.
[84] ITLOS, Case 31, para 130, 2024.
[85] Matz-Lück and Jensen (2022), p. 2.
[86] Young (2012), p. 92; Van Asselt (2014), p. 210.

various legal fields,[87] including the law of the sea, trade, human rights, environmental law and intellectual property rights.[88]

The relation between these different fields is emblematic of the complexities within "regime complexes", which often operate without clear hierarchies, creating both opportunities and challenges for effective governance.[89]

The interaction of various international regimes underscores the absence of an overarching structure or hierarchy among their institutions and regulations. This lack of structure or hierarchy constitutes a primary political characteristic of a regime.[90] For instance, the regime complex for mitigating climate change encompasses numerous mechanisms integral to the UN framework, specifically the UNFCCC and the Kyoto Protocol, as well as specialised agencies within the UN, such as the UN Development Programme (UNDP) and the UN Environment Programme (UNEP), and various bilateral and multilateral framework agreements.[91]

These overlapping structures reflect the fragmented yet dynamic nature of international environmental governance, with regime interactions often facilitating cooperation or exacerbating governance challenges, as demonstrated in the broader literature on regime interaction.[92]

Indeed, interaction between legal regimes can help reduce uncertainties and clarify ambiguous areas of the law, while also identifying and potentially addressing regulatory gaps. In this scenario, lessons can be drawn from existing areas of interaction within the Law of the Sea, including examples of "best practices" that demonstrate how mutually supportive engagement can be operationalised and reinforced through institutional mechanisms.[93]

The ocean regime is also characterised by "complexity". The UNCLOS is widely acknowledged as the "Constitution of the Ocean"[94] due to its extensive thematic scope and universal acceptance, serving as a foundational legislative framework within the Law of the Sea.[95] Both general Law of the Sea and the UNCLOS specifically engage with numerous thematic areas across international law and policy, intersecting with domains such as the protection of marine biodiversity, international human rights, and climate change, among others.[96]

Although UNCLOS does not explicitly address climate change, it mandates to preserve and protect the marine environment, as outlined in Part XII, underscoring

---

[87] Jakobsen et al. (2021), p. 375.

[88] Nwabueze and Techera (2021). Op. cit., p. 228–229.

[89] Young (2012). Op. cit., p. 92.

[90] Zhang and Bai (2023), p. 4.

[91] Zhang and Bai (2023), p. 4.

[92] Van Asselt (2014). Op. cit., p. 212.

[93] Matz-Lück and Jensen (2022). Op. Cit., p. 11.

[94] Expression formulated by Tommy T.B. KOH (Singapore), President of the third UN Conference on the Law of the Sea: "A constitution for the Oceans", 11 December 1982, 5 p.

[95] For a comprehensive historical overview of the development, please refer to Proells' UNCLOS Commentaries.

[96] Matz-Lück and Jensen (2022). Op. Cit., p. 5.

the intrinsic connection between the two regulatory frameworks. This interconnection introduces a novel dimension, explicitly managing the integration of various activities conducted in marine areas. Evolving demands and the rapid advancements of emerging technologies in the context of climate change exacerbate this challenge.

For instance, the delineation and establishment of offshore wind farms for renewable energy production, alongside the application of geoengineering techniques to mitigate excess GHG present in the atmosphere,[97] underscore the substantial role that the Law of the Sea can fulfil in furthering the objectives delineated in other legal instruments, not necessarily part of the ocean governance (e.g. the Paris Agreement).

UNCLOS may also be regarded as a dynamic instrument, in addition to its comprehensive approach and universality. Its characterisation as a living organism, capable of promoting the looping of "updates", imposes the reflection on how to balance the legislative evolution necessary in the context of climate change and the stability relevant to reliable legal frameworks.[98]

For example, due to the omission of direct measures addressing the management of the marine biodiversity of Areas Beyond National Jurisdiction (ABNJ), states perceived it as essential to establish an international legally binding instrument (LBI) to regulate that matter under UNCLOS.[99]

The sophisticated architecture of the "Biodiversity Beyond National Jurisdiction (BBNJ) Agreement" attests to the complexity of the ocean regime, as it expressly acknowledges the climate emergency (e.g. Annex II—non-exhaustive list of capacity-building and transfer of marine technology measures). Nonetheless, the BBNJ Agreement falls short in its capacity to ensure (or at least to work on) not undermining existing agreements and conventions.[100]

In this scenario, the relationship between legal frameworks governing the Law of the Sea and biological diversity can be examined from both formal and substantive angles, with significant implications for core principles of marine environmental protection—highlighting the interplay between the UNCLOS and the Convention on Biological Diversity (CBD).

The negotiation process leading to the BBNJ Agreement has highlighted significant differences in terminology and regulatory scope between UNCLOS and the CBD, reflecting the complexity of their respective conceptual frameworks. These divergences underscore the need for continued examination of the interaction between the two regimes—not only throughout the treaty-making process under

[97] This essay will refrain from analysing contentious issues such as the potential adverse effects of geoengineering technologies as carbon sinks.

[98] Jakobsen et al. (2021). Op. cit., p. 377.

[99] This represents the third realisation of an implementation agreement, constituting a multilateral commitment addressing issues or perspectives not encompassed by UNCLOS. In addition to the BBNJ Agreement, UNCLOS has two other implementing agreements, namely the 1994 Agreement on mining-related activities in the Area and the 1995 UN Fish Stock Agreement on the management of migratory species.

[100] Article 4 of the BBNJ Agreement states that XX.

UN auspices, but also during the subsequent stages of interpreting and implementing the newly adopted legal provisions.[101]

This illustrates how the nature of interactions between different regimes—whether they are mutually reinforcing or largely operate in parallel—must be assessed in relation to specific contexts.[102] Determining the extent to which such interactions have occurred—or could occur–, and the potential advantages they may yield requires careful, context-specific analysis.[103]

These complexes can leverage synergies and provide institutional transformation, where collaborative arrangements are altered or supplanted due to political changes within the regime complex.[104] For example, climate issues cut across several spheres (e.g. environmental and socio-economic) and frequently exhibit transboundary characteristics.[105]

Furthermore, litigation cannot be overlooked in this context, as it plays a crucial role in addressing gaps or conflicts between regimes and in promoting dialogue across legal systems. ITLOS has, in fact, served as a key forum for addressing disputes that arise from regime interactions, particularly in cases where environmental protection and economic activities overlap.

The role of litigation in enhancing the coherence of international law is critical, as legal adjudication plays a key role in clarifying and strengthening the relationships between competing or overlapping regimes. Through judicial processes, tensions between these regimes can be addressed, contributing to the harmonisation of legal frameworks and fostering more effective cooperation in areas where legal domains intersect.[106]

Examining regime interaction within the framework of the Law of the Sea goes beyond theoretical inquiry. It holds practical relevance for international organisations, policymakers, and both national and international judicial bodies, which must continually assess the ways in which legal rules and frameworks intersect and influence one another.

New collaborative initiatives rarely emerge from the ground up—global governance solutions demand that international organisations either recognise the need to develop, coordinate, and enact policy resolutions within a broad regime complex or

[101] Matz-Lück and Jensen (2022). Op. Cit., p. 7.

[102] Alter and Raustiala (2018), p. 333.

[103] Matz-Lück and Jensen (2022). Op. Cit., p. 6.

[104] The relationship between ocean and climate change regimes may appear straightforward upon examining the examples mentioned earlier. However, a thorough analysis of the interconnections, as well as the identification of synergies and challenges present at the intersection of these regimes, is required. This is particularly pertinent in discerning how various mechanisms and bodies will effectively accommodate each other to ensure feasible coexistence or allow for overlaps when necessary. Such compliance, derived from a nuanced understanding of the interactions among these regimes, has the potential to foster a cohesive regulatory structure. Kim (2023), p. 192.

[105] Jakobsen et al. (2021). Op. cit., p. 384.

[106] Young (2012). Op. cit., p. 90.

strive to establish a cohesive regime that addresses all aspects of the problem. Although the latter solution is rarely adopted.[107]

A roadmap for a better governance of the ocean could be established by determining the potential challenges of the interaction between the ocean and the climate change regimes, as well as by identifying the opportunities for integration.[108] In this scenario, the ITLOS—at the centre of this complexity—has deemed it feasible to accommodate the COSIS's request and issue an AO.[109]

The Tribunal, thus, affirms the legitimacy of recognising the interactions among these regimes by providing the AO. This outcome examines the legal and scientific frameworks pertinent to climate change, serving as a strategic guide for enhanced ocean governance and fostering coherence within the existing legal structure.[110]

As both the climate and ocean regimes evolve in response to emerging global challenges, their interconnectedness becomes increasingly evident. Effective cooperation between them is not only desirable but essential for addressing the multifaceted threats posed by climate change.

Instead of concentrating only on possible conflicts between different treaty regimes—including the institutional issue of specific courts and tribunals interpreting the law –, however, we align with the view that the debate should be widened, emphasising the potential benefits of such interactions.[111]

5 Concluding Remarks

The ITLOS Advisory Opinion represents a significant milestone in the interaction of the climate change regime with the Law of the Sea. By reinforcing the importance of international cooperation in addressing emerging global challenges, the Tribunal not only clarified the scope of specific obligations under UNCLOS in the context of climate change but also signalled the growing normative relevance of regime interaction. This essay has examined the Advisory Opinion through the lens of the ocean-climate nexus, highlighting the increasingly integrated nature of legal and environmental governance.

As the international community comes to terms with the accelerating impacts of climate change, it becomes imperative to foster collaborative legal and institutional frameworks that transcend traditional governance silos. The evolution of legal instruments and cooperative efforts—exemplified by initiatives such as the COSIS

[107] Alter and Raustiala (2018). Op. cit., p. 337.

[108] Kim (2023). Op. cit., p. 186.

[109] Sabin Center For Climate Change Law (2024).

[110] Kim (2023). Op. cit., p. 186.

[111] One focus of the current debate is on identifying mutual supportiveness and potential benefits rather than enumerating the challenges. In: Matz-Lück and Jensen (2022). Op. cit., p. 5.

and the proactive developments within recent COP negotiations—reflects an emerging consensus on the interconnectedness of environmental regimes.

The path forward demands sustained engagement from all stakeholders—governments, scientists, civil society, and international organisations—to develop adaptive strategies that ensure the resilience of marine environments while combating climate change. By reinforcing the synergies between ocean health and climate action, we can not only safeguard vulnerable ecosystems but also enhance global efforts to achieve sustainable development for all, particularly for SIDS communities, which are on the front lines of these challenges.

Ultimately, addressing climate change effectively requires a comprehensive legal understanding of the ocean's central role in the global climate system. Legal frameworks must evolve to reflect the complexity of environmental interdependence, reinforcing collective responsibility and enabling coherent governance in an era of planetary transformation.

References

Abram N et al (2019) Framing and context of the report. In: IPCC special report on the ocean and cryosphere in a changing climate. Cambridge University Press, Cambridge

Alliance of Small Island States (AOSIS) (2023) We are Small Island Development States

Alter KJ, Raustiala K (2018) The rise of international regime complexity. Ann Rev Law Soc Sci 14:333

Barros-Platiau AF et al (2015) Correndo para o mar no antropoceno: a complexidade da governança dos oceanos e a estratégia brasileira de gestão dos recursos marinhos. Revista de Direito Internacional 12(1)

Commission of Small Island States on Climate Change and International Law (COSIS) (2022) About COSIS

Commonwealth Foundation (2021) Agreement for the establishment of the Commission of Small Island States on Climate Change and International Law

Conference of the Parties (COP) 27 (2022). Sharm el-Sheikh Implementation Plan. Decision -/CP.27

Cremean D et al (2021) Marine pollution law. In: Techera E et al (eds) Routledge handbook of international environmental law, 2nd edn. p 173

Food and Agriculture Organization of the United Nations (FAO) (2014) Natural Resources Management and the Environment in Small Island Development States (SIDS)

Gallo N, Victor D, Levin L (2017) Ocean commitments under the Paris Agreement. Nature Climate Change 7:835

Hoegh-Guldberg, O., Northrop, E., Lubchenco, J. (2019) The ocean is key to achieving climate and societal goals 365 Science, 1372

House of Commons International Development Committee (2024). The UK Small Island Developing States Strategy Fourth Report of session 2023–24

Information Unit for Conventions (IUC) (2000) Climate Change Information Sheet 17. The international response to climate change: A history. Information Unit for Conventions – UN Environment Programme

Intergovernmental Oceanographic Commission (IOC-UNESCO) (2017) One planet, one ocean: the Intergovernmental Oceanographic Commission of UNESCO, 2017

Intergovernmental Panel on Climate Change (IPCC) (2023) Summary for Policymakers. Climate Change 2023: Synthesis Report. A Report of the Intergovernmental Panel on Climate Change.

In: Core Writing Team, Lee H, Romero J (eds) Contribution of Working Groups I, II and III to the Sixth Assessment Report of the Intergovernmental Panel on Climate Change. IPCC, Geneva
IOC-UNESCO (2020) The Science we need for the ocean we want: the United Nations Decade of Ocean Science for Sustainable Development (2021–2030)
ITLOS (2024). Request for an Advisory Opinion submitted by the Commission of Small Island States on Climate Change and International Law (Request for Advisory Opinion submitted to the Tribunal)
Jakobsen IU, Johansen E, Nickels PP (2021) The Law of the sea as part of the climate-change regime complex. In: Johansen E, Busch SV, Jakobsen IU (eds) The law of the sea and climate change: solutions and constraints. Cambridge University Press, p 375
Keohane RO, Victor DG (2011) The regime complex for climate change. Perspect Polit 9(1):7–23
Kim SW (2023) Synergizing climate change and ocean regimes: a comprehensive international legal approach for ocean acidification governance. Ocean and Polar Research, p 192
Kumar P et al (2018) Determination of hierarchical relationships among sustainable development goals using interpretive structural modeling. Environ Dev Sustain 20:2120
Laffoley D, Baxter J et al (2021) Aquatic Conservation: Marine and Freshwater Ecosystems 31(6):1512–1534
Lubchenco J, Haugan PM (2023) Transformations for a sustainable ocean economy: a vision for protection, production and prosperity. In: The Blue Compendium: from knowledge to action for a sustainable ocean economy. Springer International Publishing, pp 907–915
Luomi M (2020) Global climate change governance: the search for effectiveness and universality. IISD Earth Negotiations Bulletin, n° 6
Matz-Lück N, Jensen Ø (2022) From fragmentation to interaction? A law of the sea perspective on regime interaction and interdisciplinary interfaces. In: The law of the sea normative: context and interactions with other legal regimes, 1st edn. Routledge, London, p 2
Mead L (2021) Small Islands, large oceans: voices on the frontlines of climate change. Earth Negotiations Bulletin
Morgera E et al (2023) Addressing the ocean-climate nexus in the BBNJ agreement: strategic environmental assessments, human rights and equity in ocean science. Int J Marine Coast Law 447
National Aeronautics and Space Administration (2024). The Ocean and Climate Change
National Oceanic and Atmospheric Administration (NOAA) (2024). How many oceans are there? Home, Ocean Facts, United States
Nusdeo AMO (2016) Pagamento por Serviços Ambientais. Direito Ambiental e Sustentabilidade. Eds. Arlindo Philippi Jr., Vladimir Passos de Freitas, Ana Luiza Silva Spíndola. Barueri, SP: Manole, 2016. Coleção Ambiental 18:619–643
Nwabueze JN, Techera E (2021). International environmental law and climate change. In: Techera E, Lindley J, Scott KN Telesetsky A (eds) Routledge handbook of international environmental law, 2nd edn
OECD (2016) The Ocean Economy in 2030. OECD Publishing, Paris, p 16. https://doi.org/10.1787/9789264251724-en
Popova E et al (2019) Ecological connectivity between the areas beyond national jurisdiction and coastal waters: Safeguarding interests of coastal communities in developing countries. Marine Policy 104:90–102
Pörtner HO, et al (2019) The ocean and cryosphere in a changing climate. In: IPCC Special Report on the Ocean and Cryosphere in a Changing Climate, 1155
Pörtner HO et al (2021) IPBES-IPCC co-sponsored workshop report on biodiversity and climate change. IPBES and IPCC
Sabin Center for Climate Change Law (2024) Request for an Advisory Opinion submitted by the Commission of Small Island States on Climate Change and International Law
Servaes J (2017) Introduction: from MDGs to SDGs. In: Sustainable development goals in the Asian context. Commun Cult Change Asia 2:9
Shelton C et al (2024) Disaster risk in Caribbean fisheries: how vulnerability is shaped and how it can be reduced in Dominica and Antigua and Barbuda. Marine Policy 160

Taylor P (2023) Ocean acidification and the anthropocene: an emergency response. In: Burdon PD, Martel J (eds) The Routledge handbook of law and the anthropocene, 1st edn

Telesetsky A, Bratspies R (2021) Marine environmental law: UNCLOS, ocean governance and fisheries. In: Techera E, Lindley J, Scott KN, Telesetsky A (eds) Routledge handbook of international environmental law, 2nd edn

UN (1992) United Nations Conference on Environment & Development Rio de Janerio, Brazil, 3 to 14 June 1992 AGENDA 21

UN (1994a) Global Conference on the Sustainable Development of Small Island Developing States, 26 April-6 May 1994, Bridgetown, Barbados

UN (1994b) Report of the Global Conference on the Sustainable Development of Small Island Developing States Bridgetown, Barbados, 26 April-6 May 1994

UN (2015) Transforming our World: the 2030 Agenda for sustainable development. A/RES/70/1, New York

UN(2020) Report of the Global Environment Facility to the Conference of the Parties. Framework Convention on Climate Change, FCCC/CP/2020/1, 23 October 2020

UN (2021) How is climate change impacting the world's ocean

United Nations Environment Programme (UNEP) (2016) The first global integrated marine assessment: World Ocean Assessment. The Group of Experts of the Regular Process. Lorna Inniss and Alan Simcock (Joint Coordinators) Amanuel Yoanes Ajawin; et al

United Nations Framework Convention on Climate Change (UNFCCC) (2023) First global stocktake Proposal by the President Draft decision -/CMA.5 Outcome of the first global stocktake. FCCC/PA/CMA/2023/L.17

Van Asselt H (2014) Regime interactions in global climate governance. In: The fragmentation of global climate governance: consequences and management of regime interactions. New Horizons in environmental and energy law series. Edward Elgar Publishing, p 210

Voigt C (2023) Oceans and climate change: implications for UNCLOS and the UN climate regime. In: The environmental rule of law for oceans: designing legal solutions. Cambridge University Press

Vousdoukas MI, Athanasiou P, Giardino A et al (2023) Small Island developing states under threat by rising seas even in a 1.5 °C warming world. Nat Sustain 6:1552–1564

World Climate Conference, 1979. XX

Young MA (2012) Regime interaction in creating, implementing and enforcing international law. In: Regime interaction in international law: facing fragmentation. Cambridge University Press, p 92

Zhang L, Bai E (2023) The regime complexes for global climate governance. Sustainability 15(11):4

Adriana Isabelle Barbosa Sá Leitão Di Pasquale is a PhD in International and European law fromat the University of Pisa (UniPi - Italy) and the Federal University of Ceará (UFC - Brazil).

Julia Schutz Veiga is Visiting fellow at the Nippon Foundation Ocean Voices Programme, University of Edinburgh, Edinburgh, UK; PhD Candidate at NOVA School of Law, Universidade Nova de Lisboa, Lisbon, Portugal.

Tarin Cristino Frota Mont'Alverne is Professor at the Faculty of Law of the Federal University of Ceará (UFC); PhD in international environmental law from the University of Paris and the University of São Paulo (USP); and master's degree in public international law from the University of Paris. Fortaleza, Brazil.

The Legal Treatment of Ecocide and Climate Litigation in Brazil: A Perspective on the Need for Behavior Change

Ana Elizabeth Lapa Wanderley Cavalcanti and Gianpaolo Poggio Smanio

1 Introduction

The global concern regarding environmental preservation is not new. Many environmental catastrophes could have been avoided. On a Brazilian national level, and more recently, we can cite the dam collapses in Mariana (MG) and Brumadinho (MG), as well as the fires in the Pantanal and the Amazon Rainforest and also the floods that occurred in the southern region of Brazil in 2024, as events that have caused extreme destruction to both the environment and the lives within it. It is important to highlight that such harmful events also affect the climate, bringing important changes and negative impacts.

However, climate change has been driving discussions and negotiations about the best ways to establish limits and regulations for human activities that may potentially cause environmental damage.

It should be noted that, even with the existence of international standards on the protection of the environment and climate, there is an issue that still needs to be consolidated, namely, the recognition of ecocide as a crime against humanity.

The major debate surrounding the global recognition of ecocide is tied to the jurisdiction of the International Criminal Court (ICC)—specifically, whether ecocide could be classified under the Rome Statute as a crime against humanity. On the other hand, there is also a call for the explicit inclusion of ecocide in the list of crimes under the ICC's jurisdiction.

The right to a balanced environment is classified as a fundamental right in the Brazilian Constitutional legislation (1988), encompassing both present and future generations. Despite the importance of this constitutional protection, given the

A. E. L. W. Cavalcanti (✉) · G. P. Smanio
Mackenzie Presbyterian University, São Paulo, Brazil
e-mail: ana.cavalcanti@mackenzie.br; gianpaolo.smanio@mackenzie.br

V. E. de Aquino et al. (eds.), *Climate Litigation in a Changing World*, Ius Gentium: Comparative Perspectives on Law and Justice 130,
https://doi.org/10.1007/978-3-032-05530-9_8

increasingly frequent and large-scale environmental degradation—resulting not only from global warming but also from high-impact human activity in favor of development at any cost or personal interests, which often places sustainability in a secondary position, there arises the need for more effective legislation. This legislation should address these major events of ecosystem destruction in the country, such as fires, storms, and floods, as environmental crimes of ecocide, with harsh and decisive consequences.

Some countries have already understood the importance of this issue and have incorporated the classification of the crime of ecocide into their legal frameworks, as seen in Vietnam, Russia, Ecuador, and France, for example. In pursuit of this recognition, two bills are currently under consideration in the Brazilian legislature. These aim to amend the Brazilian Environmental Crimes Law, including the criminal offense of ecocide, thus criminalizing acts that destroy nature on a large scale and pose definitive or hard-to-repair risks to the forms of life involved, whether plant, animal, or even human life.

In this regard, the deductive method was chosen for the development of this research, based on an analysis of Brazilian legal doctrine and legislative proposals and the Brazilian Supreme Court decisions about climate litigation. The main objective of research is to examine the possibility of recognizing the crime of ecocide in Brazil and on the international stage and what would be the beneficial of the climate litigation to the recognition of the crime of ecocide in Brazil. To achieve this, the research will first review the historical evolution and concept of ecocide, then analyze the current state of environmental protection within Brazilian legislation. Finally, it will demonstrate how Brazil has been addressing the criminalization of ecocide domestically and how this issue has been approached internationally in recent times, so that, in the end, cam be demonstrate the benefits of the judgment of climate and environmental litigation by the Brazilian Federal Supreme Court in search of a paradigm shift that allows the recognition of the crime of ecocide in Brazil.

2 Brief Notes on the History and Evolution of the Concept of Ecocide

The word *ecocide* comes from the combination of the Greek root *oikos*, meaning house or habitat, and the Latin suffix *cidium*, meaning to kill or destroy. The term is inspired by the concept of genocide, which relates to the intent to destroy an entire human group.

The act of destroying or devastating "enemy" land as a military strategy has occurred for centuries. The scorched earth tactic has been employed numerous times, with the goal of causing and deepening agricultural crises, and destroying food, shelters, and essential resources for the survival of local inhabitants. Over time, this destructive tactic has evolved, causing increasingly severe environmental damage. The Vietnam War can be considered a symbolic milestone in the emergence of biological weapons that cause large-scale ecological destruction. This moment in history intensified legislative efforts on a global scale to ban such techniques. Nevertheless, more work is needed to establish international regulations on ecocide.[1]

In light of this, various activists began using the term *ecocide* in the 1970s to condemn the United States for its use of the defoliant Agent Orange during the Vietnam War to destroy Asian jungles and expose enemy hideouts.

After this war episode and seeking to hold the U.S. government accountable for war crimes committed during the Vietnam War, the *Conference on War Crimes and American Conscience* took place in 1970. In this Conference, one of its participants, biologist Arthur W. Galston (2001), presented the findings of his work on herbicides, concluding that what had occurred in Vietnam should be called "ecocide." At that time, the term was defined as the "deliberate and permanent destruction of the environment in which a people can live as they choose."[2]

It is important to highlight that when coining the term *ecocide*, Arthur Galston compared it to the term *genocide*, which was defined in the 1948 *Convention on the Prevention and Punishment of the Crime of Genocide* as a result of acts committed during World War II and the work conducted at the Nuremberg Trials. Galston argued that ecocide, in the same manner, should be considered a crime against humanity due to the impact such crimes have on human beings.[3]

Following the dissemination of Galston's proposed definition, other authors offered their own definitions of the term. One notable example is Barry Weisberg,[4] who in his 1970 book *Ecocide in Indochina: The Ecology of War*, defined *ecocide* as the "premeditated assault by a nation and its resources against the individuals, culture, and biological fabric of another country and its surroundings." As Keith Buchanan[5] pointed out, this definition proved to be more comprehensive than Galston's, as it identified the specific targets of the attacks, including the population, culture, and nature, not just the human beings who live or could live in the affected territory.

The geography professor at Victoria University of Wellington, Keith McPherson Buchanan, defined ecocide as the "destruction of the living environment that would sustain yet-to-be-born groups," also drawing a comparison to the crime of genocide. He believed that the techniques used and refined in Indochina marked the next stage in the means of warfare utilized after that event.

Furthermore, regarding the definition of the term *ecocide*, during the *Stockholm Conference on the Environment* in 1972, a document titled the *Convention on Ecocidal War* was created, calling on the UN to recognize ecocide as an

[1] Kowalska (2023), p. 5.

[2] Zierler (2011), p. 114.

[3] Zierler (2011), p. 19.

[4] Weisberg (1970), p. 04.

[5] Buchanan (1971).

international war crime. However, ecocide ultimately did not make it into the text of the Stockholm Convention. Despite this, it is important to note that the *Stockholm Declaration on the Human Environment* in 1972 emphasized the need for legal accountability of states, individuals, and legal entities for the effects caused by human activities on the environment. This indirectly encompasses the issue of ecocide, referring to the extensive damage caused by humans that significantly alters the environment.

Similarly, the topic of ecocide was revisited in 1977 in an effort to expand the scope of the 1948 *Genocide Convention*. The *Subcommission on Prevention of Discrimination and Protection of Minorities* sought to recognize the inclusion of ecocide and cultural genocide in its list of crimes.

3 Concept and Legal Treatment of Ecocide in Current Times

The most widely adopted definition of ecocide in the contemporary international community is the one formulated by Scottish lawyer and environmentalist Polly Higgins.[6] According to Higgins, ecocide is defined as "the extensive damage to, destruction of, or loss of one or more ecosystems, by human action or other causes, to such an extent that the enjoyment of the right to peace and quality of life by the inhabitants of that territory has been severely impaired." In this sense, Polly Higgins argues in her book *Eradicating Ecocide* for the need to create an amendment to the Rome Statute, classifying ecocide as an autonomous crime, the fifth crime against peace.[7,8]

Thus, the importance of international legislation in the evolution and history of ecocide becomes evident.[9] It is worth noting that the Rome Statute addresses crimes of such gravity that they pose a threat to the peace, security, and well-being of humanity, such as genocide, crimes against humanity, war crimes, and the crime of aggression[10] [11] (Article 5).[12]

In this sense, Claudia Loureiro,[13] states that:

> The historical interpretation of ecocide contributes to the consolidation of the understanding that this crime is covered by the Rome Statute, either as a crime against humanity or as genocide, since it is a consequence of the reinterpretation of the meaning of these crimes,

[6] Higgins (2015).

[7] A law of ecocide, as the 5th crime against Peace, could effectively protect the planet and its future by addressing environmental crimes and promoting an Earth jurisprudence approach (Higgins 2015).

[8] Higgins (2015).

[9] Ecocide Law (2024).

[10] The inclusion of the crime of aggression occurred in the fourth version of the Statute in 2018.

[11] The crime of aggression is defined as the use of armed force by one state against the sovereignty, territorial integrity, or political independence of another state.

[12] Brazil (2002).

[13] Loureiro (2023), p. 346.

which should be applied in the contemporary context and not merely from the perspective of modernity.[14]

Facing this interpretation offered by the Brazilian professor Claudia Loureiro, it is also important to remember that the Rome Statute, known as the Rome Statute of the International Criminal Court, began to be outlined in 1994 by the UN International Law Commission, and in 1995 the first negotiations on its text commenced. At this point, the PrepCom, a preparatory committee, was created with the objective of proposing a draft of the Statute. The Committee met several times between 1996 and 1998, when it then presented the draft text. Thus, the international treaty was developed to establish the powers and competencies of the ICC, defining its principles, jurisdiction, composition, and functions. In 2002, the necessary quorum for the establishment of the International Criminal Court was reached, and it began its activities in 2003. Brazil became a signatory to the Treaty in 2002 when it ratified it with Decree 4,388/2002.[15]

It is further argued that ecocide is anticipated, even if in an abstract form, as a crime against humanity, since Article 7(k) of the Rome Statute, and consequently of Decree 4,388/2002, provides for "other inhumane acts of a similar character, intentionally causing great suffering, or seriously affecting physical or mental integrity or health."[16]

In this context, according to the Rome Statute, the ICC is empowered to punish acts that cause environmental damage in the context of war, as can be inferred from the reading of Article 8, item 2, letter iv:

1. The Court shall have jurisdiction in respect of war crimes in particular when committed as part of a plan or policy or as part of a large-scale commission of such crimes.
2. For the purpose of this Statute, "war crimes" means:
   (a) Grave breaches of the Geneva Conventions of 12 August 1949, namely, any of the following acts directed against persons or property protected under the provisions of the relevant Geneva Convention:
      (i) Wilful killing;
      (ii) Torture or inhuman treatment, including biological experiments;
      (iii) Wilfully causing great suffering or serious injury to body or health;
      (iv) Extensive destruction or appropriation of property, not justified by military necessity and carried out unlawfully and wantonly;

[14] In the original text: A interpretação histórica do ecocídio contribui para a consolidação do entendimento de que referido crime está contemplado pelo Estatuto de Roma, como crime contra a humanidade ou como genocídio, uma vez que é decorrência da releitura do significado desses crimes, que deve ser aplicado no contexto contemporâneo e não apenas sob a perspectiva da modernidade.

[15] Brazil (2002).

[16] Brazil (2002).

(v) Compelling a prisoner of war or other protected person to serve in the forces of a hostile power;
(vi) Wilfully depriving a prisoner of war or other protected person of the rights of a fair and regular trial;
(vii) Unlawful deportation or transfer, or unlawful confinement;
(viii) Taking of hostages.

(b) (…)

On the other hand, the Rome Statute, in its Article 7, presents the concept of crimes against humanity, where ecocide could be categorized under letter K of Article 7, as follows:

Crimes Against Humanity
Article 7

1. For the purposes of this Statute, "crime against humanity" means any of the following acts when committed as part of a widespread or systematic attack directed against any civilian population, with knowledge of the attack:

(a) Murder;
(b) Extermination;
(c) Enslavement;
(d) Deportation or forcible transfer of a population;
(e) Imprisonment or other severe deprivation of physical liberty in violation of fundamental norms of international law;
(f) Torture;
(g) Rape, sexual slavery, enforced prostitution, forced pregnancy, enforced sterilization, or any other form of sexual violence of comparable gravity;
(h) Persecution against any identifiable group or collectivity on political, racial, national, ethnic, cultural, religious, gender as defined in paragraph 3, or other grounds that are universally recognized as impermissible under international law, in connection with any act referred to in this paragraph or any crime within the jurisdiction of the Court;
(i) Enforced disappearance of persons;
(j) The crime of apartheid;
(k) Other inhumane acts of a similar character intentionally causing great suffering, or serious injury to body or to mental or physical health.

2. (….)

It is evident that the Rome Statute does not limit the ICC's jurisdiction to war crimes alone, as can be seen from the reading of the mentioned Article 5 of the Rome Statute, which states that it is the competence of the ICC to judge the crimes: (a) The crime of genocide; (b) Crimes against humanity; (c) War crimes; (d) The crime of aggression.

And, that is a fact, many environmental damage events that have occurred and are currently taking place, which could be considered ecocide, occur outside a war environment, meaning they also happen in times of peace.

Another significant point of reflection regarding the recognition of ecocide as a similar crime to genocide is to check the meaning of genocide in the Rome Statute (Article 6), which states that "genocide" means any of the following acts committed with intent to destroy, in whole or in part, a national, ethnical, racial or religious group, as such: killing members of the group; causing serious bodily or mental harm to members of the group; deliberately inflicting on the group conditions of life calculated to bring about its physical destruction in whole or in part; imposing measures intended to prevent births within the group; forcibly transferring children of the group to another group.

It is necessary to note that for genocide, as defined in the Rome Statute, the acts described in the definition must be committed with the intent to destroy, in whole or in part, a national, ethnic, racial, or religious group.[17] And, it is relevant to think if for crime of ecocide it is also necessary the intention to cause the environment damage. That is an important question. In environmental degradation, the intention is often not clear in the harmful result, but the harmful conduct is certainly repeatedly negligent, and the intention is reflected in the idea of not caring, not taking precautions, simply letting it happen.

On the other hand, crime against humanity, also provided for in the Rome Statute, is not tied to the intention to exterminate a particular group of persons, a specific group, but rather to a series of generalized attacks on any segment or part of the human population. In this respect, a more nuanced examination of the legal treatment of ecocide, both at the international and national levels, as a crime against humanity appears to be quite helpful.

However, including ecocide as a crime against humanity does not provide an entirely ideal framework for legal actions against conduct that results in serious environmental damage. Nonetheless, for the time being, it seems to be the best course of action[18] until an amendment to the Rome Statute is made to formally include ecocide as a crime subject to the jurisdiction of the ICC.

It's also important to highlight that in September 2016, the Office of the Prosecutor of the ICC[19] published a document titled *Policy Paper on Case Selection and Prioritization*. This document indicates that, given the significance of the issue, the ICC should prioritize the selection of cases involving environmental damage: "[...] it will pay particular attention to the prosecution of crimes under the Statute that are committed through, or that result in, inter alia, the destruction of the environment, the illegal exploitation of natural resources, or the illegal appropriation of land."[20]

---

[17] Gordilho and Ravazzano (2017), p. 692.

[18] Panigaj and Berníková (2023), p. 08.

[19] ICC (2016), p. 5.

[20] ICC (2016), p. 5.

Meanwhile, it should be noted that the *Policy Paper on Case Selection and Prioritization* is an administrative document, lacking binding force, and is used solely as a working guide for the Office of the Prosecutor, which does not have the authority to establish a new crime within the Rome Statute on its own. Nevertheless, the emphasis placed on environmental cases demonstrates the importance of the topic and the potential for advancing discussions around the legal recognition of ecocide.

The need for the legal definition and recognition of ecocide as a crime in the ICC was driven in the past decade by civil and scientific movements that have worked to define concepts, treatments, and establish policies to combat environmental violations considered as ecocide.[21] In this context, the **Stop Ecocide**[22] campaign emerged, with one of its main voices being Jojo Mehta, president of the **Stop Ecocide Foundation**[23] (2019), and international law jurist Valérie Cabanes, spokesperson for the movement **End Ecocide on Earth**. Their aim is to achieve concrete effects on international legislation as well as on the legislation of the member countries of the Court.

These international civil society movements have been and continue to be extremely important for discussing the issue and fostering greater engagement from civil society, which has the power to drive the legal debate on the subject. The discussions stemming from these movements have led to the current legal definition of ecocide.

A new classification of a crime against humanity was proposed by a Panel of Independent Experts, an international commission of 12 jurists, in 2020, convened by the Stop Ecocide Foundation at the request of Swedish lawmakers. At that time, an extensive public consultation was held, and the final draft of the document was completed in 2021. This text was then submitted to the countries signatories of the Rome Statute to initiate discussions on the recognition of ecocide at the international level.[24]

The text of the proposal begins with the amendment of paragraph 2 of the Preamble of the Rome Statute, aiming to incorporate the following phrase:

> Concerned that the environment is daily threatened by severe destruction and deterioration, gravely endangering natural and human systems worldwide. (…).

Subsequently, the document suggests an amendment to Article 8 of the Rome Statute, which would be rephrased as follows:

> For the purpose of this Statute, "ecocide" means unlawful or wanton acts committed with knowledge that there is a substantial likelihood of severe and either widespread or long-term damage to the environment being caused by those acts.

---

[21] Currently, the definition of ecocide provided by the Stop Ecocide movement is: "unlawful or wanton acts committed with knowledge that there is a substantial likelihood of severe, widespread, or long-term damage to the environment caused by those acts." https://ecocidelaw.com/. Accessed on 08.20.2024.

[22] Stop Ecocide (2024a).

[23] Stop Ecocide (2024b).

[24] Stop Ecocide Foundation (2021).

Finally, as a proposal for the amendment of Article 1, the following definitions are suggested:

For the purpose of paragraph 1:

a. "Wanton" means with reckless disregard for damage which would be clearly excessive in relation to the social and economic benefits anticipated;
b. "Severe" means damage which involves very serious adverse changes, disruption or harm to any element of the environment, including grave impacts on human life or natural, cultural or economic resources;
c. "Widespread" means damage which extends beyond a limited geographic area, crosses state boundaries, or is suffered by an entire ecosystem or species or a large number of human beings;
d. "Long-term" means damage which is irreversible or which cannot be redressed through natural recovery within a reasonable period of time;
e. "Environment" means the Earth, its biosphere, cryosphere, lithosphere, hydrosphere and atmosphere, as well as outer space.

In light of the above, it becomes evident that there is a need for international recognition of ecocide as a crime against humanity, a threat that requires solutions both at the level of domestic legislation and through a global strategy aimed at the future.[25] However, while such recognition is not yet directly implemented, some states have already opted to include ecocide in their national legislation, and others are studying and preparing for this, such as Brazil, a situation that will be explored further in this work.

In this context, the European Union, for instance, approved a Directive in March 2024 with strict sanctions to protect the environment. This Directive includes a qualifier that applies when an infringement referred to in the directive is committed intentionally and causes irreversible or lasting destruction or damage to the environment. This situation can be viewed as "comparable"[26] to ecocide, marking the beginning of a new era in the legal treatment of environmental crimes.[27]

4 Brief Comments on Environmental Protection and Recent Environmental Events in Brazil

The protection of the environment in Brazil is provided for in the Federal Constitution of 1988, which in Article 225 states: "Everyone has the right to an ecologically balanced environment, which is a common good essential to a healthy quality of life, and it is the duty of the Government and the community to defend and preserve it for present and future generations."

[25] Kowalska (2023), p. 01.

[26] Stop Ecocide (2024b).

[27] Council of Europe (2024).

It is evident from the wording of the Federal Constitution that Brazilian legislation qualifies the right to an ecologically balanced environment as a fundamental right, serving as a value to ensure human dignity for present and future generations and, more broadly, for all forms of life, with the aim of ensuring the continuity of life on the planet as well as sustainable development. With this multifaceted nature, possessing dual dimensions—individual and collective—the constitutional legislation also imposes a duty regarding the protection and non-degradation of the environment, as a responsibility of both the Government and the entire community.[28]

As a Brazilian professor Solange Teles da Silva[29] demonstrates, the duty not to degrade the environment should be viewed as a general obligation involving both positive actions and negative conduct, including abstentions in the development of human activities, encompassing those that involve the use, enjoyment, and exercise of property rights.

On the other hand, the duty to defend and protect the environment also includes the responsibility of landowners where natural resources and various biomes are found, to facilitate their transmission to future generations.[30]

Brazil has a robust legal framework for environmental protection, supported by conventions and international documents such as the Stockholm Conference of 1972, the Kyoto Protocol of 1997, the UN Convention on Biological Diversity of 1992, the UN Framework Convention on Climate Change of 1992, and the recent 2030 Agenda for Sustainable Development. This framework is anchored in the Federal Constitution of 1988 and in laws such as the National Environmental Policy (Law 6,938 of 1981), the Environmental Crimes Law (Law 9,605 of 1998), the National System of Nature Conservation Units (Law 9,985 of 2000), Law 12,187 of 2009, which deals with the National Policy on Climate Change and the Native Vegetation Protection Law, known as the Brazilian Forest Code (Law 12,651 of 2012), which revoked the previous code from 1965. However, challenges persist, particularly due to recent modifications to environmental policies that pose a threat to the effectiveness of the legal system for environmental protection. It is important to highlight that active participation from civil society and the scientific community is crucial to ensuring the continuous protection of the environment in Brazil.

The recently revised Brazilian Forest Code addresses crucial aspects of terrestrial ecosystems and land tenure, including the protection of remnants of agricultural fragments and cultivated lands. The National Environmental Policy Law was the first to include a legal definition of the environment and established the National Environmental System, as well as the National Environment Council. However, Brazil has been experiencing legislative and judicial measures that, in some ways, weaken environmental protection, resulting in increased deforestation and reduced environmental fines.

[28] Silva (2014), p. 172.

[29] Silva (2014), p. 175.

[30] Silva (2014), p. 178.

It is also crucial to highlight that active participation from civil society and the scientific community is essential to ensuring the continuous protection of the environment. This issue has raised concerns and intense social debates, particularly due to significant and devastating climate events that have changed the lives and daily routines of people.

Environmental disasters and degradation in Brazil are not rare, but since 2015, devastating events have been noted, such as the collapse of the Fundão dam at the Mariana mine in Minas Gerais. This event resulted in numerous fatalities and caused significant environmental and climate imbalance in the surrounding area, inflicting irreparable damage to the Doce River, forever changing the lives of hundreds or thousands of people who depended directly or indirectly on the river. This is an event that people will have difficulty forgetting—a tragedy to be remembered forever.

Another case of overwhelming proportions occurred in 2019 with the collapse of the dam at the Córrego do Feijão mine in Brumadinho, Minas Gerais. It was an unimaginable tragedy for the people of Brumadinho and for all those who were directly or indirectly affected by the resulting environmental and social imbalance. Even today, the local population continues to feel the impacts of the destruction caused—something that will persist for many years to come.

It is a fact that such events have been fundamental for legal changes regarding the safety and management of mining dams in the country. However, it is always important to remember that we should not wait for damage when it comes to environmental protection; we must think in terms of precaution and prevention of environmental damage, which, in most cases, is irreparable or difficult to remedy, affecting all of humanity.

Unfortunately, Brazil has long suffered from environmental damage, and besides the cases mentioned above, numerous episodes of oil spills in rivers and oceans along the Brazilian coast can be cited, particularly the wildfires in the *cerrado, pantanal*, and national forests.

It is known that climate change, recognized as changes in climate and temperature patterns caused by human activity, directly or indirectly, affects and will continue to affect the world as a whole, whether through global warming (the increase in the planet's average surface temperature) or the consequences that arise from this temperature increase, such as droughts, wildfires, melting polar ice caps, storms, floods, rising sea levels, and water scarcity.[31] Beyond all this, we must also consider the impact of these Brazilian events on the global climate, given that Brazil holds a large portion of the world's green area and is a cradle of biodiversity.

This environmental imbalance was driven by the Industrial Revolution and has been exacerbated by human activity since the eighteenth century, especially with the increased burning of fossil fuels such as oil, natural gas, and coal. According to the UN,[32] the history of environmental imbalance intensified after World War II,

[31] UNICEF (2024a, b).

[32] UN (2020).

which marked the beginning of the nuclear age, creating a new type of pollution and increasing global concern about environmental degradation.

Notably, other factors are also directly related to the current environmental imbalance. For example, deforestation, the unchecked growth of industrial activities, land-use conversion, and even the expansion of agriculture and its limitless exploitation. All these and other human-driven activities emit large amounts of CO_2, the main greenhouse gas, which has been a driving force behind global warming. However, as Elizabeth Mrema, the deputy executive director of UNEP,[33] stated, the current generation is the first to fully understand the immense threats to the Earth, and it may be the last generation with the chance to reverse the course of destruction. The priority now is, without a doubt, the restoration of ecosystems, avoiding irreversible effects.

Analyzing the above statement, it is important to recognize the existence of the problem, namely, the growing and irreversible destruction of the environment. However, stating that the current generation is fully aware of the problem prompts reflection. It is essential to highlight that a large group, typically acting out of self-interest and economic motivations, seems not to have acknowledged this catastrophe and continues to pollute despite numerous indications from the environment that something is wrong. Unfortunately, this is a reality that needs to be confronted. It is indeed a challenging reality, but it is a necessary battle. Hence, the importance of public policies and, particularly, legislation at both the international and national levels.

The increased use of fossil fuels has enabled greater economic development but has also resulted in higher levels of pollution. Additionally, other factors such as deforestation, accelerated industrialization, land-use conversion, and agriculture without the necessary care and limits have similarly contributed to the rising levels of CO2 in the atmosphere, which is the primary greenhouse gas.[34]

It is evident that the concern over the destruction of nature is not recent; however, much still needs to be done. Despite the existence of extensive discussions, protection organizations, international legislation, etc., there remains little effectiveness in combating the significant ecological degradations caused directly or indirectly by humans, especially regarding environmental protection through legal channels. Indeed, there are international documents aiming to ensure the protection of a balanced environment; nevertheless, more action is required. We must perceive the current moment as it deserves. Environmental damage is no longer local or regional, as it might have been treated in the past. In today's interconnected society,[35] the scope of these disasters and degrading events impacts all of humanity, affecting both present and future generations. Therefore, it is essential to address the issue on local, regional, and international levels. In this regard, the importance of strengthening the study and regulation of ecocide becomes clear.

---

[33] UN (2024).

[34] UNICEF (2022).

[35] Castells (2016).

5 Legislation on Environmental Protection and Large-Scale Environmental Degradations: The Legal Treatment of Ecocide in Brazil

In Brazil, although ecocide is a relatively new topic and still not widely discussed legally, movements have been underway since 2019 to create laws addressing the subject. The changes proposed so far aim to amend the Environmental Crimes Law of 1988. The first movement occurred in 2019, following the dam collapse in Mariana, Minas Gerais, in 2015, and Brumadinho, Minas Gerais, in 2019, with a draft bill related to the recognition of ecocide, addressing issues such as ecological disasters and dam breaches. The second significant movement took place in 2023 with the presentation of another draft bill focused on the recognition of ecocide, grounded in the significant episodes of climate change.

Thus, in 2019, the Brazilian Chamber of Deputies[36] approved Draft Bill 2,787/19,[37] which proposes amendments to the provisions of Law 9,605/98 (Environmental Crimes Law),[38] recognizing the crime of ecocide and the criminal conduct of those responsible for disasters related to dam breaches. The crime is defined as follows:

> Article 54-A. Causing an environmental disaster with significant destruction of flora or mortality of animals, resulting in atmospheric, water, or soil contamination recognized in a forensic report:
>
> Penalty - Imprisonment from four (4) to twelve (12) years, and a fine.
>
> §1. If the crime is negligent:
>
> Penalty - Detention from one (1) to three (3) years, and a fine.
>
> §2. If the crime results in the death of a person, the penalty is applied independently of the penalty provided for the crime of homicide.[39]

In the legislative process, the 2019 Draft Bill[40] underwent modifications during the analysis and judgment phase in the Chamber of Deputies. Changes were made to the original text regarding the concept of ecocide and a reduction in the proposed penalty, which was initially set at a maximum of 20 years of imprisonment but was

---

[36] Chamber of Deputies (2024).

[37] Brazil (2019).

[38] Brazil (1998).

[39] Art. 54-A. Dar causa a desastre ambiental com destruição significativa da flora ou mortandade de animais, do qual decorra contaminação atmosférica, hídrica ou do solo reconhecida em laudo pericial: Pena – reclusão, de 4 (quatro) a 12 (doze) anos, e multa. § 1° Se o crime é culposo: Pena – detenção, de 1 (um) a 3 (três) anos, e multa. § 2° Se do crime resulta morte de pessoa, a pena é aplicada independentemente da pena prevista para o crime de homicídio.

[40] Brazil (2019).

lowered to 12 years, allowing for the accumulation of penalties with homicide when applicable.

After its approval, the 2019 Draft Bill[41] was forwarded to the Senate Federal's Committees on Environment (CMA) and Constitution and Justice (CCJ).[42] In this legislative process, Senator Alessandro Vieira was appointed as the rapporteur for the bill in the CMA and did not add anything to the proposal. However, Senator Luiz Carlos Heinze requested a review of the bill and presented an amendment to alter the wording of proposed Article 54-A. Following this movement, a new report was presented by Senator Alessandro Vieira, revising Article 54-A to read: "Causing an environmental disaster of large proportion or producing a state of public calamity, with significant destruction of flora or mortality of animals, due to contamination or pollution of the atmosphere, water, or soil." Additionally, the rapporteur proposed the inclusion of a new article, Article 54-B, aimed at defining and punishing the actions of public agents who unjustifiably fail to immediately provide containment measures and damage reduction, as well as to repair the area affected by an environmental disaster. Currently, Draft Bill 2,787/19 has been pending in the Federal Senate since late 2019 and has been awaiting the appointment of a rapporteur since February 2023.[43]

Subsequently, in 2023, another Draft Bill 2,933/23 was presented in the Chamber of Deputies, also seeking to define the crime of ecocide by inserting it into Law 9,605/98 - the Environmental Crimes Law (Brazil, 1998). The proposed text is as follows:

> Article 69-B. Engaging in illegal or reckless acts with the awareness that they create a substantial probability of severe and widespread or long-term damage to the environment:
>
> Penalty - Imprisonment for 5 to 15 years and a fine.
>
> §1. For the purposes of the provisions in the caput, the following definitions apply:
>
> I - Illegal act: one that is contrary to current law, license, or authorization issued by environmental authorities.
>
> II - Reckless act: one carried out with the knowledge of the risk of creating clearly excessive damage in relation to the anticipated social and economic benefits of an activity;
>
> III - Severe damage: damage resulting in very serious adverse changes, disturbances, or harm to any element of the environment, including significant impacts on human life, biodiversity, or natural, cultural, or economic resources;
>
> IV - Widespread damage: damage extending beyond a limited geographical area, crossing national borders, or affecting an entire ecosystem or species or a large number of beings;

[41] Brazil (2019).

[42] Federal Senate (2024).

[43] National Congress (2024).

V - Long-term damage: irreversible damage or damage that cannot be repaired through natural recovery within a reasonable timeframe.

§2. The crime of ecocide targets high-level executives responsible for decisions that lead to the promotion, planning, financing, agency, contracting, management, and execution of activities that fall under the provisions of this article's caput.

§3. The crime of ecocide does not apply to indigenous and traditional populations that continue to live in their traditional manner and in their territories.[44]

Draft Bill 2,933/23 proposed in the Chamber of Deputies originated from concerns regarding the increase in damage, degradation, and large-scale environmental crimes that have recently affected the world. It aligns with the international proposal for the criminalization of ecocide. Notably, it targets, in §2, the highest level of responsibility, including executives responsible for decisions that manage the execution of activities defined by law as ecocide.

In the justification for the proposed Draft Bill 2,933/23, the rationale for its presentation emphasizes the need to adopt a legal system capable of "curbing the increasing and uncontrolled environmental degradation driven by illegal and unjustified agro-industrial extractive activities, which fuel climate change, especially in the regions of the Cerrado and the Amazon". The proposed law further highlights that this growing and uncontrolled environmental degradation "generates a series of other forms of systematic and widespread violence against vulnerable people and social groups who depend on forests and nature for their livelihood, particularly indigenous and traditional populations within these biomes."[45]

---

[44] Art. 69-B. Praticar atos ilegais ou temerários com a consciência de que eles geram uma probabilidade substancial de danos graves e generalizados ou de longo prazo ao meio ambiente:

Pena - reclusão de 5 a 15 anos e multa.

§ 1° Para efeitos do disposto no caput, consideram-se:

I - ato ilegal: aquele em desacordo com a lei vigente, licença ou autorização expedida pelos órgãos ambientais.

II - ato temerário: aquele com conhecimento do risco de se criarem danos claramente excessivos em relação aos benefícios sociais e econômicos previstos em uma atividade;

III – dano grave: dano que implique em mudanças adversas muito graves, perturbação ou dano a qualquer elemento do meio ambiente, incluindo graves impactos à vida humana, à biodiversidade ou aos recursos naturais, culturais ou econômicos;

IV - dano generalizado: dano que se estenda para além de uma área geográfica limitada, cruza as fronteiras nacionais ou é sofrido por todo um ecossistema ou espécie ou por um grande número de seres;

V – dano de longo prazo: dano irreversível ou que não pode ser reparado por meio de recuperação natural dentro de um período de tempo razoável.

§ 2° O crime de ecocídio dirige-se a altos dirigentes responsáveis por decisões que levem à promoção, planejamento, financiamento, agenciamento, contratação, gerenciamento e execução de atividades que se enquadrem na hipótese prevista no caput deste artigo.

§ 3° O crime de ecocídio não se aplica a populações indígenas e tradicionais que sigam vivendo em seu modo tradicional e em seus territórios.

[45] Chamber of Deputies (2024).

The Draft Bill from 2023 is still in progress, awaiting the designation of a rapporteur in the Committee on Constitution, Justice, and Citizenship (CCJC) since November 2023. In the Committee on Environment and Sustainable Development (CMADS), the rapporteur, Deputy Nilto Tatto, has already expressed support for the text as presented, and the report was approved in November 2023. In August 2024, another Draft Bill (DB 2,875/24) on the same subject was appended to the 2023 Draft Bill.

The new Draft Bill presented in 2024 (DB 2,875/24) also aims to classify ecocide as a crime but proposes a new wording for Articles 54-A and 54-C outlined in Draft Bill 2,787/19, which has already been approved by the Chamber of Deputies and is awaiting judgment in the National Senate. Additionally, it includes a proposal for a new article, Article 54-C, which mandates that the Union, states, municipalities, and the Federal District, within their respective jurisdictions, must promote actions to prevent and mitigate the effects of ecocide, with the objective of ensuring environmental protection and the preservation of life in all its forms.[46]

It is evident that after the catastrophic events in Mariana (MG) and Brumadinho (MG), in 2015 and 2019, Brazil has witnessed a series of social movements advocating for stricter accountability and penalties in cases of large-scale environmental crimes. As of today, actions seeking accountability from the companies involved in the aforementioned events have not been concluded, highlighting that Brazilian justice still has much progress to make in handling such cases. For this to occur, significant changes to criminal legislation are necessary, particularly emphasizing the importance of amending the Environmental Crimes Law (Brazil, 1998), as sought by the aforementioned Draft Bills.

It is important to note that both Draft Bills (Brazil, 2019 and 2023) address ecocide. They emerged during periods of massive environmental degradation and served as an urgent response for accountability. The 2019 proposal has a more conceptual focus on defining and criminalizing the act, while the 2023 proposal, due to its timing, not only emphasizes the formal recognition of ecocide as a criminal offense but also reflects administrative and economic concerns, as well as a broader and stricter accountability with more severe legal consequences. This is particularly interesting since the existence of harsher penalties or fines can create a preventive and educational effect. Therefore, it can be observed that both Draft Bills under consideration share the same goal but with different intentions. Nonetheless, their existence highlights Brazil's concern with legally and criminally formalizing the crime of ecocide. However, it is clear that the sluggishness of the Brazilian legislative process places the country among those with "backward" legislation. For a nation with such rich biodiversity and ecological importance as Brazil, being "behind" in protecting and preventing complex environmental crimes like ecocide is not an ideal position.

[46] Chamber of Deputies (2024).

While there is no uniform treatment of the crime of ecocide at local or regional levels, international law assumes a crucial and necessary role. Hence, recognizing the jurisdiction of the ICC to adjudicate cases of ecocide becomes essential.

6 Reflections on the Legal Recognition of the Crime of Ecocide in Current Times

In light of the relevance of the topic and the need to develop more adequate and effective mechanisms for environmental protection, one might question: to what extent would the criminalization of ecocide and its introduction into the catalog of crimes against humanity contribute to the enforcement of constitutional environmental protection? For those advocating for the enhancement of legal and penal protection of the environment, defining environmental crimes as crimes against humanity and peace would not only be more effective but would also yield positive results, enabling the accountability of countries and companies before international criminal justice. A solid international environmental regulation would mean that the adoption of risk strategies could compel agents to face international consequences. As a signatory to the Rome Statute, Brazil recognizes the jurisdiction of the ICC and the new provision. In the case of proven ecocide, victims would be allowed to appeal to the Court to seek the conviction of the perpetrators of the crime.

However, even if ecocide is recognized as a crime against humanity, the underlying hypothesis guiding this essay suggests that the categorization and criminal accountability before Brazilian and international courts could lead to the erroneous conclusion that criminal legislation is the ideal path to solving the severe contemporary environmental crisis. Ultimately, the creation of the penal types in question is unlikely to change the growing environmental degradation in the country, serving, as occurred in Brazil with Law 9,605/98, merely as a symbolic response to the problem. Even if the ICC concluded that ecocide should be classified as a crime against humanity, it is important to highlight the existence of legal, economic, and political obstacles that could significantly hinder the realization of the Court's understanding.

In this context, one may question whether the ICC is the appropriate court for such a purpose. As Rodrigo Andrade Viviani points out:[47]

> Therefore, due to the points of contact between environmental protection and human rights, it is worth asking whether certain environmental aggressions, with the potential to compromise elements of the biosphere (more precisely, those that would affect the living conditions of humans on the planet), could be criminalized within the scope of International Criminal Law, in the sense of being subjected to the judgment of an International Criminal Court.[48]

---

[47] Viviani (2018), p. 2.

[48] Por isso, em razão dos pontos de contato entre a proteção do meio ambiente e os direitos humanos, caberia indagar se determinadas agressões ambientais, com potencialidade de comprometer

It is important to note that the International Criminal Court, established in 1998 and regulated by the Rome Statute, is a permanent court located in The Hague, Netherlands, responsible for judging individuals who have committed war crimes, aggression, genocide, or crimes against humanity, and who have not been adequately punished within the internal systems of each state.

Moreover, it is the successor to several ad hoc international courts, such as those in Nuremberg, Tokyo, and the former Yugoslavia. As a permanent court, the ICC distinguishes itself from its predecessors by adhering to a fundamental principle of Criminal Law: the principle of legality, as its regulation by the Rome Statute allows for crimes to be established in advance without infringing upon the rights of the accused, as was the case previously.

By operating according to the principle of complementarity, the ICC exercises jurisdiction only when the internal justice system of each member state is unable or unwilling to act or when there is fraud. The ICC has played a significant role in combating impunity, especially of heads of state or military leaders, as seen in the numerous convictions of individuals from African nationalities, who hold substantial influence in their countries and thus have escaped punishment domestically.

Furthermore, the Court stands out for providing for the accountability of individuals, unlike other traditional international courts, such as the International Court of Justice, where only states are held accountable. In this regard, the Court's role is to promote the individual application of penalties, preventing individuals responsible for unimaginable atrocities from remaining unpunished.

Thus, having delineated the main characteristics of the Court, it is essential to delve into the relationship between the ICC and ecocide. In the last decade, various environmental groups have argued that the Court already has jurisdiction over cases of ecocide, as this concept is already included as a crime against humanity and therefore falls within the ICC's material jurisdiction. Polly Higgins (2015), however, belongs to another school of thought, advocating in her book *Eradicating Ecocide* for the need to create an amendment to the Rome Statute that would classify ecocide as a fifth autonomous crime.

In this vein, there is a proposed amendment titled the *Ecocide Act*, formulated by the organization End Ecocide on Earth, which has been submitted to the Secretary-General of the United Nations. This proposal defines the concept of ecocide and outlines certain changes to the Rome Statute itself, aimed at enabling the accountability of legal entities, which are currently prohibited.

os elementos da biosfera (mais precisamente aqueles que afetariam as condições de vida humana no planeta), poderiam ser criminalizadas no âmbito do Direito Internacional Penal, no sentido de serem submetidas ao julgamento de uma Corte Penal Internacional.

7 Considerations on Climate Litigation and Its Connection to the Recognition of the Crime of Ecocide in Brazil

Climate issues are immensely discussed these days due to the various catastrophes that have been taking place in different parts of the world. It is known that climate change is a reality, that global warming is no longer a fact of the future, the world is already suffering the harmful consequences of global warming and climate change.

Brazil has recently suffered a wave of climatic disasters such as the heavy rains and catastrophic floods that occurred in the southern of Brazil, which show that urgent action must be taken to change the direction of environmental protection. What has been done so far does not seem to be enough.

An intrinsic conflict that clearly points out to climate issues can be observed, with controversies spread in a disaggregated way in the social environment, opposing the interests of individuals and groups, thus forming poles of disagreement. These disputes happen to show the characteristics of political choices according to the social positions involved, further aggravated by the irreparable nature of the environmental damage caused, whose compensation metrics are far from guaranteeing the reparability of existing environmental conditions.

The judiciary has a special role to play here. There is a lot of talk about climate litigation around the world. The UN (2023), in its *Global Climate Litigation Report: 2023 status review*, points out that climate litigation has been often used to ensure environmental protection on several fronts. According to the UN,[49] considering the number of surveying litigation starting in 2017, the global number of litigations has more than doubled, showing that "climate litigation is becoming an integral part of ensuring climate action and justice". Based on the UN Report, in 2017 there were 884 cases, while in 2022 the number rose to 2180 cases. Most cases have taken place in the United States. However, there has been a significant increase in Latin American countries.

According to the *Global Climate Litigation Report: 2023 status review*, based on a review of climate change-focused cases collected up to December 31, 2022, in a partnership between the UN and the Sabin Center for Climate Change Law at Columbia University, climate policies are far below what is needed to keep global temperatures at an adequate level, with extreme weather phenomena and overwhelming heat, the planet is already much hotter and this reality has pushed people to pressure governments and private sectors for change and responsibility. The report also provides an overview of key climate litigation cases, including historic breakthroughs. Indeed, as climate litigation grows, so does the body of legal precedent, forming an increasingly well-defined legal regime. On the other hand, the increase in demand may also demonstrate that the measures taken so far by governments and states may not be achieving the necessary effectiveness. It is paramount to ponder about this. Litigation should serve as a wake-up call, a warning to put measures in place and to demonstrate the discontent of civil society mainly.

---

[49] UN (2023).

The report also cites some emblematic cases, such as the Brazilian Supreme Court's decision that recognize the Paris Agreement as a human rights treaty and therefore has supranational status. Thus, this decision shows that Brazilian society has been questioning and taking relevant environmental protection issues to court and, due to the relevance of the judgment, it will be used as an example to address the current state of climate litigation in the Brazilian Supreme Court.

The decision above mentioned has the following background: Brazilian legislation dealing specifically with climate protection dating since 2009 (Law 12.187/2009). The law, although imperfect and with substantial gaps,[50] defines targets for reducing greenhouse gas emissions, measures for mitigating and adapting to climate change and creates the National Policy on Climate Change—PNMC.

Despite the existence of such an important law and other legislation designed to protect the environment, not all cases are covered by it and this situation exposes the issue to jurisprudential decisions. This is the case of the Brazilian Supreme Court decision in ADPF 708 on the Climate Fund.

It should be noted that this Fund was created by Law 12.114/2009 and its purpose is to secure resources to support projects and studies aimed at mitigating and adapting to climate change. The Arguition of Noncompliance with a Fundamental Precept (ADPF) No. 708 was filed in 2020, due to the fact that the aforementioned Fund had not been implemented until then, with the understanding that despite the law, the Brazilian State had not yet fulfilled its role, violating the environmental protection precept provided for in the Federal Constitution. In a final decision, published in 2022, the Federal Supreme Court ruled that the Brazilian State must comply with legal provisions, including with regard to the effectiveness of human rights treaties that have "supra-legal status", as in the case of the Paris Agreement, which deals with climate change issues, and that any action or omission contrary to this is a direct violation of the Constitution and human rights, the Court ordered Brazil to fulfill its commitments, and the Ministry of the Environment must resume activities to put the Climate Fund into practice.[51]

It is important to note that there are other important cases in the Brazilian judiciary. These are direct or indirect climate litigation cases. In this context, direct cases would be those that include direct requests for an immediate cut in greenhouse gas emissions, the closure of oil and coal-fired power stations, among other situations that are directly related to the climate. Indirect climate litigation, on the other hand, involves environmental protection that indirectly helps to mitigate unwanted climate emissions.[52]

It should be noted that environmental issues seem to have taken a definitive place in the Brazilian judiciary with the creation in 2022 of the Supreme Court Green Agenda, which put to priority seven lawsuits related to various environmental causes (such as deforestation, protection of the Amazon, inspection, licensing and

---

[50] Wedy (2017).

[51] Sarlet et al. (2022).

[52] Modoti (2024), p. 64.

the climate crisis)[53] and with the presentation of the Climate Statements by the National Council of Justice (CNJ), for example, demonstrating that the beginning of a new era in Brazilian Courts, the era of creating sustainable jurisprudence in the environmental field, including climate issues, is becoming more effective.[54]

One of these Green Agenda cases, ADPF No. 760, deals with climate litigation indirectly. Its focus is on reducing deforestation in the Amazon, a situation that greatly benefits climate change mitigation. However, the issue of climate damage was used in this case as one of the grounds for convincing the Supreme Court of the need to halt deforestation in the Amazon region. The case was recently judged, in March 2025, and the Brazilian Supreme Court ordered the federal government to present an action plan to prevent and control deforestation in the Legal Amazon, setting a deadline for the measures to be taken, so that by 2027 deforestation must be reduced by 80% and by 2030 the reduce must be 100%. It is important to say that, although the reporting Justice Carmén Lúcia was in favor of recognizing an *Unconstitutional State of Affairs in Environmental Matters* applicable to the case, understanding that there had been a massive, widespread and systematic affront to the environment, the Brazilian Court final decision went in the opposite direction, allowing the federal government to establish the necessary policies to remove the risks arising from the lack of adequate protection.

The decision cited above, although not directly related to climate change, has served and will certainly serve as an incentive and foundation for many other decisions related directly or indirectly to the issue. Thus, it can be said that climate litigation influences and also benefits from decisions on other environmental issues that indirectly impact the climate.

Another Brazilian case framed as climate litigation, and which indirectly used the issue of climate change for liability for environmental disasters was the Rio Doce River vs. Federal Union and State of Minas Gerais lawsuit (Mariana Disaster).[55] The lawsuit was filed by Rio Doce River, represented by the Pachamama Association, against the Federal Government and the State of Minas Gerais due to the collapse of the Samarco mining company's tailings dam in the municipality of Mariana/MG. It sought to recognize the Rio Doce River Basin as a subject of law and to hold the Federal Government and the State of Minas Gerais responsible for omissions in disaster prevention measures. Among the arguments was that the National Policy on Climate Change - PNMC (Law 12.187/2009) had not been complied with. For procedural reasons, the lawsuit was dismissed due to the lack of legal standing of the

[53] Dentro desta pauta, encontram-se ações importantíssimas que discutem, em especial, atos e políticas ambientais do Governo Federal como: a ADPF 760 que trata da redução do desmatamento da Amazônia legal; ADPF 735 sobre a valorização do IBAMA – Instituto Brasileiro do Meio Ambiente; ADPF 651 – Defesa da democracia participativa na defesa coletiva do meio ambiente; ADO 54 – Omissão do Governo Federal quanto à proteção e conservação da Amazônia; ADO 59 – Defesa do Fundo Amazônia; ADI 6148 – Qualidade do ar e redução dos gases de efeito estufa e ADI 6808 – Combate à licença ambiental automática.

[54] Wedy (2025).

[55] Juma (2024).

Rio Doce River Basin.[56] In fact, the situation did not fit the legal and procedural possibilities of Brazilian legislation, but it did demonstrate that disasters such as the one in Mariana—Minas Gerais, as well as causing irreversible environmental degradation also causes severe climatic effects.

Faced with the difficulty presented by the Brazilian State in recent years in adequately complying with what is established in the Federal Constitution (art. 225) on the protection of the environment, climate litigation has become a powerful tool in changing attitudes towards environmental protection, whether by governments, civil society, private institutions and, above all, the Brazilian judiciary. The Paris Agreement seems to represent an important milestone in this awakening, albeit slowly, driving a change in behavior regarding judicial decisions, drawing attention to the importance of properly implementing environmental public policies.

Climate litigation characterized by a set of judicial and administrative actions urging the judiciary to take a stand on climate issues, has contributed to promoting the understanding that environmental protection is a human right and as such deserves everyone's full respect. In the same vein, it can be said that climate litigation opens up space for States, private institutions and society to seek to reduce climate impacts, as a way of realizing human rights, under penalty of being held responsible in court for climate change, in other words, as a benefit beyond the climate issue, climate litigation can consolidate a culture in favor of the climate and the environment across the globe.

However, which is the connection between ecocide and climate litigation?

The recent environmental and climate disasters and catastrophes in Brazil have had an impact on public policies, legislative output and judicial decisions in environmental and climate matters. The year 2024 was a milestone in this "new" vision of environmental protection that has been emerging, and which is demonstrated by the most recent decisions of the Brazilian Courts, especially the Brazilian Supreme Court with the ADPF 708 and ADPF 760 decisions, cited above.

In fact, this was not a movement that occurred only in Brazil. The International Court of Human Rights has already handed down decisions recognizing environmental protection as a *jus cogens* norm, as in the La Oroya case, as Ingo Sarlet and Tiago Fensterseifer[57] say:

> By adopting this understanding, the IA Court has raised the legal status of environmental protection, recognizing it as an imperative norm of international law and an interrogable universal principle imposed on States, in a similar way to the prohibitions on genocide, slavery, apartheid, forced disappearance and crimes against humanity.

In addition, the IA Court of Human Rights has recognized that the duty to protect human rights affects the regulation of activities undertaken by public and private companies, so States must take appropriate measures to guarantee these rights by any means, such as judicial, administrative and legislative, including stipulating effective redress mechanisms.[58] And the fact that Brazil recognizes the "supra-legal

[56] Juma (2024).

[57] Sarlet and Fenterseifer (2025).

[58] Sarlet and Fenterseifer (2025).

status" of international treaties in environmental and climate matters, through the Brazilian Supreme Court ruling on ADPF 708, makes it possible to start changing the course of environmental due diligence in the country. Furthermore, the recent ADPF 760 judgment worked on this idea of protection and violation of human rights, emphasizing that it is not up to the State to define what to protect. The protection of the environment and climate is mandatory and the State's omissive, deficient or insufficient stance appears unconstitutional. In other words, the State must really commit to preserving and defending the environment and the climate.

The decisions handed down in Brazilian climate litigation that have recognized and emphasized the state of environmental emergency present today, as in the case of deforestation, floods and fires that have occurred in recent years, make the case that environmental protection needs to be reshaped on all fronts. This change, it seems, has been adopted by the Brazilian judiciary, with the cases cited in this paper showing a more advanced stance on environmental protection that has also been presented in the Brazilian Legislative Branch, with legal changes and the offering of new Bills, such as the Bills that provide for the classification of the crime of ecocide as an environmental crime in Brazil, which was only possible because of horrible and unforgettable events, such as the collapse of the Mariana-MG and Brumadinho-MG dams.

At the end, disasters often teach and allow changing courses. But it's much better to make the necessary changes without such catastrophes and irreparable damage. The environment has already changed, but it's still time to prevent further damage. Appropriate national and international legislation and Courts focused on the protection of human and collective rights are essential in this quest, but achieving what is intended in terms of environmental protection will only be possible through appropriate public policies and a change in the behavior of global society. And this change is also being sought by climate litigation, which is driving discussions about the effects of environmental damage around the world.

In the case of Mariana Dam in Minas Gerais, which occurred in 2015, more than 600,000 people are known to have been direct or indirect victims of the disaster. The dam collapse killed 19 people and spread destruction over 49 cities, causing irreparable damage to the Rio Doce River basin. In February 2025, 9 years after the disaster, more than 100 kilometers of riparian forest have been destroyed, in the reservoir of the Risoleta Neves Hydroelectric Power Plant in Candonga – Minas Gerais, more than 9 million cubic meters of tailings are still causing impacts in the region, in addition to contamination of the soil, subsoil and various areas with sediments, compromising aquatic fauna and the safety of riverside populations. The landscape along the Rio Doce basin still bears deep scars from the disaster.[59]

In the case of the Brumadinho Dam in Minas Gerais, case that served to propose a legal change to create the crime of Ecocide in Brazil, the victims are still waiting for effective accountability for the culprits. Six years after the tragedy that decimated 272 lives, destroyed communities and permanently degraded the

[59] IBAMA (2025).

environment, the lawsuits are still pending in the Courts of Brazil. The sense of impunity for the victims' families is latent. The judiciary plays an extremely important role in environmental issues. However, it is hoped that all the movement on climate litigation will also benefit the listening necessary to transform the position of the Federal Government, Legislative and Judiciary on effective environmental protection, which is so necessary today.

In this context, it is understood that the recognition of environmental crimes that affect the whole of humanity can also help to create a position that is more favorable to accountability regarding climate change. It is essential to think of the protection of the environment as something of global and unified importance; the environment is one and must be protected in its entirety. In this respect, justice is particularly important.

8 Conclusions

Recognizing ecocide as a crime of high severity that affects all humanity is essential, given the historical record of degradation and catastrophes that have occurred, particularly since the onset of the Industrial Revolution and accelerated by advances in new technologies.

In this regard, despite numerous voices advocating for the recognition of ecocide as a crime, there is still no consensus on the issue. Meanwhile, some countries are seeking to incorporate this crime into their domestic legislation, even though it should have an international aspect due to its implications for all humanity. It is a fact that many interests are involved in this matter, but it is necessary to view environmental protection beyond the principle of "the polluter pays." Civil accountability is not sufficient; addressing ecocide from a penal perspective fosters a sense of global responsibility. There is a need to consider the preventive protection of the environment, and criminalization can play a significant role in that.

The discussion regarding the possibility of categorizing ecocide as genocide or as a crime against humanity, transferring the jurisdiction to the ICC, is merely one avenue to address the issues related to these harmful events or excessive destruction that results in severe alterations to global common goods or Earth's ecological systems. However, simply recognizing the ICC's jurisdiction will not resolve the problem.

It is necessary to overcome economic and political interests that somehow hinder the implementation of an international criminal policy aimed at promoting and safeguarding the environment. Until that happens, each state has the obligation to defend the environment as the highest good. Allowing harmful events to degrade the environment is to condemn all of humanity; it is a global crime that must be punished.

Brazil is far from having the best policies, legislation, and positioning on this issue. However, there is at least a legislative movement to include ecocide in the domestic legal framework. And environmental litigation can contribute as an effective instrument for changing behavior in recognizing the importance of considering large-scale disasters as crimes that need to be duly punished.

Recognizing the crime of Ecocide is not much, it is true, and having a law that merely punishes or is not adequately enforced will be of no use. It is not enough to criminalize conduct or omission; the most important aspect is the awareness, education, and sense of responsibility that everyone must have to protect Mother Nature, the climate, the planet, our home. This is a public policy issue, and it is urgent!

References

Brazil (2002) Decree 4388 of 2002. Decree No. 4,388, of September 25, 2002. Promulgates the Rome Statute of the International Criminal Court. Available at: https://www.planalto.gov.br/ccivil_03/decreto/2002/d4388.htm. Accessed on 05/05/2024.

Buchanan KM (1971) Ecocide in Indochina. Victoria University Student Newspaper. New Zealand 34(14). Available at: http://nzetc.victoria.ac.nz/tm/scholarly/tei-Salient34141971-t1-body-d12.html. Accessed 5 May 2024

Castells M (2016) A Sociedade em rede. Paz e Terra, São Paulo

Chamber of Deputies (2024) Ficha de Tramitação PL 2787/2019. Available at: https://www.camara.leg.br/proposicoesWeb/fichadetramitacao?idProposicao=2201529. Accessed 90 Sept 2024.

Columbia Law School. Columbia Climate School – Sabin Center for Climate Change law. Available at: https://climate.law.columbia.edu/. Accessed 4 Apr 2025.

Council of Europe (2024). Available at: https://www.consilium.europa.eu/en/press/press-releases/2024/03/26/environmental-crime-council-clears-new-eu-law-with-tougher-sanctions-and-extended-list-of-offences/. Accessed on 20 Aug 2024

Ecocide Law (2024). https://ecocidelaw.com/history/. Accessed 20 Aug 2024

Galston AW (2001) Falling leaves and Ethical Dilemmas: Agent Orange in Vietnan. In: Galston AW Shurr EG (eds) New Dimensions in Bioethics Science, Ethics and the Formulation of Public Policy. Springer, Boston, MA. https://doi.org/10.1007/978-1-4615-1591-3_7

Gordilho HJ d S, Ravazzano F (2017) Ecocídio e o Tribunal Penal Internacional. Revista Justiça do Direito 31(3)

Higgins P (2015) Eradicating Ecocide. , 2ª edição. Shepheard-Walwyn Publishers, London

IBAMA (2025) A caminho da recuperação ambiental de Mariana (MG), Ibama realiza vistoria técnica. Available at: https://www.gov.br/ibama/pt-br/assuntos/noticias/2025/a-caminho-da-recuperacao-ambiental-de-mariana-mg-ibama-realiza-vistoria-tecnica. Accessed 4 Apr 2025

ICC (2016) International Criminal Court. Policy Paper on Case Selection and Prioritization. Available at: https://www.icc-cpi.int/itemsDocuments/20160915_OTPPolicy_Case-Selection_Eng.pdf. Accessed 30 May 2024

JUMA (2024) Plataforma de Litigância Climática no Brasil – PUC/RJ. Available at: https://litigancia.biobd.inf.puc-rio.br/visualizacao_caso/543/0/. Accessed 4 Apr 2025

Kowalska S (2023) Ecocídio: uma ameaça ao tecido biológico e à segurança ecológica. Revista Veredas do Direito. 20

Loureiro, Cláudia Regina de Oliveira Magalhães da Silva (2023) O ecocídio perante o Estatuto de Roma. Revista de Direito Internacional, UNICEUB. Brasília, 20(2).

Modoti AdeM (2024) Litigância Climática no Estado de São Paulo. Revista da Procuradoria Geral do Estado de São Paulo - PGE/SP. n. 100. São Paulo. Available at: https://revistas.pge.sp.gov.br/index.php/revistapegesp/article/view/1594/1664. Accessed 4 Apr 2025

Panigaj J, Berníková E (2023) "Ecocide - a New Crime Under International Law?". Tribuna Juridică 1:5–20. https://www.ceeol.com/search/article-detail?id=1222654. Accessed 6 Oct 2024

Sarlet I, Fenterseifer T (2025) Direitos fundamentais, meio ambiente e clima em 2024: uma retrospectiva na perspectiva jurisprudencial. Conjur: 2025 Available at: https://www.conjur.com.br/2025-jan-10/direitos-fundamentais-meio-ambiente-e-clima-em-2024-uma-retrospectiva-na-perspectiva-jurisprudencial/. Accessed 4 Apr 2025.

Sarlet I, Wedy GT, Wefenterseifer T (2022) A equiparação dos tratados ambientais aos tratados de direitos humanos. Conjur. Available at: https://www.conjur.com.br/2022-jul-15/direitos-fundamentais-equiparacao-tratados-ambientais-aos-direitos-humanos/. Accessed 4 Apr 2025

Silva STda (2014) Direito Fundamental ao Meio Ambiente Ecologicamente Equilibrado Avanços e Desafios. Cadernos Do Programa De Pós-Graduação Em Direito - PPGDir./UFRGS, (6). https://doi.org/10.22456/2317-8558.51610

Stop Ecocide (2024a) History. Available at: https://www.stopecocide.earth/. Accessed 20 Aug 2024.

Stop Ecocide (2024b) Council of Europe Votes to Criminalize Ecocide. https://www.stopecocide.earth/2024/eu-council-votes-to-criminalise-cases-comparable-to-ecocide. Accessed 20 Aug 2024

Stop Ecocide Foundation (2021) Access to the Report of the Independent Expert Panel for the Legal Definition of Ecocide: Commentary and Core Text, June 2021. Stop Ecocide Foundation. Available at: https://ecocidelaw.com/definition/. Accessed 20 Aug 2024

UNICEF (2022) Afinal o que são mudanças climáticas. Available at: https://www.unicef.org/brazil/historias/afinal-o-que-sao-mudancas-climaticas. Accessed 6 Oct 2024

UNICEF (2024a) Compreendendo as mudanças climáticas/ Available at: https://www.unicef.org/brazil/blog/compreendendo-mudancas-climaticas. Accessed 6 Oct 2024

UNICEF (2024b) Os desastres brasileiros e suas relações com as mudanças climáticas. Available at: https://www.unicef.org/brazil/blog/os-desastres-brasileiros-e-suas-relacoes-com-mudancas-climaticas. Accessed 6 Oct 2024

United Nations (2020) A ONU e meio ambiente. Available at: https://brasil.un.org/pt-br/91223-onu-e-o-meio-ambiente. Accessed 20 Sept 2024

United Nations (2023) O litígio climático mais do que dobra em cinco anos, atualmente uma ferramenta fundamental para garantir justiça climática. Available at: https://www.unep.org/pt-br/noticias-e-reportagens/comunicado-de-imprensa/o-litigio-climatico-mais-do-que-dobra-em-cinco-anos. Accessed 3 Apr 2025

United Nations (2024) Dia Mundial do Meio Ambiente: ONU lança campanha para restaurar terras degradadas. Available at: https://brasil.un.org/pt-br/268559-dia-mundial-do-meio-ambiente-onu-lan%C3%A7a-campanha-para-restaurar-terras-degradadas. Accessed 20 Sept 2024

Viviani RA (2018) Intervenção do direito internacional penal para a tutela do meio ambiente: protagonismo por meio de uma Corte Penal Internacional. Editora Lumen Juris, Rio de Janeiro

Wedy GT (2017) Climate legislation na litigation in Brazil. Columbia Law School. Sabin Center for climate change law. Available at: https://climate.law.columbia.edu/. Accessed 4 Apr 2025

Weisberg B (1970) Ecocide in Indochina. Canfield Press: San Francisco. 1970. Available at: https://archive.org/details/ecocideinindochi00weis/page/n3/mode/2up?view=theater&q=ecocide. Accessed 6 Oct 2024

Zierler D (2011) The invention of ecocide: agent orange, vietnam, and the scientists who changed the way we think about the environment. University of Georgia Press, Athens, Georgia, p 114. E-book

Ana Elizabeth Lapa Wanderley Cavalcanti is Professor of Postgraduate and Undergraduate Law at Mackenzie Presbyterian University.

Gianpaolo Poggio Smanio is Professor of Postgraduate and Undergraduate Law at Mackenzie Presbyterian University.

The Ecological Footprint: A Tool for Decision-Making in the Field of Climate Litigation

Ana María Bonet, Cósimo Gonzalo Sozzo, and María Cristina Alé

1 Introduction

The concept of ecological footprint has been associated with an integrated assessment methodology for establishing socio-environmental impact indices. Environmental impact assessment is the tool centrally used by law to measure the ecological effects of human activity. The legal approach offered by the environmental impact approach is oriented toward the quantification of negative environmental effects. It fails to consider diffuse, indeterminate, or residual effects. Furthermore, its origin is associated with the anthropocentric discursive model, which places humans at the center and non-humans as the environment. Therefore, it fails to overcome the anthropocentric logic that underlies socio-environmental crises.

This chapter proposes, as an essay, that the concept of ecological footprint can provide law with a perspective corresponding to the socio-ecological demands of the Anthropocene, helping to define discursive tools to address the complexity of socio-environmental crises based on the configuration of ecological responsibilities. Among these crises is climate change, as an aspect of global environmental change. Climate change is part of the consequences of human action and, therefore, of the ecological footprint on the planetary ecosystem. Therefore, reducing the ecological

A. M. Bonet (✉)
IHUCSO/CONICET–UCSF, Santa Fe, Argentina
e-mail: abonet@santafe-conicet.gov.ar

C. G. Sozzo
FCJS/UNL – Institute for Advanced Studies of the Litoral, Santa Fe, Argentina

M. C. Alé
UCSF - UM, Mendoza, Argentina
e-mail: maria.ale@um.edu.ar

V. E. de Aquino et al. (eds.), *Climate Litigation in a Changing World*, Ius Gentium: Comparative Perspectives on Law and Justice 130,
https://doi.org/10.1007/978-3-032-05530-9_9

footprint of individuals and businesses constitutes a key mandate for addressing the climate issue.

The concept of ecological footprint has important links to climate change, specifically to the problem of greenhouse gas emissions. Indeed, one aspect of the ecological footprint, along with waste production and the consumption of natural resources, is the generation of emissions, which is the main cause of climate change.

The concept can contribute to a comprehensive approach to climate change from a complexity perspective, considering not only the problem of emissions and their effects on the climate, but also other systemic factors, such as environmental, social, economic, and cultural factors, which come together in each climate litigation case.

In a more technical sense, the ecological footprint plays a central role in litigation seeking to establish corporate liability for the harmful consequences of climate change, seeking remediation. In this type of climate litigation, measuring the footprint offers a method that can be used, both to prove the existence of damage and, on the other, to quantify it. Also on a technical level, the ecological footprint constitutes the central point of the legal debate in another subtype of climate litigation against companies: that aimed at attacking the practice of *climate washing*, seeking its cessation.

The first section presents the challenges and limitations that socio-environmental issues pose for law and offers a mapping of the approaches that law has been offering to these issues. The second section outlines how the concept of ecological footprint can contribute to its legal approach, in relation to its translation into administrative, legislative, and regulatory decisions, as well as in relation to judicial decisions. Possible implementations in climate litigation are specified, particularly as a tool for preventing future damages and for quantifying damages incurred.

2 The Law in the Face of Socio-Ecological Crises

The management of ecological crises constitutes one of humanity's greatest challenges, along with food and energy production and waste management. The approach to ecological problems has varied over time. This has been due, on the one hand, to the various scientific and technological developments that have made it possible to address them from different contexts. On the other hand, due to the different dimensions and dynamics that these problems have taken on.

2.1 Ecological Crises as Traces of Human Action

The pre-modern perspective of threatening nature placed humans as victims of natural disasters. The *quasi-* passive human role in relation to the effects of natural events seemed almost to recognize a natural, or divine, action in what are understood as contingencies of the non-human world (cf. Hermitte 2007).

Over time, it became evident that the power that modernity enabled to human action, unleashing it, led to a definitive transformation of natural systems, reducing and weakening them (Latouche 2012; Bonet 2017). Indeed, human-driven planetary transformations have reached such a point that they already enabled the emergence of the concept of the Anthropocene in the twenty-first century, to describe the geological era characterized precisely by such human involvement in the modifications of the ecological system of planet Earth (Crutzen 2002).

The recognition of this transformative potential of human action is accompanied by the question of the corresponding responsibilities regarding the effects of such transformations on planetary coexistence (Berger and Carrizo 2019).

2.2 *The Question of Adjusting the Action to the Limits*

Early modernity established the idea of linear, infinite progress as a paradigm (cf. Estermann 2021). Based on rationalist humanism, linear political philosophy, capitalist economics, and strong anthropocentrism,[1] it presented the economic problem as unrelated to natural resources, which it considered to be superabundant.

Thus, from the mid-eighteenth century, a dynamic relationship with nature was established that consisted of enabling humanity to indefinitely transgress natural limits (Bourg 2018, pp. 184–185). This empowerment even existed legally: transgression was proclaimed as a right (Latouche 2012, p. 14) under the condition of obedience to a rule of law founded on human reason. Such a transgressive dynamic did not consider the question of the limits to human action; it even encouraged behaviors intended to surpass them.

The succession of crises linked to science and technology, however, led to a review of this thinking, triggering an adjustment to it, around the second half of the twentieth century. Since then, studies have warned[2] about planetary limits (Rockström et al. 2009)[3] and the relationship between the reach of these limits through an urgent global collapse and the process of the "great acceleration" (Steffen et al. 2015) generated by human beings since the industrial revolution. Unlimited

[1] The anthropocentric narrative has underpinned law since modern times, and this has even been reflected in the development of environmental law. Law has approached non-humans as objects of human dominion, from a hierarchical, top-down perspective, which has enabled their transformation into resources and, consequently, their exploitation (Bonet 2017).

[2] The report "The Limits to Growth," developed in the 1970s by an academic group at the request of the Club of Rome, a group of interested experts, is considered emblematic and pioneering. Despite the criticism it received, it marked a trend in the study of the limits of the planet's resources and the effects of the development model on the global ecosystem. The report was updated several times. Cf. Meadows et al. (1973, 1992, 2006).

[3] Planetary boundaries theory is a framework that identifies nine processes essential to the integrity of the Earth system and defines safety thresholds that should not be exceeded to preserve the ecological balances necessary for development on Earth. Cf. Rockström et al. (2009).

and continuous economic growth is warned as incompatible with the finiteness of natural resources and with the preservation of ecological balance (Daly 1974).[4]

The exposure of these limits was accompanied by the recognition of the relationship between development and socio-ecological crises. This generated a discursive transformation in international forums, which began to warn, at least for certain currents of economic thought, that development must conform to—and be limited to—the physical limits imposed by the scarcity of natural resources. In this conception of limits linked to scarcity (Larrère 2020, pp. 138 ff.), what is relevant to ensuring the development trajectory is the transmission to the future generation of a stock—a heritage—of natural resources similar to that received by the previous generation.

With the socio-ecological crises of development, there is a discursive shift that emphasizes the existence of limits in natural resources and illuminates a new alternative narrative to the concepts of environmental crisis, environmental law, and weak sustainable development.[5]

When criticism of the Meadows Report[6] led to a decline in the discussion about limits, a new generation of work on limits proposes shifting the focus of the discussion from resource scarcity to the biosphere's resilience to maintain a safe zone for life (Boutard and Gondran 2020). The idea of measuring the ecological footprint then renewed the ecological debate in the 1990s (Boehly 2023, p. 180), also introducing the question of the biosphere's capacity to absorb the negative effects of human activity. Due to its simplicity, it is presented as a key instrument in establishing a new approach to the impact that humans, businesses, cities, and countries have on the Earth system (Boehly 2023, pp. 189–190).

The persistence and deepening of socio-ecological crises at the global level has given rise, already in the twenty-first century, to the emergence of the concept of the

[4]The steady-state economic theory presents an economic model that limits production and consumption, promoting an economy that operates within the framework of the use of the limited resources offered by the planet (Daly 1974).

[5]The first international instruments on the subject date back to the beginning of the twentieth century and presented an approach to resources on an individual basis, such as fisheries treaties, aimed at managing them as *res nullius*. These treaties implied an initial recognition of the negative effects of the development model. It was only in the mid-twentieth century that the environmental issue emerged as a global problem. This problematization deepened during that half of the century along with the emergence of the postulate of environmental protection at the Stockholm Conference (1972), Rio Conference (1992), and Rio+20 Conference (2012). The recognition of the link between environmental crises and the development model led to a rethinking of the model that gave rise to the concepts of sustainable development and sustainable development# and led to the creation of the sustainable development goals (UN 2018).

[6]Criticism of the Meadows Report (1972) focused on several aspects, including that the models used were considered overly simplified, failing to incorporate potential technological advances or changes in global policies, thus limiting their predictive capacity (Meadows et al. 1992). Furthermore, a catastrophic determinism was pointed out in its narrative, accusing it of underestimating human capacity to adapt and generate innovative solutions to environmental challenges (Latouche 2012). Finally, the focus on discussions about sustainable growth was questioned, influencing the perception of public policies around these issues.

Anthropocene. This concept illustrates the persistent, transformative, and irreversible imprint of humankind on the planetary ecosystem. It allows us to critically understand the close link between human action and the negative transformation of the state of natural systems, as well as the inadequacy of the adjustment brought about by the narratives associated with the terms environmental crisis, environmental law, and weak sustainable development. At the same time, it underpins the discourse of socio-ecological transition, as a process of transformation of modes of coexistence at the global level, which particularly considers planetary boundaries in the design of human action (Rockström et al. 2009).

The concept of the Anthropocene highlighted the fact that socio-ecological problems can no longer be addressed as emerging crises or temporary issues. Instead, they are a permanent and definitive situation of decline and weakening of natural systems. This structural crisis calls for consideration not only of the scarcity of natural resources in terms of sustaining human activity but also of the capacity of natural systems to absorb the negative impacts of the human life system (Latouche 2012).

2.3 The Environmental Approach to Law

The law has been addressing ecological crises, especially in their preventive aspect, based on environmental administrative law, particularly through three instruments: environmental impact assessments, environmental urban planning, and territorial planning (cf. Salinas Chávez 2013).

Environmental impact assessment is a central component of the management apparatus of the sustainable development model, the mechanism that modern law designed from the third third of the twentieth century onwards to address environmental problems, attempting to adjust and reconcile the idea of economic development with the idea of protecting natural systems. It is a systematic study that identifies, predicts, and interprets the environmental impacts of projects, plans, or programs, in order to prevent negative consequences for human health, social well-being, and ecological balance (IAIA 2007; Vidal de los Santos and López 2009). Its calculation is based on quantitative and qualitative environmental indicators, such as pollutant emission levels, natural resource consumption, biodiversity loss, and alterations in water, soil, and air quality, evaluated at different times: before, during, and after project implementation. The assessment is primarily carried out during the planning stage, which allows for the analysis of different alternatives and the selection of the most sustainable and environmentally friendly options (Weston 2000; Morgan 2012).

Urban planning, for its part, is a strategy for managing urban development, which involves forecasting and organizing growth, ordering it based on criteria, which may include environmental criteria (Hall and Tewdwr-Jones 2010; UN-Habitat. 2009).

In turn, territorial planning constitutes a regulatory tool of administrative law oriented towards the organization of the territory according to the functions that the population intends to grant it (FAO 1993).

3 Potential of the Ecological Footprint Concept for the Legal Approach to Ecological Issues

The concept of ecological footprint has the potential to incorporate the question of planetary boundaries into law, since it considers not only the resources needed to sustain lifestyles but also the limited capacity of ecological regulation mechanisms (Boutard and Gondran 2020, p. 16). It reflects, in fact, the relationship of dependence between human needs and nature (cf. Wackernagel 1994, p. 70; Gareis 2022).

The emergence of the term ecological footprint is associated with global processes of environmental degradation. In the 1990s, it was developed as a concept and indicator for measuring socio-environmental impact.[7] Conceptually, it finds its roots in theories that link growth or development with human needs and resource scarcity, and methodologically, in sustainability measurement studies that combine metrics of energy, resource use, carrying capacity, and social impact.[8] Data collection and consideration of information on the ecological footprint of individuals, businesses, cities, and states are key tools for substantiating the idea of the limits of human action.

The methodology calculates the land area and resources required to produce and regenerate the resources consumed and to absorb the waste and emissions generated (Martinez Castillo 2007; Carabelli et al. 2022). It allows for the identification of the resources needed to sustain the lifestyles of different societies and the calculation of their capacity to regenerate within the available land area (cf. Nicholson et al. 2003; Husain et al. 2021).

This section seeks to analyze how the concept can become a legal tool for managing ecological issues. It first outlines its potential in discursive terms, then outlines, in essay-like fashion, its potential as a legal tool.

---

[7] William Rees and Mathis Wackernagel carried out this development between 1990 and 1994 at the University of British Columbia in Vancouver (Canada) in the context of the latter's doctoral thesis, supervised by the former.

[8] Authors recognize the concept's roots in theories that link development or growth with resource availability. In this regard, a certain trigger is detected in a Platonic postulate about the need to align population with resources (Durham 1994), as well as in the link established by Quesnay (1758) between land productivity and wealth creation, and also in Malthusian warnings about planetary boundaries in relation to the requirements implied by population growth (Malthus 1798). The methodological background includes the analysis of energy flows in relation to the functioning of economic and ecological systems (Jevons 1985; Lotka 1925; Georgescu-Roegen 1971) that took place after the industrial revolution; also the modelling of systems and the simulation of planetary boundaries (Meadows et al. 1973). For a development of the subject, see: Wackernagel (1994), pp. 70 et seq.

3.1 Discursive Contributions of the Idea of Ecological Footprint

In discursive terms, the concept has the potential, on the one hand, to reverse the anthropocentric logic that has sustained law since modernity and, on the other, to integrate sociocultural aspects into the approach to issues affecting non-humans.

Although the term ecological is often identified with the environment, it can provide a more integrated and complex perspective for addressing issues of coexistence between humans and non-humans. The concept of ecology refers to the relationships between the organisms that make up an ecosystem.[9] If planet Earth is understood as an ecosystem, terrestrial ecology would encompass all living beings within it, both human and non-human.

From this perspective, the prefix "socio" before the word ecological would not be necessary to refer to the relationships between humans and non-humans, although the limitations of common usage and understanding warrant a clarification. This would enable an integrated consideration of the effects of a human initiative on the planetary ecosystem, considering both the impact on non-humans and humans in an articulated manner.

Regarding the anthropocentric review, the approach to the problems of human-nonhuman coexistence based on the concept of the environment places the human at the center and the nonhuman as the environment. This approach is based on a hierarchy that considers the human as the subject and the nonhuman as the object, thus enabling their treatment as a resource, as a commodity. This treatment is embodied in the concept of dominance, which enables the exploitation that lies at the root of serious ecological crises. The term ecological, by referring to the relationships between all beings that coexist in an ecosystem, would place these beings, both human and nonhuman, in relationships of interdependence, which imply both competition and cooperation. Ecology is more closely identified with the concept of the network than with the vertical hierarchy of dominance.

3.2 Legal Contributions of the Idea of Ecological Footprint

The ecological footprint, as a tool for measuring socio-ecological impact, can be translated into socio-environmental policy, regulatory, and judicial instruments.

[9] The term was coined by Ernst Haeckel, a German biologist, to refer to the study of the relationships between living organisms and their environment, based on the combination of the Greek words *oikos* (house) and *logos* (reason/science). Cf. Malacazza (2013), p. 28.

3.2.1 Footprint and Responsibility

The concept of ecological footprint refers to the permanent systemic consequences of human action. It highlights the lack of harmlessness of human actions and, consequently, their relevance in terms of responsibility. The dimensionality of the consequences of an action enables the activation of a system of responsibility. Taking into account the consequences of human actions makes humans responsible.

Discursively, the ecological footprint narrative can contribute to raising awareness of individual and collective responsibility for the consequences of each action. In legal and political terms, it offers elements both for adopting more sustainable measures and for establishing ecological responsibility for the global consequences of human action.

At the individual level, it could eventually be used to calculate citizens' ecological responsibility based on the resources each individual consumes. This could translate into tax compensation or restrictions. For example, individuals who exceed a certain footprint in a given period would have to pay a higher tax burden. Another mechanism for managing the individual footprint could be the allocation of a certain number of hectares per individual for a given period. Once these hectares are used, the individual would face restrictions or a higher cost of action. The social issue can be seen as a limit to the economic compensation system, as individuals with greater purchasing power could purchase their environmental freedom through compensation.

At the business level, the footprint mechanism could be used in enabling processes. A business could be enabled if it has a compensable footprint or if its estimated footprint does not exceed a certain threshold. Estimating a business's footprint considers not only the resources consumed, but also the emissions generated and the waste produced, which would also involve considering post-consumption accountability mechanisms.[10]

At the state level, it can become a cross-cutting approach to public policy. Every state initiative should consider its socio-ecological footprint. This consideration would limit measures that imply a footprint that cannot be absorbed or offset by the ecological system and promote others that do.

3.2.2 Technical and Legal Implications

In procedural terms, this tool could be used in the field of environmental administrative decisions, as a preventive measure, in response to any initiative that could have a socio-environmental impact.

[10] Post-consumer responsibility, also known as Extended Producer Responsibility (EPR), establishes that financial and physical responsibility for products after their useful life is transferred from municipalities to manufacturers or brand owners. Thus, companies should participate in the circular economy by repurchasing products once they have been used by consumers (Tumu et al. 2023).

In the administrative sphere, it offers elements for establishing limits, setting objectives, quantifying achievements, and evaluating policies (Nogueira López 2019, p. 9). By calculating the hectares needed to sustain a certain human activity—whether individual, business, institutional, population-based, or state-based—it can be implemented as a complement to environmental impact assessments, but can also be considered in land use plans and strategic urban planning.

Calculating the ecological footprint would allow for a review of some of the instruments with which environmental law attempted to capture the idea of sustainable development, introducing the perspective of limits and thus contributing to establishing a strong idea of sustainable development.

Indeed, if the ecological footprint were used in environmental impact assessment processes for projects, it would make it easier to highlight more diffuse or distant aspects of negative impacts. At the same time, considering the ecological footprint of human activity in territorial and urban planning would make it possible to identify which human activities are contributing most to increasing the ecological footprint (cf. Mcmanus and Haughton 2006). It would facilitate, for example, identifying the ecological footprint of urban mobility, the way buildings are constructed, or the way in which gases emitted by the city's landfill are managed.

The ecological footprint of these actions would enable the design of political actions to reduce their impact or calculate from the planning stages the hectares necessary to sustain the lifestyle of the local population, considering spaces for resource reserves, waste absorption, and ecological compensation (cf. Márquez and Valenzuela 2008).

Furthermore, as a measurement tool, the ecological footprint can contribute to periodic monitoring of the effectiveness of certain policies, programs, and actions.

In the regulatory field, it could be implemented to support the implementation of a set of legislative or regulatory rules that generate incentives for different actors within the framework of a public policy for ecological transition by clearly showing which actions lead to the greatest impact on ecosystems.

In the judicial sphere, it can function as a tool for judicial decision-making, primarily as a preventive or precautionary measure, but also for the purpose of establishing liability aimed at restoring or repairing ecological damage. Indeed, by offering impact indicators, it can contribute to determining liability. It could play a role in proving the probability of damage in actions aimed at preventing environmental damage. It would also allow for meeting the requirement set by the Supreme Court of Justice of the Nation for applying the precautionary principle of minimum proof of the existence of possible future damage. Finally, in the area of actions for the restoration or repair of ecological damage, it could play a dual role. On the one hand, it would allow for the establishment of diffuse causal relationships as a mechanism for quantifying damages in actions for the restoration and repair of environmental damage. On the other hand, the ecological footprint can be used to measure residual environmental damage, that is, irreparable damage that cannot be compensated. The footprint reflects a permanent and non-compensable transformation, thus making it possible to consider systemic consequences.

3.2.3 Application in Climate Litigation

In terms of climate litigation, two implementations of the environmental footprint can be identified: one in the preventive sphere, to stipulate and quantify corporate responsibilities in terms of climate compensation, and another in the compensatory sphere: to quantify the damage and determine compensatory measures. In both cases, these would involve climate litigation against companies.

Climate litigation has two areas of action: litigation against States and litigation against companies. This second area is further divided between actions to prevent future damage through injunctions and actions seeking reparation for damages already incurred.

Preventive actions include those aimed at limiting *climate washing practices*, that is, advertisements that overestimate companies' climate performance. These advertisements tend to create an image of the company as reducing or eliminating its carbon footprint through slogans such as "carbon neutral" or "zero emissions," which usually respond to mechanisms for offsetting their emissions through voluntary carbon markets. Companies would only be carbon neutral if they manage to remove as much carbon from the atmosphere as they produce (Peacock and Markets 2023, pp. 368–369). If they portray themselves as offsetting but only offset a minimum of their carbon production, they would be engaging in *climate washing*. The objective of these climate actions is preventive, looking to the future, and discusses whether the company has exaggerated its results or promises regarding its climate footprint or offset.

In climate litigation for reparation of damages already incurred, the ecological footprint can also play a central role, but this time in terms of proof of damage and its quantification through expert evidence.

Recognizing the ecological footprint as a legal criterion for proving damage, causality, and quantification, as well as a tool for establishing the existence or absence of *climate washing* in climate litigation, would allow progress toward building more effective climate justice, providing the law with tools to address the climate crisis with an approach based on environmental responsibility and equity.

4 Conclusions

The ecological footprint constitutes a discursive and metric device for assessing the socioecological consequences of certain human activities and, consequently, human responsibility for those consequences. As a discursive device, it can be understood in a broader sense and scope than that generated by the methodology focused on ecosystem capacities to sustain lifestyles. It can offer a conceptual framework for developing contributions to the definition of ecological responsibilities, even beyond the emerging conceptualization of ecological responsibility in tort law.

In this broad sense, its particular potential lies in the articulation of the different human consequences on ecosystems, particularly the resources consumed, the emissions generated, the waste produced, and the affected communities. In a more restricted sense, linked to the impact measurement methodology, it can translate these variables into hectares, determining the biologically productive area necessary to sustain a given activity. While it has been criticized for its inadequacy in encompassing or measuring the complexity of the ecological issue (Giampietro and Saltelli 2014), it offers relevant information for determining the capacity of systems to support the ecological burden, that is, to be self-sufficient on the one hand, that is, to generate the resources necessary to sustain themselves, and to absorb systemic waste on the other (Goldfinger et al. 2014).

In legal terms, it could constitute a fundamental pillar for the design and promotion of socio-ecological transition mechanisms, that is, for the regulation of more sustainable models of human coexistence. Instrumentally, this could translate, first and foremost, into the review and strengthening of the legal instruments of environmental administrative law, enabling an integrative approach to the limits of territorial planning, urban planning, and impact assessments. In the judicial sphere, it can function as a mechanism for quantifying damages, calculating compensation or sanctions from a systemic perspective. Particularly in the area of climate litigation, it could contribute to systemically assessing the climatic effects of certain human actions in relation to the other dimensions of the ecological footprint, allowing their quantification in hectares based on the provision of both reparation and compensation mechanisms. In procedural matters, it can offer tools for determining compensatory liabilities as well as for stipulating damages and compensatory measures.

The ecological footprint could thus activate the functionality of law for the transition toward more ecologically sustainable planetary coexistence systems, fulfilling the law's vocation to regulate and design human ways of life, considering coexistence between humans and with non-humans, creating a more habitable, more livable world.

References

Berger M, Carrizo C (eds) (2019) Environmentally affected people. conceptual and practical contributions to the struggle for the recognition and guarantee of rights. Science and Democracy Publishing House

Boehly A (2023) Dernières limits. Learn to live in a finite world. Rue de l'échiquier

Bonet AM (2017) The "dispropriation" of nature. Rethinking the rules of access to goods based on Laudato si'. Italian Journal of. Philos Theol XXXI(2):253–269

Bourg D (2018) Une nouvelle Terre. Desclée Brouwer, Paris, pp 184–185

Boutard A, Gondran N (2020) Planetary limits. Discover it

Carabelli FA, Forti LL, Baroli CA (2022) The ecological footprint applied to the analysis of the human-nature relationship in small- and medium-scale socioeconomic communities in Patagonia. In: 5th patagonian forestry conference - 3rd Southern Patagonian Forestry conference, Bariloche

Crutzen PJ (2002) Geology of mankind. Nature 415(6867):23. https://doi.org/10.1038/415023a

Daly HE (1974) The steady-state economy. Demogr Urban Stud 8(03):357–365. https://doi.org/10.24201/edu.v8i03.246

Durham D (1994) Carrying capacity revisited: Plato to Malthus
Estermann J (2021) Overcoming eurocentrism. Selected texts. Poliedro
Food and Agriculture Organization (FAO) (1993) Guidelines for land use planning
Gareis MC (2022) The ecological footprint: an analysis of its conceptual origin and methodological transformations. J Marit Soc Stud 20:187–208
Georgescu-Roegen N (1971) The entropy law and the economic process. Harvard University Press, Cambridge. https://doi.org/10.4159/harvard.9780674281653
Giampietro M, Saltelli A (2014) Footprints to nowhere. Ecol Indic 46. https://doi.org/10.1016/j.ecolind.2014.01.030
Goldfinger S, Walckernagel M, Galli A, Lazarus E, Lin D (2014) Footprint facts and fallacies: A response to Giampietro and Saltelli (2014) "Footprints to Nowhere". Ecol Indic 46. https://doi.org/10.1016/j.ecolind.2014.04.025
Hall P, Tewdwr-Jones M (2010) Urban and regional planning. Routledge
Hermitte MA (2007) The legal foundation of a scientific and technical society through crises and risks. In: Díaz Varella MD (ed) Law, society and risk: contemporary society seen through the concept of risk. Latin American and European Network on Risk Governance. UniCEUB, UNITAR
Husain D, Garg P, Prakash R (2021) Ecological footprint assessment and its reduction for industrial food products. Int J Sustain Eng 14(1):26–38. https://doi.org/10.1080/19397038.2019.1665119
IAIA (2007), EIA Follow-Up. International best practice principles, special publication series N6
Jevons WS (1985) The coal question; an inquiry concerning the progress of the nation, and the probable exhaustion of our coal mines. Macmillan and Co, London
Larrère C (2020) Les limites planétaires: la portée juridique du changement climatique. In: AAVV, Marta Torre Schaub (ed) Droit et Changement climatique comment répondre à l'urgence climatique. Mare & Martin, Paris, p 138 et seq
Latouche S (2012) L'âge des limits. Mille et une nuits, Paris
Lotka AJ (1925) Contributions to the analysis of energy flows
Malacazza L (ed) (2013) Ecology and environment. Ecology of the city. UNLP, AUGM, Montevideo Group, La Plata. https://www.academia.edu/56503177/Ecolog%C3%ADa_y_ambiente
Malthus TR (1798) An essay on the principle of population
Márquez CG, Valenzuela E (2008) Ecological structure and environmental land use planning: a conceptual and methodological approach based on the accounting process. Gestión y Ambiente 11(2):137–148
Martinez Castillo R (2007) Some aspects of the ecological footprint. Int Sedes VII(14)
Mcmanus P, Haughton G (2006) Planning with ecological footprints: a sympathetic critique of theory and practice. Environ Urban 18(1):113–127. https://doi.org/10.1177/0956247806063963
Meadows D, Meadows D, Zahn E, Milling P (1973) Die Grenzen des Wachstums: Bericht des Club of Rome zur Lage der Menschenheit. In: Bericht des Club of Rome zur Lage der Menschenheit. Rowohlt
Meadows D, Meadows D, Randers J (1992) Die neuen Grenzen des Wachstums: Die Lage der Menschheit: Bedrohung und Zukunftschancen. In: Die Lage der Menschheit: Bedrohung und Zukunftschancen. Deutsche Verlags-Anstalt
Meadows DH, Randers J, Meadows DL, Pawlowsky S (2006) The limits to growth: 30 years later. Galaxia Gutenberg
Morgan RK (2012) Environmental impact assessment: the state of the art. Impact Assess Proj Apprais 30(1):5–14
Nicholson IR, Chambers N, Green P (2003) Ecological footprint analysis as a project assessment tool. Eng Sustain 156
Nogueira López A (2019) The ecological footprint. The establishment of environmental indicators and their significance for law. Catalan. J Environ Law 10(1). https://doi.org/10.17345/rcda2589
Peacock C, Markets M (2023) Consumer protection in the age of climate washing. W Va Law Rev 126:367. Available at: https://researchrepository.wvu.edu/wvlr/vol126/iss1/12
Quesnay F (1758). Tableau Économique

Rockström J, Steffen W, Noone K, Persson Å, Chapin S, Lambin E, Lenton TM et al (2009) Planetary boundaries: exploring the safe operating space for humanity. Ecol Soc 14(2) http://www.jstor.org/stable/26268316

Salinas Chávez E (2013) Reflections on the role of territorial planning in environmental planning and management. Geogr Persp 18(1):141–156

Steffen W, Broadgate W, Deutsch L, Gaffney O, Ludwig C (2015) The trajectory of the Anthropocene: the great acceleration. Anthropocene Rev 2(1):81–98. https://doi.org/10.1177/2053019614564785

Tumu K, Vorst K, Curtzwiler G (2023) Global plastic waste recycling and extended producer responsibility laws. J Environ Manag 348:119242. https://doi.org/10.1016/j.jenvman.2023.119242

UN (2018) The 2030 agenda and the sustainable development goals: an opportunity for Latin America and the Caribbean (LC/G. 2681-P/Rev. 3)

UN-Habitat. (2009) Planning sustainable cities: global report on human settlements. United Nations Human Settlements Programme

Vidal de los Santos E, López JF (2009) Environmental impact: a tool for sustainable development. AGT Editor, Mexico

Wackernagel M (1994) Ecological footprint and appropriate carrying capacity: a tool for planning toward sustainability. University of British Columbia. https://open.library.ubc.ca/collections/ubctheses/831/items/1.0088048

Weston J (2000) EIA, decision–making theory and screening and scoping in UK practice. J Environ Plan Manag 43(2):185–203

Ana María Bonet Researcher at CONICET – IHUCSO – UCSF. Associate Researcher at the Global Studies Programme – FLACSO. Postdoctoral Fellow, CONICET. PhD in Law (University of Bremen, Germany). Master of Laws – LL.M (University of Freiburg, Germany). Lawyer (UNL, Argentina), Mediator. Director of the Socio-Eco-Legal Research Team, UCSF, Argentina. "Legal regulation of access for the realization of (socio-)ecological rights." Visiting Researcher at the Max Planck Institute for International Law (Heidelberg, Germany). Visiting Research Fellow at the Institute for Sustainability, University of Kassel, Germany.

Cósimo Gonzalo Sozzo Director of the Institute for Advanced Studies of the Litoral. Full Professor at FCJS–UNL. Visiting Professor at the University of Limoges, France. Member of the Advisory Board of the International Panel on Social Progress. PhD in Legal and Social Sciences. Principal Investigator of the CAID+D UNL project: "The concept of regulation and institutionalization of climate change mitigation and adaptation in subnational states: the role of major cities and the business sector."

María Cristina Alé Master of Laws (LL.M) in Human Rights and International Humanitarian Law from the European University Viadrina (Germany). Lawyer (University of Mendoza). Editorial Board Member of the legal journal República y Derecho (RYD), National University of Cuyo, Argentina. Member of the Law and Development Research Network (LDRN), the Legal Network for Food Sovereignty (REDASA), and co-founding member of the International Network on Climate Change, Energy, and Human Rights (RICEDH). Lecturer in Public International Law and Regional Integration Law (University of Mendoza).

The Guarani Aquifer and the Transboundary Environmental and Climate Responsibility: Navigating Cooperative Governance and Conflict Resolution in a Shared Water Resource

Natalia Lorena Losccoco and Cássius Guimarães Chai

1 Introduction

Water scarcity and environmental degradation have become pressing global concerns, necessitating effective management of transboundary water resources. Among these resources, the Guarani Aquifer—a vast subterranean freshwater reservoir extending across Brazil, Argentina, Paraguay, and Uruguay—plays a crucial role in the water security of these nations. Covering approximately 1.2 million square kilometers, the aquifer serves as a lifeline for over 30 million people, providing essential water for agricultural activities and domestic requirements.

Despite its significance, the Guarani Aquifer faces multiple challenges that threaten its sustainability. These challenges include over-extraction, pollution, and climate change-induced variability,[1] as well as political complexities and technical difficulties associated with fragmented governance structures. The Guarani Aquifer Agreement serves as an essential legal framework aimed at fostering cooperative management among the countries involved. However, its effectiveness is hindered by inadequate enforcement mechanisms and a lack of cohesive governance strategies.[2]

[1] Cassuto et al. (2013).

[2] Eckstein and Eckstein (2005).

N. L. Losccoco (✉)
Buenos Aires University (UBA) and University of Belgrano (UB), Buenos Aires, Argentina
e-mail: nloscocco@derecho.uba.ar

C. G. Chai
Federal University of Maranhão (PPGDIR and PPGAERO/UFMA) and Vitória School of Law – (PPGD/FDV), Vitória, Brazil
e-mail: cassius.chai@ufma.br

V. E. de Aquino et al. (eds.), *Climate Litigation in a Changing World*, Ius Gentium: Comparative Perspectives on Law and Justice 130,
https://doi.org/10.1007/978-3-032-05530-9_10

The methodology emphasizes an interdisciplinary approach, integrating legal, political, and hydrological perspectives. A critical examination of the 2010 Guarani Aquifer Agreement reveals both achievements and gaps, particularly in enforcement and inter-country cooperation, which is challenged by fragmented governance and insufficient enforcement mechanisms across the nations involved. Utilizing case studies and comparative analyses with other transboundary aquifers, the study proposes adaptive management strategies that are responsive to scientific uncertainty and evolving domestic and international legal contexts. It advocates for harmonized legal frameworks, improved stakeholder engagement, and cooperative data sharing to enhance regional water security and promote sustainable resource management in response to the impacts of climate change.

This chapter seeks to illuminate these intricate challenges by first examining the legal and institutional frameworks surrounding the Guarani Aquifer, including the efficacy of the Guarani Aquifer Agreement. Subsequent sections will address the political and technical issues that complicate collaborative management efforts and highlight the importance of fostering public participation in decision-making processes. Ultimately, this analysis aims to propose concrete recommendations for enhancing cooperation and accountability, thereby reinforcing sustainable water management practices in the face of climate change and pollution.

2 The Guarani Aquifer: Characteristics and Importance

The Guaraní Aquifer System (GAS) is a critical transboundary water resource spanning Argentina, Brazil, Paraguay, and Uruguay, providing water security for over 30 million people in the region. With an estimated volume of 37,000 km^3 of freshwater, the GAS plays a vital role in supporting local populations, agricultural productivity, and economic stability across these four countries.[3] However, this crucial aquifer faces significant challenges, including over-extraction, pollution, and the impacts of climate change, all of which are exacerbated by inadequate governance frameworks.[4] However, this vital aquifer faces severe threats from over-extraction and pollution exacerbated by climate change and insufficient governance frameworks.[5]

For instance, the current resource exploitation totals 1.04 km^3 per year, with Brazil accounting for 94% of this extraction, of which 80% occurs in the state of São Paulo, followed by Uruguay (3%), Paraguay (2%), and Argentina (1%). Most of the extracted groundwater (80%) is used for public water supply, 15% for industrial processes, and 5% for geothermal spas. In Ribeirão Preto, Brazil, groundwater abstraction has grown significantly, substantially lowering water levels by an estimated 30–40 meters since 1970.

[3] Foster et al. (2009); Villar and Ribeiro (2011).

[4] Sindico et al. (2018); Eckstein (2009).

[5] Rodríguez de Taborda (2010).

The total level of groundwater abstraction in the area reached 186 Mm^3 per year in 2007, exceeding contemporary groundwater recharge. In São José do Rio Preto, Brazil, the urban water supply is provided from multiple sources, including the SAG, with intense competition between public and private abstractors. Private water wells account for a significant portion of the water supply, and efforts are being made to manage and regulate groundwater use. In Rivera, Uruguay, and Santana do Livramento, Brazil, the SAG is the principal source of water supply, with about 300 water wells providing a total of 16 Mm^3 per year. Groundwater abstraction has modified natural groundwater flow, depressing levels by 5–10 meters.[6]

Overall, the GAS is a storage-dominated system with recharge rates significantly lower than the total volume of water stored, and current extraction rates are leading to concerns about sustainability and groundwater level declines in heavily exploited areas.

While the Guaraní Aquifer Agreement of 2010 marked a positive step towards cooperative management, its implementation has been hindered by fragmented governance structures and weak enforcement mechanisms. The agreement acknowledges each state's sovereign rights over their respective portions of the aquifer. Still, there remains a pressing need for more robust institutional frameworks to facilitate data sharing, encourage public participation, and establish effective dispute resolution mechanisms.[7]

As climate change continues to impact water resources globally, the Guaraní Aquifer's sustainable management has become an environmental imperative and a crucial factor in fostering transboundary cooperation and regional stability.[8] Ultimately, the sustainable management of the Guaraní Aquifer is not merely an environmental imperative but a requirement for fostering transboundary cooperation in an era of increasing climate challenges.[9]

2.1 *Historical Context*

Over centuries, the Guarani Aquifer has served as a vital resource for diverse populations across Argentina, Brazil, Paraguay, and Uruguay, profoundly shaping their cultural and social landscape. Historically, indigenous communities have relied on their waters for sustenance, crafting a deep spiritual and practical connection to this underground treasure, often viewed as emblematic of their identity and heritage. The aquifer's cultural relevance extends to contemporary society. It underpins agricultural practices and the urban water supply, reflecting its pivotal role in economic stability and cultural continuity.

[6] Hirata and Foster (2020).

[7] Villar (2014).

[8] Sindico and Hawkins (2015); Amore and Tröger (2010); Aquifer Guaraní Agreement (2010).

[9] Cassuto et al. (2013); Grafton et al. (2014).

The Guarani Aquifer Agreement emerged from a historical backdrop of fragmented governance and regional tensions over transboundary water management. This is a response to the growing recognition of shared water resources amid escalating environmental concerns. Historically, this vital aquifer has faced significant threats from pollution, over-extraction, and climate change, compelling nations to seek sustainable solutions.

The agreement, formalized in 2010 and entered into force in 2020, sought to establish a framework for cooperation between Brazil, Argentina, Paraguay, and Uruguay, drawing upon principles of equitable resource sharing and protection against transboundary harm.[10] However, as White[11] highlighted, implementation gaps persist due to differing national policies and enforcement challenges.

2.2 Geographical and Hydrological Features of the Aquifer and Overexploitation Challenges

Deep beneath the landscapes of Brazil, Argentina, Paraguay, and Uruguay lies the Guarani Aquifer, a crucial transboundary freshwater resource recognized for its substantial geological and hydrological significance, positioning itself as a vital lifeline for increasing global water scarcity.

The formation of the aquifer is characterized by ancient sandstone layers, which facilitate substantial natural filtration processes and complicate regional water management owing to their geological variability. Water from the aquifer must navigate through porous sediment, posing challenges for sustainable extraction practices amid rising pollution concerns.[12]

The GAS faces significant environmental challenges across multiple South American nations, particularly regarding water security concerns arising from extensive groundwater exploitation and contamination. Similarly, the Caribbean region exhibits distinct vulnerabilities, as groundwater constitutes approximately half of its total water usage. In contrast, the region simultaneously contends with escalating threats from coastal hazards and rising sea levels.

Within this context, environmental degradation manifests through diverse contaminants, including naturally occurring substances such as arsenic and fluoride, alongside human-induced pollutants. The latter category encompasses agricultural chemicals, industrial waste, and emerging contaminants such as pharmaceutical residues and synthetic materials. These environmental challenges have significantly increased water-related disputes, which originate from various sources, including competing water access claims, territorial conflicts, and controversies linked to extractive industries.

---

[10] Gomez (2014).

[11] Grafton et al. (2014).

[12] Gomez (2014).

Tensions surrounding resource management have escalated markedly, with data indicating that water-related conflicts initiated between 2000 and 2019 have exceeded those of previous decades by more than fourfold. This sharp rise underscores the growing pressure on transboundary water resources and highlights the urgent need to strengthen governance mechanisms to ensure sustainable management.[13]

As surrounding countries strive for effective governance, the negotiation of equitable resource utilization will depend on rigorous adherence to environmental protection guidelines and shared scientific data.[14] Thus, understanding these hydrogeological features is essential for fostering international cooperation in the sustainable management of this transboundary aquifer.

2.3 Socioeconomic, Biodiversity, and Ecological Importance

The Guarani Aquifer has profound socioeconomic implications for Argentina, Brazil, Paraguay, and Uruguay. However, inequities in access and regulatory frameworks exacerbate tensions among nations, as differing priorities influence each country's management strategies.

This fragmented governance complicates the collaborative efforts essential for sustainable utilization. The Guarani Aquifer Agreement, a significant step toward joint management, faces challenges in implementation owing to a lack of harmonization and political will.[15] Thus, enhancing cooperative frameworks and institutional capacities is essential for ensuring equitable resource distribution, promoting socioeconomic stability, and safeguarding this vital water source for future generations.

The interdependence of biodiversity and ecological health within the context of the Guarani Aquifer is crucial for sustaining the regional environment and communities reliant upon it. As freshwater ecosystems are intricately linked to terrestrial biodiversity, the degradation of the Guarani Aquifer can lead to significant ecological ramifications, such as the loss of species that depend on these water sources for survival.[16]

As over 30 million individuals rely on the Guarani Aquifer, its sustainability is directly tied to their health and well-being.[17] Furthermore, diverse biological communities contribute to natural filtration processes and enhance water quality by mitigating pollutants. However, increasing pressure from pollution and over-extraction has worsened due to climate change, endangering these crucial ecosys-

[13] UNESCO (2022).

[14] da Silva et al. (2019).

[15] Cassuto et al. (2013); Grafton et al. (2014).

[16] Eckstein (2009).

[17] Grafton et al. (2014).

tems and necessitating strong legal frameworks and international cooperation to protect both biodiversity and human livelihoods.[18]

The imperative to sustain this aquatic resource shows a compelling intersection between ecological integrity and transboundary responsibility, underscoring the need for comprehensive policies that respect and protect ecological resilience, while ensuring equitable access to water resources.

2.4 The Role of the Aquifer in Regional Climate Resilience

The Guarani Aquifer is vital for improving regional climate resilience due to increasing climatic variability. Sustainable management has a direct impact on the availability of water in neighboring countries. This vast aquifer provides an essential buffer against the adverse effects of climate change, including droughts and flooding. Access to clean water from aquifers ensures basic health needs and bolsters agricultural productivity, especially in increasing food insecurity driven by climate challenges.

However, over-extraction, pollution, and fragmented governance threaten the potential of aquifers, undermining their role in regional stability.[19] Enhanced collaborative frameworks, as emphasized in the Guaraní Aquifer Agreement, are fundamental to overcoming these obstacles and achieving sustainable usage. They provide a pathway for all parties to synergistically address transboundary environmental challenges, while fostering resilience against climate-related shocks.[20]

2.5 Comparison with Other Transboundary Aquifers

The complexities of transboundary aquifer management are clearly illustrated when comparing the Guarani Aquifer System with other notable aquifers, such as the Nubian Sandstone Aquifer in North Africa and the Iullemeden Aquifer, which spans several countries in West Africa.

As a note of comparison and contextualization, the Nubian Sandstone Aquifer System (NSAS) is one of the world's largest fossil aquifer systems, extending over two million km^2 across Egypt, Libya, Sudan, and Chad.[21] It is comparable in scale to other major confined aquifers like the Continental Intercalaire in North Africa and the Great Artesian Basin of Australia (Hamed et al. 2012). The NSAS consists of two main aquifers: the deeper Nubian Sandstone Aquifer and the overlying Post-

[18] Grafton et al. (2014).

[19] Eckstein and Eckstein (2005).

[20] Grafton et al. (2014); Cassuto et al. (2013).

[21] Abdalla Mg (2015); Quadri (2019).

Nubian limestone aquifer in the northern portion.[22] The system's depth increases from north to south and west to east, reaching up to 4000 m in some areas.[23]

The aquifer holds an estimated 500 trillion m3 of freshwater, with groundwater ages ranging from 4000 to over one million years, indicating its non-renewable nature.[24] Interestingly, while the NSAS is primarily a fossil aquifer, some studies suggest potential modern recharge in certain areas. For instance, research indicates possible recharge from Lake Nasser and precipitation in relatively high rainfall zones.[25]

However, overexploitation has led to various issues, including spring drying, decreasing water levels and quality, land subsidence, and saltwater intrusion from the Mediterranean Sea.[26] Additionally, natural radioactivity in the groundwater poses health risks in some regions.[27] These challenges highlight the need for sustainable management practices and international cooperation among the shared countries to ensure the aquifer's long-term viability.[28] Similar to the Guarani Aquifer, these aquifer systems face challenges from over-extraction, pollution, and political disagreements among countries sharing these vital resources.

For instance, despite being subject to the 1992 Agreement on the Management of the Nubian Sandstone Aquifer System, the Nubian Aquifer still has problems with fragmented governance and unilateral actions that hinder collaborative management.[29] Conversely, the Guarani Aquifer Agreement allows for some level of cooperation by emphasizing mutual obligation and environmental protection. Nevertheless, it struggles with implementation due to insufficient legal frameworks and enforcement mechanisms.

Likewise, in African experience, transboundary waterways in Central Asia are currently facing significant water shortages, exacerbated by inefficient irrigation methods and rising demand for water resources. Critical environmental challenges, including the degradation of the Aral Sea, desertification, and biodiversity loss, are pervasive. Water resources in Central Asia are unevenly distributed among nations. Upstream countries such as Tajikistan and Kyrgyzstan predominantly utilize water for electricity generation, whereas downstream countries like Uzbekistan, Kazakhstan, and Turkmenistan employ it for irrigation purposes.

Rising temperatures are melting glaciers, which is expected to slow the flow of major rivers like the Amudarya and Syrdarya, reducing the amount of water available even more. The transition from a centralized water management system to national systems has heightened the likelihood of water conflicts among regional

[22] Hosseini et al. (2024).

[23] Hosseini et al. (2024).

[24] Hosseini et al. (2024).

[25] Sultan et al. (2013).

[26] Hosseini et al. (2024).

[27] Sherif and Sturchio (2021).

[28] Hosseini et al. (2024); Quadri (2019).

[29] Rodríguez de Taborda (2010).

governments. In response, strong treaties and effective agreements are essential to regulate water-sharing practices, ensuring an equitable and environmentally sustainable approach to transboundary water resource management.[30]

These challenges highlight the urgent need to strengthen international cooperation, adopt advanced irrigation technologies, and enhance water resource management efficiency to ensure the long-term sustainability of transboundary water resources in Central Asia.[31] The comparison with other regions demonstrates the importance of solid international cooperation and flexible strategies for managing transboundary aquifers. They also show that despite progress, significant legal and political gaps still make it difficult to use the sustainable management methods needed for environmental protection and regional stability.

2.6 Stakeholder Perspectives on Aquifer Management and Future Projection: Climate Litigation in Transboundary Aquifer Governance

The complexity of the Guarani Aquifer serves as an example of how understanding the various stakeholder viewpoints in aquifer management is necessary for the effective governance of shared water resources. Local communities emphasize the need for sustainable practices to preserve their primary water sources, while national governments often prioritize economic exploitation over environmental protection.

Climate litigation has emerged as a tool to enforce environmental accountability in transboundary contexts. Although Lhaka Honat v. Argentina (IACHR, 2020) primarily addressed Indigenous land and environmental rights, its precedent is relevant to Guarani communities reliant on the aquifer, highlighting states' obligations to prevent environmental harm. In Leghari v. Pakistan (Lahore High Court 2015) compelled the government to implement climate adaptation measures, illustrating how courts can mandate actionable policies for resource sustainability.[32]

The European Court of Human Rights ruling in López Ostra v. Spain (1994) demonstrates judicial recognition of state liability for environmental harm affecting human rights, a model that may inform legal approaches to aquifer contamination under the GAA. These cases underscore the necessity of integrating legal mechanisms for environmental accountability within the GAA to protect vulnerable populations.

In the Central Asia context, where 34 transboundary aquifers are identified, the arid and semi-arid climate makes groundwater a critical resource for socioeconomic development.[33] Similarly, in North Africa, major transboundary aquifers are experi-

[30] Narzullaev and Bekov (2024).

[31] OECD (2020).

[32] Leghari V. Federation of Pakistan - Climate Change Litigation (2018).

[33] Liu et al. (2020).

encing significant changes in groundwater storage, with some systems showing depletion due to both climate factors and increased water abstraction.[34]

The Guaraní Aquifer Agreement aims to address these perspectives by promoting collaboration among Argentina, Brazil, Paraguay, and Uruguay; however, its implementation suffers from fragmented governance and insufficient law enforcement mechanisms. Stakeholders' express concerns regarding over-extraction and pollution threats and call for robust monitoring frameworks and public participation to facilitate transparency and accountability.

Furthermore, integrating scientific and legal principles into policymaking processes can foster cooperative management to mitigate conflicting national interests.[35] This alignment among stakeholders is essential for establishing a resilient governance structure capable of addressing both environmental challenges and community needs, ultimately ensuring the sustainable future of the Guarani Aquifer.

Projected assessments of the future health of the Guarani Aquifer indicate a multifaceted challenge that intertwines environmental sustainability with socio-political dynamics among the four nations involved. Additionally, climate change scenarios suggest that variations in precipitation and temperature will further strain groundwater replenishment rates, emphasizing the urgency for collaborative adaptive management approaches that prioritize long-term sustainability over short-term needs.[36]

Ultimately, the continued decline in the aquifer's health underscores the pressing need for extensive international cooperation, robust regulatory mechanisms, and heightened public engagement to ensure its preservation for future generations.

3 Legal Framework and Governance of the Guarani Aquifer

The effective governance of the Guarani Aquifer hinges on the legal frameworks established by the nations involved. Current instruments, such as the Guaraní Aquifer Agreement, aim to foster sustainable management; however, significant deficiencies persist. Harmonizing national interests among various legal regimes is a notable example of how fragmented governance structures and uneven enforcement mechanisms undermine cooperation.

Principles such as equitable utilization and prevention of significant harm, highlighted in international treaties, should guide actions within this legal framework.[37] Political obstacles and a lack of domestic legislation frequently prevent the practical implementation of these ideals, causing conflicts in groundwater management practices.[38]

[34] Frappart (2020).
[35] Eckstein and Eckstein (2005).
[36] Eckstein and Eckstein (2005).
[37] Withanachchi et al. (2012).
[38] Eckstein and Eckstein (2005).

A robust joint monitoring mechanism is essential to achieve effective governance. It facilitates data sharing and engages stakeholders across borders, strengthening accountability and environmental responsibility in transboundary water management.

3.1 Overview of the Guarani Aquifer Agreement

To address the complexities of transboundary water management, the Guarani Aquifer Agreement exemplifies a collaborative effort among Argentina, Brazil, Paraguay, and Uruguay to ensure the sustainable use of a vital shared resource. This framework acknowledges each party's sovereign rights while establishing protocols for information-sharing and environmental safeguards.

However, the agreement faces significant challenges such as fragmented governance and the lack of robust enforcement mechanisms that hinder effective implementation. While it aims to foster cooperation and prevent environmental harm, the agreements' inadequacies may slip into obscurity without regular monitoring and public participation, as highlighted in.

By fostering a joint monitoring body and harmonizing legal approaches, stakeholders could substantially improve governance and accountability, ultimately ensuring the sustainability of the Guarani Aquifer amid increasing climate variability and resource scarcity.[39]

3.2 Analysis of Legal Provisions Within the Agreement: Climate Litigation Potential in the GAA

Legally, the Guaraní Aquifer Agreement encompasses a series of provisions aimed at sustainable management while recognizing the sovereign rights of the parties involved. The commitment to prevent environmental harm through cooperation is central to the Agreement, underscoring the necessity for shared responsibilities in managing this critical resource. Although the GAA, modeled after the International Law Commission Draft Articles on Transboundary Aquifers of 2008, provides a framework for regional cooperation designed to avoid or resolve conflicts (Tinker 2016). Notable gaps exist in its implementation, primarily because of fragmented governance structures and inadequate enforcement mechanisms.[40]

Transboundary cooperation has been slow since 2010, limited to sporadic cross-border projects and some new local/national initiatives.[41] This fragmentation in gov-

[39] Cassuto et al. (2013); Grafton et al. (2014).

[40] Eckstein and Eckstein (2005).

[41] Hirata et al. (2020).

ernance is evident in the lack of coordinated approaches and the diminishing chances of obtaining international funds. Interestingly, the absence of transboundary conflicts within the Guarani Aquifer System (GAS) has created a sense of abundance, leading to a lack of proactivity regarding agreement implementation.[42] This has resulted in outdated data and tools, disruption of cooperation and administrative networks, and lost opportunities for detailed assessments to manage the aquifer's heterogeneities and dynamics.

The GAA does not explicitly address climate-induced stressors, such as droughts or altered recharge patterns, thereby limiting its applicability in climate litigation contexts. For instance, although Article 4 highlights the principle of "equitable and reasonable utilization," it does not define thresholds for sustainable extraction under climate change scenarios (Villar and Ribeiro 2011). This gap contrasts with precedents like Urgenda Foundation v Netherlands, where the Dutch Supreme Court mandated emissions reductions to protect citizens' rights, establishing a judicial duty to mitigate climate harm.[43]

To enhance the GAA's relevance for climate litigation, amendments should include climate adaptation benchmarks, such as tying extraction limits to IPCC hydrological projections. Additionally, Advisory Opinion OC-23/17 of the Inter-American Court of Human Rights[44] reaffirms States' duty to prevent transboundary environmental harm. This principle could be operationalized within the GAA by binding climate accountability and risk mitigation clauses.

For instance, while the agreement outlines a framework for information sharing and technical cooperation, there is insufficient clarity on the roles and responsibilities of state parties, hindering effective collaboration. Additionally, as referenced in the agreement, consultation mechanisms remain underutilized, leading to missed opportunities for coordinated action against pollution and over-extraction. This impacts water security for millions within the aquifers' reach.[45] Addressing these shortcomings is essential for establishing a robust legal foundation to confront transboundary water management's complexities.

Fragmented governance impedes climate litigation by obscuring accountability. The absence of a centralized monitoring body within the GAA starkly contrasts to rulings such as Leghari v. Pakistan (2015), where the court mandated comprehensive climate vulnerability assessments. Incorporating similar evaluative mechanisms under the GAA could facilitate the quantification of harm and enable judicial mandates for remedial action in transboundary water governance.

---

[42] Hirata et al. (2020).

[43] *Urgend a Foundation V. State of the Netherlands - Climate Change Litigation* (2020).

[44] Interamerican Court of Human Rights (2017).

[45] Sindico and Hawkins (2015); Cassuto et al. (2013).

3.3 Fragmented Governance Structures and Inadequate Enforcement Mechanisms

The existing governance structures surrounding the Guarani Aquifer reveal a troubling fragmentation pattern among Argentina, Brazil, Paraguay, and Uruguay, which hinders collaborative resource management. The Guaraní Aquifer Agreement aims for sustainable use, but there are still key problems because of different national legal frameworks and a lack of unified implementation strategies. This makes it hard to enforce the environmental protections that were agreed upon.

Furthermore, the absence of a centralized monitoring body complicates efforts to oversee the aquifer's health, leading to inconsistent data sharing and decision-making processes. The complexities of regional hydropolitics, as highlighted in da Silva et al. (2019),[46] underscore how fragmented governance can exacerbate tensions over resource allocation and environmental degradation.

Because of this, the chances of managing this significant cross-border resource well are still very low without a unified approach that includes scientific knowledge and fair government.[47] Addressing these fragmentation issues is imperative for fostering cooperation and ensuring the longevity of the Guarani Aquifer.

Inadequate enforcement mechanisms fundamentally undermine the effectiveness of international agreements, such as the Guaraní Aquifer Agreement, leading to severe implications for sustainable management. While the agreement aims to promote cooperation among the parties, its weaknesses in implementation and oversight have resulted in fragmented governance that fails to address pressing issues like over-extraction and pollution.[48]

The literature highlights that the lack of robust legal frameworks contributes to limited accountability, diminishing the potential for effective transboundary management.[49] Conflicting domestic laws among the participating countries worsens the situation by making it challenging to apply coherent policies and undermining cooperative efforts.

As environmental challenges multiply, particularly in the face of climate change, the absence of solid and coherent enforcement mechanisms threatens the aquifers' sustainability. It jeopardizes regional water security, necessitating immediate and comprehensive reform of governance structures.[50]

---

[46] da Silva et al. (2019).

[47] Eckstein and Eckstein (2005).

[48] Eckstein and Eckstein (2005).

[49] Grafton et al. (2014).

[50] Aquifer Guaraní Agreement (2010).

3.4 The Role of International Law in Transboundary Water Management and Judicial Regional Perspectives

International law is fundamental because it sets rules like fair use and shared responsibility. These rules are spelled out in essential documents like the Helsinki and Berlin Rules, which affect how states deal with shared aquifers.[51]

Moreover, the necessity for clear demarcation of shared responsibilities and the obligations to prevent harm further illustrates the potential of international law to resolve disputes arising from competing national interests, creating a framework that emphasizes cooperation over conflict. Sustainable management of the Guarani Aquifer will continue to be problematic without an improved legislative framework incorporating science, public involvement, and enforceable promises.

The pivotal role of the Inter-American Court of Human Rights (IACHR) in adjudicating transboundary environmental issues is particularly salient in the context of the Guarani Aquifer, which traverses multiple national jurisdictions. The IACHR's views often show the importance of including environmental rights in the larger human rights framework. For example, Odaguiri[52] shows how access to clean water is directly linked to state accountability and individual welfare.

The Inter-American Court of Human Rights (IACtHR) jurisprudence provides a valuable roadmap for adjudicating climate-related breaches of the GAA. In Yakye Axa Indigenous Community v. Paraguay (2005), the court affirmed states' duty to protect Indigenous livelihoods from environmental degradation. This principle could be extended to cases of climate-induced aquifer depletion. Hypothetically, Guarani communities could invoke this precedent to challenge unsustainable extraction practices, exacerbating water scarcity. Similarly, the African Commission's ruling in *Social and Economic Rights Action Center (SERAC) v. Nigeria* (2001) established the principle of state accountability for environmental harm affecting human health. This framework could apply to pollution-related cases under the Guaraní Aquifer Agreement (GAA). To enhance access to justice and ensure the adequate protection of affected communities, State Parties could consider strengthening the Agreement's dispute resolution mechanisms, potentially by aligning them with human rights-based standards.

For instance, it reflects on the intersection of human rights and international environmental law, emphasizing the courts' evolving doctrine that affirms the right to a healthy environment as fundamental. Such rulings underscore that environmental degradation can breach individual rights, thereby compelling states to collaborate effectively on resource management.

Furthermore, the court's determinations push for robust legal frameworks that ensure equitable resource sharing, a crucial aspect in managing the Guarani Aquifer effectively and in alignment with the principle of sustainable development, as articulated in (Wilk et al., 2016). Addressing the judicial perspective thus draws

[51] Cassuto et al. (2013).

[52] Odaguiri et al. (2011).

attention to transboundary resource dynamics and reinforces the need for comprehensive legal obligations to uphold environmental and human rights within the region concurrently.

3.5 Domestic Legislation and Its Impact on Aquifer Management

Effective management of the Guarani Aquifer is intimately tied to the nuances of domestic legislation across the four nations it straddles. Each country—Brazil, Argentina, Paraguay, and Uruguay—operates under its legal framework concerning groundwater resources, leading to significant regulatory discrepancies and conflicts that further complicate transboundary governance.

The divergence in domestic legislation and local priorities manifests in inconsistent resource management strategies, potentially exacerbating issues of over-extraction and pollution. Therefore, reconciling these legal frameworks and fostering a cooperative regulatory environment is crucial to ensuring the aquifer's health and availability for future generations, necessitating an urgent rethinking of domestic and international legal obligations.[53]

Amid the increasing pressures on the Guarani Aquifer, adopting a multifaceted approach to enhancing the legal frameworks governing its management is crucial. The legal frameworks should be harmonized to account for discrepancies in domestic legislation, as these inconsistencies can create significant obstacles to effective aquifer management.[54] Finally, fostering broader public participation in decision-making is essential to cultivating a shared sense of responsibility and commitment to preserving this vital resource for future generations.[55]

4 Political and Institutional Challenges

Sustainable management of the Guarani Aquifer faces formidable political and institutional challenges that hinder effective governance among the four sharing nations. Fragmented governance structures and inadequate enforcement mechanisms exacerbate tensions, leading to ineffective implementation of the Guaraní Aquifer Agreement.[56] The absence of a unified legal framework complicates collaborative efforts, mainly as domestic legislation varies significantly across

[53] Cassuto et al. (2013); Grafton et al. (2014).

[54] Eckstein and Eckstein (2005).

[55] Eckstein (2009).

[56] Eckstein and Eckstein (2005).

Argentina, Brazil, Paraguay, and Uruguay, creating inconsistencies that stall progress.

Civil society involvement remains minimal, reducing public accountability and oversight while entrenching political disagreements. Reliance on unilateral actions often leads to detrimental outcomes, as evidenced by the environmental degradation and declining water quality associated with overexploitation and insufficient cooperative policies along shared borders.[57]

To address the political and institutional challenges faced in the sustainable management of the Guarani Aquifer, it is essential to explore comprehensive solutions that leverage international law and regional judicial mechanisms. Strengthening the legal frameworks governing the aquifer can enhance cooperation among the four nations by establishing uniform regulatory standards and compliance protocols.

Engaging regional courts to arbitrate disputes and enforce agreements could foster accountability and mitigate tensions, promoting a more cohesive governance model. Additionally, incorporating stakeholders, including local communities and environmental advocacy groups, into decision-making processes can enrich governance practices through a participatory approach. This reinforces public accountability and cultivates a shared sense of stewardship over the resource.

Collaborative initiatives focusing on educational outreach to raise awareness about the aquifer's significance and the importance of sustainable practices can further galvanize civil society involvement, ultimately leading to a more robust and effective governance framework.

4.1 Political Dynamics and Public Policies

Political dynamics among Argentina, Brazil, Paraguay, and Uruguay regarding the Guarani Aquifer are characterized by a complex interplay of national interests that often results in discord. The diverging priorities of these nations complicate the shared management of this vital resource, as each country possesses its distinct legal frameworks and water management policies.[58]

Although initiatives like the Agreement aim to foster collective responsibility, the lack of effective enforcement mechanisms and a tendency toward fragmented governance amplify political disagreements, as each country tends to prioritize its sovereignty over collaborative sustainability efforts.[59] This dissonance highlights the pressing need for coherent strategies that can reconcile national objectives with transboundary responsibilities to ensure the aquifers long-term viability.

Each of the four signatory countries approaches the aquifer with differing priorities shaped by local economic demands, political agendas, and environmental

[57] Withanachchi et al. (2012).

[58] Rodríguez de Taborda (2010).

[59] Eckstein and Eckstein (2005).

concerns. Brazil's inclination toward unilateral management of its portion of the aquifer exemplifies a national interest that conflicts with the collaborative objectives of sustainable resource management outlined in the Guaraní Aquifer Agreement.

This disagreement is a sign of a bigger problem: different national rules make it harder for people to work together. For example, different groundwater management laws make it hard to create a unified framework to effectively lower pollution risks.[60]

As climate change exacerbates water scarcity and alters hydrological cycles, states may prioritize immediate national security over long-term regional sustainability, leading to intensified competition rather than cooperation. Such a landscape necessitates robust mechanisms and mutual recognition of national interests aligned with regional goals to foster effective transboundary governance.[61]

The current governance surrounding the aquifer exemplifies significant shortcomings that undermine effective environmental management. Fragmented public policies across Argentina, Brazil, Paraguay, and Uruguay complicate collaborative efforts, leading to inconsistent management practices and regulatory enforcement. Specifically, it highlights the lack of a comprehensive legal framework, which impedes cooperative governance and effective resource allocation crucial for water security.

Additionally, the Guaraní Aquifer Agreement, while a step towards sustainable management, suffers from implementation gaps and insufficient enforcement mechanisms, as noted in (Hayes Vieira, 2019). These inadequacies foster an environment where environmental protection is secondary to national interests, further exacerbating over-extraction and pollution.

Furthermore, widespread pollution from unchecked farming shows that current policies are not doing enough to stop transboundary water contamination, which means that regional governance cannot protect this critical resource.[62] Ultimately, a paradigm shift towards enhanced cooperation and cohesive policy frameworks is essential to ensure the aquifer's sustainability amid growing environmental challenges.

4.2 Historical Context of Political Relations in the Region

Historical tensions and cooperative efforts surrounding shared resources, particularly the Guarani Aquifer, have significantly impacted political relations between Argentina, Brazil, Paraguay, and Uruguay. The legacy of colonialism and subsequent national independence movements has fostered cooperation and rivalry, often exacerbating resource allocation and management disputes.

---

[60] Eckstein and Eckstein (2005).

[61] Cassuto et al. (2013); Grafton et al. (2014).

[62] Gomez (2014).

The development of the Guaran Aquifer Agreement, which aims to promote sustainable usage against a backdrop of fragmented governance and inconsistent enforcement mechanisms, as highlighted in, emphasizes this complex political landscape. The diverse legal frameworks of these countries further complicate effective collaboration, leading to challenges in harmonizing water policies that reflect national sovereignty and the imperative of collective environmental responsibility.[63]

Ultimately, the historical context of political relations underscores the necessity for enhanced cooperation and the establishment of robust legal frameworks, as supported by the evolving principles of international water law gleaned from the practices outlined.[64]

4.3 Influence of Economic Factors on Environmental Policies

Economic factors profoundly shape environmental policies, particularly in the context of transboundary resources like the Aquifer. The imperative for economic development often leads nations to prioritize short-term growth over sustainable practices, resulting in policies that inadequately address critical environmental challenges, such as over-extraction and pollution. For instance, it emphasizes the necessity of collaborative governance to mitigate the threats posed by over-extraction, which can adversely impact water security for millions in the region.

Furthermore, as we have discussed before, the Guarani Aquifer Agreement aims to promote sustainable water management but encounters implementation gaps due to fragmented governance and a lack of financial resources for enforcement.[65] This demonstrates how economic constraints hinder effective environmental stewardship, underscoring the need for integrated approaches that align economic incentives with environmental protections.

Ultimately, developing robust legal frameworks like the Guarani Aquifer Agreement is vital. Yet, success remains contingent upon harmonizing economic ambitions with environmental responsibilities, thereby fostering a cooperative paradigm that benefits all stakeholders involved.

[63] Eckstein and Eckstein (2005).

[64] Gomez (2014; Grafton et al. (2014).

[65] Eckstein and Eckstein (2005).

4.4 Public Awareness and Participation in Governance

Aquifer governance of transboundary water resources, particularly in the case of the Guarani Aquifer, necessitates robust legal frameworks and active public engagement and awareness. Public participation fosters a sense of ownership and accountability, critical for sustainable resource management. As highlighted, fragmented governance structures and inadequate enforcement mechanisms within the Guarani Aquifer Agreement diminish stakeholder trust and involvement.

Involving local communities in decision-making processes can enhance the transparency and efficacy of governance, ensuring that diverse perspectives are considered, thereby enriching policy outcomes. To get more people to understand how vital the aquifers are, educational programs could also help with conservation efforts. This would align with the ideas of fair use and avoiding harm emphasized in international legal documents.[66] Fostering a collaborative governance model that prioritizes public participation is essential for addressing environmental challenges inherent in managing shared freshwater resources.

4.5 Case Studies of Successful and Failed Cooperation Efforts

The complexities surrounding transboundary aquifer management are vividly illustrated through various cooperation efforts, revealing successes and failures. The Guaraní Aquifer Agreement, though a progressive step toward sustainable management among Argentina, Brazil, Paraguay, and Uruguay, has faced notable shortcomings, notably in its implementation and enforcement mechanisms; despite robust provisions, the lack of coordinated governance has hindered meaningful progress.

On the other hand, the Franco-Swiss agreement for the Genevese Aquifer is an example of effective transboundary management. This successful implementation demonstrates how integrated monitoring networks, clear allocation protocols, and shared financial responsibilities can overcome traditional barriers to transboundary cooperation. The model's success lies in establishing a joint management authority with robust enforcement powers and standardized data collection protocols. Their implementation of a comprehensive digital monitoring system that tracks extraction rates, water quality parameters, and recharge patterns in real-time, enabling swift responses to environmental changes and potential violations, is particularly noteworthy.

This approach has proven especially effective in addressing climate-related challenges, as evidenced by their adaptive management strategies during drought and increased water demand. It shows how shared technical knowledge and making decisions together can promote sustainability.[67] These contrasting case studies

[66] Grafton et al. (2014); Sindico and Hawkins (2015).

[67] Eckstein and Eckstein (2005).

underscore the necessity for strong legal frameworks, well-defined responsibilities, and proactive engagement among stakeholders, as highlighted by the urgent need for harmonized legal approaches to prevent pollution and resource depletion.[68]

Success in managing transboundary aquifers requires innovative strategies that foster political collaboration among the nations involved. One practical approach to enhance cooperation involves establishing robust institutional frameworks prioritizing shared governance and enforcement mechanisms currently lacking in the Guarani Aquifer Agreement.[69]

Additionally, integrating scientific research into legal policies can clarify hydrological connections, supporting informed decision-making and conflict resolution. Promoting transparent data-sharing practices is crucial to building trust and accountability among stakeholders, as successful collaborative management relies on the real-time exchange of information regarding resource usage and environmental conditions.[70]

Furthermore, encouraging active public participation in decision-making can amplify community voices, legitimize governmental actions, and foster a culture of shared responsibility.[71] Ultimately, these strategies will create a more comprehensive governance model that effectively addresses the complexities of the Guarani Aquifer's management.

5 Environmental and Climate Responsibility

This aquifer exemplifies the environmental and climate responsibilities that nations must embrace to mitigate potential conflicts arising from resource depletion and pollution. It serves as a reminder of the interconnectedness of human societies and the natural world, highlighting the need for collaborative efforts in protecting our shared resources. As water scarcity becomes an increasingly pressing issue globally, it is imperative for governments and communities to prioritize sustainable management practices and conservation efforts. Failure to do so threatens the livelihoods of millions and exacerbates tensions and conflicts over access to essential resources. Affected nations must transcend traditional security paradigms and adopt a more integrative approach that aligns with principles of shared stewardship and sustainable practice.[72]

A potential framework for addressing accountability gaps in climate governance could involve a protocol inspired by climate litigation precedents and international environmental law. The Juliana v. United States case, filed in 2015, established

[68] Grafton et al. (2014); Okonkwo (2016).

[69] Eckstein and Eckstein (2005).

[70] Grafton et al. (2014).

[71] Withanachchi et al. (2012).

[72] Grafton et al. (2014).

important principles despite its dismissal.[73] The plaintiffs argued that government policies promoting fossil fuel consumption violated their constitutional rights to life, liberty, and property.[74] They asserted a fundamental right to a "climate system capable of sustaining human life". They claimed the government violated the public trust doctrine by failing to protect essential natural resources for future generations.

Furthermore, transparency mechanisms, similar to those in the Paris Agreement,[75] could be integrated into such a framework. The Paris Agreement's Enhanced Transparency Framework requires countries to report greenhouse gas emissions and progress toward climate commitments regularly.[76] For aquifer management, mandatory reporting of extraction rates compared to recharge data could create reliable evidence for climate litigation, enhancing accountability through measurement and review.[77]

Incorporating human rights principles, as articulated by the Inter-American Court of Human Rights (IACtHR), can significantly enhance environmental protection efforts. The Court has emphasized recognizing the right to a healthy environment as a fundamental human right, alongside the corresponding state obligations to prevent environmental harm. These obligations include cooperation with affected states, access to environmental information, public participation in decision-making, and access to justice. This jurisprudence provides a valuable framework for linking environmental protection with human rights, reinforcing the need for integrated and rights-based environmental governance.[78]

By fostering more robust institutional frameworks and enhancing public participation in decision-making, the region can better uphold its environmental responsibilities while promoting resilience against emerging climate challenges, ultimately safeguarding this vital resource for future generations. For example, countries in the Middle East and North Africa region are facing severe water scarcity due to overexploitation of groundwater sources and pollution from industrial activities. By implementing stricter regulations on water usage and investing in sustainable technologies, these nations can mitigate the impacts of climate change and ensure a more secure water supply for their populations.

[73] Bucher (2017).

[74] Juliana V. United States - Climate Change Litigation (2017).

[75] Paris Agreement (2015).

[76] Enhanced Transparency Framework (n.d.).

[77] Center for Climate and Energy Solutions (2017).

[78] Tigre and Urzola (2021).

5.1 *Definition and Scope of Environmental Responsibility*

Responsibility for environmental stewardship extends beyond national boundaries, particularly in regions like the Guarani Aquifer, where shared resources necessitate collective accountability. At its core, environmental responsibility encompasses the duty of states and communities to manage natural resources sustainably, ensuring that ecological integrity is preserved for future generations.

This concept is profoundly articulated in frameworks such as the Guaraní Aquifer Agreement, which seeks to balance sovereign rights with obligations to prevent environmental harm and to promote equitable utilization of resources.[79] However, ineffective enforcement mechanisms and fragmented governance structures frequently limit the practical scope of this responsibility.

Thus, a comprehensive understanding of environmental responsibility must encompass legal obligations, local governance capacities, and the dynamics of international cooperation to effectively address the myriad challenges posed by transboundary environmental management, particularly considering the escalating threats from climate change.

5.2 *Climate Change Impacts on the Guarani Aquifer*

The effects of climate change on the Guarani Aquifer are profound and multifaceted, exacerbating existing challenges linked to this vital transboundary resource. Altered precipitation patterns threaten the aquifers' recharge capabilities, impacting water availability for the millions who depend on it for drinking, agriculture, and industry.

Increasing temperatures may accelerate evaporation rates, further compounding stress on groundwater reserves while potentially leading to pollution from surrounding agricultural runoff.[80] Furthermore, intensified droughts could push neighboring countries into competition for already-strained water resources, increasing the likelihood of transboundary conflicts.[81]

While the existing Guaraní Aquifer Agreement is a step towards cooperative management, it suffers from fragmented enforcement and a lack of comprehensive regulatory frameworks to address climate-induced challenges.

The intersection of climate change impacts and governance solutions demands innovative technological approaches to aquifer management. Satellite-based monitoring systems, such as those successfully implemented in the Nubian Sandstone Aquifer System, demonstrate the potential for real-time tracking of groundwater

[79] Cassuto et al. (2013).

[80] Eckstein (2009).

[81] Grafton et al. (2014).

depletion and recharge patterns.[82] Combined with machine learning algorithms for predictive modeling, these advanced monitoring capabilities enable authorities to anticipate and respond to climate-induced changes in aquifer dynamics.[83] Implementing such technologies in the Guarani Aquifer context would significantly enhance the effectiveness of the existing legal framework by providing empirical data for enforcement actions and policy adjustments.[84]

5.3 Role of Local Communities in Environmental Stewardship

Local communities possess indigenous knowledge and a vested interest in sustainable practices, which can complement formal regulatory frameworks. In the context of the Guarani Aquifer, local populations are often first responders to environmental degradation, providing critical observations on the impacts of industrial activities and pollution.

Their engagement can facilitate monitoring efforts and enhance stakeholder accountability, fostering proactive management strategies. Collaborative governance structures that include community voices empower local residents and promote better adherence to environmental regulations, as seen in the challenges highlighted regarding implementing the Aquifer Agreements.[85]

Ultimately, recognizing and integrating the role of local communities is pivotal for cultivating a culture of stewardship, which is necessary to combat the multifaceted threats facing the aquifer and ensure its long-term sustainability.

5.4 International Obligations and Commitments of the Four Countries

Despite the framework's establishment, the implementation remains hindered by fragmented legal structures and inequitable resource allocation among the nations involved, ultimately undermining shared environmental responsibilities. Each country must recognize its commitment to prevent significant harm and promote equitable utilization of the aquifer, as highlighted in.

This responsibility includes developing standardized monitoring systems and harmonized legal frameworks to mitigate pollution risks, which are prevalent in a region heavily reliant on the aquifer for water security (Rodríguez de Taborda 2010). Failure to uphold these obligations risks exacerbating tensions over resource

[82] Eckstein and Eckstein (2005).
[83] Foster et al. (2009).
[84] Sindico et al. (2018).
[85] Rodríguez de Taborda (2010).

distribution and impeding collective efforts to combat climate change's adverse impacts on water availability.[86]

Therefore, a coherent strategy integrating scientific research, robust legal frameworks, and public participation is essential for fostering a cooperative environment and enhancing regional resilience. Current environmental policies regarding transboundary aquifers face significant challenges that undermine their effectiveness.

Despite the existence of international frameworks designed to regulate shared water resources, such as the United Nations Convention on the Law of Non-Navigational Uses of International Watercourses and the Helsinki Rules, enforcement remains fragmented and inconsistent among the involved nations. While these frameworks offer essential provisions for information sharing and environmental protection, they often lack robust compliance and dispute resolution mechanisms.

This insufficiency can hinder effective implementation and lead to conflicts regarding water use and management. For instance, in the Aral Sea Basin, multiple nations have struggled to coordinate under the framework of the Interstate Commission for Water Coordination, resulting in significant ecological and economic challenges. Moreover, the differing interpretations of international treaties can create legal ambiguities and jurisdictional disputes, further complicating cooperative management efforts.[87]

Several human rights courts, such as the European Court of Human Rights (ECHR) and the Inter-American Court of Human Rights, have addressed cases where states failed to protect access to clean water. This highlights the need for a cohesive legal framework that integrates human rights considerations into water management practices. Effective governance must tackle these legal discrepancies and advocate for stronger intergovernmental cooperation.

Recommendations for improvement include establishing a joint monitoring body tasked with enhancing data sharing and ensuring adherence to environmental standards. Such a body would facilitate better compliance and foster a more unified approach to sustainably and equitably managing shared water resources. To illustrate the necessity for this integrative approach, recent rulings—the ECHR's recognition of the right to water as part of the right to private and family life (Article 8 of the European Convention on Human Rights) and the Inter-American Court's emphasis on water as a fundamental human right—underscore the pressing need for aligning international water governance frameworks with human rights imperatives.[88]

In conclusion, enhancing the regulatory landscape for shared water resources necessitates a commitment to legal harmonization among states, improved compliance mechanisms, and a strong focus on human rights, ensuring that all stakeholders benefit equitably from these vital resources.

[86] Grafton et al. (2014), Cassuto et al. (2013).

[87] Rodríguez de Taborda (2010).

[88] Maitland and Scoones (2018); Cissé (2020).

5.5 *Integration of Climate Adaptation Strategies*

Considering the increasing threats posed by climate change, the imperative for integrating effective climate adaptation strategies into transboundary water management frameworks, particularly for the Guarani Aquifer, becomes glaringly apparent. Collaborative governance through the Guaraní Aquifer Agreement presents a foundation for mitigating these challenges.[89]

As suggested in other successful international water treaties, implementing adaptive management practices could enhance resilience and improve cooperation among the involved nations. This calls for harmonized legal frameworks and robust data-sharing protocols, allowing states to respond dynamically to environmental changes, thereby facilitating equitable and sustainable water use across borders.[90]

A more cohesive approach to climate adaptation is likely to emerge by addressing these gaps, ensuring long-term ecological and human security. Effective management of the Guarani Aquifer hinges on integrating scientific research and data sharing among the four sharing countries: Argentina, Brazil, Paraguay, and Uruguay. Sound scientific investigations are essential for assessing the aquifer's hydrological properties and understanding the environmental variables at play, such as the impacts of pollution and climate change—issues that directly threaten groundwater sustainability.

Since international cooperation is critical, establishing standardized data-sharing protocols can facilitate timely access to crucial hydrological and ecological information, fostering transparency and collective decision-making.[91] Moreover, ongoing community engagement and stakeholder participation in scientific initiatives can enhance public awareness and bolster governance efforts to enforce the Guarani Aquifer Agreement.

Successful environmental initiatives often demonstrate the power of collaborative governance in managing shared resources effectively. For instance, the Guarani Aquifer Agreement serves as a prominent case study highlighting the significance of joint management among Argentina, Brazil, Paraguay, and Uruguay. Equitable resource use, as outlined in the Agreement, embodies principles found in international frameworks, emphasizing cooperation and communication among states.

Moreover, establishing a joint monitoring body, as proposed within the context of the aquifer's governance, can enhance transparency and accountability. Such measures are reminiscent of successful initiatives seen in other transboundary contexts, where unified approaches have led to effective dispute resolution and sustainable practices, fostering a stronger collective responsibility toward environmental stewardship.[92]

---

[89] Rodríguez de Taborda (2010).

[90] Cassuto et al. (2013); Grafton et al. (2014).

[91] Eckstein and Eckstein (2005).

[92] Grafton et al. (2014); Cassuto et al. (2013).

6 Conclusion

The case of the Guarani Aquifer illuminates the complexities inherent in transboundary water governance, where distinct national interests, fragmented legal frameworks, and varied enforcement mechanisms present significant barriers to sustainable management.[93] Despite establishing the Guarani Aquifer Agreement, the limited implementation and the inconsistencies across Argentina, Brazil, Paraguay, and Uruguay underscore the difficulties in harmonizing domestic legal structures for shared resource management (Aquifer Guarani Agreement, 2010). Environmental pressures like pollution and over-extraction, which jeopardize the aquifer's long-term viability and the livelihoods of over 30 million people who depend on its waters, compound these difficulties.[94]

The study reveals that the Guarani Aquifer Agreement, while a landmark in regional cooperation, lacks the necessary enforcement provisions and institutional support to ensure effective governance.[95] This shortfall highlights a pressing need for stronger oversight mechanisms, including a joint monitoring body and standardized data-sharing protocols to facilitate real-time responses to environmental threats. Other aquifers that have been managed well show that regional cooperation, along with structured institutional frameworks, makes people more accountable and makes people more resistant to risks caused by climate change.[96]

Future research should delve deeper into the interplay between national legislation and transboundary cooperative frameworks, identifying legal and political obstacles that hinder cohesive governance. An in-depth examination of enforcement gaps within the Guarani Aquifer Agreement could uncover specific provisions requiring revision or reinforcement to bridge these divides. By addressing the deficiencies in current governance structures, stakeholders can better align local actions with regional objectives, strengthening accountability and resource management capabilities.[97]

Furthermore, integrating judicial perspectives from regional bodies such as the Inter-American Court of Human Rights could support a more holistic approach to transboundary governance, emphasizing the importance of environmental responsibility and legal accountability.[98] Such integration would illuminate the role of human rights considerations in resource governance, underscoring the broader social and environmental implications of water management.

Finally, fostering public participation in decision-making processes is crucial for aligning transboundary governance with the needs of local communities. Directly involving stakeholders, especially those who directly impact the aquifer's

93 Eckstein (2009); Eckstein and Eckstein (2005).

94 Grafton et al. (2014); Rodríguez de Taborda (2010).

95 Withanachchi et al. (2012).

96 Grafton et al. (2014); Sindico and Hawkins (2015).

97 Hayes Vieira (2019); UN-Water (2008).

98 Rodríguez de Taborda (2010).

management, can increase transparency, strengthen the idea of shared responsibility, and advance a culture of collaborative stewardship.[99] Public participation mechanisms, coupled with robust legal frameworks, would empower communities to advocate for sustainable practices, contributing to the aquifer's resilience and the equitable distribution of its resources.

The sustainability of the Guaraní Aquifer depends on integrating climate litigation frameworks into its governance architecture. Judicial precedents such as Urgenda Foundation v. The Netherlands demonstrate the capacity of courts to enforce state accountability for climate-related harm. At the same time, the Inter-American Court of Human Rights has recognized the right to a healthy environment as a fundamental human right, alongside the corresponding state obligations to prevent environmental degradation. This interpretation offers a robust normative guide for linking environmental protection with human rights. Adopting a Guaraní Aquifer Climate Protocol—establishing extraction limits based on IPCC hydrological projections and creating a regional dispute resolution body—could effectively address current enforcement gaps. By anchoring the GAA in human rights jurisprudence, stakeholders can transform it from a symbolic accord into a litigation-ready instrument, ensuring equitable water security in an era of climate uncertainty.

In conclusion, the effective management of the Guarani Aquifer depends on strengthening institutional frameworks, harmonizing legal provisions, and fostering an inclusive approach that transcends national boundaries. Addressing the gaps in the Guarani Aquifer Agreement and adopting best practices from other regional water frameworks can pave the way for a sustainable, cooperative governance model. This approach not only mitigates risks associated with environmental degradation and climate change but also secures the aquifer's future for the communities and ecosystems that depend on it. The Guarani Aquifer case underscores the broader imperative for international collaboration in transboundary water governance, setting a precedent for managing shared resources in a rapidly changing environmental landscape.

References

Abdalla Mg KS (2015) Groundwater modeling of multi-aquifer systems using GMS. J Waste Water Treat Anal 06(01):184. https://doi.org/10.4172/2157-7587.1000184

Amore L, Tröger U (2010) Transboundary guarani aquifer system and groundwater management mechanisms. In: UNESCO-IHP (ed) Transboundary aquifers: challenges and new directions. UNESCO, pp 86–95

Bucher R (2017) Juliana, et al v. United States, et al.

Cassuto DN, Sampaio RS (2013) The Importance of Information and Participation Principles in Environmental Law in Brazil, the United States and Beyond. Rev Eur Comp Int Environ Law, 22(1):68–77.https://doi.org/10.1111/reel.12019

[99] Grafton et al. (2014); Aquifer Guarani Agreement (2010).

Center for Climate and Energy Solutions (2017, October 15) Post-Paris transparency under the United Nations Framework Convention on Climate Change - Center for Climate and Energy Solutions. https://www.c2es.org/document/post-paris-transparency-under-the-united-nations-framework-convention-on-climate-change/

Cissé A (2020) Water rights as human rights: the role of international law. Water Int 45(5):553–570. https://doi.org/10.1080/02508060.2020.1804618

Da Silva LPB, Hussein H (2019) Production of scale in regional hydropolitics: An analysis of La Plata River Basin and the Guarani Aquifer System in South America. Geoforum 99:42–53. https://doi.org/10.1016/j.geoforum.2018.11.019

Eckstein Y, Eckstein GE (2005) Transboundary aquifers: conceptual models for development of international law. Ground Water 43(5):679–690

Eckstein G (2009) Water Scarcity, Conflict, and Security in a Climate Change World: Challenges and Opportunities for International Law and Policy. 27 Wis. Int'l L J 409. https://scholarship.law.tamu.edu/facscholar/333

Enhanced Transparency Framework (n.d.) World Resources Institute. https://www.wri.org/paris-rulebook/enhanced-transparency-framework

Foster S, Hirata R, Vidal A, Schmidt G, Garduño H (2009) The Guarani Aquifer initiative – towards realistic groundwater management in a transboundary context. The World Bank

Frappart F (2020) Groundwater storage changes in the major North African Transboundary Aquifer Systems during the GRACE era (2003–2016). Water 12(10):2669. https://doi.org/10.3390/w12102669

Gomez P (2014) Transboundary groundwater and unsustainable practices of water governance in the Guarani Aquifer : the case of the province of Misiones. https://doi.org/10.18297/etd/513

Grafton Q, Wyrwoll P, White C, & Allendes D (Eds.) (2014) Global Water: Issues and Insights. ANU Press. https://doi.org/10.22459/GW.05.2014

Guarani Aquifer Agreement. (2010, August 2). San Juan, Argentina: Argentina, Brazil, Paraguay, & Uruguay https://faolex.fao.org/docs/pdf/mul-143888English.pdf

Hamed Y, Demdoum A, Al-Gamal SA, Bouri S, Ben Dhia H (2012) Groundwater recharge areas of the Continental Intercalaire aquifer-hydrogeochemical and environmental isotopes: Southern Tunisia and Algeria. Quat Int. https://doi.org/10.1016/j.quaint.2012.11.011

Hayes Vieira J (2019) Market-base solutions to manage the Guarani Aquifer: Pigouvian Fee and Cap-and Trade. Master's Theses and Capstones. 1374. https://scholars.unh.edu/thesis/1374

Hirata R, Foster S (2020) The Guarani Aquifer System – from regional reserves to local use. Q J Eng Geol Hydrogeol 54(1):91. https://doi.org/10.1144/qjegh2020-091

Hirata R, Kirchheim RE, Manganelli A (2020) Diplomatic advances and setbacks of the Guarani Aquifer System in South America. Environ` Sci Pol 114:384–393. https://doi.org/10.1016/j.envsci.2020.07.020

Hosseini Z, Raeisi E, Abdollahifard I, Teatini P (2024) Comprehensive hydrogeological study of the Nubian aquifer System, Northeast Africa. J Hydrol 636:131237. https://doi.org/10.1016/j.jhydrol.2024.131237

Inter-American Court of Human Rights. (2017) Advisory Opinion OC-32/17: Human rights and the climate emergency. San José, Costa Rica. https://www.corteidh.or.cr/docs/opiniones/OC-32-17.pdf

Juliana v. United States - Climate Change Litigation (2017, June 9) Climate change litigation. https://climatecasechart.com/case/juliana-v-united-states/. Accessed 1 Apr 2025

Lahore High Court (2015) Leghari v. Federation of Pakistan. W.P. No. 25501/2015

Leghari v. Federation of Pakistan - Climate Change Litigation (2018, January 25). Climate change litigation. https://climatecasechart.com/non-us-case/ashgar-leghari-v-federation-of-pakistan/. Accessed 1 Apr 2025

Liu Y, Wang T, Ruan H, Yu J, Wang P, Cheng Y, Kulmatov R (2020) Sustainable use of groundwater resources in the transboundary aquifers of the five Central Asian countries: challenges and perspectives. Water 12(8):2101. https://doi.org/10.3390/w12082101

López Ostra v. Spain, 303-C Eur. Ct. H.R. (1994)

Maitland C, Scoones I (2018) Water justice: perspectives on human rights and sustainability. Environ Policy Gov 28(3):155–166. https://doi.org/10.1002/eet.1800

Narzullaev O, Bekov I (2024) Contemporary analysis of the use of transboundary waters in Central Asia. IOP Conf Ser Earth Environ Sci 1420(1):012035. https://doi.org/10.1088/1755-1315/1420/1/012035

OECD (2020) The use and management of water resources in Central Asia: a consultation on future directions. Green Action Task Force. http://www.oecd.org/env/outreach/green-action-task-force/

Odaguiri F (2011) Legal Analysis of the Case Concerning Aerial Herbicide Spraying (Ecuadorvs. Colombia): Possible Violations of International Environmental Law and International Human Rights Law. Direito Público, 6(30). Recuperado de. https://www.portaldeperiodicos.idp.edu.br/direitopublico/article/view/1662

Okonkwo T (2016) A Glimpse into International Regimes Governing the Use of Transboundary Freshwater Resources. Okonkwo I Journal Of Law, Policy And Globalization. https://www.iiste.org/Journals/index.php/JLPG/article/view/32680

Paris Agreement, December 12, 2015., https://treaties.un.org/doc/Treaties/2016/02/20160215%2006-03%20PM/Ch_XXVII-7-d.pdf

Quadri E (2019) The evolving framework for transboundary cooperation in the Nubian Sandstone Aquifer System. Water Int 44(3):363–377. https://doi.org/10.1080/02508060.2019.1593839

Rodríguez de Taborda J (2010) Legal framework for transboundary water management in South America. Nat Resour J 50(1):16–30

Sherif MI, Sturchio NC (2021) Elevated radium levels in Nubian Aquifer groundwater of Northeastern Africa. Sci Rep 11(1):78. https://doi.org/10.1038/s41598-020-80160-0

Sindico F, Hawkins S (2015) The Guarani Aquifer Agreement and transboundary aquifer law in the SADC: comparing apples and oranges? Rev Eur Comp Int Environ Law 24(3):318–329

Sindico F, Hirata R, Manganelli A (2018) The Guarani Aquifer System: from a beacon of hope to a question mark in the governance of transboundary aquifers. J Hydrol Reg Stud 20:49–59

Sultan M, Ahmed M, Wahr J, Becker R, Sturchio N, Yan YE, Chouinard K, Milewski A, Becker D (2013) 5.20 - Assessment of the vulnerabilities of the Nubian Sandstone Fossil Aquifer, North Africa. In: Climate vulnerability, vol 5. Elsevier, pp 311–333. https://doi.org/10.1016/b978-0-12-384703-4.00531-1

Tigre MA, Urzola N (2021) The 2017 Inter-American Court's Advisory Opinion: changing the paradigm for international environmental law in the Anthropocene. J Hum Rights Environ 12(1):24–50. https://doi.org/10.4337/jhre.2021.01.02

Tinker C (2016) The Guarani Aquifer accord. Law Practice Int Courts Trib 15(2):249–263. https://doi.org/10.1163/15718034-12341321

UN-Water. (2008). UN-Water thematic paper: Transboundary waters—Sharing benefits, sharing responsibilities. https://www.unwater.org/publications/transboundary-waters-sharing-benefits-sharing-responsibilities

UNESCO (2022) UN-Water Summit on Groundwater 2022: background documents. https://www.unesco.org/reports/wwdr/2022/fr

Urgenda Foundation v. State of the Netherlands - Climate Change Litigation (2020, January 13) Climate change litigation. https://climatecasechart.com/non-us-case/urgenda-foundation-v-kingdom-of-the-netherlands/. Accessed 1 Apr 2025

Villar PC, Ribeiro WC (2011) The Agreement on the Guarani Aquifer: a new paradigm for transboundary groundwater management? Water Int 36(5):646–660. https://doi.org/10.1080/02508060.2011.603671

Villar PC (2014) Groundwater International Cooperation and the Guarani Aquifer. FLACSO-ISA Joint International Conference: Global and Regional Powers in a Changing World, Buenos Aires, 23–25

Withanachchi SS (2012) The study of Transboundary Groundwater Governance in the notion of Governmentality: in the case of Guaraní Aquifer. AQUA mundi 1(6):9–14. https://nbnresolving.org/urn:nbn:de:0168-ssoar-349390

Natalia Lorena Losccoco, International Law Professor at Buenos Aires University (UBA) and University of Belgrano (UB). Lawyer, graduated with honors from the University of Buenos Aires, where she also completed advanced doctoral courses in law. Specialized in Environmental Law. Tutor of the International Law Working Group at the Center for International Studies of the University of Belgrano. Her areas of consultancy include International Law, Human Rights, and Environmental Law. She has been a United Nations Fellow (RCIL 2016). Former scholarship holder of the Hague Academy of International Law, the Organization of American States, the British Institute of International and Comparative Law, and the International Institute of Humanitarian Law in Sanremo.

Cássius Guimarães Chai, Full Law and Geopolitics Professor. Law Departament, Social Sciences Center, Federal University of Maranhão, Full Geopolitics and Criminology Professor Faculdade de Direito de Vitória (PPGD/FDV), State Criminal Prosecutor MPMA. International Law Association and International Political Science Association member. BRICS—Geopolitics and Democracy Research Center, Coordinator. Postdoctoral fellow, visiting Researcher Central European University, Law School. Guest Researcher Beijing Criminal College Normal University of Political Science and Law. Doctor and Master in Constitutional Law from the Federal University of Minas Gerais and Cardozo School of Law, Yeshiva University. Graduated from the Superior School of War (2019).

Climate Change and Air Pollution in Africa: Legal Precedents and Their Impact on Environmental Justice

Ibrahim Badawi

1 Introduction

Climate change: Global Warming are widely recognized terms today. These phenomena refer to significant changes in global temperature, precipitation, wind patterns, and other climate indicators that occur over several decades or longer.[1] Climate change is caused by the emissions of greenhouse gases, mostly originating from human consumption of fossil fuels that which still provide us with the essential conveniences of modern life: heat to warm our households, kinetic energy to transport us at speed over long distances, electricity to power our appliances, and power to dig, extract, melt, refine, and transform raw materials into the manufactured products we use every day.[2]

The global average temperature since 1900 A.D. has risen by about 1 °C. By 2050 A.D., it is projected to rise another 1.5 °C by 2050. According to the U.S. Government's Climate Science Special Report (CSSR), projected climate change will be seen in rising surface, atmospheric, and oceanic temperatures, and their related phenomena (i.e., melting glaciers, diminishing snow cover, shrinking sea ice, rising sea levels, ocean acidification, and increasing intensity and frequency of rainfall, hurricanes, heat waves, wildfires, and drought. Inevitability, humanity's basic needs, such as food, water, health, and shelter will be (and are) affected by climate change.

[1] UC Davis, climate change terms and definitions.

[2] Deloitte Sustainability Circular economy potential for climate change mitigation; November 2016.

I. Badawi (✉)
Seattle University, Seattle, WA, USA
e-mail: ibadawi@seattleu.edu

V. E. de Aquino et al. (eds.), *Climate Litigation in a Changing World*, Ius Gentium: Comparative Perspectives on Law and Justice 130,
https://doi.org/10.1007/978-3-032-05530-9_11

Africa is the second largest continent in the world by both size and population, after Asia. It consists of 54 countries and covers approximately 11,724,000 square miles (30,365,000 square km).[3] The continent stretches about 5000 miles (8000 km) from north to south and about 4600 miles (7400 km) from east to west. The largest country is Algeria, covering 2,381,741 square kilometers. As of 2024, Africa's population is approximately 1.522 billion, with Nigeria being the most populous country, with 232,679,478.[4]

Africa's contribution to the global greenhouse gas emissions has fluctuated between 3.4 percent and 3.9 percent.[5] Africa has the lowest emissions out of all continents with an average of 1 tonne of CO2 emitted annually by each individual, followed by South America (2.5 tonnes), Asia (4.6 tonnes), Europe (7.1 tonnes), Oceania (10 tonnes) and North America (10.3 tonnes).[6] However, Africa is one of the most vulnerable regions to the effects of climate change disasters. According to the United Nations Environment Programme (UNEP), this vulnerability is driven by the continent's low levels of socioeconomic growth. While climate change is a global issue, the poor are disproportionately affected to their lack of resources to afford goods and services they need to protect themselves and recover from its impacts.[7] Additionally, the large portion of the population lives below the poverty line, and its livelihood depends on activities that are extremely sensitive to climate changes and weather conditions.

The number of deaths registered in Africa was projected to reach 11.7 million in 2025.[8] In 2022, the average crude death rate in Africa was 8.4 deaths per 1000 people. According to the State of Global Air Report in 2019, air pollution was the second leading risk factor for death across Africa after malnutrition. In 2019, air pollution contributed to 1.1 million deaths in Africa. Of these, more than 63% were linked to exposure to household air pollution. Globally, air pollution is the fourth leading cause of death, accounting for nearly seven million deaths annually.[9]

One of the main reasons for the increasing death rates in Africa is the lack of stringent legislation and enforcement of the environmental policies across many countries. Corruption and insufficient implementation of strict regulations

---

[3] Worldometer, Available at: https://www.worldometers.info/geography/how-many-countries-in-africa/#:~:text=There%20are%2054%20countries%20in,the%20United%20Nations%20official%20statistics) (last visited Sept. 12, 2024)

[4] Encyclopaedia Britannica, https://www.britannica.com/topic/list-of-African-countries-by-population (last visited Sept. 12, 2024).

[5] Africa Report, CDP, https://www.cdp.net/en/research/global-reports/africa-report (last visited Sept. 12, 2024).

[6] Al Jazeera (2023).

[7] United Nations Environment Programme (UNEP), https://www.unep.org/regions/africa/regional-initiatives/responding-climate-change#:~:text=While%20Africa%20has%20contributed%20negligibly,socioeconomic%20growth%20in%20the%20continent (last visited Sept. 12, 2024).

[8] Number of Deaths in Africa, Statista, https://www.statista.com/statistics/1282721/number-of-deaths-in-africa/#:~:text=The%20number%20of%20deaths%20registered,slightly%20over%2012%20million%20deaths

[9] Health Effects Institute (2022).

contribute to high levels of greenhouse gas emissions and pollution. Many countries still rely heavily on coal and fossil fuels, which exacerbates air pollution and has significant health impacts on the population.

This chapter highlights the effects of climate change and air pollution on Africa, and how they significantly impact vulnerable communities. It aims to shed light on some of the critical issues related to climate change and air pollution by focusing on two landmark cases in Africa courts; the *Save Lamu* case in Kenya, which addresses climate change litigation and explores how the Paris Agreement can be invoked in court, and *Deadly Air* case in South Africa which prioritizes human rights over other interests to safeguard the health of the communities affected by air pollution and ultimately reinforcing the importance of environmental justice.

Environmental justice aims to protect individuals from disproportionate and adverse effects on human health and the environment, including risks and hazards related to climate change, cumulative impacts of environmental burdens, and the legacy of racism or other structural and systemic barriers. It advocates for equitable access to clean environmental that allow individual to live, play, work, learn, grow, worship, and engage in culture and subsistence practices.[10]

Environmental justice has been created in response to the recognition that low-income and minority communities often bear the brunt of environmental degradation, as shown in *Save Lamu* and *Deadly Air* cases, including exposure to toxic pollutant and the impacts of climate change.

These cases are central to the global discussions. By examining the impacts of climate change and air pollution in Africa alongside these important legal precedents, the paper seeks to contribute to the ongoing conversation about environmental challenges and the urgent need for effective solutions. It emphasizes the necessity for Africa to act as a unified body, united in purpose and action, in addressing these pressing challenges. Furthermore, it advocates for the adoption of union legation to address climate change and air pollution, reaffirming that Africa comprises some of the most vulnerable communities affected by these phenomena.

2 Climate changes effects on the dark continent[11]

In Africa, 2023 was one of the three warmest years in the 124 years, and was the warmest year in many countries, including Mali, Morocco, Uganda, and the United Republic of Tanzania. The average rate of warming in Africa was +0.3 °C per decade during the 1991–2022 period, compared to +0.2 °C per decade between

[10] Environmental Protection Agency (n.d.).

[11] The term "Dark Continent" was used for first time by Welsh journalist and explorer Henry Morton Stanley, he used it to describe Africa's largely uncharted landscapes and culture. The phrase is prominently featured in his book In Darkest Africa (1890), reflecting both the literal darkness of unexplored territories and the figurative darkness of misunderstanding surrounding the continent. For further reading, see Stanley (1890).

1961 and 1990. This rate is slightly above the global average. The warming has been most rapid in North Africa, where extreme heat has fueled wildfires in some countries like Algeria and Tunisia in 2022.[12]

Looking at the sea level around the Dark Continent, there are seven coastal regions: including Red Sea, Western Indian Ocean, South-west Indian Ocean, South-east Atlantic Ocean, Tropical Atlantic Ocean, North-east Atlantic Ocean and Southern Mediterranean Sea. The figure shows that from 1993 until June 2024, the sea level has increased at an average rate of 3.4 mm per year, with some regional differences.

According to the US national Oceanic and Atmospheric Administration, there are two main reasons causes sea level rise. The first is melting ice. Ice from glaciers and ice sheets in places like Greenland and Antarctica is melting into ocean, adding more water, which leads to rising sea levels. Imagine that Greenland loses about 270 billion tonnes of ice per year, while Antarctica loses around 150 billion tonnes annually. The second reason is the thermal expansion. As global temperatures rise, seawater expands because warmer water takes up more space and contributing to sea level rise.[13] This expansion, driven by the heat stored in the oceans, is responsible for up to half of the global sea level rise according to the NASA says. The past decade has been the ocean's warmest since at least 1800, and ocean temperatures reached a new high in 2023.

The question here is how the increase in temperature and sea levels, both significant indicators of climate change effects, are impacting Africa which is among the most vulnerable regions of the effects of climate change disasters.

2.1 *The Dual Threat of Coastal Erosion and Displacement: Communities at Risk*

As sea levels rise, coastal erosion and flooding are becoming more severe in low-lying areas, threatening communities living in coastal regions which creates potential refugee crises. By the end of the century as many as 410 million people could be vulnerable to rising sea levels by the end of the century. According to the OECD, the economic cost associated with rising sea level could reach as much as $5.5 trillion. Additionally, by the end of the century, around 410 million people may reside on land less than 2 meters above sea level, putting them at significant risk of coastal flooding.[14] sending 1 billion cubic feet (30 million cubic meters) of water into already inundated areas and resulting in catastrophic flooding that destroyed homes, hospitals, roads, and power lines.

---

[12] World Meteorological Organization (2024).

[13] World Economic Forum (2024).

[14] Hooijer and Vernimmen (2021).

For example, as the whole world saw, on Sunday 10 September, one of the effects of climate change struck in Libya with Storm Daniel, after it had already impacted Greece, Bulgaria and Türkiye. The storm arrived to Libya, brought strong winds and sudden heavy rainfall, causing flooding that led to the to the collapse of two dams sending 1 billion cubic feet (30 million cubic meters) of water into already inundated areas and resulting in catastrophic flooding that destroyed homes, hospitals, roads and power lines.[15] Storm Daniel triggered 52,000 displacements across several districts, mostly in Derna city and many people were killed.[16] According to WHO, The deceased health workers are among the 4333 people thus far confirmed dead following the storm. More than 8500 people are still missing.[17]

According to the IFRC "Though annual flooding is a natural phenomenon in many parts of the world, human habitation and land-use practices have led to an increase in frequency and size of floods. Floods are also predicted to become even more frequent and severe in the future due to climate change. Floods can be extremely dangerous and cause massive human, environmental and material damage to communities."[18]

As sea levels rise, coastal erosion and flooding are becoming more severe in low-lying areas, threatening communities living in coastal regions. Countries such as Senegal, Nigeria, and Mozambique are already experiencing significant coastal erosion. In 2023, disaster triggered six million displacements across Sub-Saharan Africa, making the second-highest figure since records began in 2008 and nearly double the average of the past decade. These displacements primarily resulted from heavy flooding in Horn of Africa, following years of drought. Cyclone Freddy, which traversed the Indian Ocean Basin from off the northwest coast of Australia to multiple landfalls in Africa between February 4 to March 14, 2023, was the most significant storm to impact the region. The majority of displacements occurring in Mozambique, accounting around 640,000. The cyclone struck during the harvesting season, forcing people to replant their crops and heightening food insecurity.[19]

The *World Bank* estimates that by 2050, 105 million people including North Africa (19 million), Sub-Saharan Africa (86 million), could be displaced by climate change-related events, including rising sea levels.[20]

---

[15] Disaster Philanthropy, 2023 Libya Floods, DisasterPhilanthropy.org, https://disasterphilanthropy.org/disasters/2023-libya-floods/

[16] IDMC (2024).

[17] World Health Organization (2023a).

[18] International Federation of Red Cross and Red Crescent Societies, Floods, IFRC, https://www.ifrc.org/our-work/disasters-climate-and-crises/what-disaster/floods

[19] IDMC (2024)

[20] World Bank (2021).

2.2 Climate Change and Its Impact on Agriculture and Food Security in Africa

Higher temperatures are intensifying droughts and changing rainfall patterns across Africa, while rising sea level are increasing flooding. The Horn of Africa has experienced its worst drought in 40 years, particularly affecting Ethiopia, Kenya and Somalia. Agriculture is the backbone of Africa's livelihoods and national economies, supporting more than 55% of the labor force. However, agricultural productivity growth has declined by 34% since 1961 due to climate change.[21] Both factors are threats to agriculture and food security, especially considering that Africa is already grappling with food shortage and a hunger crisis, which pose significant challenges to the continent. Approximately 429 million people in Africa were living below the extreme poverty line. According to the FAO, nearly 282 million people in Africa (about 20 percent of the population) were undernourished in 2022, an increase of 57 million people since the COVID-19 pandemic began. Additionally, around 868 million people were moderately or severely food insecure and more than one-third of them—342 million people—were severely food-insecure.[22]

In the southern part of Madagascar, climate change has led to severe lack of rainfall, resulting in prolonged droughts. As a result, many people are migrating to area near water sources, leaving behind their homes, schools in search of water. This migration has caused significant crises related to food security, hunger, illness, child mortality, and malnutrition. According to NASA, this region is experiencing its worst drought in 40 years, with persistent drought and devastation to farms leaving over a million people in southern Madagascar lacking reliable access to food.[23] In 2023, drought and floods in Somalia triggered two million displacements, the floods fueled a cholera outbreak, including among IDPs, particularly in the Amhara and Somali regions.[24]

Another example is East Africa, which has experienced frequent droughts that have affected crop production and livestock, worsening food insecurity. In addition, In the North, cereal production for 2023 was estimated at 33 million tonnes, similar to last year's drought-impacted harvest and about 10% below the 5-year average. Taking Tunisia an example, it faced the largest decline, with cereal output dropping over 80% to 30,000 tonnes due to widespread drought. Alegria reported a 12% decrease in cereal output to 3.6 million tonnes, while Morocco's output of 5.6 million tonnes showed some recovery from 2022 but remained about 30% below average.[25]

[21] World Meteorological Organization (2023).

[22] FAO, AUC, ECA and WFP (2023).

[23] NASA Earth Observatory (2020).

[24] IDMC (2024).

[25] World Meteorological Organization (2024).

2.3 *Climate Change and Its Effects on Human Health*

The Intergovernmental Panel on Climate Change highlights that tens of millions of Africans are already experiencing the negative health effects of climate change, such as heat stress, extreme weather and spread of infectious disease. Dr. Githinji Gitahi, CEO of Amref Health Africa, emphasized that many governments have not prioritized addressing the health impacts of climate change, with fewer than 20% of the countries including health in their climate action plans. He affirmed that the situation is worsening, with global warming increasingly straining both health and healthcare systems.[26]

Climate change is significantly affecting health across the Dark Continent, with increased temperatures, altered rainfall patterns, and extreme weather event worsening food insecurity and spreading diseases. Droughts in East Africa and extreme heat in North Africa have fueled health crisis. Climate variables such as temperature, humidity, and rainfall are influencing the spread of vector-born diseases like malaria, with some regions seeing higher incidences due to changing climates.[27] Diarrheal diseases, particularly in children, are also rising as temperatures and rainfall increase, further threatening progress in reducing child mortality.[28]

Health related illnesses are growing concern, with many Africa regions lacking preparedness and public awareness about the risks of extreme heat. Heat exposure during pregnancy has been linked to adverse maternal and neonatal health outcomes.[29] Moreover, flooding in coastal areas is leading to water contamination, injuries, and mental health like anxiety and depression, especially in heavy impacted cities, like Lagos in Nigeria.[30]

2.4 *Economic Effects of Climate Change*

The economic impacts of climate change vulnerability in Africa are alarmingly high. According to the 2022 African Economic Outlook (AEO), a flagship publication of the African Development Bank, the continent is currently losing between $7 billion to $15 billion annually due to the devastating effects of climate change. This figure is projected to increase to approximately $50 billion yearly by 2030,

[26] World Health Organization (2023b).

[27] Mosquito-borne diseases could reach extra one billion people as climate warms, Carbon Brief, https://www.carbonbrief.org/mosquito-borne-diseases-could-reach-extra-one-billion-people-as-climate-warms/ (last visited Sept. 25, 2024).

[28] In-depth: How climate change affects health in Africa, Carbon Brief, https://www.carbonbrief.org/in-depth-how-climate-change-affects-health-in-africa/ (last visited Sept. 25, 2024).

[29] Chamnha: Climate, Heat, and Maternal and Neonatal Health in Africa, Global Heat Health Information Network, https://ghhin.org/resources/chamnha-climate-heat-and-maternal-and-neonatal-health-in-africa/ (last visited Sept. 25, 2024).

[30] Ashton (2023).

potentially up to 7% of Africa's GDP on average. While climate change poses the most significant threat to development in Dark continent, this situation has been exacerbated by the economic impacts on food and fuel prices. According to the UNECA's African Climate Policy Centre, the loss and damage costs in Africa due to climate change are expected to range between US$ 290 billion and US$ 440 billion, depending on the degree of warming.

3 Air Pollution in Africa: A Silent Killer with Deadly Consequences

Air pollution in Africa is a growing crisis, often linked to a ghost hanging over the continent. The main resource of air pollution in Africa, include emission from transportation, industrial activates, biomass burning, crops burning, the use of kerosene, reliance on coal, and the evaporation of chemicals. These activities lead to increased greenhouse gas emissions, including carbon dioxide, nitrogen, sulfur oxides, methane, and other harmful pollutants. This has not only worsened air quality but also exacerbated the continent's vulnerability to climate change and its related health and environmental challenges.

The lack of strict legislation on air quality standers, combined with weak law enforcement mechanism, has allowed air pollution to spread and increase in Africa. Additionally, widespread corruption and the prioritization of economic interest over public health have contributed to this dangerous crisis, with human health receiving inadequate attention from government and manufactures.

According to the State of Global Air Report in 2019, air pollution was the second leading risk factor for death across Africa, following malnutrition. In that year, air pollution contributed to 1.1 million deaths in Africa.[31]

To understand the severity of the air pollution, often described as a "silent killer," it's important to note that indoor and outdoor source combine to make air pollution the second-largest cause of death in Africa, claiming more lives than tobacco, alcohol, motor vehicle accidents, and drug abuse. Only AIDS causes more deaths.[32] In 2019, air pollution contributed to 1.1 million deaths in Africa. It is important to mention here that a World Health Organization (WHO) report shows that over 99 percent of humanity breathes air below air quality guidelines.

How does air pollution cause deaths? Air pollution poses significant health risks, particularly for vulnerable populations such as the elderly, newborns, children under 5 years old. Exposure to polluted air can lead to variety of health problems, including respiratory infections, asthma, and cardiovascular diseases.

---

[31] State of Global Air, Africa, https://www.stateofglobalair.org/resources/africa (last visited Sept. 26, 2024).

[32] Boston College News, Air Pollution in Africa: A Growing Crisis, https://www.bc.edu/bc-web/bcnews/nation-world-society/international/air-pollution-in-africa.html

As older people in Africa lack access to adequate medical systems and sufficient hospitals, they suffer great from air pollution. This demographic is particularly vulnerable due to pre-existing health conditions such as heart diseases, blood disorders, and respiratory illnesses, which can be exacerbated by exposure to harmful air pollutants. Air pollution contributes to diseases like ischemic heart disease, strokes, and chronic obstructive pulmonary disease, all of which are prevalent in older populations.[33]

For the newborn and child under five, approximately 236.000 newborns in Africa died during the first months of life due to air pollution exposure, with 80% those deaths coming from household air pollution (HAP). Air pollution ranked as the third largest risk for mortality in children under the age of 5 in Sub-Saharan Africa, after malnutrition and water, sanitation, and hygiene.

The economic costs of air pollution in African cities are projected to rise by 600% over the next 18 years without immediate action, according to a report by the Clean Air Fund (CAF) published in October 2022.[34] In 2019, the economics losses attributable to air pollution-related health issues and deaths were estimated at $3.02 billion in Ethiopia (1.16% of GDP), $1.63 billion in Ghana (0.95% of GDP), and $349 million in Rwanda (1.19% of GDP).[35] However, transitioning away from polluting energy sources for transportation, heating, and electricity could have significant benefits: it could save over 120,000 lives, reduce climate change emissions by 20%, and generate $20 billion for the urban economics of Lagos, Cairo, Johannesburg, and Accra over the next 17 years. In business-as-usual scenario, air pollution is expected to incur a total cost of $115.7 billion from 2030 to 2040 across these four cities.[36]

4 Climate Change and Air Pollution Cases in Africa

4.1 Save Lamu: The Intersection of Climate Change Law and Community Rights

Lamu, is an old town located just off the shore of Kenya in the Indian Ocean, approximately 1240 miles (240 km) from Mombasa. It is managed under the National Museums and Heritage of Act 2006 and was added to UNESCO World Heritage List in 2001. Kenya's Vision violated Kenya's obligations 2030, which aims to create "a globally competitive and prosperous country with a high quality of

[33] Air Pollution, World Health Org., https://www.afro.who.int/health-topics/air-pollution (last visited Sept. 26, 2024).

[34] Clean Air Fund, Clean Air for Africa's Cities, https://www.cleanairfund.org/clean-air-africas-cities/#explore-the-report

[35] Fisher et al. (2022).

[36] Fletcher (2022).

life by 2030," was launched on 10th June 2008 and passed by the 10th Parliament as Sessional Paper No: 10 of 2012.

This long-term development plan seeks to transform Kenya into newly industrializing nation. As part of this vision, the Kenya government aimed to boost the country's power generation capacity by implementing a program to increase total energy capacity to 5000 MW. This plan included a proposed 1050 MW coal fired power plant in Lamu County at Kwasasi, near to sea. Investors claimed that this would lower the overall cost of power generation in Kenya.

The case of Save Lamu from arose from opposition to this project and was brought before the National Environmental Tribunal. a quasi-judicial tribunal established under the Environmental Management and Coordination Act (EMCA) of 1999. Its main role to hear any disputes regarding the exercise of power by the National Environmental Management Authority (NEMA). Additionally, it is primary purpose noble to ensure that NEMA effectively balances economic development with the conservation and preservation of our national heritage.[37]

The coal-fired power plant is owned and operated by AMU Power Company, the second Respondent before the Tribunal. AMU power hired Kurrent Technologies Limited to conduct an Environmental and social impacts Assessment (ESIA), to assess the project potential effects on the environmental and local community.

Kurrent Technologies Limited completed the ESIA for the proposed coal-fired power plant, which was submitted to the National Environmental Management Authority (NEMA), the first Respondent in the case. NEMA, the official agency responsible for issuing environmental impact assessment licenses in Kenya. On September 7, 2016, NEMA, granted the environmental impact Assessment (EIA) license No. NEMA/ ESIA/PSL/3798 to the second Respondent, AMU Power company, allowing the coal power plant project to proceed.

This decision, however, sparked strong opposition from local communities, led by the first Appellant, a community-based organization representing the interest of the Lamu people, along with other appellants. They were aggrieved by the issuance of the EIA license, believing that the licensing process was deeply was flawed, and that the environmental assessment did not sufficiently consider the potential negative impacts on Lamu's ecosystem and residents.

On November 7, 2016, the community group filed an appeal challenging NEMA'S decision to issue the EIA license. They raised several grounds for appeal before the Tribunal, including:

a. There was a poor analysis of alternatives and economic justification and failure to take into account economic issues and to identify and analyse alternatives to the proposed project; b. Insufficient scoping process that lacked proper Public Participation;

b. Adverse effects on the Marine Environment through the discharge of thermal effluent into the marine environment by using poor and outdated cooling system.

c. Approval of the project on land falling within an ecologically sensitive area.

d. A flawed EIA Report plagued with misrepresentations inconsistencies and omissions.

[37] Cytonn Investments (2020).

e. The Negative Impact on Kenya's Air Quality with adverse effects on human health and biodiversity

f. Contribution to climate change and making the Project inconsistent with Kenya's low carbon development commitments.

g. The Failure to put conditions in the EIA license to put in place mitigation measures to address coal pollution caused by coal handling and storage.

h. Lack of sound mitigation measures

i. Compounded unviability of the project[38]

In the end, the appellants requested several demands from the Tribunal, including setting aside NEMA's decision to grant the EIA License to the second Respondent, conducting a fresh environmental impact assessment based on current up-to-date information, and ensuring that all stakeholders, including local communities and environmental groups, were involved in the process.

The appellants' main argument was that the proposed project violated Kenya's obligations under the Paris Agreement. The Paris Agreement is a legally binding international treaty on climate change, adopted by 196 parties, include Kenya, during the UN climate change conference (COP21) held in Paris in December 2015, which entered into force on November fourth, 2016. The primary goal of this treaty is to limit the global temperature rise to well below 2 °C above pre-industrial levels, with efforts to restrict the increase to 1.5 °C.

The appellants contended that the project is inconsistent with the country's commitments to a low carbon future. However, the second Respondent countered that the Paris Agreement only came into force after the Environmental and Social Impact Assessment (ESIA) study had been completed on September 7, 2016. Additionally, the second Respondent claimed that the appellants failed to demonstrate how the project specifically breached Kenya's obligations under the Paris Agreement, particularly given the mitigation and adaptation measures outlined in the ESIA study regarding climate change risks. Furthermore, they mentioned that the ESIA study addressed climate change adaptation and identified potential risks and consequences, but there was failure to comply with the newly enacted climate change act of 2016.

For these points, the Tribunal responded that the Paris Agreement entered into force on November 4th, 2016, after the ESIA study had concluded and the EIA license was issued, and the Tribunal emphasized that "the Appellants never demonstrated how and to what extent the proposed project violates Kenya's commitments under the Agreement, especially in the light of the mitigation and adaptation measures outlined in the ESIA study regarding climate change challenge."[39]

Additionally, the Tribunal found that the ESIA study report contained mitigation measures but emphasized that these measures had not been subjected to proper public participation, raising concerns about their adequacy. However, the Tribunal concluded that the comprehensiveness of the ESIA study did not excuse the failure to

[38] Save Lamu v. National Environmental Management Authority (NEMA) & Amu Power Co. Ltd., Tribunal Appeal No. NET 196 of 2016, at 2 (Kenya Nat'l Env't Tribunal).

[39] Id at 27.

conduct effective public participation. The approval process and subsequent issuance of the license did not meet legal requirement. The Tribunal stated:

> However, the comprehensiveness of the EIA Study report did not excuse the failure to carry out effective public participation during this process, as well as after the preparation of the voluminous EIA study report. The EIA study and report thereof were thus never subjected to proper and effective public participation that would have covered most of the grievances now raised in this appeal. As we have found earlier, the 1st Respondent's approval of the ESIA Study and the consequent issuance of the ESIA license and its conditions failed to meet the requirements of the law. The 1st Respondent therefore failed in discharging its mandate as provided for under the enabling statute, EMCA, by appearing to have only formally endorsed the EIA study process and ESIA Study report contrary to its own directive. It is also clear from the 2nd Respondent's own witness that he failed to consider certain factors such as the impact of climate change in relation to the Climate Change Act to determine compliance.[40]

Finally, the Tribunal set aside the decision of the first Respondent to issue the Environmental Impact Assessment License No. NEMA/ESIA /PSL/3798 dated 7th September 2016 to the second Respondent.

The Save Lamu case stands as one of the landmark climate change litigation cases in Africa. It opened the door for a pivotal moment in the region's engagement with international climate agreements, particularly following the Paris Agreement, demonstrating how this agreement can be invoked in courts. Given that climate change is a global phenomenon impacting all continents, and with greenhouse gas emissions on the rise, this case provides insight into how looking the judicial system in Africa can address transboundary environmental challenges by referencing the Paris Agreement.

According to the Sabin Center for Climate Change Law, approximately 3479 climate-related cases have been filed worldwide, with only 17 recorded in Africa. The lack of the climate change and air pollution litigation in Africa can be attributed to several reasons, including weak legislative frameworks, sluggish processes, limited financial resources, and the underdevelopment of the NGO sector. These challenges present obstacles for potential litigants to fully exhausting domestic remedies, which is prerequisite for brining cases before the African human rights system. Moreover, climate change has not garnered as much attention in Africa as other pressing environmental issues, such as disputes over land, property rights, and natural resources.[41]

Another barrier to climate change litigation in African is the difficulty in establishing victimhood which requires substantial evidence to prove the harm suffered and the causal relationship between that harm and the actions or omissions, which underscores the importance of the robust environmental assessments. UN General Assembly defines victim as individual or groups who have suffered harm-whether physical, mental, emotional, economic, or through the substantial violation of

---

[40] Id at 30.

[41] Suedi and Fall (2024).

fundamental rights—due to acts or omissions that violate international human rights law.[42]

Furthermore, the African Court on Human and People's Rights has issued only 15 advisory opinions to date, with none related to climate change. The scarcity of advisory opinion, including in climate matters, is likely due to restrictive procedural conditions for NGOs, lengthy proceedings, and the non-binding natural of such opinions, which may discourage applicants.[43]

The scarcity of climate change and air pollution cases in Africa highlights the need for greater cooperation across the continent to address and mitigate the impacts of climate change. Currently, there is more acceptance for individual and group to pursue litigation related to climate change and air pollution, especially with the increasing prevalence of such litigation worldwide and growing movements advocating for vulnerable communities.

The Sabin Center identifies various aspects of climate change litigation, including environmental assessment and permitting (as seen in the Save Lamu case), greenhouse gas reductions and trading, human rights (as highlighted in the 'Deadly air' case), just transitions, failure to adapt, protecting biodiversity and ecosystems, public assembly, public trust, trade and investment. The majority of climate change cases fall under environmental assessment and permitting, as well as greenhouse gas reductions and trading.

Africa, with many countries highly vulnerable to climate change, faces unique and pressing challenges. Advocacy for affected communities is essential, alongside efforts to regulate projects that exacerbate climate impacts. There is a critical need for a comprehensive and enforceable legal framework that addresses climate change across the continent. It is insufficient to have laws that exist only in theory; these laws need to be actionable, with mechanisms for enforcement that extend beyond national jurisdictions. Africa must pursue greater regional cooperation to develop unified climate legislation under the umbrella of the African Union. Without a collective approach and with only fragmented efforts by individual countries, Africa risks enduring ever-worsening consequences from a problem that demands both local and global solutions.

5 Deadly Air: Landmark Climate Litigation in South Africa

This section sheds light on one of the most famous cases in Africa regarding air pollution, known as 'Deadly Air.' This case is considered a landmark moment in South Africa, as it reinforces the right to a healthy environment and holds the government accountable for air quality management. Additionally, it serves as an important

[42] UN General Assembly (2006).

[43] Suedi and Fall, Ibid. at 14.

precedent for other environmental justice cases in Africa and highlights the critical intersection between environmental health and human rights.

In the northeastern part of South Africa lies Mpumalanga, which covers an area of 76495km^2 and has a population of 4,335,964, making it the sixth most populous province in country. It is situated mainly on the high plateau grasslands of the Middleveld and is known for its tourism and agriculture, featuring many national parks like Kruger National Park, which offers a wildlife experience that ranks among the best in Africa. In terms of agriculture, the region produces a variety of crops, including subtropical fruits, nuts, citrus, cotton, tobacco, wheat, vegetables, potatoes, sunflowers, and maize.

Mpumalanga is rich in coal reserves and is home to South Africa's major coal-fired power stations. The city of Emalahleni in Mpumalanga is the largest coal producer in Africa and is also the site of the South Africa' second oil-from-coal plant, following Sasolburg.[44]

Before narrating our case, it is important to mention that the High Court of South Africa referenced in their judgment the Applicant's Supplementary Affidavit "Air pollution knows no boundary and has potential to affect everyone, but it can affect us differently…children [the] elderly and those with respiratory diseases such as asthma, are the most vulnerable to air pollution…. The most vulnerable groups…[tend] to lose if air pollution levels are not properly managed".

The Mpumalanga Highveld has been identified as one of the worst places around the world due to the high levels of air pollution. In November 2007, the Minister of environmental affairs declared the Highveld priority Area (HPA) under the National Management Air Quality Act of 2004. The HPA covers Gauteng and Mpumalanga provinces and includes towns such as Emalahleni, Middelburg, Secunda, and others, which knows as particularly poor air quality due to heavy industrial activity.

In March 2012, the South African government published the Highveld Priority Area Air Quality Management plan, which aimed to bring air pollution levels in line with national stranders by setting seven key goals to be achieved by 2020. These goals are:

- Goal 1: By 2015, organizational capacity in government is optimized to efficiently and effectively maintain, monitor and enforce compliance with ambient air quality standards
- Goal 2: By 2020, industrial emissions are equitably reduced to achieve compliance with ambient air quality standards and dust fallout limit values.
- Goal 3: By 2020, air quality in all low-income settlements is in full compliance with ambient air quality standards Effective interventions, research, awareness raising, and education are major aspects in achieving the goal.
- Goal 4: By 2020, all vehicles comply with the requirements of the National Vehicle Emission Strategy
- Goal 5: By 2020, a measurable increase in awareness and knowledge of air quality exists

[44] Municipalities.co.za, Mpumalanga, https://municipalities.co.za/provinces/view/6/mpumalanga

- Goal 6: By 2020, biomass burning, and agricultural emissions will be 30% less than current
- Goal 7: By 2020, emissions from waste management are 40% less than current[45]

However, by 2011, only 8% of the polluters had complied, and minimal steps had been taken, further exacerbating the suffering of the affected communities. This lack of action from 2011 to 2019, led to initiation of the 'Deadly Air' case in June 2019, brought before Pretoria High Court. The applicants were represented by two organizations: GroundWork, an environmental justice service and development organization that focuses on environmental concerns, and Vukanio Environmental justice Movement in Action, a community organization fighting for the environmental rights of people in the Highveld. The respondents included the Minister of Environmental Affair, National air quality officer, The President of the Republic of the South Africa and three other respondents.

In this case, the applicants argue that air pollution in the HPA remains higher than the national ambient air quality standards. On the other hand, the Minister of Environmental Affairs acknowledges that pollution levels continue to exceed these standards, as she stated, "I am aware of the unacceptably high levels of ambient air pollution in the Highveld Priority Area and the potential for that polluted ambient air to adversely impact the health and well-being of the people living and working in the area."[46]

Additionally, the Minister concedes that the government has not achieved the seven goals mentioned for them above due to the lack of regulations that were supposed to be created under Section 20 of the Air Quality Act to enforce the HPA plan, she admits, "[T]o date, the Government has not been successful in bringing the ambient air quality everywhere into compliance with the National Ambient Air Quality Standards."[47]

The applicants argue that the unsafe levels of air pollution in the HPA violate the Sections 24 (a) of the constitutional right of residents to an environment, which states "Everyone has the right (a) to an environment that is not harmful to their health or well-being". On these points the applicants argue that the Minister has legal obligation to promulgate and enforce regulations under Section 20 of the Air Quality Act to implement the HPA, but has failed to do so. They also mention that the former Minister, Nomvule Mokonyane, refused to create any regulations, which led to the launch of the present litigation.

The applicants finally seek to obtain five main remedies from the court. First, they request a declaration that the poor air quality in the HPA is a violation of Section 24(a) of the Constitution, which affirms the right to an environment that is not harmful to health or well-being. Second, they seek a declaration that the Ministry is obliged to promulgate regulations to give effect to the HPA Plan, as required by

[45] Department of Environmental Affairs (2011).

[46] Groundwork Trust v. Minister of Environmental Affairs, No. 39724/2019, at 8(Gauteng Div. Pretoria Mar. 18, 2022)

[47] Id. at 9.

Section 20 of the Air Quality Act. Third, they request a declaration that the Minister's failure to create regulations is unconstitutional and invalid. Fourth, they seek a review and setting aside of the Minister's refusal or unreasonable delay in creating regulations, under the Promotion of Administrative Justice Act, or under the constitutional principle of legality. Finally, they request an order directing the Minister to prepare and publish regulations within 6 months to implement the HPA Plan.

After reviewing all the facts and legal arguments presented by both sides, the court ruled that the poor air quality in the HPA forms a violation of the residents' constitutional right to an environment as stated on the Section 24(a). it confirmed the legal obligation of the Minister of Environmental Affairs to develop and enforce regulations for the HPA Air Quality Management Plan, noting the Minister's unreasonable delay in taking necessary action. The court directed the Minster to prepare and implement these regulations within a timeline a12-month timeline.

Additionally, the court emphasized the importance of public oversight by highlighting key considerations such as enhanced monitoring, public accessibility of emissions data, and cooperation among relevant authorities. This ruling represents a landmark decision not only for South Africa but for the entire continent.

It is a victory for vulnerable communities suffering from air pollution, ensuring that children, women, adults, and the elderly have the right to breathe a clean air and live in good health. This judgment prioritizes human rights over other interests, aiming to safeguard the health of the communities affected by air pollution and ultimately reinforcing the importance of environmental justice. We are grateful to the court for this significant decision, which stands firmly in support of community well-being.

6 United Against the Threats: Climate Change and Air Pollution in Africa

In conclusion, the effects of climate change on Africa are profound and multifaceted impacting the continent's health, economy, and environment. Africa is one of the most vulnerable regions to the effects of the climate change. The significant rise in temperature, as evidenced by the record heat in 2023 coupled with rising sea levels, poses severe threats. Moreover, health crises driven by extreme weather events and proliferation of vector-born diseases further strain already fragile healthcare System.

The case of Save Lamu underscore the importance of international agreements, like the Paris Agreement in protecting vulnerable communities from the side effects of a climate change. This case opened the door for pivotal litigation in Africa's engagement with international climate agreements, demonstrating how the Paris Agreement can be invoked in the courts to safeguard climate change impacts.

Compounding these issues in the growing crisis of air pollution in Africa, often regarded as a silent killer. The main sources of air pollution, transportation emissions, industrial activities biomass burning, and reliance on the fossil fuels—had led to increased greenhouse gas emissions and deteriorated air quality. The lake of strict air quality legislation and weak enforcement mechanisms have allowed pollution levels to rise, while corruption and economic interests often overshadow the public health concerns.

The 'Deadly Air' case in Mpumalanga, South Africa highlights the severe consequences of air pollution. In this region, pollution from coal fired power stations and industrial activities has caused health crisis particularly among vulnerable population like children and the elderly. The South Africa High Court ruling in the favor of affected communities emphasize human rights over industrial interests, reinforcing the importance of environmental justice. These cases serve as a critical reminder that environmental justice is not just about protecting the environment but also about safeguarding the rights and health of marginalized and vulnerable communities especially the low-income.

To effectively combat the dual threats of climate change impacts and air pollution, in Africa needs to adopt unified approach. Cooperation across nations, rather than isolated efforts, is essential. Strict continental union legislations, with robust law enforcement and a priority on human health and community well-being, will put Africa on the right track, especially considering the continent's growing population. The lessons from Save Lamu and Deadly air cases provide a solid foundation upon which Africa can build a united front in addressing these pressing challenges. Africa needs act as one body, united in purpose and action.

References

Africa Report, CDP. https://www.cdp.net/en/research/global-reports/africa-report

Air Pollution, World Health Organization. https://www.afro.who.int/health-topics/air-pollution (last visited 26 Sept 2024)

Al Jazeera (2023, Sept. 4) How much does africa contribute to global carbon emissions? https://www.aljazeera.com/news/2023/9/4/how-much-does-africa-contribute-to-global-carbon-emissions

Ashton K (2023, Sept. 13) Guest post: impact of climate change on mental health 'impossible to ignore'. Carbon Brief. https://www.carbonbrief.org/guest-post-impact-climate-change-on-mental-health-impossible-to-ignore/

Boston College News, Air Pollution in Africa: A Growing Crisis. https://www.bc.edu/bc-web/bcnews/nation-world-society/international/air-pollution-in-africa.html

Chamnha: Climate, Heat, and Maternal and Neonatal Health in Africa, Global Heat Health Information Network, https://ghhin.org/resources/chamnha-climate-heat-and-maternal-and-neonatal-health-in-africa/

Clean Air Fund, Clean Air for Africa's Cities. https://www.cleanairfund.org/clean-air-africas-cities/#explore-the-report

Cytonn Investments (2020) The National Environmental Tribunal: a balance between economic and environmental rights. https://www.cytonn.com/uploads/downloads/the-national-environmental-tribunal-a-balance-between-economic-and-environmental-rights.pdf

Deloitte Sustainability Circular Economy Potential for Climate Change Mitigation (2016, November)

Department of Environmental Affairs (2011) Highveld priority area air quality management plan. https://screening.environment.gov.za/ScreeningDownloads/DevelopmentZones/HIGHVELD_PRIORITY_AREA_AQMP.pdf
Disaster Philanthropy, 2023 Libya Floods, DisasterPhilanthropy.org. https://disasterphilanthropy.org/disasters/2023-libya-floods/
Encyclopaedia Britannica. https://www.britannica.com/topic/list-of-African-countries-by-population
Environmental Protection Agency (EPA) (n.d.) Learn about environmental justice. U.S. Environmental Protection Agency. https://www.epa.gov/environmentaljustice/learn-about-environmental-justice
FAO, AUC, ECA, and WFP (2023) Africa regional overview of food security and nutrition: statistics and trends. https://openknowledge.fao.org/server/api/core/bitstreams/c6c81d5f-e337-4b3e-8330-555c9ed0e741/content
Fisher S et al (2022) Air pollution and development in Africa: impacts on health, the economy, and human capital
Fletcher ER (2022, Oct. 27) Africa faces 1.1 million deaths annually from air pollution – second largest risk after malnutrition. Health & Environment
Groundwork Trust v. Minister of Environmental Affairs, No. 39724/2019, at 8 (Gauteng Div. Pretoria Mar. 18, 2022)
Health Effects Institute (2022) The state of air quality and health impacts in Africa. A report from the state of global air initiative. Health Effects Institute, Boston
Hooijer A, Vernimmen R (2021) Global lidar land elevation data reveal greatest sea-level rise vulnerability in the tropics. Nat Commun 12:3592
IDMC (2024) 2024 global report on internal displacement. Internal Displacement Monitoring Centre. https://www.internal-displacement.org/global-report/grid2024/
International Federation of Red Cross and Red Crescent Societies, Floods, IFRC. https://www.ifrc.org/our-work/disasters-climate-and-crises/what-disaster/floods
Mosquito-borne diseases could reach extra one billion people as climate warms, Carbon Brief, https://www.carbonbrief.org/mosquito-borne-diseases-could-reach-extra-one-billion-people-as-climate-warms/ (last visited Sept. 25, 2024)
Municipalities.co.za, Mpumalanga, https://municipalities.co.za/provinces/view/6/mpumalanga
NASA Earth Observatory (2020, Dec. 17) Drought in Madagascar. NASA. https://earthobservatory.nasa.gov/images/148636/drought-in-madagascar
Number of Deaths in Africa, Statista. https://www.statista.com/statistics/1282721/number-of-deaths-in-africa/#:~:text=The%20number%20of%20deaths%20registered,slightly%20over%2012%20million%20deaths
Save Lamu v. National Environmental Management Authority (NEMA) & Amu Power Co. Ltd., Tribunal Appeal No. NET 196 of 2016, at 2 (Kenya Nat'l Env't Tribunal)
Stanley HM (1890) In darkest Africa. Sampson Low, Marston, Searle, & Rivington, London
State of Global Air, Africa, https://www.stateofglobalair.org/resources/africa (last visited Sept. 26, 2024)
Suedi Y, Fall M (2024) Climate Change Litigation before the African Human Rights System: prospects and pitfalls. J Hum Rights Practice 16:146. https://doi.org/10.1093/jhuman/huad024
The term "Dark Continent" was used for first time by Welsh journalist and explorer Henry Morton Stanley, from his book In Darkest Africa (1890)
UN General Assembly (2006) Resolution 60/147. Basic principles and guidelines on the right to a remedy and reparation for victims of gross violations of International Human Rights Law, adopted 21 March 2006, A/RES/60/147
UNEP. Responding to Climate Change in Africa, https://www.unep.org/regions/africa/regional-initiatives/responding-climate-change#:~:text=While%20Africa%20has%20contributed%20negligibly,socioeconomic%20growth%20in%20the%20continent

United Nations Environment Programme (UNEP), https://www.unep.org/regions/africa/regional-initiatives/responding-climate-change#:~:text=While%20Africa%20has%20contributed%20negligibly,socioeconomic%20growth%20in%20the%20continent
World Bank (2021) Groundswell report. World Bank, Washington DC
World Economic Forum (2024, Sept) What causes sea levels to rise and how can we stop it? World Economic Forum
World Health Organization (2023a, Sept. 20) 101 Health workers killed in Libya in the aftermath of Storm Daniel. WHO EMRO. https://www.emro.who.int/media/news/101-health-workers-killed-in-libya-in-the-aftermath-of-storm-daniel.html
World Health Organization (2023b, Sept) Regional initiative to tackle health impacts of climate change in Africa Launched
World Meteorological Organization (2023) Africa suffers disproportionately from climate change. https://wmo.int/news/media-centre/africa-suffers-disproportionately-from-climate-change
World Meteorological Organization (2024) State of the climate in Africa 2023
Worldometer, Number of Countries in Africa, https://www.worldometers.info/geography/how-many-countries-in-africa/#:~:text=There%20are%2054%20countries%20in,the%20United%20Nations%20official%20statistics

Ibrahim Badawi is a Ph.D. Candidate at Seattle University, Seattle, USA.

The Role of Courts and the Legal Profession in Climate Litigation: A Tripartite Analysis of Access to the Kenyan, East African, and African Court Systems

Muriuki Sharon

1 Introduction

The Mau Forest Complex on the Western Highlands of the Great Rift Valley is one of Kenya's Water towers. Its rivers flow and water tea farms and flow onward to the Maasai Mara and the Serengeti, the setting of one of the natural wonders of the world, the Great Wildebeest Migration.[1] The Forest Complex is also home to the indigenous Ogiek. In October 2009, the Ogiek received an order to leave their home in the Mau Forest by the Kenya Forest Service.[2] The move aggrieved the Ogiek. They presented their case, through the Centre for Minority Rights Development and the Minority Rights Group International to the African Commission on Human and Peoples' Rights which in turn presented their case to the African Court on Human and Peoples' Rights.[3] On May 26th· 2917, the African Court found Kenya liable for violating the land rights of the Ogiek community.[4] The other violations cited by the Court include the right to property and religious practices. The Court ordered Kenya to pay reparations to the Ogiek on June 23rd· 2022 but as Amnesty International notes, the violations of the rights continue.[5] The apex of successful climate litigation is the enforcement of legal orders to ensure climate justice. The judgment in the

[1] Githumbi et al. (2021), pp. 229–245.

[2] See Amnesty International's commentary on the *Ogiek Case*.

[3] See the Ogiek Case.

[4] Ibid.

[5] Ibid.

M. Sharon (✉)
Human Rights Measurement Initiative, Wellington, New Zealand

V. E. de Aquino et al. (eds.), *Climate Litigation in a Changing World*, Ius Gentium: Comparative Perspectives on Law and Justice 130,
https://doi.org/10.1007/978-3-032-05530-9_12

Ogiek Case sets the tone for examining how the judicial arm of the government encounters the executive dilly-dally in ensuring the finality of the justice process.

1.1 Background of the Study

The age of litigation in the new age is upon us. Aided by education and accessibility to justice, communities and individuals alike are aware of climate justice and climate litigation. The COVID-19 pandemic provided a health-mandated shift to the use of technology by many courts, even those suffering from underfunding. Courts and court users found themselves at the crossroads of change regarding filing systems, representation, and adoption of and adaptation to neo-tech. The availability of knowledge due to technology, education, and civic education has led to an informed populace that as a matter of fact cannot 'let injustice pass' and is more informed on the pursuit of justice and accountability. It is against this background that the study focuses on Kenya and climate litigation and which laws govern and regulate this. It is not a comprehensive study of all Kenyan laws on climate justice, litigation, and enforcement as the Kenyan legal system contains numerous statutes. It also explores the structure of the East African Court and the African Court and their provision of access to justice.

1.2 Aim of Study

The study seeks to investigate the legal processes of initiating and sustaining climate litigation specifically in the Kenyan, East African, and African Courts of Justice. It presents the court's structures, modes, and documents required to institute climate justice proceedings, the key players and their appointments, and the challenges in achieving climate justice.

1.3 Literature Review

The literature review herein was conducted to introduce climate litigation, access to justice, the systems and the people affected by the initiation of such processes. To concisely address such areas, literature review herein is topical. It examines scholarly publications on specific themes of climate justice and litigation processes, access, and persons involved in such processes. International legal scholarship has been likened to a duel amongst the state, international institutions, and other influences, with the ability to adapt to fit the location and merging issues.[6] In addition, there have been calls to implement new legal approaches to ensure that legal systems effectively address the climate change problem and promote social justice.[7] It is from this starting point that this review examines the various players in the climate justice system. The aim of the literature review is to set a scholarly introduction on the subsequent analysis of Kenyan Statutes and treaties affecting access to justice and climate litigation on East Africa.

1.3.1 Climate Justice

Climate justice has been defined as a forward-looking mechanism to eliminate climate-related inequalities in the world.[8] A change social-economic systems are a necessity in ensuring climate justice.[9] The changes, called just transformations, cut across political, gender social, ethnic, religious, and location spheres. Climate ethics is identified by the unfair distribution of the effects of global warming, with individuals, communities, and countries that contribute less to climate change facing the greatest challenges of mitigating it.

1.3.2 Access to Justice

Climate justice is a human rights issue that adopts the element of human rights of the university. Access to justice is a human right.[10] The position of environmental justice as being incorporated into international law includes recognition of universal human rights, the rise of environmental awareness, internationalization of trade and business and relations and changes in governance. However, environmental justice is just a component of access to justice and since climate change affects all levels and aspects of life, it cannot be departmentalized as an environmental issue only.

1.3.3 The People

The citizenry plays an important role in climate justice mechanisms. They are the most affected by climate change and therefore should, in a balanced and well-meaning legal process, enjoy legal protection and compensation when affected by adverse effects of climate change. The citizenry herein includes the global citizenry as climate change and its effects have been described as a problem of global

[6] See Leiter Andrea and Petersman Marie (2022).

[7] See Mboya (2018), pp. 79–103.

[8] See Perkins (2023) on climate justice and participatory research.

[9] Ibid at p. 13.

[10] See Redgwell (2007), pp. 153–176.

inequalities.[11] Scholars have argued that to address climate justice, countries should adopt and implement climate policies founded on ethics to dually address policy and science.[12] This is reflected in interest in treaties, protocols, and agreements affecting climate justice and efforts by various actors to ensure that the people's voice is heard in climate negotiations.

1.3.4 The Legal System

Legal systems have been set up to promote, enforce, and ensure adherence to the rule of law. Legal systems can be localized from a village or town up to an international level. They include bylaws, national and international laws, localized tribunals, national courts and international legal systems. Three areas have been identified where legal rules can be applied in claims for climate change damage.[13] They include checking and addressing time limitations, research and investigate on responsibility by developed countries liable for greenhouse emissions, feasibility of implementation of responsibilities and reading on precedents on how laws and rules have been applied in climate justice. It is worth noting that the term 'legal systems' should be noted to include alternative and informal legal systems[14] as an all-inclusive way of bringing in sections of the society that have been left to the margins or othered by formal rigid systems. The twin issues of climate change and inequalities have been addressed. It has been posited that human rights and inequality help in viewing climate change is a social-legal lens.[15] This is important because it brings to the fore the fact that climate change is experienced differently in parts of the world, and turns climate change into a human rights issue to how rights of vulnerable sectors are exposed to abuse and limitation. While some climate justice emergencies require the enactment of new laws, some legal system mechanisms are in a state of dormancy that are activated in times of climate emergencies. It has been written of how several legal instruments such as the Public Civil Action was used by departments and agencies such as prosecutors, public defenders and observers to address the rupture and accompanying disaster of the Fundao Dam in Minas Gerais.[16]

[11] See Roser and Seidel (2017).

[12] Ibid.

[13] Farber (2017), pp. 80–106.

[14] See Mbote-Kameri and Kabira (2023), pp. 165–187.

[15] Atrey Shreya (2023), pp. 17–39.

[16] Losekann et al. (2020), pp. 199–208.

1.3.5 The Judges, the Courts and the Registries

Judges as determiners of the law are a crucial element in climate litigation and thereby enforcement of climate. Their judgments and orders not only create the law and precedents, but fundamentally affect the enforcement of climate justice. Courts are centres of litigation. In the climate justice sphere, they represent visual and audio locations where disputes are determined and legal knowledge dispensed.

The legal system, through courts, has been described by as a means where governments can be obligated to protect human rights as a climate change issue.[17] The reliance of courts on politics has been a bottleneck in ensuring that courts properly and with unfettered due processes, address climate change matters before them. It has been opined that courts should stop founding their lack or reluctance to address the climate crisis on political doctrines and suggests the usage of tort and constitutional law and apply constitutional provisions to remedy the climate crisis.[18] The registries represent the first point of contact when ensuring, filing and following up on climate justice cases and litigation. The registries acts as record centres and libraries and statistical centres as it is possible to track how many climate justice and litigation cases have been filed, the state of proceedings and enforcement of orders. Records are repositories of justice. Whether in soft copy or hard copy, they are what enforceability is all about. In the Ogiek Case, for example, the Kenyan government cannot remove itself from the duty of ensuring justice as the records have been there for 2 years. Records of climate justice legal efforts provide education and contribute a lot to legal libraries all over the world.

1.3.6 The Lawyers and Law Schools

Lawyers are legal systems representatives of individuals, companies, agencies and governments in climate litigation. Law schools at different levels, are legal ovens, where legal professionals can acquire education knowledge and professional continuous development. Legal education is an important avenue and meeting point of linking intersectionality and climate justice. They allow the application of intersectional insights which calls for synchronicity and application on intersectionality in climate justice scholarship.[19] As justice and climate litigation become globalized, so does legal education. Authors have written on the globalization of legal education as the world becomes joined through trade, treaties, migration and technology. It is possible to earn a law degree online and study for bar exams for different jurisdictions such as New York online. This internationalization of legal education has been

[17] Shuen (2021), pp. 377–410.

[18] See Novak (2020), pp. 778–743.

[19] See Mikulewicz et al. (2023), pp. 1275–1286.

described as 'transnationalization' as a component of the globalizing legal education.[20]

1.3.7 Legal Language and Records

The *lingua franca* of the justice system is an important wave when moving the climate justice ship. Words acquire different meanings upon interpretation and translation. Climate change cuts across and affects different societies and communities with diverse cultures and languages. It is imperative that legal instruments, when translated, capture the meaning that is clearly understood by the people affected but it the most. Legal discourses can take various forms as identified by authors who, when addressing the role of culture in legal languages, opine that interpretation and translation involves legislative discourse, courtroom discourse and judicial discourse.[21] Interpreters and translators, therefore, play a crucial role in court proceedings especially at the international level where judges and parties maybe alien to each other's cultures and language. Legal language used in drafting national laws, continental laws, treaties and protocols should also be easily understood and simplified to avoid differing interpretations.

It has been noted that legal discourses can be influenced by translations at various levels and the translation affects access and understanding of legal texts by judges and students as well as institutions.[22] Legal education has further been contextualized as part of education for sustainable development (ESD) which in turn is aimed at achieving social justice.[23]

1.3.8 Liability and Enforceability

The law does not act in vain as does it issue redress that cannot be enforced. Legal enforcement of orders on climate justice is the apex of every legal system. Holding governments, individuals, and companies is an obstacle in many legal systems. Addressing liability and holding responsible parties to account for causing the climate crisis is the role of the court. In other written discourses, courts have been advised to use science to identify liable parties and ensure the law's speedy and far-reaching responsibility.[24] Therefore science not only helps define climate change but its findings and predictions can be used in courts, and legal documents to assign responsibility and liability, especially in enforcing the Polluter Pays Principle,

[20] See Garth Bryant and Shaffer Gregory (2022) on the Globalization of Legal Education.

[21] See Piszcz and Sierocka (2020) on the Role of culture in legal languages, interpretation and translation, pp. 533–542.

[22] Canaperi (2023), pp. 147–170.

[23] Guth (2018), pp. 301–315.

[24] Beck (2020) on Climate Change and Climate Jurisprudence.

2 Introduction to the Kenyan Judicial System Concerning Climate Litigation

The Kenyan justice system is pillared on the Common Law System of its former colonial master, Great Britain. It has undergone legal evolution to adopt and adapt to international law and precedents from other jurisdictions especially when addressing new areas of the law such as climate litigation and digital rights. The Constitution restates the sovereignty of the people and its supremacy and places justice in the hands of individuals, meaning that individuals can approach courts for redress and interpretation of the law regarding climate change and climate justice. The Constitution of Kenya, 2010 establishes the Judiciary under Chapter 11.

It establishes tribunals, commissions, authorities, magistrates' courts, the environment and land court, the high court, the employment and labor relations court, the court of appeal, and the Supreme Court who have original or appellate jurisdiction concerning climate litigation. In this subsection, an analysis of constitutional and statutory provisions on access to justice, the structure of the courts, and judicial precedents on access to justice are examined.

2.1 Constitutional Provisions

The Constitution of Kenya begins with a preamble. Preambles have been said to serve legal and social functions.[25] Preambles constitute declarations and affirmations of sovereignty, historical narrations of a state, the goals of the society, national identity, and religion or spiritual aspirations.[26] The Preamble recognizes that Kenyans are respectful to the environment, a heritage, and will sustain it for the benefit of future generations.[27] It also recognizes the aspirations of Kenyans for a governance structure based on human rights, equality, freedom, democracy, social justice, and the rule of law.[28] Access to justice is a fundamental right and freedom expressly guaranteed under Article 48. The article proved that the state shall ensure justice for all persons and if any fee is required, such fee should be reasonable and not impede access to justice. The reading, application, and enforcement of this right must be read together with other constitutional, statutory, and case law provisions and precedents.[29]

On language, which as noted in the literature review as being part of a good access to justice system, the Constitution declares Kiswahili as the national language of Kenya and identifies Kiswahili and English languages as being the official

---

[25] See Orgad (2010) on Preamble in Constitutional Interpretation.

[26] Ibid at pp. 716–717.

[27] See Note 25.

[28] Ibid.

[29] See Note 25 at Article 48.

languages of Kenya.[30] It also calls for the promotion of other languages and access to Braille and sign languages for persons with disabilities. In addition, the constitution prohibits the discrimination of any person on the grounds of language,[31] meaning that access to justice should not be hindered by one's inability to speak the two official languages.

The Constitution further sets out the National Values and Principles of Governance that are binding on State Organs, State Officers, and all persons whenever interpreting, enacting, applying, or implementing the Constitution and other public policy decisions. In interpreting and ensuring access to justice, these include the rule of law, participation of the people, human dignity, equity, social justice, inclusiveness, equality, human rights, non-discrimination, and protection of the marginalized, good governance, integrity, transparency, accountability, and sustainable development.[32]

The Constitution entrenches the Bill of Rights under Article 19 to preserve the dignity of individuals and communities and the promotion of social justice.[33] The Bill of Rights applies to all state organs and persons. To ensure access to justice, the Constitution empowers courts, tribunals, and authorities to compel the state to implement rights if it claims it does not have resources to do so by compelling the state to furnish proof that it does not have the resources to do so and upon allocating resources, ensure that vulnerable groups and individuals are prioritized.[34] Consolidating its provision on the implementation of fundamental rights and freedoms, the Constitution obligates the state to respect, protect, promote, and fulfill fundamental rights and freedoms. This is to be done by ensuring the progressive realization of economic and social rights and adherence to international law.

The enforcement of the Bill of Rights is the right of every person whose personal or community rights have been violated, denied, infringed, or threatened.[35] The Chief Justice is mandated to make rules to ensure that people can access redress on the infringement of the Bill of Rights by ensuring the facilitation of access, ensuring minimum formalities, ensuring no fees are charged, disregarding undue procedural technicalities, and allowing for representation in a court of experts in a particular field as *amicus curiae*.[36] The absence of these rules does not preclude any person from accessing the court for determination of their petition.

In furtherance to ensuring access to justice, the Constitution guarantees the right to a clean environment and the right to health, safety, and economic interests of consumers.[37] In its duty to ensure a clean environment, the state is obligated to

---

[30] Ibid 25 at Article 7.

[31] Ibid at Article 27(4).

[32] Supra 25 at Article 10.

[33] Ibid.

[34] Ibid.

[35] Supra 25 at Article 22.

[36] Ibid.

[37] Supra 25 at Article 42 and Article 46.

ensure sustainable use of the environment and other natural resources, ensure the achievement of tree cover by at least 10% on Kenya's land mass, encourage public participation in the management, protection conservation of the environment, ensure environmental impact assessment mechanism and procedures are in place and followed, eliminate activities that endanger the environment.[38] To ensure access to and enforcement of this right, the Constitution provides that any person can seek redress and claim remedies when the right to a clean and healthy environment is violated or infringed or denied.[39] To actualize Article 70, there is no requirement to prove loss or injury, thus matters concerning climate change and climate induced losses can be brought to court as both curative and protective measures.

2.2 *Judicial Obligations with Regards to Access to Justice*

The Courts and their obligations in climate litigation is also a constitutional provision and mandate. The Constitution recognizes that judicial mandate is derived from the people and exercised by courts and tribunals.[40] To ensure access to justice in furtherance to Article 48, the courts and tribunals are required to do justice to all, regardless of status, ensure that justice is not delayed, promote alternative dispute resolution mechanisms such as reconciliation, mediation, arbitration and traditional dispute resolution and disregard procedural technicalities while promoting the spirit of the constitution.[41]

The Constitution establishes the structure, composition and functions of the courts. The Court system intersects. This means that in climate litigation, a party or person approaches a court with specific, territorial or appellate jurisdiction to hear and determine the issue. The courts system in Kenya comprises of the Supreme Court, Court of Appeal, The High Court, the Environment and Land Court (E.L.C), the Employment and Labour Relations Court (E.L.R.C), the magistracy and various tribunals with specific mandates.

The promotion and facilitation of the independence and accountability of the Judiciary is a function of the Judicial Service Commission (J.S.C) established under Article 172.[42] The JSC recruits and hires personnel working in the courts and the registries. Its functions as per the Constitution is also the preparation and implementation of programs for the continuing education and training of judges and judicial officers and advising the national government on improving the efficiency of the administration of justice.[43] To ensure that justice is accessed and facilitated, the

[38] Supra 25 at Article 69.

[39] Supra 25 at Article 70.

[40] Supra 25 at Article 159.

[41] Ibid.

[42] See Supra 25.

[43] Ibid at Article 172(1)(b).

Chief Registrar (C.J) of the Judiciary, administers the Judiciary Fund. This is done by preparing an estimate of the expenditure for the Judiciary and submitting it to the National Assembly for approval.[44]

2.3 Select Statutory Provisions on Access to Justice

2.3.1 The Advocates Act

The Advocates Act[45] governs the admission, licensing and regulation of legal practice in Kenya. With regards to access and administration of justice it ensures that persons practicing law in Kenya are qualified to so by providing the qualifications and licensing procedures of persons to do so. Advocates in Kenya are required to take out practicing licenses valid from the first of January to December 31st every year. Failure to comply makes one unqualified to practice law and any documents and legal representation maybe struck pout or declared null and thus affecting access to and promotion and preservation of justice.

2.3.2 The Appellate Jurisdiction Act

The Appellate Jurisdiction Act[46] governs the hearings and modes of procedure at the Court of Appeal. The Court of Appeal hears, among others, appeals from the Environment and Land Court. The overriding objective of this statute is the facilitation of the just, expeditious, proportionate and affordable resolution of appeals.[47] It requires advocates appearing before it, to assist it in achieving its overriding objective and participation in the Court's processes. The aims of the Court are to ensure the just determination of proceedings, efficient use of available judicial and administrative resources, timely disposal of proceedings and the use of technology in its functions.[48]

2.3.3 Arbitration Act

The Arbitration Act[49] is the procedural act governing arbitration, arbitration agreements, and arbitral awards in Kenya. With regards to access to justice, it allows persons seeking arbitration to agree on the procedures of appointing arbitrators and

---

[44] Ibid at Article 173.

[45] Cap 16, Laws of Kenya.

[46] Cap 9, Laws of Kenya.

[47] Ibid at Section 3A.

[48] Ibid at Section 3B.

[49] Cap 49, Laws of Kenya.

what to do in instances where parties cannot agree to do so.[50] The Act provides that parties in arbitral proceedings shall be treated equally and given fair and reasonable opportunities to present their cases.[51] Parties are also free to agree on the language to be used in the proceedings. It also requires that parties be given sufficient notice of hearings and meetings as well as the furnishing of documents to be relied on. International arbitration awards are enforced in Kenya under the New York Convention or any other convention Kenya is signatory relating to arbitral awards.[52]

2.3.4 Climate Change Act and the *Lamu Coal Case*

The Climate Change Act provides the regulatory framework for enhanced responses to climate change and provides the mechanisms and measures to achieve low carbon climate development..[53] One of the objectives of the statute is the provisions of mechanisms and facilitation of climate change research and development, training and capacity building. It also seeks to integrate climate change into the exercise of power and functions at all levels of governance. Thus, if these objectives are met, individuals and institutions are better equipped when approaching courts and tribunals or when dispensing climate litigation justice.

In the recent past, the Kenyan legal system has been approached by individuals and institutions alike to hear and resolve matters concerning the environment and the climate. The National Environment Tribunal was approached in 2016 by the organization 'Save Lamu' in *Save Lamu and Others V- National Environment Management Authority* and Another to determine and EIA appeal.[54] The grounds of the appeal included the following:-.

The Tribunal allowed the appeal and set aside the decision of the first Respondent to issue the Environmental Impact Assessment License No. **NEMA/ESIA / PSL/3798** dated **7th September 2016** to the second Respondent. It also made an order that, the second Respondent, should it still wish to pursue the construction and operation of the project, to undertake a fresh EIA study following the terms of reference already formulated in January 2016, and in compliance with the Director - general's directive as well as adherence to each step of the requirements of the EIA Regulations on EIA Studies. The fresh EIA study, if undertaken, is to, *inter alia*, include all approved and legible detailed architectural and engineering plans for the plant and its ancillary facilities (such as the coal storage and handling facility and the ash pit with its location in relation to the seashore), consideration of the Climate Change Act 2016, the Energy Act 2019 and the Natural Resources (Classes of

[50] Ibid at Section 12.

[51] Ibid at Section 19.

[52] Ibid at Section 36.

[53] Cap 387 A, Laws of Kenya.

[54] For further details on the case see *Tribunal Appeal No. Net 196 of 2016 Save Lamu and others –v- National Environment Management Authority*.

Transactions subject to Ratification) Act 2016 in so far as the project will utilize seawater for the plant and/ or if applicable.

Subject to these steps being undertaken, a fresh EIA study report is to be prepared and presented to the first Respondent. The first Respondent was directed to comply with the provisions of regulations 17 and 21, engage with the lead agencies and the public, in the manner and strict timelines provided for under the said law. The first Respondent is to share its memorandum of reasons for reaching its decision whether for or against the project with the relevant parties and publish its decision on the grant or refusal to issue an EIA license accompanied with a summary of its reasons within 7 days of its decision. Such publication should be in a newspaper with nationwide circulation.'[55]

The Tribunal noted that these extraordinary measures are necessary to ensure sufficient access to information by the public on a project that will be the first of its kind in Kenya and the East African region.

2.3.5 Commission on Administrative Justice Act

The Commission on Administrative Justice Act[56] creates the Commission on Administrative Justice. This Commission investigates conduct in public administration, investigates complaints of abuse of power, investigates administrative injustices, sets up complaint-handling sectors of public service, promotes Alternative Dispute Resolutions, recommends compensation and remedies, provides advisory opinions, publishes periodic reports on administrative justice in Kenya, promotes public awareness on administrative procedures, promotes and protects fundamental human rights and freedoms and collaborates with the Kenya National Commission on Human Rights to ensure efficient, effective and complementarity in their functions.[57] The Commission has powers to investigate complaints and matters arising out of the administrative actions of a public office, a state corporation and other bodies and agencies not limited under Section 30.

2.3.6 The Commissions of Inquiry Act

The Commissions of Inquiry Act makes the procedural and regulatory provisions governing the appointment of commissioners to inquire into matters of public nature referred to them by the president, prescribing of powers, privileges and duties.[58] Commissions formed under this Act inquire matters that are of public interest. Commissions regulate proceedings and are bestowed with powers to summon and

[55] See the *Lamu Coal Case*.

[56] Cap 7 J, Laws of Kenya.

[57] Ibid at Section 8.

[58] Cap 102, Laws of Kenya.

examine witnesses. The hearings can also take the form of judicial proceedings ensuring that the commissions are guided by the laws of natural justice.

2.3.7 The Consumer Protection Act

The Consumer Protection Act is aimed at protecting the consumer and preventing unfair trade practices in consumer protection.[59] The Act actualizes Article 46 of the Constitution.[60] With regards to climate litigation, the Act provides that class action suits can be commenced against suppliers who are under an obligation to ensure that goods and services are of merchantable quality.[61] Thus degraded and goods arising out of climate neglect, omission and injustices can be subject to court proceedings. This law prohibits false, misleading and deceptive representation which is terms as unfair practice.[62] Misrepresentation and deception may, for climate litigation practice, include misrepresentation on quality, approval, grade and status.

2.3.8 The Energy Act

The Energy Act aims at establishment, powers and functions of the energy sector entities, promotion of renewable energy, exploration, recovery and commercial utilization of geothermal energy, regulation of petroleum and coal activities and the production, regulation and supply of electricity in Kenya.[63] Despite the link between energy and climate change, this statute lacks clear, express provisions on climate injustices and climate litigation. It prescribes offences such as extraction of wells, drills extractions and uses of geothermal energy in contravention of the Act removal of pegs and beacons and damaging of property as major offences. This notwithstanding, this statute has been used in litigation in Kenya in recent years.

2.3.9 The Environmental Management and Coordination Act

The Environment Management and Coordination Act (EMCA)[64] provides the legal and institutional framework for the management of the environment by providing definitions and principles of environmental management as well as establishing duties and responsibilities. These include administration, environmental planning and protection and conservation of the environment, integrated environmental

---

[59] Cap 50, Laws of Kenya.

[60] Supra 25.

[61] Supra 58, Section 5.

[62] Ibid at Section 12.

[63] Energy Act, Cap 314, Laws of Kenya.

[64] Environmental Management and Coordination Act, Cap 387, Laws of Kenya.

impact assessment, environmental audit and monitoring, environmental restoration orders, quality and standards, inspection, analysis and records, the role of international treaties, conventions and agreements, environmental offences and other incidental provisions. EMCA creates the National Environment Tribunal which hears grievances arising out of grant of licenses or permits, imposition of conditions, limitations or restriction of licenses, revocation or variation of licenses and imposition of environmental restoration or improvement orders.[65]

2.3.10 The Environment and Land Court Act

The Environment and Land Court Act establishes the Environment and Land Court, a superior court that hears and determines disputes relating to the environment and the use, occupation and title to land.[66] Like the Energy Act it does not have 'Climate Change' or 'Climate Injustice' in it interpretation section but is nevertheless the court with jurisdiction to hear and determine such matters when they relate to climate issues, land and the environment and any adverse effects arising. The principal objective of the statute is to establish the ELC to ensure just, expeditious, proportionate and accessible resolutions of disputes governed by the statute.[67] Parties who approach the court through petitions, plaints and originating summons can be granted reliefs such as interim or permanent preservative orders including injunctions, prerogative orders, award of damages, compensation, specific performance, restitution, declarations or costs.[68]

Section 18 provides the 'Guiding Principles of Kenya's Environment Land Court'.[69] They include the principle of sustainable development such as public participation, cultural and social principles, international cooperation, intergenerational and intragenerational equity, the polluter pays and the precautionary principle. The others include the principles of land policy and judicial authorities, the national values and principles of governance and the values of public service under Articles 60 (10), Article 159, Article 10(20 and Article 232 (1)of the Constitution respectively. The Court is not tied down by technicalities of procedure and can adopt, implement alternative dispute resolution mechanisms either on its own motion or upon request by the parties before it. Apart from the use of the English language, the ELC is mandated and obligated to 'facilitate the use of indigenous languages, the Kenyan Sign Language, Braille and other communication formats and technologies accessible to persons with disabilities'.[70] It can also direct that proceedings be

[65] See Section 129 of EMCA.

[66] Environment and Land Court, Cap 8D, Laws of Kenya.

[67] Ibid at Section 3.

[68] Ibid at Section 13(5).

[69] Ibid at Section 18.

[70] Supra Section 23.

conducted electronically such as tele-conferencing and video conferencing among other electronic means.

2.3.11 The Fair Administrative Action Act

This statute defines administrative actions as 'powers, functions and duties exercised by authorities or quasi-judicial tribunals or any act, omission or decision of an person, body or author that affects the legal rights or interests of any person to whom such action relates'.[71] The Act restates the constitutional right to administrative action which is expeditious, efficient, lawful reasonable and procedurally fair.[72] Every administrative action should be in written form, given within reasonable time. In compliance with the laws of natural justice, every person has a right to be heard and make representation, has a right of review or internal appeals, provided with a statement of reasons against them, right to legal representation, right to cross examination and information.[73] Administrative actions that may affect a group of persons or the general public can occur. In such instances a public notice should be issued inviting views from the public, consider all views represented as well as all relevant material and facts, give reasons for the action, issue notices on internal mechanisms available[74] and specify the time period in which any appeal should be lodged.

A person or institution aggrieved by a fair administrative action can file judicial review proceedings in a court or tribunal. Such review may occur when a person who carried out the administrative action, lacked empowering legal authority to do so, acted in excess of jurisdiction or power, acted in delegated authority in contravention of the law, was biased or suspected to be biased and denied reasonable opportunities to the aggrieved party to present their case.[75] In addition, a decision may be reviewed where a mandatory/material procedure was not complied with, the action and decision were procedurally unfair, there was material influenced founded on an error of the law, the decision was made with ulterior motives and prejudicial to the applicant, failure to take relevant considerations, acting on the direction of unauthorized body or person, decisions made in bad faith, irrational decisions, abuse of discretion, delay, decisions which are not proportionate and unfair decisions.

Applications and Appeals under this law should be heard and determined within ninety (90) days of filing.[76] Orders from proceedings of judicial review include a declaration of the rights of the parties, restraining acts or continuing breach of duty directing an administrator to give reasons for their decision, prohibiting an

[71] Cap 7 L, Laws of Kenya.

[72] Ibid at Section 4.

[73] Ibid at Section 4(3).

[74] Ibid at Section 5.

[75] Ibid Section 7.

[76] Ibid at Section 8.

administrator from acting in a particular manner, compelling administrators to perform their legal duties, setting aside the administrative action, granting a temporary interdict and an award of costs.[77]

2.3.12 The Foreign Judgments (Reciprocal Enforcement Act)

This law provides for the enforcement of judgments given in countries outside Kenya which accord reciprocal treatment to judgments given in Kenya.[78] In climate litigation, awards for compensation may happen in foreign jurisdictions and the purpose of this law is to ensure their enforcement in Kenya. These judgments may include orders for payment of money, delivery of movable property, appeals and award in arbitration proceedings.[79]

2.3.13 The Judiciary Fund Act

The statute provides the regulation of the Judiciary Fund.[80] This is a constitutional provision as noted earlier I noted in 2.2 The objective of the Fund are to safeguard the financial and operational independence of the Judiciary, ensure accountability for funds allocated to the Judiciary and ensure that the Judiciary has adequate resources to enable its functions.[81] The Fund is to be utilized to provide for the administrative expenses of the Judiciary as well as acquisition and proper maintenance of buildings, rounds and other assets of the Judiciary.[82] His means that this fund can be used to construct courts in far flung places as well as build ramps and elevators for the differently abled court users and staff.

2.3.14 The Legal Aid Act

The purpose of the Legal Aid Act is to facilitate access to justice and social justice, establish the National Legal Aid Service and provide legal aid and funding of legal aid.[83] The act defines legal aid to include legal advice, legal representation, assistance in resolving disputes by way of alternative dispute resolution, drafting relevant documents, giving effect to out-of-court-settlements, creating awareness through legal information and law-related education and recommending law reform

---

[77] See Section 11of the FAA.

[78] Cap 43, Laws of Kenya.

[79] Ibid at Section 3.

[80] Cap 8B, Laws of Kenya.

[81] Ibid at Section 3.

[82] Ibid at Section 6.

[83] Cap 16 A Laws of Kenya.

and undertaking advocacy work on behalf of the community.[84] Legal aid providers include advocates under the Law Society of Kenya *pro bono* programmes, civil society organizations, public benefits organizations, paralegals, law firms, universities and accredited government agencies.[85]

The objects of the Acts are to provide accessible, affordable, sustainable, credible and accountable legal service, provide legal aid schemes in accessing legal aid, promote legal awareness, support community legal services and promote alternative dispute resolution methods to enhance justice.[86] On climate litigation, the act does not expressly define people affected by the effect of climate change but does make provisions for the provision of legal aid to people who make applications for legal aid defined as 'Applicants' and an 'indigent person' who has been defined as a person who cannot afford to pay for legal services.[87]

Legal aid is funded through the Legal Aid Fund with funds allocated by Parliament, grants, gifts, donations, loans, endowments and money from lawful sources.[88] Legal Aid Service maybe provided in civil, criminal, children, constitutional and matters of public interest[89] which are all areas where climate litigation can take shape. Legal aid is available to citizens of Kenya, children, refuges, victims of human trafficking, internally displaced people and stateless people,[90] providing avenues for judicial representation for people displaced by climate change. Legal aid is not available to companies, corporations, trusts, civil society, NGOs and other artificial entities or persons.[91]

2.3.15 The Magistrates' Court Act

The law confers jurisdiction, functions, powers, and procedures of the magistrates' courts.[92] Magistrates' courts have jurisdiction to hear and determine claims relating to environmental planning and protection, climate issues, land use planning, title, tenure, boundaries, rates, rents, valuations, mining, minerals, and other natural resources.[93] In regards to access to justice, the Act establishes the office of the court administrator which maintains the registry, accepts, transmits serves and keeps documents, facilitates the enforcement of decisions of the magistrate's court, certifies orders and decisions of the court, keeps records and minutes of meetings of the

---

[84] Ibid at Section 2.

[85] See the objectives of the Legal Aid Act.

[86] Ibid at Section 3.

[87] See note 82 at Section 2.

[88] Ibid at Section 29.

[89] Ibid at Section 35.

[90] Ibid at Section 36.

[91] Ibid at Section 37.

[92] Cap 10, Laws of Kenya.

[93] Ibid at Section 9(i).

court, manages staff, carries out daily administration of the court and managing the courts' library.[94]

2.3.16 The Mining Act

The purpose of this Act is to provide the framework for the prospecting, mining, processing, refining, treatment, transportation and other dealings in minerals.[95] From the onset the act removes itself from ammeters relating to petroleum and hydrocarbon gases. The extractive industry is one of the major causes of climate change. This law is generally silent on climate justice and climate litigation. It has a provision that a mineral right is granted under the conditions of protecting the environment, community development and the health of persons in such activities. The law further provides that prospecting license can only be issued when an applicant has submitted an environmental rehabilitation and restoration plan.[96] An environmental and social impact assessment report and environmental management plan are required before the granting of a mining license.[97] Furthermore, the environmental protection bond provided under Section 181 is silent on climate change and injustices as well as provisions on the application of the Polluter Pays Principle.

2.3.17 The Office of the Attorney-General Act

The Office of the Attorney-General advices government ministries, departments, constitutional commissions and State Corporations on legislative and other matters.[98] It also advices the government on all matters relating to the Constitution, international law, human rights, consumer protection and legal aid.[99] This office also negotiates, drafts, vets and interprets local and international documents, agreements, and treaties. It also coordinates reporting obligations to international human rights treaty bodies to which Kenya is a member and obligated to report to.[100] It also represents the Government in matters before foreign courts and tribunals.[101] In essence, this office acts as an agent for the people of Kenya when seeking access to international justice. Locally, the Attorney-General has a right to an audience in matters of public interest and can be enjoined in such suits.[102]

---

[94] Ibid at Section 12.

[95] Cap 306, Laws of Kenya.

[96] Ibid at section 72(3) (c).

[97] Ibid at Section101 (2) (i) and 176.

[98] Cap 6 A of the Laws of Kenya. See the functions of the office under Section 5.

[99] Ibid.

[100] Ibid.

[101] Ibid.

[102] See Section 7 of Note 88.

2.4 The East African Court of Justice

The East African Court of Justice is treaty-created. It is one of the organs of the East African Community. The East African Community is a partner state-centre community whose members are Burundi, Tanzania, Kenya, Uganda, The Democratic Republic of Congo, Rwanda, South Sudan and Somalia. The Court is headquartered in Arusha, Tanzania. It is established under Article 9 of the East African Community Treaty of 1999.[103] The Court has a registry, registrars, and runs the East African Law Reports. The Court structure is jurisdictional based. It has the Fists Instance Division and the Appellate Division. A glance at the case database reveals that individuals, governments, government agencies, and organizations can institute proceedings in the Court.

The Treaty empowers the court to hear and determine cases before it on issues where:

a. A Partner State against another Partner State, an organ or institution of the Community which has failed to fulfill an obligation or has infringed a provision of the Treaty;
b. Legal or natural person seeking a determination on the legality of any Act, regulation, directive decision or action of a Partner State on the ground that it is or unlawful or infringes the Treaty;
c. Employees of the Community on disputes concerning the terms and conditions of their employment;
d. The Secretary General of the EAC may file a Reference, under the direction of the EAC Council of Ministers, against a Partner State that fails to fulfill Treaty;
e. Parties to commercial contracts may seek arbitration if their agreements have an arbitration clause giving the Court jurisdiction
f. The EAC Council of Ministers or a Partner State may request for an Advisory Opinion;
g. National Courts and Tribunals can seek an interpretation or application of the Treaty or on questions of the validity of the regulations, directives, decisions, or actions of the Community.[104]

Thus the Court's power cuts across many areas where climate and climate justice are concerned. According to the EACJ website, these are the powers of the courts and instances where the Court can render directions, judgments, rulings, and opinions. The Court has been approached to settle disputes concerning the environment and climate change. In Reference No. 39 of 2020, *Center for Food and Adequate Living Rights (CEFROHT) Limited & 3 others V. The Attorney General Republic of Uganda, The Attorney General of The United Republic of Tanzania and The Secretary General of The East African Community* filed under Articles 5(3)(c), 6(d) & 7 (2), 8 (1)(c), 71(1) (d), 101, 111(1)(b) & (d), 114(1) & (2) 105(2), 112, 114,

[103] See details on the East Africa Court of Justice.

[104] Ibid.

116, 120 (c) of the EAC Treaty, Articles 2, 3, 4, 6(a), (e), (c), 12 and 13 of the *Protocol for Sustainable Development of Lake Victoria Basin to the EAC Treaty (2003)*, Articles 24, 25, 31, and 40(3) of *the Protocol on Environment and Natural Resource* Management to the EAC Treaty; and Rule 25 of the *EACJ Rules of Procedure 2019.*

The subject matter concerns the environment.

I wish to quote the EACJ Registry which summarizes the Case as follows

> The Applicants allege that the act of signing of the Host Government Agreement by the 1st Respondent with the East African Crude Oil Company Limited and the Intergovernmental Agreement between the 1st and 2nd Respondent to build a pipeline that goes through protected areas which has adverse impacts on the livelihoods, biodiversity, climate change, and social-economic aspects is a violation of the provisions of the EAC Treaty and Protocols therein.[105]
>
> The Applicants also allege that the signing of the two agreements without a certificate of approval of the Environmental and Social Impact Assessment is a violation of the EAC Treaty and Protocols therein. Moreover, that the signing without notification, submission, and approval of the environmental and Social Impact Assessment by the 3rd Respondent and the Council of Ministers violates the provisions of the EAC law because the project has deleterious environmental and ecological effects.
>
> The Applicants state that the 3rd Respondent, the Secretary General of the East African. Community failed to discharge his legal obligation under the Treaty of the undertaking, whether On his initiative or otherwise of such investigations, collection of information, or verification of matter affecting the community that appears to merit examination. The Applicant therefore seeks a declaration by the Court that the actions of the Respondents infringe the Treaty, the Protocol for sustainable development of Lake Victoria Basin to the EAC Treaty, and The Protocol on Environmental and Natural Resource and Natural Resource Management to the EAC Treaty.
>
> The 1st Respondent, the Attorney General of the Republic of Uganda contends that prior to the signing of the Host Government Agreement on the project an environment and social impact assessment was conducted and approved by the National Environment Management Authority of Uganda. He also contends that the Protocol on Sustainable development on L. Victoria Basin does not require the submission of the environment and social assessment impact report to the 3rd Respondent and or approval of Council of Ministers before signing of the Agreements Between the 1st and the 2nd Respondents.
>
> The 1st Respondent further contends that the Reference raises no matters for interpretation of the EAC Treaty, is time barred and cannot be adjudicated on by this Honorable Court hence should be dismissed with costs.
>
> The 2nd Respondent, the Attorney General of United Republic of Tanzania states that the Applicants were aware of the EACOP project and on several occasions attempted to challenge the EACOP project in different forums.
>
> He further states that, prior to the signing of the agreement an environment and social impact assessment was carried out and approved by the relevant authority in which case the 2nd Respondent had the Certificate of ESIA issued by the National Environmental

---

[105] East African Court of Justice. *Centre for Food and Adequate Living Rights (Cefroht) & 3 Others v. The Attorney General of the Republic of Uganda, the Attorney General of United Republic of Tanzania and the Secretary General of the East African Community*. Available at: https://www.eacj.org/?cases=centre-for-food-and-adequate-living-rights-cefroht-3-others-v-the-attorney-general-of-the-republic-of-uganda-the-attorney-general-of-united-republic-of-tanzania-and-the-secretary-general-of-the

> Management Council (NEMC) and Human Rights Impact Assessment (HRIA) before implementation of the said project.
>
> The 2nd Respondent therefore prays that the entire Reference be dismissed with costs for want of merit as well as jurisdiction and that it is time barred. He also seeks a declaration that the EACOP project is in compliance with the EAC Treaty, Protocol on Environment and Natural Resources Management and the Protocol for Sustainable Development of Lake Victoria Basin. The 3rd Respondent, The Secretary General of the East African Community represented by Counsel to the Community states that the signing of the agreements related to the project of building a pipeline that allegedly goes through protected areas was entirely between two Governments in exercise of their sovereign rights and was a properly informed decision and therefore, there is no cause of action against the third Respondent. That he should be expunged from the proceedings as he has no case to answer. He therefore prays that the Reference against him be dismissed with costs.

The *CEFROHT Case* herein is used to highlight the challenges of accessing justice at the East African Court of Justice. The first paragraph of the quote shows disregard of international treaties and duty obligations by national governments. They reveal the fracture between the gains of capitalism and economic development on one hand and absolute use of government power to put up infrastructure on community lands that compounded with climate change, adversely affects lives and the environment. The second paragraph of the quote shows a dereliction of state's duty to ensure due diligence, community involvement, consultations and application of the law in aiding the wheels of justice.

The third paragraph highlights the importance of environmental impact assessment at all levels of environmental justice. Environmental impact assessment cannot be wished away, after all climate change is not a localized problem. The impacts of climate change are global and the outcomes of climate litigation brings international law to localities and villages far removed from internationalized litigation. The fourth paragraph indicates the importance of time and awareness for affected litigants to file claims within the stipulated time period. Filing cases out of time and using the wrong documents have been defence mechanisms and legal shields for individuals, companies and governments. It internationalizes the mantra of 'Ignorance of the law is not a defence'.

For climate litigation to be successful, all players in the legal process should be aware of time limits and the critical need to have documents and records ready. The issue of costs and finances and effects of poverty and their effect on climate justice can be gleaned from this case. The fifth paragraph can be deduced in various ways. It shows the availability of other juridical avenues to prosecute such cases. It also shows the applicability and effectiveness of alternative dispute resolution mechanisms in resolving and settling climate justice disputes. The seventh paragraph positions international law and international agreements as important pillars in enforcing international judgments. Cordial relations amongst neighbors have the double-sided ability of early resolution of disputes or the swift enforcement of international judgments and orders.

In addition, lawyers have a role play in climate litigation in regional courts. They are a voice of the law. Lawyers have been approaching the East African Court for litigation of public interest cases. Legal expertise allows regional courts to hear and determine filed by law societies and deal with issues in different litigation areas. In *Reference No 19 of 2019, Legal And Human Rights Centre & Tanganyika Law Society V. The Attorney General of The United Republic of Tanzania,*[106] the East African Court of Justice delivered a judgment on 27th March 2024 in which it dismissed a reference by the Applicants which sought to have the government of Tanzania held accountable for assenting to laws that the TLS felt were contrary to the East African Community Treaty on matters of trade and movement of people.

2.5 The African Court of Human and People's Rights and the African Commission

The African Court on Human and People's Rights also known as the African Court is established under Article. It is the judicial arm of the African Union based in Arusha, Tanzania.[107] Article 1 of the *Protocol to the African Charter on Human and Peoples' Rights on the Establishment of an African Court on Human and Peoples' Rights.*[108] This Protocol was adopted on 9 June 1998 in Ouagadougou, Burkina Faso, and entered into force on 25 January 2004 after it was ratified by 15 African States, as prescribed under article 34(3). The African Court complements the protective mandate of the African Commission on Human and Peoples' Rights (the African Commission—often referred to as the Banjul Commission), which is a quasi-judicial body charged with monitoring the implementation of the African Charter.[109] Article 4 of the Protocol empowers the Court to give advisory opinions on legal matters concerning the African Charter and others related to other human rights instruments.[110]

On access to justice, Article 5 of the African Charter provides that the following can file claims in the Court

- The Commission i.e. The African Commission
- State Party which has lodged a complaint to the Commission
- State Party against which a complaint has been lodged at the Commission
- State Party whose citizen whose citizen is a victim of human rights violation
- African Intergovernmental Organizations

---

[106] See the Decision on of the East African Court of Justice cited as Reference No 19 of 2019, *Legal and Human Rights Centre & Tanganyika Law Society V. The Attorney General of the United Republic of Tanzania.* Available at https://www.eacj.org/wp-content/uploads/2024/03/Reference-No.-19-of-2019.pdf

[107] See The African Court on Human and People's Rights (The African Court) in brief. Available at https://www.african-court.org/wpafc/basic-information/

[108] Ibid.

[109] See more on the African Court.

[110] See the Protocol to the African Charter on Human and Peoples' Rights on the Establishment of an African Court on Human and Peoples.

According to Sub article 3, the Court can allow Non-Governmental Organizations and relevant individuals to appear before the Commission. The proceedings of the Court are public. Parties before the Court are entitled to legal representation and free legal representation when the laws of natural justice require.[111]

2.5.1 The African Commission (Banjul Commission)

The African Commission on Human and People's Rights is headquartered in Banjul, the Gambia.[112] It is established under...Article 30 of the African Charter on Human and People's Rights.[113] It comprises eleven members elected through secret ballot and who serve for a 6-year term each. The African Commission performs tasks, which may be entrusted to it by the Assembly of Heads of State and Governments. Its main mandates are

a. the protection of human and people's rights
b. the promotion of human and people's rights
c. the interpretation of the African Charter on Human and Peoples' Rights.

Article 45 of the Charter provides an opportunity for access to justice for parties and researchers. It empowers the Commission to collect documents, undertake research and studies, organize seminars, disseminate information, interact with national and local institutions, and make recommendations to governments.[114] In addition, the Commission formulates principles and rules to solve legal problems concerning human rights, cooperation with African and international institutions, ensure the protection of human rights, and interpret the Charter. Articles 47 to 54 provide for the processes of receiving of complaints of human rights violations till the presentation of reports to the Assembly of Heads of States and Governments.

The Ogiek Case is a good example of understanding how the African Commission and the African Court work. In this case, the Centre for Minority Rights Development and the Minority Group International presented a complaint to the African Commission which in turn presented the case to the African Court for determination in 2012.[115]

---

[111] Ibid.

[112] See the functions and responsibilities of the African Commission on Human and People's Rights. Available at https://achpr.au.int/en/about

[113] See the African Charter on Human and People's Rights. Available at https://au.int/sites/default/files/treaties/36390-treaty-0011_-_african_charter_on_human_and_peoples_rights_e.pdf

[114] See the African Charter.

[115] Supra 2.

3 Legal Societies: The Role of Lawyers

3.1 Law Society of Kenya

The Law Society of Kenya is established by the Law Society of Kenya Act. It has the power to sue and be sued thus can represent victims and interested parties in human rights cases.

The functions and objects of the Society are set out under Section 4 of the Act to—

(a) Assist the Government and the courts in matters relating to legislation, the administration of justice and the practice of law in Kenya;

(b) Uphold the Constitution of Kenya and advance the rule of law and the administration of justice;

(c) Ensure that all persons who practise law in Kenya or provide legal services in Kenya meet the standards of learning, professional competence and professional conduct that are appropriate for the legal services they provide;

(d) Protect and assist the members of the public in Kenya in matters relating to or ancillary or incidental to the law;

(e) Set, maintain and continuously improve the standards of learning, professional competence and professional conduct for the provision of legal services in Kenya;

(f) Determine, maintain and enhance the standards of professional practice and ethical conduct, and learning for the legal profession in Kenya;

(g) Facilitate the acquisition of legal knowledge by members of the Society and ancillary service providers, including paralegals through promotion of high standards of legal education and training;

(h) Represent, protect and assist members of the legal profession in Kenya in matters relating to the conditions of practice and welfare;

(i) Formulate policies that promote the restructuring of the legal profession in Kenya to embrace the spirit, principles, values and objects the Constitution of Kenya;

(j) Facilitate the realization of a transformed legal profession that iscohesive, accountable, efficient and independent;

(k) Establish mechanisms necessary for the provision of equal pportunities for all legal practitioners in Kenya;

(l) Protect and promote the interests of consumers of legal services and the public interest generally, by providing a fair, effective, efficient and transparent procedure for the resolution of complaints against legal practitioners;

(m) Develop and facilitate adequate training programmes for legal practitioners; and

(n) Do all such other things as are incidental or to the foregoing functions.[116]

With this expansive mandate, the LSK has mechanisms to facilitate and be a legal representative in climate litigation especially in public interest matters.

[116] See the Law Society of Kenya Act. Available at https://lsk.or.ke/wp-content/uploads/2024/06/Law-Society-of-Kenya-Act-21of-2014.pdf

3.2 *East African Law Society*

The East African Law Society is the regional bar association for East Africa founded in 1995.[117] Its functions include:

a. Fast tracking the integration of East African communities through targeted support to cross-border commerce, the legal profession, civil societies, business communities and governments.
b. Developing the capacity of the legal profession to respond to emerging challenges to businesses, governance and trade, among other areas.
c. Promoting rule of law, good governance and human rights through strategic litigation at the East African Court of Justice and the African Court, and through capacity building initiatives to members and communities-based organizations.
d. Support EAC institutions of EALA, EACJ and the Secretariat, and the Apex bodies in developing tools aimed at realizing the EAC integration.

The EALS has official Observer Status, the East African Community, and the African Commission on Human and People's Rights, It conducts training in law and technology, international trade, business and human rights, artificial intelligence, cybercrime and forensic evidence, among other areas and collaborations with the International Bar Association and other global institutions.

4 Conclusion: Factors Limiting Access to Green, Brown, and Blue Justice

This research concludes by identifying factors limiting access to green, brown, and blue justice. They are highlighted as follows:

a. Costs.

Litigation is an expensive undertaking. It requires legal fees, filing fees and other logistical monies. Geography too, plays a role in increased costs. Filing fees, lawyer bills and general costs of commencing and sustaining a legal clam are beyond the reach of many citizens. If for any reason, a claimant s unable to attend court and their suit is dismissed, they are burdened with costs of the suit which can turn into incarceration for failure to pay the debts. Literal legal distance and travel costs for litigants, lawyers and witnesses add to expenses that are more often than not, unbudgeted in the developing world.

b. Citizenry and Government Disinterest.

The registries of the courts mentioned reveal few climate justice cases filed. This is paradoxical in a region hosting the African Court and fully functioning regional

[117] See the East African Law Society. at https://ealawsociety.org/objectives/

court. This disinterest could be because of perceived ineffectiveness of judicial decisions. The non-enforcement of the *Ogiek Case* is an example to government still-water disregard of judgments. It remains unenforced by the Kenyan authorities. Indeed the Ogiek people continue to suffer eviction from their ancestral homes.

c. Emerging Areas of Law.

Kiswahili language speakers have a saying '*Sheria ni msumeno, hukata mbele na nyuma'* which, when loosely and literally translated, means 'the law is like a power saw, it cuts both ways'. This paper concludes that the non-static nature of legal attention has lawyers, especially young lawyers, focusing elsewhere in line with modernity and current happenings. Novels legal areas aided by tech and pop culture are more likely to interest lawyers and increased funding, leaving out traditional and established legal spheres such as human rights law and environmental law.

References

Beck H (2020) Locating liability for climate change: a comparative analysis of recent trends in climate jurisprudence. Environ Law 50:885–917

Canaperi M (2023) Intralingual and intersemiotic translation for accessibility in educational and social environments-focus on legal language. Comp Legaling 56:147–170

Farber D (2017) How legal systems deal with issues of responsibility for past harmful behavior. In: Meyer LH, Sanklecha P (eds) Climate justice and historical emissions. Cambridge University Press, Cambridge, pp 80–106

Garth Bryant and Shaffer Gregory (2022) The globalization of legal education: a critical perspective. Oxford University Press, Oxford

Githumbi EN et al (2021) Late Pleistocene and Holocene Afromontane vegetation and headwater wetland dynamics within the Eastern Mau Forest, Kenya. Quat Sci 38:229–245

Guth J (2018) Social justice: education for sustainable development in law schools. In: Chris A, Paul MK (eds) Social justice and legal education. Cambridge Scholars Publishing, Newcastle upon Tyne, pp 301–315

Leiter Andrea and Petersman Marie (2022) Tech-based prototypes in climate governance: on scalability, replicability and representation. Law Critique 33:39–333

Losekann C et al (2020) The Rio doce mining disaster: legal framing in the Brazilian Justice System. Extr Ind Soc 7:199–208

Mbote-Kameri P, Kabira N (2023) Gender equality and climate change in plural legal contexts: a critical analysis of Kenya's law and policy. In: Albertyn C et al (eds) Feminist frontiers in climate justice. Edward Elgar Publishing, Camberley, pp 165–187

Mboya A (2018) Vulnerability and the climate change regime. Environ Law 36(1):79–103

Mikulewicz M et al (2023) Intersectionality and climate justice: a call for synergy in climate change scholarship. Environ Polit 32(7):1275–1286

Novak S (2020) The role of courts in remedying climate chaos: transcending judicial nihilism and taking survival seriously. Georget Environ Law Rev 32:778–743

Orgad L (2010) The preamble in constitutional interpretation. Int J Const Law 8(3):714–738

Perkins P (2023) Climate justice and participatory research: building climate-resilient commons. LCR Publishing Services, Calgary

Piszcz A, Sierocka H (2020) The role of culture in legal languages, legal interpretation and legal translation. Int J Semiot Law 33(3):533–542

Redgwell C (2007) Access to environmental justice. In: Franconi F (ed) Access to justice as a human right. Oxford University Press, Oxford, pp 153–176
Roser D, Seidel C (2017) Climate justice: an introduction. Routledge, London and New York
Shreya A (2023) The inequality of climate change and the difference it makes: feminist frontiers. In: Albertyn C et al (eds) Climate justice. Edward Elgar Publishing, Camberley, pp 40–67
Shuen R (2021) Addressing a constitutional right to a safe climate: using the court system to secure climate justice. Gender Race Just 24(2):377–410

Muriuki Sharon, M.A, Colonial and Post-Colonial Studies, Linnaeus University, Post-Graduate Diploma in Law, Kenya School of Law, LL.B Moi University, Country Ambassador, Human Rights Measurement Initiative, Advocate of the High Court of Kenya, Nairobi, Kenya.

Challenges in Climate Litigation in India: Analyzing the Legal Framework and Its Effects on Climate Action

Shuma Talukdar

1 Introduction

Since the mid of twentieth century, India started experiencing the impact of climate change with rise in average temperature and sea levels rise, decrease in monsoon rainfall (since 1950s), increase in extreme temperature and melting of glacier, droughts (since 1970s), and the intensity of severe cyclones.[1] In 1987 and 2002–2003 half of India's crop areas were affected by drought, resultantly fall in crop production.[2] Despite numerous early warnings, India continues to lack a comprehensive legislation to tackle climate change concerns.

However, India framed policies for tackling the impact of climate change. National Action Plan at the national level and State Action Plans at the state level were formulated to show India's commitment to address the issue of climate change. Despite these commitments, there are concerns about the pace and scale of India's efforts. The Climate Action Tracker has assessed India's existing policies and efforts and categorized them as "Insufficient" in relation to what would be considered a fair contribution.[3] This assessment suggests that India's climate initiatives and actions must undergo significant enhancements to align with the target of limiting global temperature rise to 1.5 °C.[4] Implementing these policies effectively in absence of legal

[1] The World Bank (2013).

[2] The World Bank (2013).

[3] Climate Action Tracker (2023).

[4] Ibid.

S. Talukdar (✉)
Mahindra University, Hyderabad, India

V. E. de Aquino et al. (eds.), *Climate Litigation in a Changing World*, Ius Gentium: Comparative Perspectives on Law and Justice 130,
https://doi.org/10.1007/978-3-032-05530-9_13

sanction has become a huge challenge because of multiple reasons, like lack of political will, institutional bottlenecks, and dependency on fossil fuel.

Tackling climate change is pertinent for protecting the larger population of the country (the poorer section). The most severe consequences of climate change are disproportionately felt by impoverished communities. India, as the world's most populous nation with a significant number of people living in poverty, has been grappling with the effects of climate change for many decades. Rapid lose of land due to rise in sea level is contributing to the poverty of the people and making them even more vulnerable, which is going to multiply with the passing generations.[5] By 2030 even India's GDP could be at risk due to climate change. The Reserve Bank of India estimated 4.5% GDP loss for India.[6] In light of the current circumstances, it is imperative to reconsider whether our existing policies are adequate in addressing the challenges posed by climate change. We may have reached a point where the enactment of climate change legislation is crucial, as the absence of such legislation stands as a major hindrance to climate-related legal actions within the country. In the case of Indian Council for Enviro-Legal Action (ICELA) v. MoEF (2014), the tribunal correctly emphasized that the matter of climate change in India is predominantly influenced by international policy, specifically the United Nations Framework Convention on Climate Change (UNFCCC). Consequently, the absence of local legislation renders the courts ill-equipped to handle climate change concerns.

2 Existing Legal Framework on Climate Change

The key goal of climate litigation is to reduce, response, and redress. Reduce GHG, response to climate treat, and redress damages caused by climate change.[7] India possesses an extensive array of legal measures and regulations aimed at safeguarding the environment, boasting a comprehensive set of over 200 laws dedicated to environmental protection. In addition, there exists the National Green Tribunal (NGT), a specialized court established to address cases related to environmental matters.[8] The regulations such as the Environmental Protection Act of 1986 and the Air Prevention and Control of Pollution Act of 1981 play a vital role in controlling pollutant emissions, thereby contributing to the reduction of greenhouse gas emissions.[9] Other than this, conservation efforts are bolstered by the Forest Conservation Act of 1980 and the Wildlife Protection Act of 2002, both of which are geared towards safeguarding forests and wildlife.[10] This not only aids in preserving biodiversity but also assists in carbon sequestration. Additionally, the Energy Conservation Act of 2001 provides a

---

[5] BBC (2007).

[6] Greenly (2023).

[7] Wentz et al. (2022).

[8] Patel (2022).

[9] Sherwani and Gupta (2020).

[10] Forest Conservation Act of 1980: To ensure the protection of forests and address related or supplementary matters and the Wildlife Protection Act of 2002: Enacted to safeguard the well-being

structured approach to enhance energy efficiency, thus curbing energy consumption and, ultimately, greenhouse gas emissions.[11]

National Building Code of 2016,[12] Compensatory Afforestation Fund of 2016,[13] Clean Energy Cess Rules of 2010,[14] Finance Bill of 2010,[15] the Disaster Management Act of 2005,[16] and Electricity Act of 2003[17] also add to the legislative measures of India to address the issues of climate change.[18] These legislative measures collectively constitute a framework that recognizes the significance of climate change and its potential impact on the environment and society. They aim to provide guidelines, regulations, and financial mechanisms to promote sustainable practices, reduce greenhouse gas emissions, and enhance India's resilience to climate-related challenges.

Lastly, India's commitment to international climate agreements, including the United Nations Framework Convention on Climate Change (UNFCCC), Kyoto Protocol, and Paris Agreement, reinforces its pledge to decrease greenhouse gas emissions on a global scale.

3 Critical Assessment of the Existing Legal Framework

The legal landscape in India pertaining to climate change has garnered criticism on several fronts. India lacks a comprehensive legislative framework dedicated specifically to climate change.[19] Instead, it relies on a multitude of laws that indirectly

of wildlife, avian species, and flora, along with any related issues or associated aspects, in order to uphold the ecological and environmental stability of the nation.

[11] Energy Conservation Act of 2001: This act enables the central government to reward energy-efficient consumers and obliges those who use more energy than recommended to buy energy-saving certificates to meet the guidelines. The law also mandates large energy users to meet consumption standards, new buildings to follow energy-efficient construction codes, and appliances to meet energy efficiency criteria and display consumption labels.

[12] National Building Code of 2016: This code sets out guidelines and standards for construction and urban development, with an emphasis on sustainable and eco-friendly practices. It aims to reduce the carbon footprint of buildings and infrastructure projects.

[13] Compensatory Afforestation Fund of 2016: This funds support compensatory afforestation. It's based on the idea of net present value, which includes services like flood control and carbon storage. The Act also forms the CAMPA and defines its structure and authority. In May 2020, the government pledged Rs 6000 crore to create jobs for indigenous tribes to boost afforestation and ecosystem protection.

[14] Clean Energy Cess Rules of 2010: These rules outlines India's Clean Energy Cess, which is a tax imposed on coal, lignite, and peat.

[15] Finance Bill of 2010: The Bill introduced the National Clean Energy Fund, aimed at supporting clean energy technology ventures and research.

[16] Disaster Management Act of 2005: This Act serves as the primary law for coordinating India's approach to both human-caused and natural disasters. It outlines clear guidelines for enhancing readiness, disaster preparedness, and risk reduction.

[17] Electricity Act of 2003: This act governs the generation, distribution, transmission, and trading of electricity in India.

[18] LSE (n.d.).

[19] Kumar and Naik (2019).

touch upon the subject, resulting in a fragmented approach. This fragmentation often leads to inconsistencies and gaps within the legal system, hampering the effective response to climate change-related challenges.[20]

There is also a notable dependence on judicial activism to bridge the gaps in climate change law.[21] While the Indian judiciary has demonstrated a willingness and capability to incorporate emerging principles of climate change into the legal framework, this approach introduce an element of uncertainty and unpredictability.[22] Furthermore, there are challenges related to the enforcement and implementation of even sound climate-related policies, often stemming from resource limitations, capacity issues, or a lack of political will.[23]

These collective critical views underscore the need for India to establish a more comprehensive, predictable, and effectively implemented legal framework that can proactively address the climate risks the nation faces, both at the national and state levels. Efforts should be made to develop structured processes for assessing and managing climate risks, ensuring that the legal response to climate change is not only robust but also responsive to the evolving challenges posed by this global issue.

4 Climate Change Litigations in Indian Courts

Climate litigation in India is still at a very nascent stage compared to other jurisdictions, with only a limited number of cases directly addressing climate change concerns. Most Indian cases so far have been framed within the broader contexts of environmental protection or constitutional rights (particularly the right to life under Article 21), rather than explicitly under the banner of "climate litigation." However, these early efforts lay important groundwork by recognizing the link between state obligations, environmental governance, and the impacts of climate change. In the following table, the main points of all climate-related cases in India, including their issues, legal basis, law(s) invoked, and outcomes or current status, are highlighted.

5 Challenges and Obstacles Facing Climate Litigation in India

A fundamental challenge in climate change litigation lies in the establishment of causation, specifically in connecting governmental or corporate inaction on climate change with its adverse effects on human rights.[24] The table of case laws mentioned above (Table 1) clearly illustrates that many challenges in climate litigation are not just

[20] Ibid.

[21] Chaturvedi (2021).

[22] Ibid.

[23] Ibid.

[24] Guruparan and Moynihan (2021).

Table 1 List of Climate Litigations in India

	Issue	Law/Article Invoked	Status/Grounds
Supreme Court of India (SCI)			
Hindustan Zinc Ltd. v. Rajasthan Electricity Regulatory Commission (2015)	Challenged the power of Rajasthan Electricity Regulatory Commission imposing captive power plants to procure 'green power' for strengthening renewable energy market.	The Electricity Act 2003; The National Electricity Policy 2005; The Tariff Policy 2006	The Supreme Court upheld captive power plants can be subjected to purchase renewable energy (green power).
Association for Protection of Democratic Rights v. The State of West Bengal and Others (2018)	Challenged the Calcutta HC's decision on granting permission of the cutting down 356 trees for the construction of a public project.	Constitution of India (Article 21, 48-A); Paris Agreement; National Action Plan on Climate Change 2008	Pending before the SCI.
Hanuman Laxman Aroskar v. Union of India (2018)	Whether the Indian government's approval of a new airport adequately considered environmental impacts	Paris Agreement; Constitution of India (Article 142)	SCI initially suspended the environmental approval but subsequently lifted the suspension. Along with other environmental commitments the project approval is also subjected to commitment to make it a "zero carbon airport operation."
Ranjitsinh et al. v. Union of India et al. (2024)	Balancing the interplay between safeguarding biodiversity by preservation of the Great Indian Bustard and mitigating the impacts of climate change.	Constitution of India (Article 21 & 14 Right to Life and Equality) WildLife Act, 1972	Admitting the nuanced interplay between safeguarding biodiversity and mitigating the impact of climate change, the court appointed an expert committee to balance facilitation of solar power generation and implement conservation efforts.
National Green Tribunal (NGT)			
Sukhdev Vihar Welfare Residents Association v. Union of India (2013)	Challenged the operation of waste-to-energy plant in a densely populated area leads to GHG emissions.	NGT Act 2010 [Section 14, 29, 30, 38(5)]	The tribunal permitted the operation relying on scientific evidence that showed emission is within the permissible limits.

(continued)

Table 1 (continued)

	Issue	Law/Article Invoked	Status/Grounds
Society for Protection of Environment & Biodiversity v. Union of India (2016)	Challenged the draft notification that exempted building and construction projects from the environmental clearance.	Environmental Impact Assessment Regulation 2006; Environmental Protection Act 1986 (Section 3, 5)	NGT quashed those parts of the notification that exempt construction sector from environmental clearance.
Rajiv Dutta v. Union of India (2016)	Petition filed against the uncontrolled forest fires damaging the States of Uttarakhand and Himachal Pradesh and stressed the need to develop forest fire management plans.	NGT 2010; Environmental Protection Act 1986 [Section 3(1), 5]	The NGT directed the central and respective state governments to formulate national policy and guidelines for forest fire prevention and control.
Indian Council for Enviro-Legal Action (ICELA) v. MoEF (2014)	Whether the government should formulate new climate policies to regulate HFC-23.	NGT 2010; Environmental Protection Act 1986 (Section 3); Constitution of India [Article 47, 48A, 51A(g)]	The petition is disposed of by stating tribunal have the jurisdiction, however, lack of specific domestic law to address the issue is accepted. The tribunal further mentioned this aspect is presently governed entirely by global policy (UNFCCC).
Mahendra Pandey v. Union of India (2016)	Petition filed to direct formulation and implementation of Delhi climate action plan by the Delhi State Government.	National Action Plan on Climate Change; Paris Agreement	The NGT directed the state government to prepare and submit the climate action plan to MoEFCC and directed MoEFCC to approve within 4 weeks.
Gaurav Bansal v. Union of India (2014)	Questioned if the State governments have formulated and implemented climate action plans at the state level.	National Action Plan on Climate Change; Paris Agreement	The NGT directed the state government to prepare the draft and submit it to MoEFCC for approval.

(continued)

Table 1 (continued)

	Issue	Law/Article Invoked	Status/Grounds
In re Court on its own motion v. State of Himachal Pradesh and others (2013)	Court relied on Art 48A of the Constitution (requires the state to protect and improve the environment), Art 51A (requiring a citizen to protect and improve the natural environment) and Art 21 (protecting the right to life as a fundamental right) of the Constitution of India.	NGT 2010; Constitution of India (Article 48A, 51A, and 21)	Court on its own motion issued restrictions to curb black carbon emissions, among other things.
Pandey v. India (2017)	India's commitment to the Paris Agreement was questioned along with adequacy of its climate change mitigation efforts vis-a-vis Public Trust Doctrine and other legal obligations.	Paris Agreement; Environment Protection Act 1986 (Section 6 and 25); Biodiversity Act 2002 (Section 36); Forest Conservation Act, 1980.	The NGT dismissed the case, reasoning, climate change is covered in the process of impact assessments under the Environment Protection Act of 1986, and therefore, "There is no reason to presume that Paris Agreement and other international protocols are not reflected in the policies of the Government of India or are not taken into consideration in granting environment clearances."

Source: Processed by author, 2024

theoretical concerns, they are being encountered on the ground. For example, in Pandey v. India (2017), the court's reluctance to fully engage with claims of inadequate climate action underlines the difficulty of establishing a direct causal link between government policies (or inaction) and the adverse impacts on human rights. This is a recurring theme: proving that specific administrative decisions directly cause environmental harm requires robust scientific evidence, a challenge compounded by the absence of a clearly defined legal mechanism to do so.

Similarly, cases such as Hanuman Laxman Aroskar v. Union of India (2018) and the self-initiated restrictions in In re Court on its own motion v. State of Himachal Pradesh (2013) highlight the judiciary's struggle with the justifiability of intervening in what is traditionally the domain of the executive. The question of justifiability concerns are pivotal in determining the court's role in these matters, casting doubts on whether the courts possess the authority to entertain claims regarding executive decisions related to climate change. Deciding when and to what extent the judiciary should step in to influence or overrule executive decisions related to climate policies is a complex matter. This issue delves into the scope and boundaries of the judiciary's jurisdiction in climate matters.[25] This involves weighing the separation of powers, ensuring that courts respect the executive's domain while also ensuring that constitutional rights and human rights are upheld. The concerns regarding judicial overreach surface, with the judiciary sometimes exceeding its bounds in addressing environmental issues and potentially undermining other branches of government, also adds to the obstacles.[26] These instances reveal the inherent tension between the need to protect constitutional rights and the risk of judicial overreach, raising important questions about the scope of judicial authority in climate-related matters.

The listed cases also show the practical effects of these challenges. In Ranjitsinh et al. v. Union of India et al. (2024), for instance, the court was forced to balance the dual imperatives of promoting renewable energy while safeguarding biodiversity, a reflection of the complex interplay between development and conservation goals. Similarly, in the case of Society for Protection of Environment & Biodiversity v. Union of India (2016), the NGT's decision to quash parts of a notification demonstrates the difficulties in striking a balance between easing regulatory burdens on the construction sector and upholding rigorous environmental standards.

Moreover, the concept of standing adds another layer of complexity.[27] The persistent issue of standing is underscored across several cases. Strict standing rules in India often prevent affected communities or environmental groups from bringing forward claims, thereby limiting access to justice even when the environmental and public health stakes are high. In India, the stringent application of standing rules by the courts poses a substantial obstacle for plaintiffs seeking recourse in climate change litigation. The legal principle of standing essentially determines who has the legal right to initiate a lawsuit, and the strictness of its application hamper access to justice in climate cases.[28] The issue of *locus standi*, or legal standing, is a hurdle in climate litigation. Some individuals or organizations may not meet the criteria required to initiate legal action, and this can hinder the pursuit of climate-related lawsuits.

The financial and temporal burdens associated with litigation, stands as another barrier, especially when pursued against powerful entities such as governments and corporations; create an inherent imbalance of resources and influence. This power asymmetry presents yet another formidable challenge in climate change litigation.[29] Preparing and presenting a case in court can be a costly endeavor. This can deter individuals and organizations from pursuing climate-related legal action, particularly in a jurisdiction like India, where resources for such endeavors are limited. Financial constraints and the burden of producing comprehensive scientific evidence further exacerbate these challenges, as seen in Sukhdev Vihar Welfare

[25] Ibid.

[26] Kodiveri (2020).

[27] Malik (2023).

[28] Ibid.

[29] Ibid.

Residents Association v. Union of India (2013) where the tribunal relied on scientific benchmarks to justify permitting the operation of a waste-to-energy plant. The intricate nature of scientific evidence complicates matters for the courts.[30] As scientific evidence is crucial in climate litigation as it forms the backbone of any case, the lack of comprehensive, up-to-date, and context-specific scientific data hinder the ability to build a strong legal argument. This includes data that supports claims of causation between specific activities or policies and their impact on the environment and human rights. The challenge of comprehending and adjudicating complex scientific data often hinders the expeditious resolution of climate-related disputes.

In addition to these judicial and evidentiary challenges, the broader socio-political context, ranging from competing ideologies in environmental conservation to the influence of corporate lobbying (as highlighted by recent instances involving major industrial players), adds another layer of complexity. The influence of corporate lobbying further obstructs climate litigation efforts.[31] It is a significant obstacle in many countries, including India, where powerful corporate interests influence government policies and regulations to favor their industries.[32] Business-Government relation in third-world is not a noble concept[33] nor is it globally. In India, Vedanta has recently lobbied to weaken the environmental regulations during the pandemic.[34] These kinds of lobbying create an uphill battle for climate activists and those seeking legal redress for climate-related injustices.

The Indian environmental movement grapples with competing ideologies, vacillating between the interests of marginalized communities and exclusive conservation practices, where the rights of local forest-dwelling communities may be violated.[35] In India, the Forest Rights Act of 2006 (FRA)[36] and the Indian Forest Act of 1927 (IFA)[37] establish two distinct approaches to the conservation of forests, running in parallel, and creating complexities.[38] These factors, combined with a general lack of public awareness and political will,[39] create an environment where even well-founded legal arguments can struggle to gain traction in the courts.

---

[30] Guruparan and Moynihan (2021).

[31] Sullivan et al. (2023).

[32] Ibid.

[33] Kochanek (1996).

[34] Deshmane (2023).

[35] Kodiveri (2022).

[36] The primary objectives of the Act are to rectify past injustices faced by forest-dwelling communities, guarantee land rights and sustenance for Scheduled Tribes and traditional forest inhabitants, and empower Forest Rights holders with the responsibility and authority to enhance forest conservation, promote sustainable resource usage, preserve biodiversity, and maintain ecological equilibrium.

[37] The law was put into effect with the aim of protecting and securing the woodlands. It was implemented in 1927, granting the British government the authority to designate any wooded area as a government forest and establish regulations for its management.

[38] Bhadauria (2019).

[39] Sharma (2023).

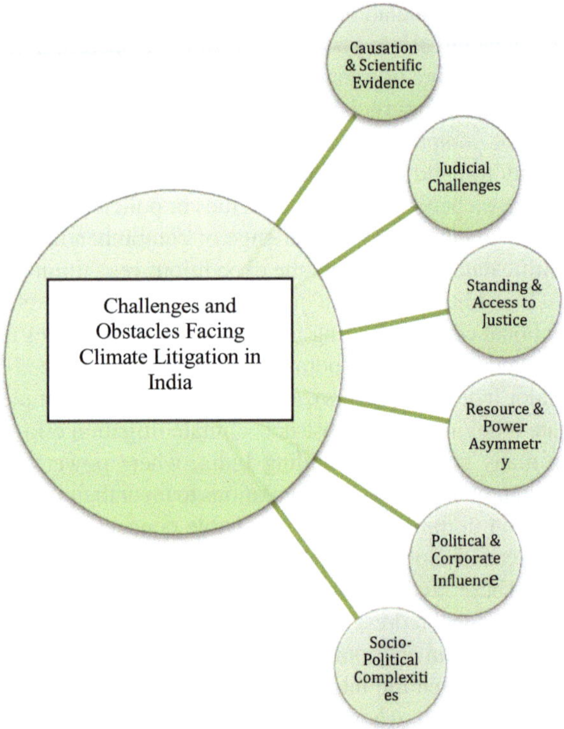

Fig. 1 Diagram Layout on Challenges and Obstacles Facing Climate Litigation in India. Source: processed by author, 2025

Largely, the mentioned case laws serve as concrete examples that encapsulate the multifaceted obstacles of climate litigation in India, from the struggle to prove causation and overcome strict standing rules to the challenges of balancing developmental needs with environmental conservation (see Fig. 1). They confirm that, despite judicial interventions aimed at catalyzing government action, systemic issues in the legal and political framework continue to impede robust climate litigation.

6 Final Remark

Although India has established an extensive array of both domestic and international legal mechanisms, including the Environmental Protection Act of 1986, the Air Prevention and Control of Pollution Act of 1981, the Forest Conservation Act of 1980, the Wildlife Protection Act of 2002, the Energy Conservation Act of 2001, along with other acts and has also been signatory to global agreements like the United Nations Framework Convention on Climate Change, the Kyoto Protocol, and the Paris Agreement, its performance in the realm of climate change litigation has not kept pace with the potential afforded by these legal frameworks. India's engagement in climate change-related legal actions and advocacy lags significantly behind what one might expect given the presence of these established laws and international commitments.

The absence of a comprehensive legal framework designed to effectively tackle the pressing problem of climate change is a significant shortcoming in our current legislative landscape. This deficiency has resulted in an overreliance on judicial activism to bridge the gap and address environmental concerns. Furthermore, even when environmental laws do exist, their enforcement and practical implementation remain inadequate, contributing to the inefficacy of these regulations. These combined issues underscore the pressing need for a more robust and holistic legislative approach to combat climate change and ensure its effective enforcement.

Climate litigation in India faces several significant challenges, primarily stemming from the absence of a robust legal framework that can definitively establish a causal connection between climate change and its impact on human rights. These hurdles encompass various facets, including justifiability, or the court's rationale for interfering in executive decision-making processes, as well as the concept of *locus standi*, which addresses who has the legal standing to bring such cases.

Moreover, the dearth of comprehensive scientific evidence, financial constraints, the status of the environmental movement, limited public awareness, political will, and corporate lobbying all contribute to the complexity of climate litigation in the India. The multifaceted challenges we face emphasize the complexities and obstacles that come with using legal actions to promote climate action in India. To surmount these challenges successfully, it is imperative that we establish comprehensive climate-related laws, enhance public awareness, and demonstrate a more robust political dedication to confronting climate change directly. Resolving these issues is absolutely crucial for the advancement of climate justice in India. Dealing the multifaceted challenges inherent in employing litigation as a tool for driving climate action in India requires the immediate enactment of comprehensive climate legislation, heightened public awareness, and a more resolute political commitment to addressing climate change.

Succinctly, climate litigation in India faces a multifaceted and complex set of challenges, encompassing legal, scientific, financial, social, political, and corporate dimensions. Addressing these obstacles requires a coordinated effort from various stakeholders, including the legal community, environmental activists, policymakers, and the public.

Further study could examine the long-term impact of climate litigation on shaping environmental policy and regulatory reforms in India through a mixed-methods study. The study could analyze landmark cases and subsequent policy responses. Such an approach would help illuminate how litigation outcomes influence legislative change and identify best practices to overcome challenges like evidentiary burdens, strict standing rules, and corporate lobbying.

References

Anderson K (2023) Why is climate change a huge challenge for India. Greenly. https://greenly.earth/en-gb/blog/ecology-news/why-is-climate-change-a-huge-challenge-for-india#:~:text=Extreme%20climate%20events%20such%20as,the%20impacts%20of%20climate%20change. Accessed 6 Oct 2023

Bhadauria V (2019) Forest Rights Act vs Indian Forest Act: conservation or conservatism. News Click. https://www.newsclick.in/forest-rights-act-indian-forest-act-conservation-conservatism. Accessed 13 Oct 2023

Chaturvedi E (2021) Climate change litigation: Indian perspective. Ger Law J 22(8):1459–1470. https://doi.org/10.1017/glj.2021.85

Climate Action Tracker (2023) India. Climate Action Tracker. https://climateactiontracker.org/countries/india/policies-action/. Accessed 11 Oct 2023

Deshmane A (2023) As the COVID-19 pandemic swept across India, major mining and oil company Vedanta quietly lobbied the government to dilute environmental safeguards regulating the oil and mining industries. OCCRP. https://www.occrp.org/en/investigations/inside-indian-energy-and-mining-giant-vedantas-campaign-to-weaken-key-environmental-regulations. Accessed 11 Oct 2023

Guruparan K, Moynihan H (2021) Climate change and human rights-based strategic litigation. Chatham House. https://www.chathamhouse.org/2021/11/climate-change-and-human-rights-based-strategic-litigation/challenges-facing-rights-based. Accessed 11 Oct 2023

Harrabin R (2007) How climate change hits India's poor. BBC. http://news.bbc.co.uk/2/hi/south_asia/6319921.stm. Accessed 6 Oct 2023

Kochanek SA (1996) Liberalisation and business lobbying in India. J Commonw Comp Polit 34(3):155–173

Kodiveri A (2020) The promises and challenges of climate change litigation in India. Open Global Rights. https://www.openglobalrights.org/promises-and-challenges-of-climate-change-litigation-in-india/. Accessed 11 Oct 2023

Kodiveri A (2022) Climate change litigation in India: its potential and challenges. In: Rodríguez-Garavito C (ed) Litigating the climate emergency: how human rights, courts, and legal mobilization can bolster climate action, Globalization and human rights. Cambridge University Press, Cambridge, pp 364–375. https://doi.org/10.1017/9781009106214.025

Kumar P, Naik A (2019) India's domestic climate policy is fragmented and lacks clarity. Engage. https://www.epw.in/engage/article/indias-domestic-climate-policy-fragmented-lacks-clarity. Accessed 11 Oct 2023

LSE (n.d.) Climate change laws of the world. Grantham Research Institute on Climate Change and the Environment. https://climate-laws.org/search?l=india&c=Legislation. Accessed 13 Oct 2023

Malik K (2023) Climate change litigation: an emerging frontier in ESG law. Enterslice. https://enterslice.com/learning/climate-change-litigation-an-emerging-frontier-in-esg-law/#Legal_Challenges_in_Climate_Change_Litigation_in_India. Accessed 11 Oct 2023

Patel A (2022) India's interest groups and the environment – how many are there and how do they operate? Kings College, London. https://www.kcl.ac.uk/indias-interest-groups-and-the-environment-how-many-are-there-and-how-do-they-operate. Accessed 11 Oct 2023

Sharma S (2023) India's climate change policy: challenges and recommendations. Indian School of Public Policy. https://www.ispp.org.in/indias-climate-change-policy-challenges-and-recommendations/29174/. Accessed 11 Oct 2023

Sherwani F, Gupta A (2020) India: climate change – Indian law and judiciary. Mondaq. https://www.mondaq.com/india/clean-air%2D%2Dpollution/945304/climate-change%2D%2D-indian-law-and-judiciary. Accessed 11 Oct 2023

Sullivan R, Black R, Kyriacou G (2023) What is climate change lobbying? Grantham Research Institute on Climate Change and the Environment. https://www.lse.ac.uk/granthaminstitute/explainers/what-is-climate-change-lobbying/. Accessed 11 Oct 2023

Wentz J, Merner D, Franta B, Lehmen A, Frumhoff PC (2022) Research priorities for climate litigation. Earth's Future 11(1):e2022EF002928. https://doi.org/10.1029/2022EF002928

World Bank (2013) India: climate change impacts. The World Bank. https://www.worldbank.org/en/news/feature/2013/06/19/india-climate-change-impacts#:~:text=In%201987%20and%202002%2D2003%2C%20droughts%20affected%20more,fall%20in%20crop%20production.%20What%20could%20happen. Accessed 6 Oct 2023

Shuma Talukdar is a Corporate Lawyer and Governance Professional. She is also a Ph.D. Research Scholar at Mahindra University, Hyderabad (India). Her educational qualifications include B.A., M.P.A., LL.B., LL.M (Business Law). She holds professional membership of the IUCN-WCEL (Biodiversity Law and Climate Change Law) specialist group and Ethics Task Force. Her scholarly publications include an co-edited volume *Judicial Responses to Climate Change in the Global South: A Jurisdictional & Thematic Review* (Switzerland: Springer, 2023) and papers in peer-reviewed journals and edited collections. She has also published in popular media and presented at international conferences in Asia, Europe, and North America.

Third Sector's Contributions

El-Hinnawi's Legacy and His Contribution to Climate Litigation

Thiago Giovani Romero and Mariana Cofferri Ferreira da Silva

1 Introduction

This chapter seeks to present not only the legacy of Essam El-Hinnawi, who introduced this very important new concept of environmental refugees in a historical context of environmental disasters and climate change but also highlight the importance of reviewing and updating concepts and legal systems, so that legal protection is increasingly ensured across all international, national, and alternative dispute resolution systems.

El-Hinnawi's pioneering work in the 1980s laid the groundwork for understanding the complex relationship between environmental degradation and human displacement. His definition of environmental refugees encompassed those who are forced to migrate due to severe ecological changes, including natural disasters and the gradual deterioration of their living conditions. This recognition was groundbreaking, as it expanded the traditional understanding of refugees to include those affected by environmental crises, thereby intertwining the issues of human rights, environmental justice, and migration policy.

In the realm of climate litigation, El-Hinnawi's concept of environmental refugees is increasingly recalled considering the need for legal protection and support for individuals displaced by extreme weather events and environmental degradation. The urgency of this issue is underscored by the growing frequency and intensity of climate-related disasters, which have led to significant population displacements globally. This reality prompts a critical examination of existing legal

T. G. Romero (✉)
IBMEC/SP and Universidade Federal de Uberlândia (UFU), São Paulo, Brazil

M. C. F. da Silva
IBMEC/SP and Universidade Federal de Uberlândia (UFU), Brasília, Brazil

V. E. de Aquino et al. (eds.), *Climate Litigation in a Changing World*, Ius Gentium: Comparative Perspectives on Law and Justice 130,
https://doi.org/10.1007/978-3-032-05530-9_14

frameworks and the need for innovative solutions that can adequately address the rights and needs of environmental refugees.

That is the reason why it is relevant to analyze how the growing awareness of the impacts of climate change has driven debates on shared responsibilities, adaptation, and mitigation, as well as the necessity for robust legal mechanisms to address emerging challenges. As nations grapple with the implications of climate change, there is a pressing need to foster international cooperation and develop comprehensive policies that recognize the plight of environmental refugees.

By connecting El-Hinnawi's legacy with climate litigation, this article seeks to identify integrated and collaborative approaches to recognize and protect the rights of environmental refugees, showing the challenges in addressing global climate issues. The discourse surrounding climate change and migration is evolving, and it is imperative that legal systems adapt to these changes to ensure that vulnerable populations receive the support and protection they deserve.

El-Hinnawi's concept of environmental refugees provides a crucial framework for understanding the link between environmental degradation and human displacement and as seen in this article his idea has gained increasing recognition in international law, influencing court decisions and legal doctrines. Notably, discussions at the United Nations and regional human rights courts have explored environmental degradation as grounds for refugee status.

Furthermore, it is important to remember that these decisions often combine principles from international environmental law, human rights law, and refugee law, creating a comprehensive legal approach to protecting environmental refugees' rights.

When we come to the practical field, these rulings set important precedents for holding states accountable for failing to protect citizens from environmental harm and displacement, as seen in the Öneryıldız v. Turkey (2004) and Kovačić v. Croatia (2008) cases.

In matter of fact, there is a strict conection between these author studies with the hard cases of today, mainly to provide the evolution of discourse on environmental refugees and climate litigation.

An inductive method is employed, starting from El-Hinnawi's pioneering idea and definition of environmental refuge, to explore how this concept might shape discourse and policies related to environmental refugees, emphasizing the urgency of collective actions and sustainable solutions to protect the most vulnerable in the face of climate change. Through this analysis, we aim to contribute to the ongoing dialogue on climate justice and the imperative for a comprehensive legal response to the challenges posed by environmental displacement.

2 Climate Change

2.1 What are Climate Change and Environmental Degradation

Nowadays, the existence of climate change is undeniable. In 2023, the United Nations, through the World Meteorological Organization (WMO), confirmed data[1] showing a rise in global temperatures. According to the Secretary-General of the WMO, "*climate change is the greatest challenge humanity faces. It is affecting everyone, especially the most vulnerable*." It is from this perspective that the article revisits El-Hinnawi's concept of environmental refugee and seeks to intertwine it with the current climate litigation movement, focusing on protecting the most vulnerable.

In this sense, to achieve the primary objective of this research, which is to understand El-Hinnawi's legacy and his contribution to climate litigation, some concepts are necessary. Initially, it is essential to understand what climate change and environmental degradation are.

Climate change refers to long-term alterations in temperature, precipitation, and other atmospheric conditions on Earth, such as burning fossil fuels, industrial processes and deforestation, which in consequence are far-reaching global warming, extreme weather events, sea level rises, and other environmental new consequences that are discovered every day.

Those processes reflect on the deterioration of natural systems, especially due to human activities. Pollution of forests and seas, soil degradation, loss of biodiversity are just "small" examples. Recently, humanity has discovered that the consequences are far more nocives, like the resurgence of diseases and the emergence of new viruses and bacteria[2] due to climate change. This brief context on climate change and environmental degradation is provided to establish a foundation for the elements that will compose this article and to ensure the importance of analyzing all factors intrinsic to the main debate.

2.2 Historical Context

The concept of environmental refugees, introduced by Essam El-Hinnawi in 1985, emerged in a historical context marked by growing concerns about the consequences of environmental and climate changes. This concept not only expanded the traditional definition of refugees but also highlighted the intersection between human rights, migration, and environmental degradation. To fully understand the relevance and evolution of this concept, it is essential to explore the historical context that

[1] United Nations (2023).

[2] Pan American Health Organization (2024).

surrounded it, as well as the events and trends that shaped global perceptions of forced displacement caused by environmental disasters.[3]

Historically, the term "refugee" referred to individuals who were forced to leave their countries of origin due to political persecution, wars, or armed conflicts. The formal definition of a refugee was established by the 1951 Refugee Convention, which focused on issues of persecution and security. Over time the understanding of what constitutes a refugee began to expand occurred particularly because of the environmental crises and their social consequences. The concept of a refugee now encompasses not only those fleeing violence and oppression but also individuals displaced by natural disasters and climate change.[4]

During the 1970s and 1980s, the world began to recognize the impacts of environmental changes, including pollution, ecosystem degradation, and climate change. These factors not only affected biodiversity but also had direct consequences on human life, including the displacement of entire communities. Events such as severe droughts, floods, and natural disasters began to be seen not only as environmental crises but also as humanitarian crises.[5]

In 1985, Essam El-Hinnawi, in his work titled "Environmental Refugees" presented a new paradigm by identifying and defining "environmental refugees." He argued that people who are forced to leave their homes due to environmental disasters or environmental degradation should be recognized and protected in the same way as traditional refugees.[6] This definition was a significant milestone, as it brought to light the need for a more inclusive and comprehensive approach to dealing with issues of forced displacement.

The recognition of environmental refugees began to gain momentum in the following decades, as the international community faced an increasing number of people displaced by natural disasters and climate change. International organizations, such as the United Nations (UN) and the United Nations High Commissioner for Refugees (UNHCR), started to explore the legal and political implications of environmental displacement, although formal legal protection for environmental refugees remained limited.

The Role of International Conferences on environment and development, such as the United Nations Conference on Environment and Development (Rio-92) and the United Nations Climate Change Conferences, also played a crucial role in the discussion about environmental refugees. These meetings helped raise awareness about the need to address the root causes of forced displacement and promote policies that consider the rights of individuals affected by environmental disasters.

Despite advances in awareness and policy formulation, environmental refugees face several challenges. The lack of clear legal recognition and the absence of specific protection mechanisms hinder adequate assistance and support for these

---

[3] Black (2001).

[4] El-Hinnawi (1985).

[5] Black (2001).

[6] El-Hinnawi (1985).

vulnerable populations.[7] Additionally, climate change continues to intensify environmental crises, increasing the number of displaced people and further complicating the situation.[8]

Considering this scenario, the need for collective action and sustainable solutions becomes increasingly urgent. Protecting the rights of environmental refugees requires an integrated approach involving governments, non-governmental organizations, civil society, and the international community. Promoting policies that recognize and address the causes of environmental displacement is essential to ensure that the voices of the most vulnerable are heard and their needs met.

3 The Concept of an Environmental Refugee by El-Hinawi

3.1 Concept and Legacy

Once more, to understand the legacy of El-Hinnawi and how his ideas are crucial to nowadays discussions about climate litigation, it is necessary to present his main concept, and the essential elements associated with it.

Within international refugee law, the author identified a normative and conceptual gap reflecting the increase in climate change and environmental disasters and their migratory consequences, in a way that surpasses and attempts to include some form of international protection for this differentiated category of vulnerability. The concept of a refugee centers around the realization of a fear of persecution, and according to the 1951 Convention Relating to the Status of Refugees,[9] a refugee is defined as someone who:

> [...] fearing persecution for reasons of race, religion, nationality, membership in a particular social group, or political opinions, is outside the country of their nationality and is unable or, due to such fear, unwilling to avail themselves of the protection of that country, or who, not having a nationality and being outside the country of their former habitual residence as a result of such events, is unable or, due to such fear, unwilling to return to it.

It is noted that the initial concept of a refugee does not mention any environmental elements as grounds for granting asylum and refugee status to a vulnerable person. It was from this perspective that Essam El-Hinnawi coined the concept of an environmental refugee in 1985, as seen:

> Environmental refugees are defined as those individuals who have been forced to leave their traditional habitat, temporarily or permanently, due to severe environmental disruption, whether from natural risks and/or human-caused factors such as industrial accidents or permanent displacement due to large economic development projects, or who have been

[7] El-Hinnawi (1985).

[8] Black (2001).

[9] The 1951 Refugee Convention. Available at: https://www.unhcr.org/about-unhcr/who-we-are/1951-refugee-convention; Accessed in August 2024.

forced to migrate due to improper handling and disposal of toxic waste, putting their existence at risk and/or severely affecting their quality of life.

Thus, by introducing this important definition into international law, El-Hinnawi included not only "natural" environmental disasters, such as tsunamis and earthquakes, but also anthropogenic disasters, where human action results in industrial catastrophes that harm the environment so aggressively that it becomes uninhabitable.

For these assertions, it is also important to present that the author classifies this concept into three categories. The first category includes refugees who are temporarily displaced due to environmental pressures such as earthquakes and cyclones. The temporary nature implies that there will be a return to the original habitat once the triggering event is resolved. One of the most emblematic examples that perfectly illustrates the author's concept of this is the Fukushima nuclear disaster in 2011 in Japan, which resulted in the temporary displacement of those who lived there.

In the second category of human displacement, we encounter situations of permanent displacement due to irreversible changes in habitat, such as dam collapses or the creation and expansion of lakes. The disasters involving the Fundão Dam in Mariana (2015) and the Córrego do Feijão Dam in Brumadinho (2019) in Brazil serve as paradigm examples of this type of displacement.[10] These events not only devastated local ecosystems but also rendered vast areas uninhabitable, forcing communities to relocate indefinitely.

The Mariana disaster released approximately 40 million cubic meters of toxic mining waste, contaminating the Doce River and destroying villages like Bento Rodrigues, where homes, farmland, and infrastructure were buried under toxic mud, preventing residents from returning. Similarly, the Brumadinho disaster unleashed 12 million cubic meters of tailings, obliterating settlements and resulting in the deaths of 270 people. Both events caused extensive environmental damage that permanently altered the landscape, leading to long-term soil and water contamination and significant biodiversity loss.[11] Unlike temporary displacements caused by other disasters, survivors of these dam failures face a permanent severance from their homes and livelihoods. The inability to restore the devastated habitats or mitigate their toxic legacies underscores the permanence of these displacements. These incidents also highlight the anthropogenic nature of such displacements, where human negligence and corporate misconduct played central roles in the disasters.[12]

From a legal perspective, these cases illustrate significant gaps in protecting those permanently displaced by environmental harm. Brazil's obligations under international agreements, such as the Convention on Biological Diversity (CBD), emphasize the necessity for stricter enforcement mechanisms to prevent such disasters. However, the aftermath of Mariana and Brumadinho reveals shortcomings in accountability and remediation efforts, leaving affected communities vulnerable

[10] Silva and Ferreira (2020), pp. 1–20.

[11] Costa and Almeida (2018), pp. 1–10.

[12] Costa and Almeida (2018), pp. 1–10.

without clear legal recognition as environmental migrants.[13] These events underscore the challenges within international environmental law regarding permanent displacement. They call for a re-evaluation of existing legal definitions and protections to include individuals displaced by irreversible human-induced environmental damage. This situation illustrates the profound consequences of neglecting environmental stewardship and community resilience, serving as a stark warning for future governance of natural resources and disaster prevention.

Finally, the third category presents those who are necessarily permanently displaced due to the search for better living conditions, as the original habitat was unable to meet the minimum living needs, with the progressive degradation of basic natural resources. Desertification and flooding are two examples of environmental factors that cause this type of displacement. A big example of this category can be illustrated by the situation in Kiribati,[14] an archipelago in the Pacific Ocean that is sinking due to the exponential rise in sea levels. Some of its islands are already submerged, and the population has been seeking refuge, which has been denied by New Zealand.

It is interesting to observe that the first two categories can reflect both internal and external displacements, depending on the severity of the natural disasters. And as discussed, even if these are entirely natural disasters, it cannot be denied that current human actions directly influence the maintenance, persistence, and increase of these degrading effects. Within the years and the increase of climate changes it is possible to affirm that the third category will be the most prospective scenario.

El-Hinnawi's legacy introduced various scholars who support these ideas. In Brazil, for example, the author Lopes[15] advocates for the inclusion of this new category within the original concept provided by Brazilian national legislation, arguing that it is necessary to understand the reasons and needs for this forced migration:

> It is necessary to understand that forced migration is characterized by the necessity imposed on individuals or certain groups to leave their place or country of origin due to causes beyond their control, which may be of economic, social, natural disaster, or other relevant factors that cause crises or situations where the social organization system cannot ensure the fulfillment of the essential survival needs of the population. Refugees, in turn, represent a specific category within the 'forced migrants' genre, that is, those who fall under the definition of Article 1 of Law No. 9474/97[16] (Brazilian legislation).

[13] Silva and Ferreira (2020), pp. 1–20.

[14] Due to the floods, a resident of that country applied for refuge on an environmental basis to the Supreme Court of New Zealand, which denied the grant of refugee status. The Court argued that, among other reasons, the cause of the floods in that region was human intervention in greenhouse gas production, rather than an unforeseen environmental catastrophe. Thus, New Zealand could reject the application.

[15] Lopes (2018), p. 143.

[16] Article 1: An individual shall be recognized as a refugee if they: I - Due to well-founded fears of persecution based on race, religion, nationality, social group, or political opinions, are outside their country of nationality and are unable or unwilling to seek the protection of that country; II - Not having a nationality and being outside the country where they previously had their habitual residence, are unable or unwilling to return to it due to the circumstances described in the previous

Another idea inherited from El-Hinnawi is presented by Meyers and Kent,[17] who indicate that the socio-political context combined with environmental factors are determinants for the forced migration of individuals from their original habitats, considering that climate change (and the resulting disasters) is the result of global warming, misuse of environmental resources, water scarcity, soil erosion, desertification and environmental overload. Thus, countries with more fragile economies and social contexts are more likely to suffer from these human-caused disasters.

Understanding the origins of this primordial concept, even though not codified, we will now analyze how environmental litigation uses these ideas to achieve its objectives and to produce decisions in accordance to the evolution of the law and climate changes.

4 Environmental Litigation

4.1 Concept of Environmental Litigation

The concept of environmental litigation has gained prominence in recent years due to the increasing awareness of climate change and its far-reaching impacts. This field of law deals with disputes related to environmental issues, often involving individuals, organizations, and governments. As is known, one of the foundational figures in this area is Essam El-Hinnawi, who introduced the concept of environmental refugees in the 1980s. His pioneering work highlighted the intersection of human rights, environmental protection, and migration, emphasizing the need to address the plight of those displaced by environmental disasters and climate change.

section; III - Due to serious and widespread violations of human rights, are compelled to leave their country of nationality to seek refuge in another country. Law 9.474/97. Available at: http://www.planalto.gov.br/ccivil_03/leis/l9474.htm

[17] Meyers, Norman; Kent, Jennifer. Environmental Exodus: An Emergent Crisis in the Global Arena Washington DC: Climate Institute: "Environmental refugees are people who can no longer lead a secure life in their homeland due to unusual environmental factors. These factors include drought, desertification, deforestation, soil erosion, and other forms of land degradation; resource deficits such as water scarcity, the decline of urban habitats due to massive overloads on city systems, emerging issues such as climate change, especially global warming, and natural disasters such as cyclones, storms, floods, and earthquakes, with impacts exacerbated by poor human management. There may be additional factors that exacerbate environmental problems and often result, in part, from environmental issues: population growth, widespread poverty, hunger, and pandemic disease. Other factors include inadequate development policies and government systems that marginalize people economically, politically, socially, and legally. Under certain circumstances, several factors may serve as immediate 'triggers' for migration, such as major industrial accidents and the construction of large dams. Among these multiple factors, several may act together, often with compounded impacts. Faced with environmental problems, affected people feel that they have no alternative but to seek sustenance elsewhere, either within their own countries or in other countries, on a semi-permanent or permanent basis."

Climate litigation has evolved significantly since El-Hinnawi's time,[18] driven by the increasing frequency and severity of climate-related events. Legal actions are now being used as tools to hold governments and corporations accountable for their contributions to climate change and to compel action to mitigate its effects.[19]

El-Hinnawi's concept of environmental refugees is particularly relevant in the context of climate litigation. As climate change exacerbates the frequency and intensity of environmental disasters, the number of individuals displaced by these events is expected to rise. This creates a pressing need for legal mechanisms to protect and support environmental refugees.

One of major challenges in protecting environmental refugees is the lack of a clear and universally accepted definition. El-Hinnawi's work provides a foundational framework, but further refinement is needed to address contemporary realities.[20] Currently, there is no specific international legal instrument that addresses the rights of environmental refugees. The 1951 Refugee Convention[21] does not cover those displaced by environmental factors, highlighting a significant gap in international law. Although the United Nations Environment Programme (UNEP) recognizes the term 'environmental refugees' (*at least in light of El-Hinnawi's thought*) both the International Organization for Migration (IOM) and the United Nations High Commissioner for Refugees (UNHCR) do not acknowledge it. This discrepancy complicates efforts to establish a coherent international response to the plight of those displaced by environmental changes, as these agencies prefer terms like "environmental migrants" or "climate-displaced persons" which do not carry the same legal implications as "refugees".

In other words, the concepts and ideias of this author started a movement of legal environmental thoughts that consequently permitted the development of climate litigation, as will be seen.

Some countries and regions are beginning to develop legal frameworks to address the needs of environmental refugees. For example, New Zealand has considered special visas for individuals displaced by climate change in the Pacific. Similarly, Australia has begun granting visas to individuals impacted by climate change, reflecting an emerging recognition of the necessity to accommodate those displaced by environmental factors. Climate litigation can play a crucial role in driving policy changes and expanding legal protections for environmental refugees. By challenging inadequate government responses and advocating for stronger protections, litigation can help ensure that the rights of environmental refugees are recognized and upheld. Addressing the challenges faced by environmental refugees requires a

[18] El-Hinnawi (1985).

[19] Faculty of Public Health (FPH) (2024).

[20] El-Hinnawi (1985).

[21] The 1951 Refugee Convention. Available at: https://www.unhcr.org/about-unhcr/who-we-are/1951-refugee-convention; Accessed in August 2024.

collaborative and integrated approach. Climate change is a global problem that necessitates shared responsibilities and collective action.[22]

Efforts to enhance the resilience of communities to climate change can help reduce the number of environmental refugees. This includes investing in infrastructure, developing early warning systems, and implementing sustainable land management practices. Reducing greenhouse gas emissions is crucial to slowing the pace of climate change and minimizing its impacts. International agreements like the Paris Agreement provide a framework for global cooperation on mitigation efforts. The Paris Agreement is also a significant milestone in advancing mitigation and adaptation plans. However, it is important to note that the mechanism for addressing loss and damage remains at a very nascent stage, leaving substantial gaps in providing adequate support for countries already experiencing severe climate impacts.

Strengthening international agreements to include provisions for environmental refugees is essential. This could involve amending existing treaties or developing new instruments specifically focused on environmental displacement. Countries need to develop and implement national legislation that recognizes and protects the rights of environmental refugees. This includes providing legal status, access to social services, and pathways to permanent residency or citizenship. Regional organizations can play a pivotal role in addressing environmental displacement. Initiatives like the Nansen Initiative in the Pacific and the Kampala Convention in Africa provide valuable models for regional cooperation on this issue. In addition to the Kampala Convention, which expands the concept of refuge, it is also worth mentioning the Cartagena Declaration (1984), which further contributes to the protection of individuals displaced due to environmental factors in Latin America.

The increasing impacts of climate change and the rising number of environmental refugees underscore the urgency of collective actions and sustainable solutions. Protecting the most vulnerable requires a multi-faceted approach that integrates legal, policy, and practical measures. Addressing environmental displacement requires collaboration across multiple disciplines, including law, environmental science, human rights, and migration studies. This holistic approach can help develop comprehensive strategies to protect environmental refugees. Involving affected communities in the decision-making process is crucial. Their insights and experiences can inform the development of effective and culturally appropriate solutions. Raising public awareness about the plight of environmental refugees and the broader impacts of climate change is essential for garnering support for necessary policy changes and actions.

Investing in green technologies can help mitigate the impacts of climate change and reduce the need for displacement. This includes renewable energy, sustainable agriculture, and eco-friendly infrastructure. The United Nations' Sustainable Development Goals (SDGs) provide a comprehensive framework for addressing the root causes of environmental displacement. Goals related to climate action,

[22] Grad and Rockett (1970), p. 742.

sustainable cities, and reduced inequalities are particularly relevant. Adequate funding and resources are critical for implementing effective adaptation and mitigation measures. This includes financial support for developing countries, which are often disproportionately affected by climate change.

4.2 *State, Courts, Accountability, and Due Diligence*

The increasing awareness of the impacts of climate change has driven crucial debates on shared responsibilities, adaptation, and mitigation. This awareness has also emphasized the need for robust legal mechanisms to address the emerging challenges posed by climate change. Through examining the connection between El-Hinnawi's legacy and climate litigation, it is possible to identify integrated and collaborative approaches to recognize and protect the rights of environmental refugees.

This examination also sheds light on the challenges of addressing global climate issues. By employing an inductive method, starting from El-Hinnawi's pioneering idea and definition of environmental refuge, we can identify the potential of this concept to shape discourse and policies related to environmental refugees. This process highlights the urgency of collective actions and sustainable solutions to protect the most vulnerable in the face of climate change.

Doctrine, jurisprudence, and precedents of international courts play a pivotal role in shaping the legal landscape surrounding environmental refugees. The concept of environmental refugees, as introduced by El-Hinnawi, provides a foundational framework for understanding the intersection of environmental degradation and human displacement.[23] This framework has been increasingly recognized and incorporated into international legal doctrines and court decisions. For instance, the recognition of environmental degradation as a legitimate cause for refugee status has been debated in various international forums, including the United Nations and regional human rights courts.

International courts have begun to address the issue of environmental displacement more directly. In particular, the International Court of Justice (ICJ) and regional human rights courts, such as the European Court of Human Rights (ECHR), have issued decisions that acknowledge the severe impacts of environmental degradation on human rights.

These decisions often draw on principles of international environmental law, human rights law, and refugee law, creating a comprehensive legal framework for addressing the rights of environmental refugees. The jurisprudence of these courts reflects an evolving understanding of state responsibility and accountability in the context of climate change and environmental displacement. For example, the ICJ's advisory opinions on the legal implications of environmental harm have

[23] United Nations (2007).

underscored the duty of states to prevent significant harm to the environment and protect the rights of individuals affected by environmental degradation. These opinions highlight the principle of due diligence, which requires states to take proactive measures to prevent environmental harm and mitigate its impacts on vulnerable populations.[24]

That is one of the biggest connection between an author's concept and a hard case litigation, that shows since the construction of and idea to the application.

Moreover, regional human rights courts have issued landmark rulings that emphasize the connection between environmental protection and human rights. The ECHR has recognized that severe environmental degradation can violate fundamental human rights, such as the right to life and the right to a healthy environment. For instance, in the case of *Öneryıldız v. Turkey* (2004), the Court ruled that the failure to prevent a dangerous landfill explosion violated the right to life. In *Kovačić and others v. Croatia* (2008), the ECHR also found a violation of the right to respect for private and family life due to environmental pollution. These rulings have set important precedents for holding states accountable for failing to protect their citizens from environmental harm and displacement. These rulings have set important precedents for holding states accountable for failing to protect their citizens from environmental harm and displacement.

State accountability and due diligence are central concepts in the discourse on environmental refugees and climate litigation. States have a legal and moral obligation to protect individuals from the adverse impacts of climate change and environmental degradation. This obligation is rooted in international human rights law, environmental law, and refugee law, which collectively provide a framework for addressing the rights and needs of environmental refugees.

The principle of state accountability requires that states be held responsible for their actions or inactions that contribute to environmental harm and displacement. This includes both direct actions, such as policies that exacerbate environmental degradation, and failures to take necessary measures to prevent or mitigate such harm. International courts and legal doctrines have increasingly recognized the need to hold states accountable for their contributions to climate change and their failure to protect vulnerable populations.[25]

Due diligence, as a complementary principle to state accountability, requires states to take proactive and preventive measures to address environmental risks and protect individuals from displacement. This principle is well-established in international environmental law, which mandates that states must take all necessary steps to prevent significant environmental harm, even in the absence of explicit international agreements.[26] Due diligence encompasses a range of actions, including the development and implementation of effective environmental policies, monitoring

---

[24] Net Impact (2023).

[25] World Health Organization (WHO) (2022).

[26] Venghaus et al. (2022).

and assessing environmental risks, and ensuring that affected populations have access to legal remedies and support.

The intersection of state accountability and due diligence is particularly relevant in the context of climate litigation. Legal actions aimed at addressing the impacts of climate change often focus on whether states have fulfilled their obligations to protect their citizens from environmental harm. These actions seek to compel states to adopt and enforce measures that mitigate the effects of climate change, such as reducing greenhouse gas emissions, investing in renewable energy, and enhancing the resilience of vulnerable communities.[27]

Climate litigation has emerged as a powerful tool for holding states accountable and ensuring that they fulfill their due diligence obligations. Notable cases, such as the Urgenda Foundation v. The State of the Netherlands have demonstrated the judiciary's role in enforcing climate policies and compelling states to take more aggressive action to combat climate change. In this case, the Dutch government was ordered to reduce greenhouse gas emissions significantly, based on the argument that the state's inaction violated its duty of care to protect its citizens from the harmful effects of climate change.[28]

Such judicial decisions have set important precedents for climate litigation and state accountability. They highlight the potential for courts to drive policy changes and ensure that states meet their obligations to protect the environment and human rights.[29] These decisions also underscore the importance of integrating principles of environmental protection, human rights, and refugee law to address the complex challenges posed by climate change and environmental displacement.

5 Conclusion

The historical context that led to the formulation of the concept of environmental refugees is complex and multifaceted, reflecting the interconnectedness between environmental changes, human rights, and migration. Essam El-Hinnawi's contribution was fundamental in opening the debate about the need to protect those forced to leave their homes due to environmental disasters. As the world faces increasing climate challenges, the urgency of recognizing and supporting environmental refugees becomes even more critical, requiring a collaborative and effective global response.

There would be a serious delay on the formulation of climate litigation if not from his concept. This text provides an overview of the historical context that shaped the discussion about environmental refugees, highlighting the importance of continuing to explore and develop policies that ensure the protection and rights of

[27] Venghaus et al. (2022).

[28] Venghaus et al. (2022).

[29] Venghaus et al. (2022).

these vulnerable populations. El-Hinnawi's pioneering work on environmental refugees laid the foundation for a critical area of study intersecting human rights, environmental protection, and migration.

In the context of climate litigation, his legacy underscores the urgent need for robust legal mechanisms to protect individuals displaced by environmental disasters and climate change. Currently, the most cited examples of environmental refugees do not involve countries considered "powerful" or developed. Consequently, there is limited concern to legislate in favor of vulnerable populations or to envision mechanisms beyond the existing legislative gaps. Nonetheless, climate change and environmental disasters are persistent phenomena that will increasingly affect more populations.

The rise in temperatures, rainfall, and sea levels is a fact. Perhaps only when these issues impact those with the power to legislate will meaningful results be seen—at least in a way that enables states to better shelter and support the displaced. If it is not possible to codify El-Hinnawi's remarkable concept, efforts should at least be made to seek other methods through climate litigation to build mechanisms that minimize the legal and social effects caused by environmental disasters.

As climate litigation continues to evolve, it has the potential to drive significant policy changes and expand legal protections for environmental refugees. Addressing the challenges posed by environmental displacement requires a collaborative and integrated approach, involving international cooperation, national legislation, and sustainable solutions. Recognizing and addressing the rights of environmental refugees can lead to meaningful steps towards a more just and sustainable future. The urgency of collective actions and sustainable solutions cannot be overstated, as the impacts of climate change continue to threaten the most vulnerable populations worldwide.

Through the legacy of El-Hinnawi and ongoing efforts in climate litigation, there is an opportunity to shape a more equitable and resilient world for all. In conclusion, the legacy of Essam El-Hinnawi and the concept of environmental refugees continue to shape the discourse and legal frameworks surrounding climate litigation. The evolving doctrines, jurisprudence, and precedents of international courts reflect an increasing recognition of the rights of environmental refugees and the obligations of states to protect them. State accountability and due diligence are central to this discourse, emphasizing the need for proactive and preventive measures to address environmental risks and protect vulnerable populations.

The connection between El-Hinnawi's pioneering work and the current debates on climate litigation demonstrates that integrated and collaborative approaches are essential for recognizing and protecting the rights of environmental refugees. The challenges posed by global climate change require collective actions and sustainable solutions to ensure that the most vulnerable are not left behind. By strengthening international legal frameworks, holding states accountable, and promoting due diligence, the international community can take meaningful steps towards a more just and sustainable future for all.

References

Black R (2001) Environmental refugees: myth or reality? University of Sussex
Costa AA, Almeida JS (2018) Impact of the Fundão Dam disaster on water quality in the Gualaxo do Norte and Carmo Rivers, Mariana, Minas Gerais. Floresta e Ambiente 25(3):1–10
El-Hinnawi E (1985) Environmental refugees. United Nations Environment Programme, Nairobi. https://digitallibrary.un.org/record/121267?ln=en&v=pdf. Accessed June 2024
Faculty of Public Health (FPH) (2024) From analysis to action: climate change litigation - guide for public health professionals. Faculty of Public Health. https://www.fph.org.uk/media/iqkft-mug/climate-litigation-report.pdf
Grad FP, Rockett LR (1970) Environmental litigation - where the action is. Nat Resour J 10:742
Lopes RSR (2018) Direito internacional público: À luz dos direitos humanos e da jurisprudência internacional, 2nd edn. Editora JusPodvm, Salvador, p 143
Net Impact (2023) Unlocking the three levels of climate knowledge: Moving from awareness to action. Net Impact
Pan American Health Organization (2024) The impact of climate change on emerging viral diseases. Pan American Health Organization. https://www.paho.org/en/health-emergencies/disasters-newsletter-n132-health-emergency-challenges-times-climate-crisis-1. Accessed August 2024
Silva AC, Ferreira F (2020) Desastre da Samarco/Vale/BHP: Um campo de estudo sobre desastre socioambiental. Rev Bras Hist 40(1):1–20
UN (2007) Business and climate change: Rising public awareness creates significant opportunity. UN
UN (2023) UN confirms that 2023 sets record for global temperature. https://brasil.un.org/pt-br/257750-onu-confirma-que-2023-bate-recorde-de-temperatura-global#:~:text=Seis%20conjuntos%20de%20dados%20internacionais,limite%20do%20Acordo%20de%20Paris. Accessed August 2024
Venghaus S, Henseleit M, Belka M (2022) The impact of climate change awareness on behavioral changes in Germany: Changing minds or changing behavior? Energy Sustain Soc 12(8)
WHO (2022) Raising awareness on climate change and health. WHO

Thiago Giovani Romero Postdoctoral in Law at the Federal University of Uberlândia (UFU). Ph.D. in Public and Comparative International Law from the Faculty of Law at the University of São Paulo. Master's degree in law from São Paulo State University "Júlio de Mesquita Filho." Professor of Public and Private International Law at IBMEC/SP, Fundação Educacional de Penápolis and Damásio Educacional.

Mariana Cofferri Ferreira da Silva Master's Candidate in Law at Centro de Ensino Unificado de Brasília (CEUB). Postgraduate in International Law (Specialist) at Faculdade Damásio de Jesus/SP. Bachelor of Laws at União Pioneira de Integração Social (UPIS). Bachelor of International Relations from the Institute of Higher Education of Brasília (IESB). Lawyer, specialist in International Law and Civil Appeals. Public servant at the Ministry of Justice and Public Security (MJSP), working in the Department of Asset Recovery and International Legal Cooperation.

Climate Emergency and Human Rights: Perspectives of the Consultative Process of the Inter-American Court

Javier Palummo Lantes

1 Introduction

Climate change has emerged as one of the most critical challenges of our era, not only because of its devastating effects on the environment, but also because of its profound implications for the enjoyment and protection of human rights. As extreme weather events become more frequent and intense, the impact on communities in the most vulnerable situations is increasingly evident, compromising human rights such as access to water, health, and adequate housing. This global crisis, exacerbated by human activity, has led the international community to recognize that the fight against climate change must be integrally integrated into the protection of human rights, particularly for those groups in the most vulnerable situations who face disproportionate risks.

This chapter addresses the relationship between climate change and human rights from the perspective of the Inter-American Human Rights System and aims to present and analyze the process of preparation and implications of the Advisory Opinion on Climate Emergency and Human Rights before the Inter-American Court of Human Rights (IACtHR). In addition, it explores the fundamental role played by the Special Rapporteurship on Economic, Social, Cultural, and Environmental

This text was fully translated by the organizers from Spanish to English.

The opinions expressed in this article are strictly personal and do not necessarily represent the positions of the institutions to which the author belongs. The author would like to thank María Paula Roncancio for her valuable support in preparing the first draft of this text.

J. P. Lantes (✉)
Inter-American Commission on Human Rights, Washington, DC, USA

V. E. de Aquino et al. (eds.), *Climate Litigation in a Changing World*, Ius Gentium: Comparative Perspectives on Law and Justice 130,
https://doi.org/10.1007/978-3-032-05530-9_15

Rights (SRESCER, in Spanish REDESCA) of the Inter-American Commission on Human Rights (IACHR) in this context.

Throughout the article, several key aspects are examined. First, climate change is introduced as a human rights issue, exploring the interdependence between the environment and human rights, as well as the specific impact of climate change on various rights and regional vulnerability. Then, a detailed analysis of REDESCA-IACHR Resolution 3/2021, its objectives, and its influence on the development of inter-American standards is presented. Next, the process of preparing the Advisory Opinion is described, highlighting the contributions of REDESCA in clarifying state obligations. Finally, the implications of the Advisory Opinion in strengthening a regional legal framework based on the protection of human rights in the context of the climate crisis are reflected upon.

2 Climate Change as a Human Rights Issue

Climate change is a central threat to the protection of human rights today. The intersection between environmental impacts and human rights underlines the urgent need to address this crisis from a perspective that transcends the traditional boundaries of environmental policy. Recognizing that the effects of climate change have profound implications for the enjoyment of rights such as life, health, and access to basic resources has led the international community to redefine its approaches and strategies.

In this context of redefinitions in the relationship between the environment and human rights, organizations linked to international environmentalism, social movements, representatives of indigenous peoples and local communities on the front line, as well as the human rights movement itself, have developed innovative strategies. These strategies involve the use of norms, mechanisms and institutions of international human rights law to address issues traditionally dealt by International Environmental Law.

One of the main ways for this integration is the "environmentalization" of human rights through their interpretation. This approach has consisted of interpreting human rights from an environmental perspective, incorporating relevant considerations within the scope of existing rights. By combining elements of international environmental law with international human rights law, the aim is to harmonize these branches of international law and strengthen the protection of human rights in the face of growing environmental threats. This environmentalization of human rights can be enriched by using principles of international environmental law to guide the interpretation and application of human rights. However, while the relevance of these principles is recognized, a clear and systematic approach to their implementation is still required. In this way, the strategies developed by local and global actors not only open new perspectives in the protection of human rights and the environment, but also promote a normative convergence that is essential to face contemporary environmental challenges.[1]

It should be remembered that international environmental law is a relatively young legal field, encompassing a multitude of political and legal issues that have not developed in a uniform manner. At the global level, its content can be described as diluted due to the high degree of commitment required to negotiate multilateral environmental agreements, such as the Paris Agreement. In addition, several of its principles can only be based on soft law norms, contained in declarations following international conferences, recommendations of treaty bodies, and other initiatives whose common denominator is their non-binding nature. All of these actions have the potential to create customary norms, a task that is often left to international courts.[2]

In general terms, international environmental law has established a constellation of instruments with few links between them, on the protection of specific environmental issues, such as climate change, biodiversity conservation, protection of the marine environment, oceans or certain species, among other purposes. In many cases, the structure is based more on the establishment of voluntary goals and commitments than on specific obligations for States. In this context, addressing environmental issues from the perspective of human rights represents something positive in terms of achieving greater protection.

Thus, the preamble of the Paris Agreement highlights that "climate change is a problem for all of humanity and that, when adopting measures to address it, States Parties should respect, promote and take into account their respective obligations relating to human rights, the right to health, the rights of indigenous peoples, local communities, migrants, children, persons with disabilities and persons in situations of greater vulnerability and the right to development, as well as gender equality, women's empowerment and intergenerational equity."[3]

The challenge lies not only in mitigating the effects of climate change, but in doing so in a way that protects and respects human rights, especially those in vulnerable situations. In this section, we will explore how climate change affects these rights, the growing regional vulnerability, and the responsibilities that States have in this context. The response to this phenomenon requires a comprehensive approach that combines environmental protection with the safeguarding of human rights.

[1] Donald (2023), p. 50.

[2] Bendel (2023), p. 18.

[3] United Nations, Preamble of the Paris Agreement (2015).

2.1 Impact of Climate Change and Regional Vulnerability

Climate stability and the integrity of the biosphere are essential for the health of ecosystems, and their destabilization seriously jeopardizes the full exercise of human rights. The interrelationship between climate change and human rights has gained international recognition, establishing that the increase in greenhouse gas (GHG) emissions amplifies the risks for societies, people and natural systems.

Climate change, according to the United Nations Framework Convention on Climate Change (UNFCCC), is defined as a change in climate attributable directly or indirectly to human activity, which alters the composition of the global atmosphere, in addition to natural climate variability.[4] Its adverse effects include significant alterations in the physical environment or biota, which have harmful effects on the composition, resilience, productivity of ecosystems, as well as on human health and well-being.[5]

In this context, climate change represents a significant threat to human well-being and the health of the planet. The risks, projected impacts and associated losses intensify with each increase in global warming. In addition, non-climatic factors are increasingly interacting, generating compounding and cascading risks that are difficult to manage.[6] Since the adoption of the UNFCCC, it has been recognized that human activities have increased concentrations of greenhouse gases (GHGs) in the atmosphere, intensifying the natural greenhouse effect and causing additional warming of the Earth.[7]

The Intergovernmental Panel on Climate Change (IPCC) has confirmed that human activities, mainly through GHG emissions, are responsible for global warming.[8] Between 2011 and 2020, the global surface temperature was 1.1 °C higher than in the period 1850–1900.[9] REDESCA has noted a direct relationship between the increase in GHG emissions and the frequency and intensity of extreme weather events.[10] The IPCC has also highlighted that the degradation of ecosystems increases the vulnerability of people, especially for indigenous peoples and communities that directly depend on ecosystems.[11]

Additionally, the Inter-American Court has stressed that the effects of climate change can cause floods, desertification, storms, erosion and landslides, affecting water supply, agriculture and fisheries, as well as destroying land and homes.[12]

---

[4] United Nations (1992), article 1.1; REDESCA (2023a), p. 8.

[5] Ibid.

[6] REDESCA (2023a), p. 8; IPCC (2023), p. 1–34.

[7] United Nations (1992), article 1.2; REDESCA (2023a), p. 8.

[8] IPCC (2023), pp. 1–34.

[9] Ibid.

[10] REDESCA (2023a), p. 9.

[11] IPCC (2022), p. 12.

[12] IACtHR (2017), footnote 126.

These impacts alter the natural cycles of ecosystems, generating droughts, floods, heat waves and fires.[13]

The OAS has recognized the causality of climate change as accelerating its effects, making it difficult to adapt and create adequate living conditions. The geographic location of Latin America and the Caribbean, influenced by the Pacific and Atlantic oceans, as well as phenomena such as El Niño, significantly affect rainfall and temperature patterns in the region.[14]

Sea level has risen in the region at a rate higher than the global average in some areas, threatening coastal populations with aquifer contamination, coastal erosion and flooding.[15] In 2022, the average temperature in Latin America and the Caribbean was one of the highest on record, with thermal anomalies reaching up to +3 °C in some areas.[16]

The IPCC Sixth Assessment Report indicates a likely increase in the intensity and frequency of extreme heat events and a decrease in extreme cold events in Central and South America, as well as an increase in intense rainfall in southeastern South America.[17] REDESCA has also observed how extreme events such as hurricanes, storms, floods, fires and droughts have been exacerbated by the climate emergency and environmental degradation.[18]

In 2022, 78 extreme weather events were recorded in Latin America and the Caribbean, with storms and floods being the main causes of casualties and economic damage.[19] SRESCER has observed that climate impacts are particularly severe for populations that are in a situation of greater vulnerability, such as women, children, indigenous peoples and people living in poverty.[20]

Climate change also causes forced displacement. It is estimated that up to 216 million people could be internally displaced due to climate change by 2050,[21] affecting their rights to food, water, housing and health.[22] In 2021, around 1.7 million people were internally displaced in the Americas, mainly due to climate disasters.[23]

---

[13] IACHR-REDESCA (2021), p. 5.

[14] General Secretariat of the OAS (2022), p. 8.

[15] World Meteorological Organization (2023a), p. 23.

[16] Ibid., p. 7.

[17] World Meteorological Organization (2023b).

[18] REDESCA and IACHR (2024a), REDESCA and IACHR (2024b), REDESCA (2024), REDESCA (2023c), paragraph. 8; REDESCA (2023a), p. 11.

[19] World Meteorological Organization (2023c), p. 21.

[20] REDESCA (2023c), para. 63.

[21] REDESCA (2023b), para. 264; See World Bank, Groundswell Report, 13 Sep. 2021; UN General Assembly, Report of the Special Rapporteur on the promotion and protection of human rights in the context of climate change: Promotion and protection of human rights in the context of climate change mitigation, loss and damage, and participation A/77/226, 26 July 2022.

[22] Special Rapporteur on the promotion and protection of human rights in the context of climate change (2023), párr. 16.

[23] Internal Displacement Monitoring Centre (2021).

Finally, the 2021 Global Report on Internal Displacement highlights that climate disasters are the main cause of displacement in the Americas.[24] In response, the international community has underlined the urgent need to act to mitigate the adverse effects of climate change and protect human rights.[25] There is currently a rapidly closing window of opportunity to take action to enable a sustainable future for humanity.[26]

2.2 *Groups That Are in a Situation of Greater Vulnerability*

Extreme climate events disproportionately impact groups that are most vulnerable, such as people living in poverty, indigenous peoples, women, children, and people with disabilities. These groups, due to their limited access to resources and capacities to adapt to climate change, face aggravated vulnerability, which puts their access to economic, social, cultural and environmental rights at risk.

The IACHR and REDESCA have identified that the risk of harm is particularly high for segments of the population that already face situations of marginalization or vulnerability, or that, due to pre-existing discrimination and inequalities, have limited access to decision-making and resources.[27] These groups include women, children and adolescents, indigenous peoples, people with disabilities, inhabitants of informal settlements, migrants, peasants, and residents of rural areas. REDESCA has highlighted that, although these groups have contributed marginally to greenhouse gas emissions, they are the most affected by the climate crisis[28]. An example of this situation was evident during the fires of August 2019 that affected the Brazilian and Bolivian Amazon, as well as the Chaco region in Paraguay. In these cases, it was observed that indigenous peoples were the most harmed by these fires, in part due to the lack of control over forest management[29].

Climate change exacerbates existing inequalities, marginalization and exclusion, further increasing vulnerabilities. The intersection of factors such as gender, race, class, ethnicity, indigenous identity, age, disability, income, and geographic location—among others—intensifies vulnerability to the effects of climate change, exacerbating inequality. Furthermore, people belonging to these groups are also those who, due to various factors, may be forced to move for climate reasons, which further increases their situation of vulnerability due to involuntary human mobility caused or exacerbated by the climate emergency[30].

---

[24] Ibid.

[25] Human Rights Council (2017), preamble.

[26] IPCC (2023), p. 1–34. Retrived from: REDESCA (2023a), p. 12.

[27] IACHR-REDESCA (2021), p. 6.

[28] Ibid.

[29] Ibid.

[30] REDESCA (2023b), para. 314.

The IACHR has also highlighted the need for differentiated approaches in decision-making processes on public policies on climate matters. These approaches must prioritize equity, climate justice, social justice, inclusion and just transition processes that allow for adaptation and ambitious mitigation actions. In addition, it is essential to strengthen adaptation measures with greater support to regions and people in situations of greater vulnerability to the effects of climate change[31]. The loss of ecosystems and their services has long-term impacts, especially on indigenous peoples and local communities who directly depend on them to meet their basic needs[32].

In this regard, the IACHR has stressed that States have a reinforced obligation to guarantee and protect the rights of persons or groups in vulnerable situations or who are particularly vulnerable to the damage and adverse impacts of climate change[33]. To this end, States must immediately adopt measures that incorporate gender equality and intersectionality perspectives, as well as differentiated approaches that make visible the aggravated risks to the human rights of these groups[34].

2.3 *Impact of Climate Change on Specific Rights*

Climate change has a profound impact on a wide range of human rights. Among the rights most compromised are the right to water, health, food, housing and the right to a healthy environment[35]. Extreme weather events such as droughts, floods and heat waves have devastating effects, particularly on the most vulnerable populations, who face greater difficulties in adapting and protecting themselves. These impacts underscore the urgency of integrating environmental protection into human rights guarantees.

The Inter-American Court of Human Rights has noted that, in addition to the right to a healthy environment, environmental damage can affect all human rights, since the full enjoyment of these rights depends on a favorable environment[36]. However, some human rights are especially vulnerable to certain types of environmental damage.[37]

---

[31] Ibid., para. 313; REDESCA (2021), p. 15.

[32] Ibid; IPCC (2023), p. 15.

[33] Ibid., Para. 312; REDESCA (2021), p. 17.

[34] Ibid.

[35] IACtHR (2017), para. 54.

[36] REDESCA (2023b), para. 358.

[37] *Cfr.* Human Rights Council, Preliminary Report of the Independent Expert on the issue of human rights obligations relating to the enjoyment of a safe, clean, healthy and sustainable environment, John H. Knox, 24 December 2012, UN Doc. A/HRC/22/43, para. 19, and Human Rights Council, Compilation Report of the Independent Expert on the issue of human rights obligations relating to the enjoyment of a safe, clean, healthy and sustainable environment, John H. Knox, 30 December 2013, UN Doc. A/HRC/25/53, para. 17. Cited in REDESCA (2023b), para. 358.

Rights closely linked to the environment have been classified into two categories:

- **Substantive rights:** These are rights whose enjoyment is particularly susceptible to environmental degradation and the effects of climate change. Key examples include the right to life, personal integrity and health. Environmental degradation can endanger people's lives and health, as well as compromise their well-being and quality of life.[38]
- **Procedural rights:** These are rights whose exercise contributes to better formulation of environmental policies and the fight against climate change. These include the rights to freedom of expression and association, the right to information, the right to participate in decision-making, and access to justice. The exercise of these rights is essential to ensure the protection of the environment and for communities to be able to actively participate in decision-making that affects their lives and their environment[39]. In relation to these latter rights and the protection of defenders, at the regional level there is a specific regional instrument of the United Nations, such as the Escazú Agreement.

In this sense, climate change not only threatens specific rights such as water, health and housing, but also affects people's ability to exercise other human rights that are crucial for the formulation of adequate environmental policies. The protection of these rights is vital to effectively address the climate crisis and ensure a safe environment.

3 Right to a Healthy Environment

As previously stated, climate change is a phenomenon that impacts and is closely related to a number of human rights. Consequently, the right to a healthy environment has emerged as an autonomous human right, protected under the framework of the American Convention on Human Rights, and it is also explicitly recognized in the Protocol of San Salvador.

This right, which transcends the mere protection of the natural environment, is deeply interrelated with other human rights, highlighting its indivisible and interdependent nature. Through the analysis of the jurisprudence of the Inter-American Court of Human Rights and the pronouncements of the Inter-American Commission

[38] Cfr. Human Rights Council, Preliminary Report of the Independent Expert on the question of human rights obligations relating to the enjoyment of a safe, clean, healthy and sustainable environment, John H. Knox, 24 December 2012, UN Doc. A/HRC/22/43, para. 17. With regard to substantive rights, the Inter-American Court has referred to the right to life, in particular with respect to the definition of a dignified life, as well as to personal integrity, the right to property, and the right to health. See, inter alia, Case of the Yakye Axa Indigenous Community v. Paraguay. Merits, Reparations and Costs. Judgment of 17 June 2005, para. 163. Cited in: REDESCA (2023b), para. 358.

[39] Ibid.

on Human Rights, it is established that States have clear and specific obligations in relation to the protection of this right. This section examines the progressive development of this right, its recognition as an autonomous right, and the responsibilities that States must assume for its effective protection, especially for groups in situations of vulnerability to the impacts of climate change and environmental degradation.

Article 26 of the American Convention imposes on the States Parties the obligation to seek the progressive development of the economic, social, cultural and environmental rights (ESCER) contained in the Charter of the Organization of American States (OAS), in accordance with the general obligations established in Articles 1.1 and 2 of the same Convention. The IACHR has emphasized that, in the analysis of a specific case under Article 26, it is first necessary to determine whether the right in question is derived from the economic, social, educational, scientific and cultural norms of the OAS Charter. This process involves resorting to other auxiliary texts, such as the American Declaration of the Rights and Duties of Man, to identify the rights recognized by this treaty.[40]

Once it is established that a right is derived from the OAS Charter, it must be assessed whether the State has failed to comply with its obligation to progressively advance towards the full effectiveness of said right, or whether it has failed in its obligation to respect and guarantee it. According to the IACHR, Article 26 not only imposes the prohibition of regressiveness, but also establishes immediate and enforceable obligations, such as respect, guarantee, non-discrimination, adoption of measures to ensure the enjoyment of rights, and the provision of effective remedies for their protection[41]. In addition, States have the obligation to satisfy certain essential levels of these rights immediately, without being subject to progressive development[42].

Regarding the right to a healthy environment, both the IACHR and the Inter-American Court of Human Rights have recognized it as an autonomous right protected by Article 26 of the American Convention. In its Advisory Opinion 23, the Court stressed that the right to a healthy environment not only protects the components of the environment, such as forests, rivers, and seas, but does so for their intrinsic value, independently of their usefulness for human beings. This approach highlights the importance of protecting nature for its own value and its relevance for other living organisms, which also deserve protection[43].

Various international instruments recognize the right to a healthy environment, such as the Paris Agreement (2015) and the Rio Declaration on Environment and Development (1992). The former has recognized the relationship between human

[40] IACHR (2018), para. 129.

[41] IACHR (2018), para. 134.

[42] United Nations Committee on Economic, Social and Cultural Rights (2017), para. 236 y 237.

[43] IACtHR (2017), para. 57.; See also IACtHR. Case of Kichwa Indigenous People of Sarayaku v. Ecuador. Fund and Repairs. Judgment of June 27, 2012. Series C No. 245. Cited in: REDESCA (2023c), para. 83–84.

rights and environmental protection,[44] and the latter underlines that environmental protection is integral to the development process and that States must apply the precautionary principle in situations of serious or irreversible environmental damage.[45]

The Rio Declaration is key, as it significantly expanded the scope of environmental law, consolidating its influence on the international agenda. This process not only allowed for greater attention to the introduction of effective instruments or combinations of instruments to address environmental challenges, but also integrated environmental policies and considerations with other key areas of law, such as human rights law, economic law, energy law and public procurement law. This intersectoral approach recognises that environmental protection cannot be addressed in isolation, but is intrinsically linked to sustainable development and the guarantee of human rights.[46]

The right to a healthy environment has both individual and collective dimensions. In its collective dimension, it is understood as a universal interest that benefits both present and future generations. In its individual dimension, its violation can directly affect people, as it is connected to other rights such as health, personal integrity and life. Therefore, a healthy environment is fundamental for human existence.

3.1 Interdependence and Indivisibility of the Right to the Environment with Other Human Rights

The IACHR reiterates the interdependence and indivisibility of civil and political rights with economic, social, cultural and environmental rights. These rights must be understood in an integral manner and without hierarchies among them, and must be enforceable before the competent authorities. The Inter-American Court has identified that several rights, such as life, personal integrity, health, water, food and housing, are particularly vulnerable to environmental damage. In addition, environmental degradation can lead to forced displacement, which often results in violent conflicts.

The United Nations Special Rapporteur on Human Rights and the Environment has established 16 framework principles that reinforce the interdependence between human rights and environmental protection. These principles emphasize that a safe, clean, healthy and sustainable environment is necessary for the full enjoyment of human rights such as life, health and access to safe drinking water. They also

[44] United Nations (2015), preamble.

[45] Rio Declaration on Environment and Development (1992), principle 4.

[46] Kars y Weishaar (2023), p. 4

underline that the exercise of rights such as freedom of expression, participation and access to effective remedies is essential for environmental protection[47].

International instruments such as the Escazú Agreement and the Aarhus Convention also emphasize the procedural dimensions of the right to the environment, recognizing the importance of public participation and access to justice in environmental matters.

The right to a healthy environment is intrinsically linked to the principles of equality, non-discrimination and protection of vulnerable groups. The organs of the Inter-American System have recognized that environmental damage affects these populations more intensely, which imposes on States the obligation to address these vulnerabilities in accordance with the principle of equality and non-discrimination.

3.2 *State Obligations in Relation to the Right to a Healthy Environment*

According to Article 1.1 of the American Convention, States Parties have the obligation to respect the rights established in the treaty, which includes refraining from actions that may violate those rights. In the context of the right to a healthy environment, the Inter-American Court has held that States must refrain from conduct that may unlawfully contaminate (or pollute) the environment in such a way as to affect the conditions necessary for a dignified life[48].

The Inter-American Court stressed that, in addition to the obligation of respect, States also have the obligation to guarantee the right to a healthy environment, which includes preventing violations of this right. This obligation of prevention is not limited to the actions of State agents, but also extends to the private sphere, requiring States to adopt all necessary measures, whether legal, political, administrative or cultural, to prevent third parties from violating the protected rights[49].

In this order of ideas, States are obliged to ensure that both public and private entities respect, mitigate and account for the damage they may cause to the environment and the climate, in compliance with their duties of respect and guarantee.[50]

[47] United Nations General Assembly (2018), para. 14.

[48] IACtHR (2017), para. 117; IACtHR (2020), para. 207.

[49] IACtHR (2005a), para. 111; IACtHR (2005b), para. 170.

[50] IACHR. Business and Human Rights: Inter-American Standards. Special Rapporteur on Economic, Social, Cultural and Environmental Rights. November 1, 2019, para. 247.

3.3 Obligations of Prevention and Guarantee in the Context of the Climate Emergency

In the context of the climate emergency, prevention and guarantee obligations are essential for States to fulfill their duty to protect human rights against the adverse impacts of climate change. These obligations have been exhaustively addressed in the written observations submitted by the IACHR and REDESCA to the Inter-American Court of Human Rights.

The duty of prevention, recognized by the organs of the inter-American system, covers all measures necessary to safeguard human rights and avoid significant environmental damage[51]. This principle, part of customary international law, obliges States to take ex ante measures to prevent environmental damage[52], including those that may occur within or outside their territory[53].

The obligation to prevent is conditioned by the magnitude of the potential damage. For example, the United Nations Framework Convention on Climate Change (UNFCCC) obliges States to anticipate, prevent or minimize the causes of climate change and mitigate its adverse effects.

Likewise, international treaties and the jurisprudence of the Inter-American Court recognize that the obligation to prevent environmental damage is linked to the significance of the potential damage. The obligation of prevention requires States to use all means at their disposal to prevent activities under their jurisdiction from causing significant damage to the environment[54].

Significant harm includes any impact on the environment that may lead to a violation of the right to life or personal integrity. The Court has indicated that the significant nature of the harm must be assessed on a case-by-case basis, taking into account the particularities of each situation[55].

Once environmental damage has been caused, the duty of prevention takes on a different scope, especially in the context of climate change. This duty includes the obligation to mitigate the effects of climate change, implement adaptation measures and remedy the resulting damage[56].

Regarding the measures necessary to comply with the duty of prevention, the Inter-American Court has stated that it is not possible to make an exhaustive list of the preventive measures that States must adopt, since these vary according to the right in question and the specific circumstances of each State[57]. However, the precautionary principle, included in the UNFCCC, establishes that when there is a

[51] IACtHR (2009), para. 252.

[52] IACtHR (2020), para 208.

[53] IACtHR (2017), para. 133.

[54] TIDM (2011), para. 117.

[55] IACtHR (2017), para. 140.

[56] IACHR-REDESCA (2021), para 15.

[57] Christian Courtis (2023), p. 8.

threat of serious or irreversible damage, the lack of scientific certainty should not be used as an excuse to postpone the adoption of preventive measures.

The IACHR emphasizes that human rights obligations are applicable not only to decisions on climate protection, but also to the mitigation and adaptation measures that States must adopt[58]. These include reducing greenhouse gas emissions and implementing adjustments to ecological, social or economic systems in response to the impacts of climate change.

The Commission concludes that, in order to comply with their obligations in the context of the climate emergency, States must take appropriate measures to mitigate the effects of climate change, implement adaptation measures, require and approve social and environmental impact studies, and supervise regulated conduct, all in accordance with available scientific evidence and under a framework of constant re-evaluation[59].

States therefore have an inescapable obligation to respect and guarantee the right to a healthy environment, which implies not only the adoption of proactive measures to prevent environmental damage, but also the implementation of effective mechanisms for mitigation and adaptation to the effects of climate change. These responsibilities extend to both the public and private spheres, requiring the active participation of all actors involved to protect populations that are in a situation of greater vulnerability in the face of adverse environmental impacts.

In light of these considerations on the relationship between climate change and human rights, it is essential to address the regulations and standards that have been established to guide state actions in this matter. In this context, Resolution 3/2021 of SRESCER and the IACHR stands out as an instrument that reinforces the inter-American obligations in the area of human rights in the face of the climate emergency that have already been set out. Its approach, which covers both mitigation and adaptation to climate change, and its emphasis on protecting the rights of the most vulnerable groups, lays the foundations for the creation of policies and regulatory frameworks that recognize the interdependence between environmental protection and the realization of human rights[60]. The resolution also reinforces the idea that States must be held accountable not only for their direct actions, but also for the policies they promote at the international level that may have adverse effects on the climate[61]. This approach contributes to strengthening State responsibility in the area of international cooperation and ensures that political decisions are aligned with human rights commitments.[62]

[58] Special Rapporteur on the issue of human rights obligations relating to the enjoyment of a safe, clean, healthy and sustainable environment (2016), para. 33.

[59] REDESCA (2023c), para. 121.

[60] Ibid., para. 30.

[61] Ibid., para. 31.

[62] Ibid., para. 32.

4 Advisory Opinion on Climate Emergency and Human Rights

The States of Chile and Colombia brought the aforementioned discussion before the Inter-American Court of Human Rights, requesting an Advisory Opinion that would clarify State obligations in the context of the climate emergency. Below, we explore the process of preparing this Advisory Opinion, a legal milestone that will establish more concrete and binding standards for States in their fight against climate change.

4.1 Process for Elaborating the Advisory Opinion

The request for an Advisory Opinion to the IACtHR arose from the need to clarify the obligations of States in the context of the climate emergency and its impact on human rights. Given the concern about the adverse effects of climate change, the States of Chile and Colombia submitted, on January 9, 2023, a formal request to the IACtHR. Their main objective was to obtain a clear legal interpretation that would guide States in developing policies and programs that effectively respond to the climate crisis, in line with their commitments under the American Convention on Human Rights and other international treaties[63].

The requesting States stressed the importance of the Court clarifying the scope of State obligations, both individual and collective, to address the climate emergency, with special emphasis on the differentiated impacts suffered by the most vulnerable populations. This Advisory Opinion would not only serve as a guide for the requesting States, but also for all countries in the region, by offering a normative framework that facilitates the adoption of urgent, equitable and sustainable measures.[64]

In response to the request, the IACtHR opened a public consultation process, inviting all interested parties to submit comments before December 18, 2023. The request from Chile and Colombia was organized around six general themes, each addressing key aspects of state obligations in the face of the climate emergency:[65]

i. **Obligations to prevent and guarantee human rights:** The scope of the duty of prevention that States have in the face of climate phenomena derived from global warming is explored, as well as the differentiated measures necessary to protect vulnerable populations according to everything set out in the previous section.
ii. **Right to life and survival:** This topic addresses the obligations of States regarding the production and access to environmental information, and how these

[63] IACtHR (2023), pp. 1–14.

[64] Ibid.

[65] Ibid.

obligations are fundamental to guarantee other rights, such as life, health, and participation in environmental decisions.

iii. **Differential obligations towards children and new generations:** The nature of State obligations to protect the rights of children and adolescents, as well as new generations, in the face of the long-term risks of climate change, including their participation in decisions that affect their future, is analyzed.
iv. **Consultation procedures and judicial remedies:** This section examines the duty of States to provide effective judicial remedies and how prior consultation should incorporate the climate consequences of the activities in question.
v. **Protection and prevention for environmental defenders and groups in a situation of greater vulnerability:** This section focuses on the measures that States should adopt to protect environmental defenders, as well as women, indigenous peoples and Afro-descendant communities in the context of the climate emergency.
vi. **Shared and differentiated responsibilities:** Finally, it addresses how States should act both individually and collectively to comply with their obligations of cooperation and reparation in the face of climate damage, with a focus on the most affected regions and populations.

These six general themes provide a structure for the IACtHR to develop a normative framework to guide States in the implementation of effective and fair policies to address the climate crisis, with a particular focus on the protection of human rights.

4.2 REDESCA's Contributions

REDESCA, together with the IACHR, played a fundamental role in the process of preparing the Advisory Opinion requested before the IACtHR by the States of Chile and Colombia. The observations presented by REDESCA and the IACHR not only offered a critical and detailed perspective on the issues raised, but also constitute a significant contribution to the development of inter-American standards on the matter.

The main contributions in this process are the following:[66]

i. **Human rights approach to climate action:** REDESCA stressed that climate change mitigation and adaptation measures must be guided by principles of climate justice, intergenerational equity and respect for human rights, especially those of the most vulnerable groups. They stressed that climate change is not only an environmental problem, but a direct threat to the enjoyment of human rights such as life, health, and access to food and water.
ii. **Right to a healthy environment as an autonomous right:** The autonomous nature of the right to a healthy environment, protected under Article 26 of the

[66] REDESCA (2023a), pp. 1–119.

American Convention, was also emphasized. This right, in addition to being intrinsically related to other human rights, has its own value, protecting nature and ecosystems as legal interests in themselves. This approach reinforces the need for States to implement effective policies for environmental conservation.

iii. **Interdependence and indivisibility of human rights:** The observations highlighted the interconnection between civil, political, economic, social, cultural and environmental rights. The violation of environmental rights has a direct impact on other rights, such as health, food and access to water, which underlines the need for State obligations to be understood and applied in a comprehensive and coordinated manner.

iv. **Obligations of prevention and guarantee:** The obligations of States to adopt preventive measures to avoid environmental damage that may violate human rights were also explored in depth, as set out in previous sections. This includes regulating and monitoring activities that could aggravate the climate crisis, as well as implementing public policies that effectively protect human rights. It was stressed that the obligation to prevent not only requires proactive actions, but also the implementation of legal frameworks that ensure environmental sustainability.

v. **State obligations regarding procedural rights:** The importance of ensuring access to information, public participation in environmental decision-making, and access to justice in the context of the climate emergency was emphasized. REDESCA stressed that access to information is crucial for people to exercise control over decisions that affect their environment, and that public participation is essential to ensure that climate policies are inclusive and equitable. In addition, it was highlighted that States must ensure that effective judicial remedies exist to challenge decisions that violate environmental rights and guarantee adequate reparations. Regarding the right to reparation, it was emphasized that any violation of human rights generated by the climate crisis must be adequately remedied. Reparation measures include restitution, compensation, satisfaction and guarantees of non-repetition, and must be proportional to the severity of the violation and the damage caused. The need for States to implement national and international reparation programmes to address the damage caused by the climate emergency, especially in relation to the rights of future generations, was also stressed.

vi. **Common but differentiated responsibilities:** The comments also stressed that, while all States share the responsibility to combat climate change, those with greater capacities and that have contributed most to the problem have a reinforced obligation to lead mitigation and adaptation efforts. Furthermore, the importance of international cooperation was underlined as a key element to effectively address the climate crisis, promoting climate justice at the global level.

In summary, the observations presented represent a key contribution to framing the legal debate on the climate emergency in the context of human rights, providing a comprehensive vision that integrates the principles of climate justice, equity and protection of the rights of groups in the most vulnerable situations.

4.3 Reflections on the Legal Milestone in the Inter-American System

The issuance of the Advisory Opinion by the Inter-American Court of Human Rights in response to the request of the States of Chile and Colombia will have profound implications for the development of international human rights law in the context of the climate emergency. This Opinion will not only offer an authoritative interpretation of State obligations in the face of climate change, but will also establish legal standards that will guide countries in the region in the adoption of public policies and legislation aligned with human rights principles.

One of the main implications of this Opinion will be the clarification of States' obligations under international human rights law. The Court will provide a detailed interpretation on how States should act to prevent, mitigate and remedy the damage caused by climate change, especially in relation to human rights such as life, health, food, housing and a healthy environment. This clarification will allow States to better understand their responsibilities at both the national and international levels, ensuring a more coordinated and effective response to climate challenges.

Furthermore, the Advisory Opinion will have a significant impact on the protection of groups that are most vulnerable to climate change, such as indigenous peoples, women, children and adolescents, persons with disabilities, and Afro-descendant and rural communities. The Court is likely to emphasize the need for differentiated approaches and specific measures to protect the rights of these groups, which will prompt States to design more inclusive and equitable public policies, effectively addressing inequalities exacerbated by the climate crisis.

The Opinion will also contribute to the establishment of regional standards on the relationship between human rights and climate change, providing normative guidance that States in the region should follow when implementing their climate policies. By defining these standards, the Court will strengthen the inter-American legal framework and promote greater harmonization of national legislation on climate change and human rights, fostering a collective and coherent response throughout the region.

The implications of this Opinion will not be limited to the inter-American level, but will also influence national and international jurisprudence. National courts will be able to use it as a reference to resolve cases related to climate change and human rights, which could lead to a greater judicialization of these issues in domestic judicial systems. Moreover, the Opinion could serve as an inspiration for other international and regional courts, contributing to a more uniform development of international human rights law in relation to the climate crisis.

Another key implication will be the reinforcement of international cooperation among States in the region. The Court will likely underline the importance of international cooperation and solidarity in facing the climate crisis, considering the principle of common but differentiated responsibilities.

Finally, the Advisory Opinion could serve as a catalyst for States to take more ambitious, sustainable and fair climate action. By providing a clear normative framework, the Court will incentivize States to fulfill their international obligations in ways that respect and promote human rights. This could include implementing just transition policies, promoting renewable energy, protecting critical ecosystems and taking measures to ensure the resilience of communities that are in a situation of greater vulnerability.

In short, the issuance of this Advisory Opinion has the potential to transform the way States address the climate emergency from a human rights perspective, setting legal precedents that will have long-lasting repercussions in the region and even beyond.

5 Conclusion

The analysis carried out in this article highlights the critical intersection between the climate emergency and the protection of human rights within the Inter-American System. The future issuance of the Advisory Opinion by the Inter-American Court of Human Rights will represent a legal milestone in the consolidation of regional standards that address this complex relationship, in a context where climate change threatens the validity of human rights. The role played by the IACHR and REDESCA has been especially relevant in guiding this process, providing a comprehensive vision that prioritizes climate justice.

The recognition of the climate emergency as a human rights crisis, the special protection of groups that are in a situation of greater vulnerability, and the insistence on international cooperation, constitute fundamental pillars that must guide public policies in this matter. In addition, the incorporation of procedural rights, such as access to information and participation in decision-making, is essential to ensure that responses to the climate crisis are inclusive, equitable, and effective.

Extreme weather events are destroying the economic and social foundations of entire communities, intensifying food insecurity and forcing the displacement of thousands of people. Forest fires, such as those that have occurred in recent months in South America and with unusual severity in Bolivia and Brazil, not only destroy vast areas of biodiversity and carbon sinks, but also have a serious impact on the human rights of communities that are in a situation of special vulnerability. That the inter-American system can continue to advance along this path, with advances from the Inter-American Court, the IACHR and REDESCA, is necessary in a context in which decades of discussions in multilateral settings on climate change have not led to sufficiently ambitious commitments to reduce greenhouse gas emissions, nor to seriously address reparations for those who suffer climate damage. Meanwhile, the effects of climate change are progressively aggravating the already severe inequalities in the region.

References

Asamblea General de Naciones Unidas (2018) Informe del Relator Especial sobre la cuestión de las obligaciones de derechos humanos relacionadas con el disfrute de un medio ambiente sin riesgos, limpio, saludable y sostenible. A/HRC/37/59, párr. 14

Bendel J (2023) Litigating the Environment: Process and Procedure Before International Courts and Tribunals. Edward Elgar Publishing

Centro de Monitoreo de Desplazamiento Interno (2021) Informe Mundial sobre Desplazamiento Interno

CIDH (2017) Informe sobre pobreza y derechos humanos en las Américas. 7 de septiembre, párrs. 236–237

CIDH-REDESCA (2021) Resolución 3/2021 Emergencia Climática: Alcance de las obligaciones interamericanas en materia de derechos humanos. Aprobada el 31 de diciembre

Consejo de Derechos Humanos (2016) Informe del Relator Especial sobre la cuestión de las obligaciones de derechos humanos relacionadas con el disfrute de un medio ambiente sin riesgos, limpio, saludable y sostenible. 1 de febrero, Doc. ONU A/HRC/31/52, párr. 33

Consejo de Derechos Humanos (2017) Resolución 35, titulada "Los derechos humanos y el cambio climático." Adoptada el 19 de junio, Doc. ONU A/HRC/35/L.32, preámbulo

Corte IDH (2005a) Caso Comunidad Indígena Yakye Axa Vs. Paraguay. Fondo, reparaciones y Costas. Sentencia de 17 de junio, párr. 163

Corte IDH (2005b) Caso de la "Masacre de Mapiripán" Vs. Colombia. Sentencia de 15 de septiembre, Serie C No. 134, párr. 111

Corte IDH (2009) Caso González y otras ("Campo Algodonero") Vs. México. Excepción Preliminar, Fondo, Reparaciones y Costas. Sentencia de 16 de noviembre, Serie C No. 205, párr. 252

Corte IDH (2017) Medio ambiente y derechos humanos (obligaciones estatales en relación con el medio ambiente en el marco de la protección y garantía de los derechos a la vida y a la integridad personal - interpretación y alcance de los artículos 4.1 y 5.1, en relación con los artículos 1.1 y 2 de la Convención Americana sobre Derechos Humanos). Opinión Consultiva OC-23/17 de 15 de noviembre. Serie A No. 23, párrs. 54, 57, 117, 126, 133, 140

Corte IDH (2020) Caso Comunidades Indígenas Miembros de la Asociación Lhaka Honhat (Nuestra Tierra) Vs. Argentina. Fondo, Reparaciones y Costas. Sentencia de 6 de febrero, Serie C No. 400, párrs. 207, 208

Corte IDH (2023) Solicitud de Opinión Consultiva presentada por Chile y Colombia ante la Corte Interamericana de Derechos Humanos de 9 de enero, pág. 2

de Graaf KJ, Weishaar SE (2023) Introduction to the future of environmental law. In: Weishaar SE (ed) The future of environmental law: ambition and reality. Edward Elgar Publishing

Donald M (2023) The role of principles of international environmental law in greening the interpretation of human rights: the case of the UN Committee on Economic, Social and Cultural Rights. In: de Graaf KJ (ed) The future of environmental law: ambition and reality. Edward Elgar Publishing

Euroclima (2017) Medidas de adaptación y mitigación frente al cambio climático en América Latina y el Caribe, pág. 7. Disponible en https://www.cepal.org/sites/default/files/news/files/sintesis_pp_cc_medidas_de_mitigacion_y_adaptacion.pdf

IPCC (2022) Summary for Policymakers [H.-O. Pörtner, D.C. Roberts, E.S. Poloczanska, K. Mintenbeck, M. Tignor, A. Alegría, M. Craig, S. Langsdorf, S. Löschke, V. Möller, A. Okem (eds.)]. In: Pörtner H-O, Roberts DC, Tignor M, Poloczanska ES, Mintenbeck K, Alegría A,

Craig M, Langsdorf S, Löschke S, Möller V, Okem A, Rama B (eds) Climate change 2022: Impacts, adaptation and vulnerability. Contribution of Working Group II to the sixth assessment report of the intergovernmental panel on climate change. Cambridge University Press, Cambridge, p 12

IPCC (2023) Summary for policymakers. In: Core Writing Team, Lee H, Romero J (eds) Climate change 2023: Synthesis report. Contribution of Working Groups I, II and III to the sixth assessment report of the intergovernmental panel on climate change. IPCC, Geneva, pp 1–34

Naciones Unidas. Convención Marco de las Naciones Unidas sobre el Cambio Climático (CMNUCC). Adoptada el 9 de mayo de 1992, 1771 UNTS 107; entrada en vigor el 21 de marzo de 1994

Naciones Unidas (2015) Acuerdo de París

Organización Meteorológica Mundial (2023a) El círculo vicioso del cambio climático se agrava en América Latina y el Caribe. 5 de julio

Organización Meteorológica Mundial (2023b) Estado del Clima en América Latina y el Caribe en 2022. Ginebra

Organización Meteorológica Mundial (2023c) La Organización Meteorológica Mundial anuncia la prevalencia de unas condiciones que pueden indicar el inicio de un episodio de El Niño. 4 de julio

Peritaje de Christian Courtis ante la Corte Interamericana de Derechos Humanos (2023) Caso Comunidad de La Oroya V. Perú, p 8

REDESCA (2023a) Observaciones de La Comisión Interamericana de Derechos Humanos y de La Relatoría Especial Sobre Los Derechos Económicos, Sociales, Culturales y Ambientales a La Solicitud de Opinión Consultiva Sobre Emergencia Climática y Derechos Humanos Presentada Por Las Repúblicas de Chile y Colombia

REDESCA (2023b) Pobreza, Cambio Climático y DESCA en Centro América y México. OEA/Ser.L/V/II. Doc. 158, 28 de julio, párr. 264

REDESCA (2023c) VI Informe Anual de la Relatoría Especial sobre Derechos Económicos, Sociales, Culturales y Ambientales (REDESCA), Capítulo IV Informe Especial: Emergencia Climática y Derechos Humanos en las Américas. OEA/SER.L/V/II Doc. 50, 6 marzo, párrs. 8, 63

REDESCA (2024) La REDESCA insta a una acción urgente ante la crisis ambiental en América del Sur provocada por los incendios forestales, Comunicado de prensa

REDESCA y CIDH (2024a) La CIDH y REDESCA hacen un llamado a la solidaridad internacional ante la emergencia en los países afectados por el huracán Beryl, Comunicado de prensa

REDESCA y CIDH (2024b) Brasil: CIDH y REDESCA se solidarizan con la tragedia ambiental en Rio Grande do Sul y reafirman la importancia de promover acciones de mayor alcance ante la emergencia climática, Comunicado de prensa

Secretaría General de la OEA (2022) Cambio Climático: Vida, Democracia, libertad, justicia, igualdad. Noviembre, pág. 8

TIDM (2011) Responsabilidades y Obligaciones de los Estados respecto de actividades en la Zona. Opinión Consultiva de 1 de febrero, párrs. 117, 158

Javier Palummo Lantes is the Special Rapporteur on Economic, Social, Cultural, and Environmental Rights (REDESCA) at the Inter-American Commission on Human Rights (IACHR). He previously served as Chair of the Advisory Committee of the United Nations Human Rights Council and was Director of Research and Information Management at the Institute of Public Policies on Human Rights of MERCOSUR. Human rights PhD (Universidad Nacional de Lanús, Argentina) and law social sciences PhD (Universidad de la República, Uruguay).

Final Reflections

Valéria Emília de Aquino, Claudia Loureiro, and Vinicius Villani Abrantes

Climate litigation emerges as an essential tool to address the global inequalities exacerbated by climate change, connecting the fight for climate justice to the recognition of the interdependence between human rights and sustainability. But beyond its legal nuances, climate litigation also has a social dimension, which consists of giving voice and visibility to those who suffer most from the harmful effects of climate change, highlighting that the climate crisis is also a social and moral crisis, since the core issue is precisely inequality.

Inequality is one of the world's greatest evils, because it segregates and widens the gap between the poorest and most vulnerable and the richest, who are unlikely to give up their lifestyles and profits at the expense of nature and the rest of society. It is unfair that the richest 1% in the world hold approximately two-thirds of the world's wealth, and it is also unfair that those who pollute the most do not reduce their emissions and do not help the most vulnerable countries and communities.

The idea of economic growth propagated for decades by the Global North must be replaced by the notion of sustainable development,[1] and in this context, the voices of the Global South cannot be ignored, especially the voices of indigenous

[1] Pahuja (2011).

V. E. de Aquino (✉)
Federal University of Goiás, Goiânia, Goiás, Brazil

C. Loureiro
Federal University of Uberlândia, Uberlândia, Minas Gerais, Brazil
e-mail: claudia.loureiro@ufu.br

V. V. Abrantes
Direito Internacional sem Fronteiras, Juiz de Fora, Minas Gerais, Brazil
e-mail: viniciusabrantes@ufmg.br

V. E. de Aquino et al. (eds.), *Climate Litigation in a Changing World*, Ius Gentium: Comparative Perspectives on Law and Justice 130,
https://doi.org/10.1007/978-3-032-05530-9_16

peoples and traditional communities, black people, women, children, the elderly, among other groups that find themselves in a situation of extreme vulnerability in the face of the triple planetary crisis, which require an intersectional analysis.[2]

Thus, it is the role of climate litigation to advocate for climate justice, in other words, to advocate for equality. It is also the duty of national, regional and international courts and tribunals to look after the interests of the majority, who need a healthy environment to have their other human rights guaranteed, and not of the wealthy minority, who will continue to exploit the environment.[3]

It is worthless having so many international documents focused on the climate issue if the signing of these agreements is not followed by real change in favor of climate actions to combat inequality. It urges that international society, international organizations and courts monitor the actions of each of these countries that have committed to protecting the environment and reducing their emissions. And even further than that: it urges that the entire society mobilizes efforts to supervise the actions of other international actors, especially large companies and transnational corporations, which continue to sustain inequality throughout the world.

Each advisory opinion or judgment issued by these courts must take into account that human rights are interdependent, indivisible and inalienable, and that a healthy, safe and sustainable environment is therefore essential for the enjoyment of other human rights. Furthermore, the environment is also an indispensable and essential element for many peoples and cultures, constituting an important element of their subsistence and ancestry. Consequently, Nature is not only a common heritage of mankind, but its protection is also a value that should guide our society.

Each case presented, despite its own particularities, shows us the desire of a society that wants to change, of a society that cares about the future. However, it is not only the future that is at stake, but also the present, since we are increasingly experiencing floods, droughts, storms, rising sea levels, among other phenomena. What is at stake is not only the survival of human life, but of all nature, of all ecosystems, and if we do not understand that everything is interconnected, it may be too late for our planet.

Each paper presented in this work sought to demonstrate that climate litigation is a necessary tool for the realization of human rights and human life. Many of these articles sought to denounce structural inequalities in our society, and to show that this crisis affects some people much more than others, such as women, children, the elderly, black people, traditional peoples, among others.

As discussed in the book, this movement articulates efforts by nations and international courts to hold states and corporations accountable for their contribution to the climate crisis, especially when the impacts disproportionately affect the most vulnerable communities, as presented by Rodrigues, Bhattacharya, Medina and Cabete in their analysis of disparities between the Global North and South.[4]

---

[2] Robinson (2021).

[3] Bullard (2000).

[4] Rodrigues et al. (2025).

In Wenzel's chapter, the emphasis on the procedural rights guaranteed by the Aarhus Convention exemplifies how climate litigation also seeks to guarantee access to information, public participation and environmental justice. In other words, there is no environmental or climate justice unless these rights are guaranteed to everyone, and NGOs have been exhaustively working to promote and advocate for human rights at national and international levels.[5]

These rights are often violated by states that prioritize economic interests over collective well-being, connecting directly to Hartwig and Wedy's discussion in this book of how climate-washing and disinformation undermine transparency and social mobilization. This intersection shows that strengthening the right to information is fundamental to building a more engaged and aware global environmental citizenship.[6]

The cases presented in the book also highlight the transnational dimension of climate litigation, connecting jurisdictions and regions. The role of regional and international courts, as addressed by Loureiro and Oliveira in their study of the European and Inter-American systems, is essential to creating precedents that promote climate justice. These institutions connect different perspectives and realities, fostering dialog and cooperation between states.[7]

Although Oceania lacks a regional human rights system, such as the European, Inter-American and African systems, Aquino and Rosa sought to analyze national cases to identify the challenges faced by Australia and New Zealand, concluding that these are not the same challenges faced by small island states in the Pacific, which are highly threatened by rising sea levels. Whether due to differences in the resilience of ecosystems or economic and political differences, it is clear that inequality is once again at the heart of the issue.[8]

Rising sea levels are undoubtedly causing a cascade of human rights violations for individuals living in areas most vulnerable to this phenomenon. Along with the loss of arable land and housing, the culture, subsistence and history of these people are also at risk of being silently erased. Beyond an anthropocentric perspective, the chapter by di Pasquale, Mont'Alverne and Veiga sought to address the intersections between the oceans, environmental protection and climate change, drawing on ITLOS' jurisprudence.[9]

In this context, Cavalcanti and Smanio sought to study the legal possibility of the crime of ecocide in Brazil, assuming that these human rights violations arise from the action or inaction of States, and in certain cases, from the actions of non-State entities. The existence of a deliberate political project to dismantle the environmental-climate regime, especially by the far-right, shows the need to criminalize any action (or inaction) that results in ecocide. The authors also emphasized that collaboration

---

[5] Wenzel (2025).

[6] Hartwig and Wedy (2025).

[7] Loureiro and Oliveira (2025).

[8] Aquino and Rosa (2025).

[9] Di Pasquale et al. (2025).

between local and international actors is indispensable for tackling the climate crisis effectively.[10]

These efforts converge with Bonet, Sozzo and Alé perspective on the need for technical tools, such as the ecological footprint, to support legal and political decisions.[11] Besides, the authors touched on an important point for the environmental-climate area: the responsibility of States for their ecological footprint, since environmental damage often crosses borders.

In this sense, Loscocco and Chai also addressed the transboundary issue from the perspective of the sharing of natural resources, as for example in the case of the Guarani Aquifer, shared by Argentina, Brazil, Paraguay and Uruguay. The analysis carried out by the authors allows us to verify the importance of the norms of International Law regarding the shared responsibility for these resources, which is also reflected in the international climate regime.[12]

Therefore, the international responsibility of States in the climate regime involves two essential points: responsibility for violations of individual and collective human rights, such as in the cases addressed in this book, and responsibility towards other States, towards society itself and towards ecosystems, since environmental-climatic damage is not restricted to national borders.

These reflections dialogue with Badawi's analysis of the vulnerability of the African continent, where climate disasters intensify social, agricultural and food security crises.[13] From the discussion addressed by the author, it is clear that the climate crisis is also a social crisis, which consists of the failure of international systems and of States themselves to prevent the collapse of the environment.

Similarly, the Muriuki's contribution, in analyzing African legal systems, shows that climate litigation can be bureaucratic, and sometimes relies on incipient laws, making it necessary to use other means to complement them, whether through dialogue with other international courts and tribunals, or through doctrine, as well as jurisprudence of regional courts, such as the African Court on Human Rights and Peoples' Rights.[14]

Finally, Talukdar's analysis of the Indian legal scenario demonstrates how the challenges of one country can offer lessons applicable in other regions, underlining the importance of an interconnected global legal system.[15] Hence, the climate regime and climate litigation can and should draw on positive examples from other countries, in order to incorporate laws that will benefit and strengthen environmental protection at all levels.

The last part of this book aimed to bring two contributions to highlight that building more inclusive and effective environmental governance relies on cooperation

[10] Cavalcanti and Smanio (2025).

[11] Bonet et al. (2025).

[12] Loscocco and Chai (2025).

[13] Badawi (2025).

[14] Muriuki (2025).

[15] Talukdar (2025).

between experts, activists and institutions. Romero and Silva addressed El-Hinnawi's legacy,[16] and demonstrated that academic research can and should be taken to international forums, since climate governance depends not only on policy makers, but above all on the role played by scientists, given that it is an interdisciplinary area that requires cooperation and efforts towards a common goal: environmental protection, and consequently, human rights protection.

By creating the term 'environmental refugees', El-Hinnawi gave visibility and voice to environmental migrants as well as climate migrants. Furthermore, the researcher reinforced the connection between environmental impacts and human rights. Without an adequate international legal framework, climate migrants will continue to be exposed to rights violations, highlighting the importance of integrating environmental and humanitarian agendas. This issue also highlights the need for climate justice, which, as discussed in different chapters, must include technical and financial support for the communities and countries most affected.

It is also important to highlight and acknowledge the valuable and indispensable work carried out by experts in human rights, such as the role of Special Rapporteurships on human rights, climate change and environmental protection. Their work consists of true advocacy and campaigning work in favor of the promotion and defense of human rights for present and future generations.

The chapter by the Special Rapporteur of REDESCA before the Inter-American Commission, Dr. Javier Palummo Lantes, pointed out that several professionals are deeply committed to not only investigating serious human rights violations, but also exposing and naming violating States, often risking their own lives when making their recommendations and criticizing the legal systems of these countries.[17]

All the authors converge in the conclusion that the necessary transformation requires an integrated and global approach. Climate litigation is more than a legal resource: it is a movement that seeks to redesign the foundations of international cooperation and promote a transition to sustainable and inclusive development models. As highlighted throughout this book, tackling climate inequality and demanding more ambitious emission reduction commitments are fundamental steps towards guaranteeing a fair and balanced future for all generations.

Each chapter not only interacts with each other, demonstrating similarities in the challenges and obstacles faced, but also represents important contributions from researchers who dedicate their lives to studying the environment and climate. We hope that the work can serve as a reference for other professionals and, especially, for those who advocate for a better, greener and sustainable world. Generosity, compassion, empathy, fraternity and solidarity must guide our society towards a more humane, fair and equal world.

[16] Romero and Silva (2025).

[17] Palummo Lantes (2025).

References

Aquino VE, Rosa MA (2025) Climate litigation in Oceania: the case of insular countries. In: Aquino VE, Loureiro C, Abrantes VV (eds) Climate litigation in a changing world – a comparative analysis of similarities, challenges and pathways (this volume). Springer Nature, Berlin

Badawi I (2025) Climate change and air pollution in Africa: legal precedents and their impact on environmental justice. In: Aquino VE, Loureiro C, Abrantes VV (eds) Climate litigation in a changing world – a comparative analysis of similarities, challenges and pathways (this volume). Springer Nature, Berlin

Bonet AM, Sozzo G, Alé MC (2025) The ecological footprint: a tool for decision making in the legal field. In: Aquino VE, Loureiro C, Abrantes VV (eds) Climate litigation in a changing world – a comparative analysis of similarities, challenges and pathways (this volume). Springer Nature, Berlin

Bullard RD (2000) Dumping in dixie: race, class and environmental quality. Westview Press, Boulder

Cavalcanti AELW, Smanio GP (2025) The legal treatment of ecocide in Brazil. In: Aquino VE, Loureiro C, Abrantes VV (eds) Climate litigation in a changing world – a comparative analysis of similarities, challenges and pathways (this volume). Springer Nature, Berlin

Di Pasquale AIBSL, Veiga JS, Mont'alverne TCF (2025) Diving into the synergies between the climate and ocean emergencies: An analysis of the International Tribunal for the Law of the Sea Advisory Opinion on Climate Change. In: Aquino VE, Loureiro C, Abrantes VV (eds) Climate litigation in a changing world – a comparative analysis of similarities, challenges and pathways (this volume). Springer Nature, Berlin

Hartwig EM, Wedy G (2025) Climate disinformation and climate-washing: litigation in defense of human rights and transparency. In: Aquino VE, Loureiro C, Abrantes VV (eds) Climate litigation in a changing world – a comparative analysis of similarities, challenges and pathways (this volume). Springer Nature, Berlin

Loscocco NL, Chai CG (2025) Transboundary environmental and climate responsibility: the Guarani aquifer. In: Aquino VE, Loureiro C, Abrantes VV (eds) Climate litigation in a changing world – a comparative analysis of similarities, challenges and pathways (this volume). Springer Nature, Berlin

Loureiro C, Oliveira AS (2025) Recent trends in climate justice before the European and Inter-American Human Rights Systems. In: Aquino VE, Loureiro C, Abrantes VV (eds) Climate litigation in a changing world – a comparative analysis of similarities, challenges and pathways (this volume). Springer Nature, Berlin

Muriuki S (2025) The role of courts and the legal profession in climate litigation: a tripartite analysis of access to the Kenyan, East African, and African Court Systems. In: Aquino VE, Loureiro C, Abrantes VV (eds) Climate litigation in a changing world – a comparative analysis of similarities, challenges and pathways (this volume). Springer Nature, Berlin

Pahuja S (2011) Decolonising international law: development, economic growth and the politics of universality. Cambridge University Press, New York

Palummo Lantes J (2025) Climate emergency and human rights: perspectives of the consultative process of the Inter-American Court. In: Aquino VE, Loureiro C, Abrantes VV (eds) Climate litigation in a changing world – a comparative analysis of similarities, challenges and pathways (this volume). Springer Nature, Berlin

Robinson M (2021) Justiça climática. Esperança, resiliência e a luta por um futuro sustentável. Civilização Brasileira, Rio de Janeiro

Rodrigues JN, Bhattacharya S, Medina JC, Cabete DCR (2025) The role of international and national courts in climate disputes. In: Aquino VE, Loureiro C, Abrantes VV (eds) Climate litigation in a changing world – a comparative analysis of similarities, challenges and pathways (this volume). Springer Nature, Berlin

Romero TG, Silva MCF (2025) El-Hinnawi's legacy and his contribution to climate litigation. In: Aquino VE, Loureiro C, Abrantes VV (eds) Climate litigation in a changing world – a comparative analysis of similarities, challenges and pathways (this volume). Springer Nature, Berlin

Talukdar S (2025) Challenges in climate litigation in India: analyzing the legal framework and its effects on climate action. In: Aquino VE, Loureiro C, Abrantes VV (eds) Climate litigation in a changing world – a comparative analysis of similarities, challenges and pathways (this volume). Springer Nature, Berlin

Wenzel A (2025) Litigation for climate justice: the case of procedural rights under the Aarhus Convention. In: Aquino VE, Loureiro C, Abrantes VV (eds) Climate litigation in a changing world – a comparative analysis of similarities, challenges and pathways (this volume). Springer Nature, Berlin

Valéria Emília de Aquino Lawyer and Human Rights Consultant, Human Rights PhD (Federal University of Goiás). Master in Fundamental Rights and Sustainability (Federal University of Uberlândia). Member of the Editorial Board and Senior Research Member of 'Direito Internacional sem Fronteiras' (Brazil). Researcher at 'Global Crossings' (Jean Monnet Chair at Federal University of Uberlândia), former scholar at CAPES and FAPEG. International Law and Environmental Law Professor. Researcher in International Law, Environmental Law, International Security, and Human Rights. Former Visiting fellow at the Mercosur Institute of Public Policies on Human Rights (Argentina).

Claudia Loureiro Coordinator of the Jean Monnet Chair at the Federal University of Uberlândia with the GLOBAL CROSSINGS Project. Post-Doctorate in Law at Nova School of Law - Lisbon (2021), in Human Rights from the Faculty of Law of the University of Coimbra (2016) and International and Comparative Law completed by the Faculty of Law of the University of São Paulo (2019). PhD in Law from Universidade Nova de Lisboa (2020). PhD (2015) and Master (2006) in Comparative Civil Law from the Pontifical Catholic University of São Paulo. Professor of Environmental Law and Biolaw at the Faculty of Law of the Federal University of Uberlândia. Permanent Professor of the Postgraduate Program in Law at the Federal University of Uberlândia. Associate member of the International Law Association - ILA BRASIL, and the Ibero-American Institute of Legal Studies - IBEROJUR. She is a researcher at the Nova Refugee Legal Clinic at Universidade Nova de Lisboa-Portugal. She is an associate member of the Brazilian Society of Bioethics-SBB. She is leader of the Biolaw and Human Rights Research Group-UFU and the Inter-American and European Observatory of Sustainable Development Goals-UFU, both certified by CNPq.

Vinicius Villani Abrantes PhD Candidate and Master in Linguistic Studies at Federal University of Minas Gerais, with an emphasis on language and migration law. Specialist in "Public Law" and "International Law" at Centro Universitário União das Américas (UniAmérica). He has "Applied Practical Training in Human Rights in the Brazilian Context" from Centro de Direito Internacional (CEDIN); Founder and General Director of the "Direito Internacional sem Fronteiras - Brazil" Research Center.